BOWIE

STARDUST, RAYGUNS & MOONAGE DAYDREAMS

BOWIE

STARDUST, RAYGUNS & MOONAGE DAYDREAMS

SCREENPLAY BY

STEVE HORTON & MICHAEL ALLRED

TECHNICOLOR CINEMATOGRAPHY

LAURA ALLRED

DIRECTED BY

MICHAEL ALLRED

EDITED BY

MARK IRWIN

COLOR ASSISTS BY

HAN ALLRED

FOREWORD BY

NEIL GAIMAN

INSIGHT
COMICS

San Rafael, California

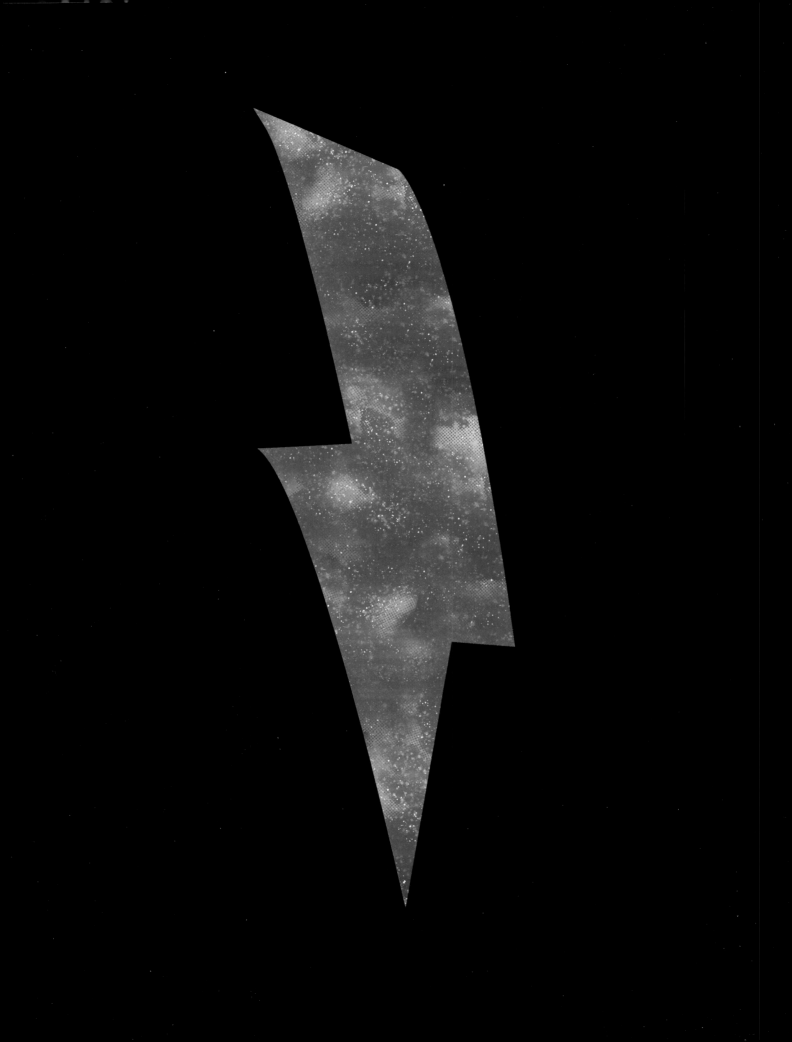

IF WE CAN SPARKLE HE MAY LAND TONIGHT

BY NEIL GAIMAN

I read about David Bowie in a newspaper before I ever heard his music. I was eleven. The article in a daily newspaper was about Bowie saying he was bisexual, a term I had never previously encountered. The people who wrote the article seemed more shocked that he wore makeup. A man wearing makeup. Had you ever heard of such a thing?

Not long after that, I heard a song on the radio about a spaceman leaving his capsule on a space walk; it was being played in the school's hobby room, where the kids were allowed to go and make balsa wood airplanes. I didn't really *get* pop music at that age. I loved Gilbert and Sullivan; I loved songs that were stories, and most rock and pop wasn't. "Space Oddity" was a story, even if it left its ending wrapped in ambiguity, and it was science fiction, and I loved and understood science fiction.

And really, it was the science fiction that was the fishhook in my cheek and dragged me in, as much as the music. Perhaps more than the music. I would listen to music that I didn't love, to tease out the ideas, and play it enough that I loved every beat and bar of it. For me, it was the thread that linked *The Man Who Sold the World*—"The Supermen" and "The Man" himself—with *Hunky Dory*—which gave me "Changes" and "Quicksand"—and *The Rise and Fall of Ziggy Stardust and the Spiders From Mars*, a sci-fi journey. It started with a heartbeat that told us that we only had five years until the end of the world and took us to a room where a kid my age was listening to a Starman sending in music from outer space. The other side of the record was the story of Ziggy Stardust and his journey from fame to zombie obscurity, and I was certain that Ziggy was an alien, come to bring us music. The Starman had descended into a world that was ending in five years, and he would finish his life wandering dully, insulated from all feeling, like Thomas Jerome Newton drinking himself into painlessness.

I was twelve when *Aladdin Sane* came out, and I was bedazzled and confused, and I wanted to know who the strange ones in the dome were and why Aladdin Sane was going to fight in the third world war, and I held on to the conviction that this was science fiction. I was thirteen when *Diamond Dogs* hit, and I was so much in love I went to the school library and took out George Orwell's *1984* and

built huge sapphire-colored postapocalyptic sagas in my head out of the rest of it.

At fifteen, I bluffed my way into a showing of *The Man Who Fell to Earth*, acting old enough to be allowed in, and I bunked a day off school to go to Victoria Station for Bowie's arrival there (I didn't see him, but I met people who were different Bowies at different periods, and I saw copies of *Station to Station* flung over the wall they had put up to stop us from seeing him, and felt like I was touching magic).

The incarnations of David Bowie were, in themselves, science fictional. All I was missing was a Bowie comic, and, missing it, I would draw bad Bowie comics myself.

I met Mike Allred around 1989, at (I think) a Forbidden Planet signing. He gave me some of his art, and I loved it. I sent it to Karen Berger, my editor on *Sandman*, who had him do a tryout page and told him he wasn't quite ready yet. I continued to love his art and was proud that the world rapidly discovered how good he was and that, together, we would bring back the character Prez in the pages of *The Sandman: Worlds' End*. Later, we would make one of my favorite comics I had any part of: the *Metamorpho* story in *Wednesday Comics*, complete with a 1963-style periodic table. There was a cleanness to his lines, a joy in the image and in the construction of each page, aided and abetted by Laura Allred's precise and delightful colouring.

There was a brief moment in the early 1990s when rock-and-roll biography comics were the next big thing. It didn't last very long. None of them were like this. This is pure delight, a book made by fans who are also artists, for fans who are dreamers.

This is a book filled with visual allusions (my favorite is the *Hunky Dory* "Quicksand" first Spiders gig page). The people in these pages aren't people: They are icons—larger-than-life versions of themselves, filled with resonance. It's Bowie's life as parables and imaginary histories, a beautifully researched re-creation of something that might be better than documentary footage. It's an imaginary reconstruction of the time and lives of an imaginary figure, inspired by the life of the actor, one David Jones, formerly of Bromley and originally of Brixton.

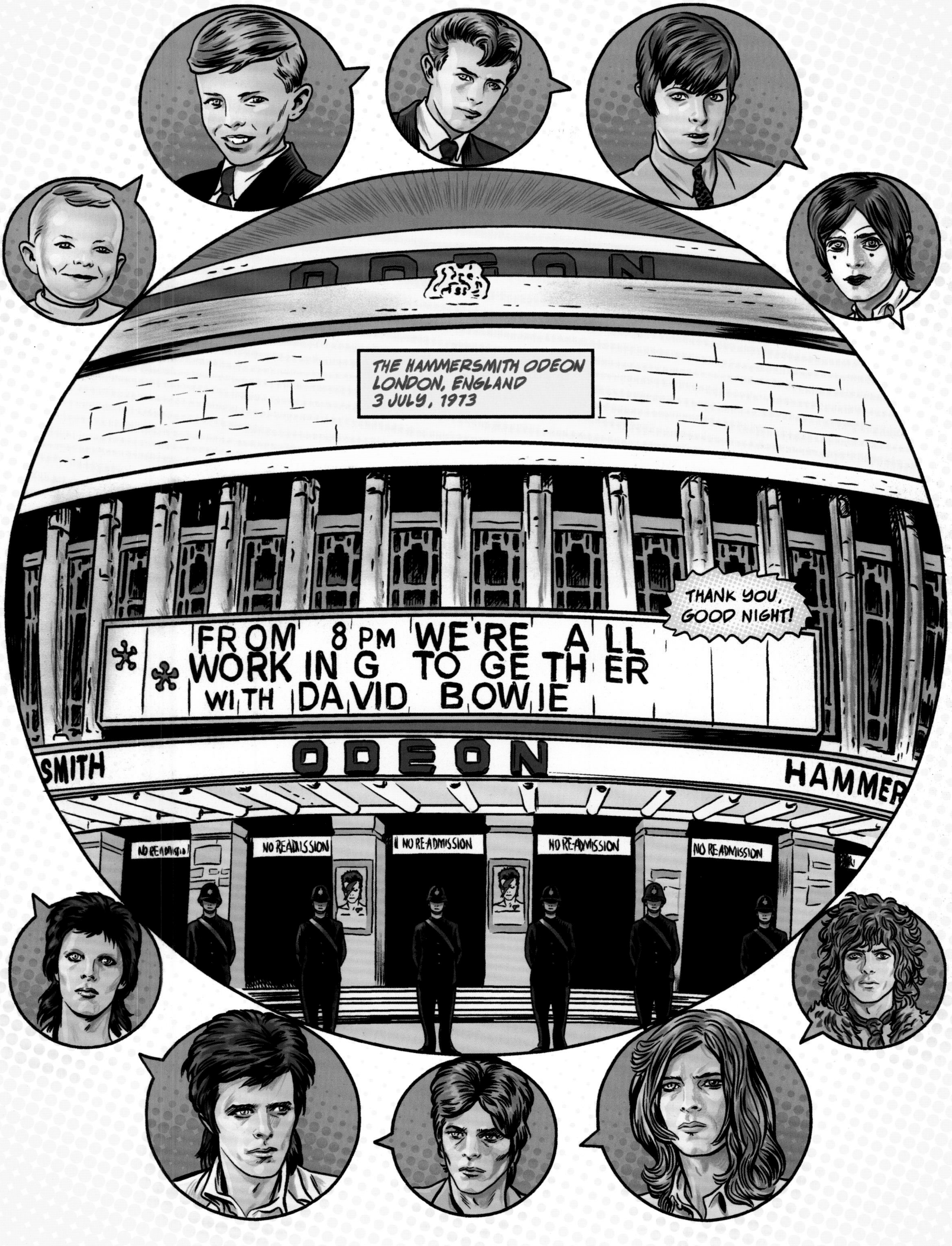

THE HAMMERSMITH ODEON
LONDON, ENGLAND
3 JULY, 1973
ODEON
FROM 8 PM WE'RE ALL
WORKING TOGETHER
WITH DAVID BOWIE
THANK YOU, GOOD NIGHT!
ODEON
SMITH
HAMMER
NO RE-ADMISSION
NO RE-ADMISSION
NO RE-ADMISSION
NO RE-ADMISSION
NO RE-ADMISSION

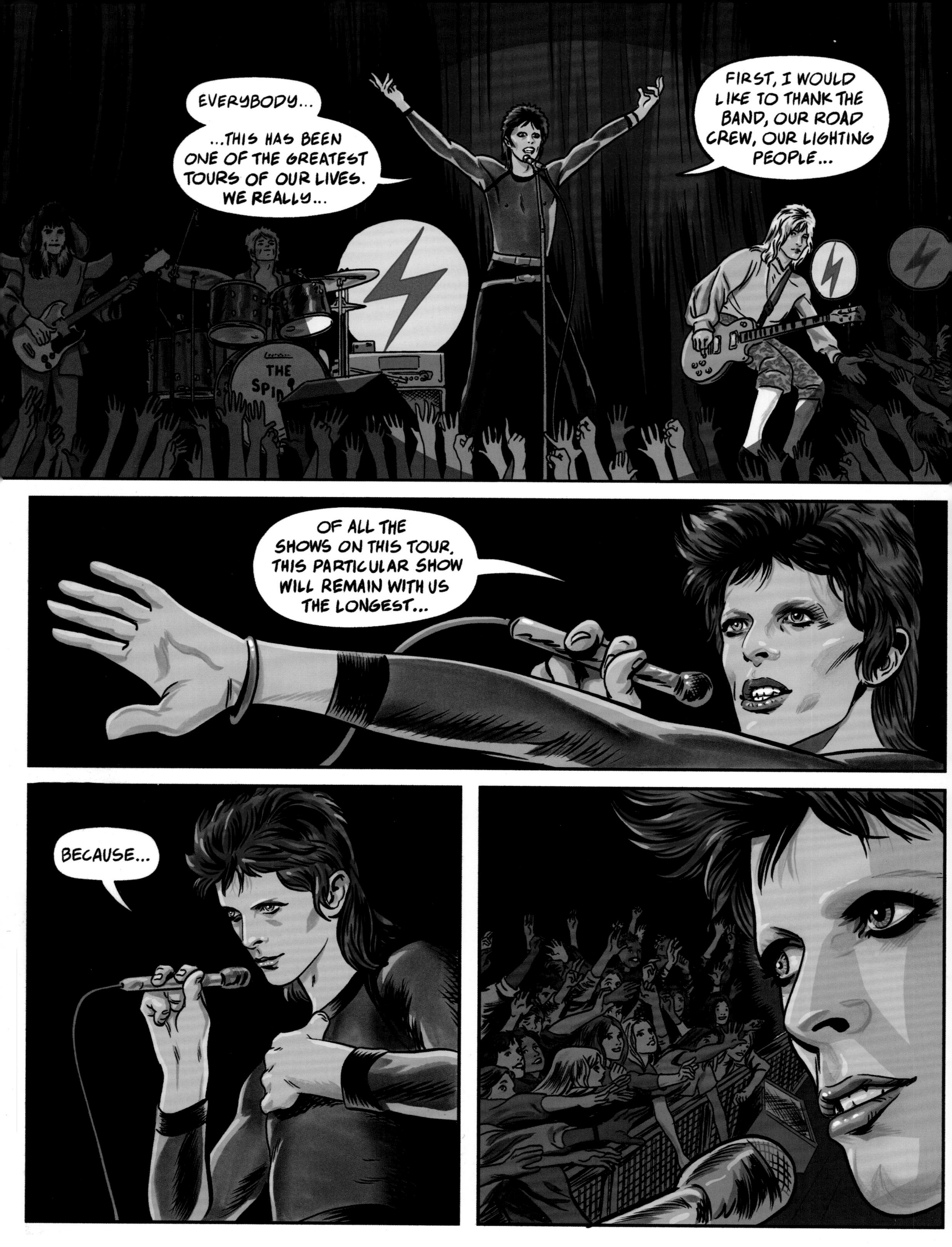
EVERYBODY...
...THIS HAS BEEN ONE OF THE GREATEST TOURS OF OUR LIVES. WE REALLY...
FIRST, I WOULD LIKE TO THANK THE BAND, OUR ROAD CREW, OUR LIGHTING PEOPLE...
OF ALL THE SHOWS ON THIS TOUR, THIS PARTICULAR SHOW WILL REMAIN WITH US THE LONGEST...
BECAUSE...

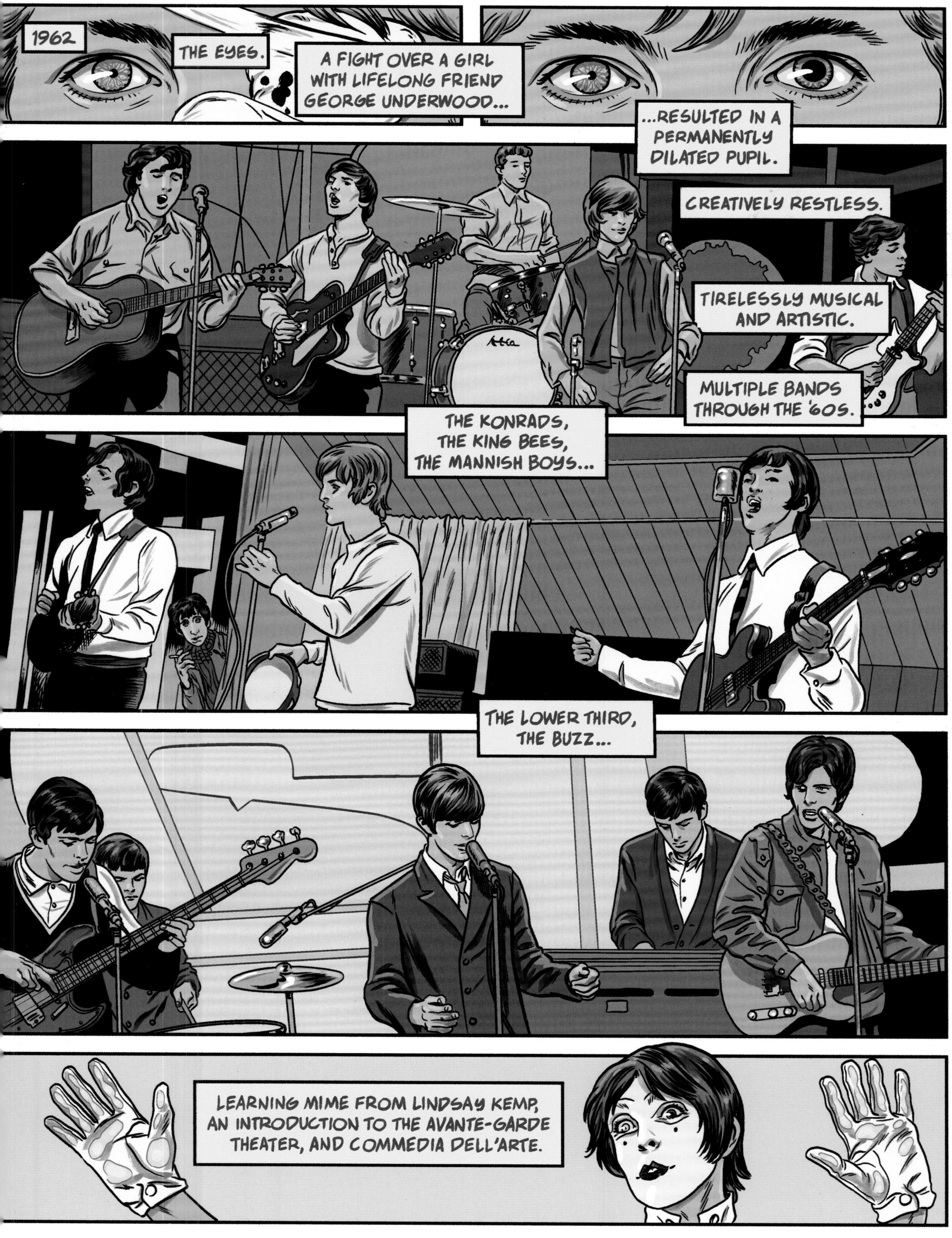

1962
THE EYES.
A FIGHT OVER A GIRL WITH LIFELONG FRIEND GEORGE UNDERWOOD...
...RESULTED IN A PERMANENTLY DILATED PUPIL.
CREATIVELY RESTLESS.
TIRELESSLY MUSICAL AND ARTISTIC.
MULTIPLE BANDS THROUGH THE '60S.
THE KONRADS, THE KING BEES, THE MANNISH BOYS...
THE LOWER THIRD, THE BUZZ...
LEARNING MIME FROM LINDSAY KEMP, AN INTRODUCTION TO THE AVANTE-GARDE THEATER, AND COMMEDIA DELL'ARTE.

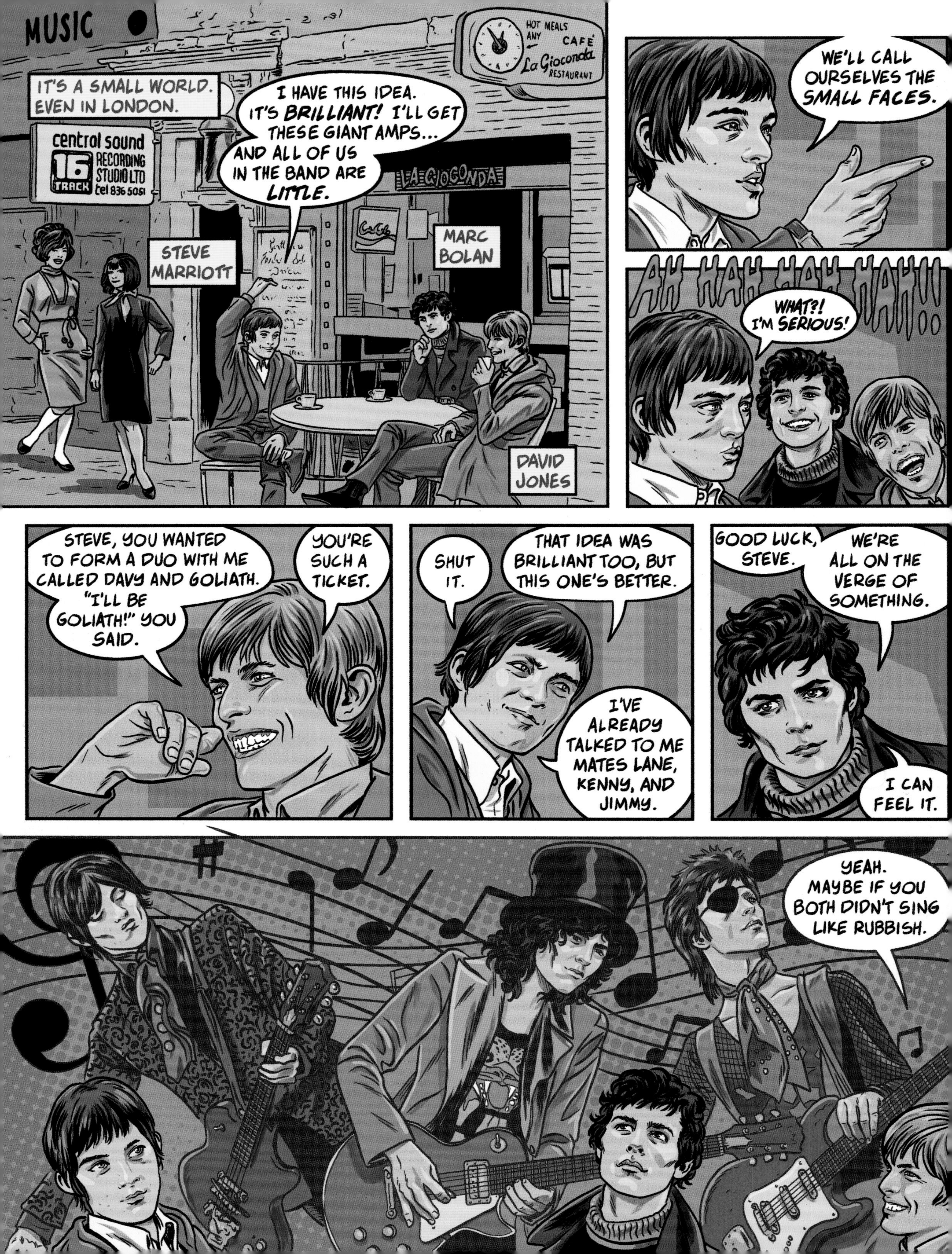
MUSIC
HOT MEALS ANY CAFÉ La Gioconda RESTAURANT
IT'S A SMALL WORLD. EVEN IN LONDON.
central sound 16 TRACK RECORDING STUDIO LTD tel 836 5051
I HAVE THIS IDEA. IT'S BRILLIANT! I'LL GET THESE GIANT AMPS... AND ALL OF US IN THE BAND ARE LITTLE.
LA GIOCONDA
STEVE MARRIOTT
MARC BOLAN
DAVID JONES
WE'LL CALL OURSELVES THE SMALL FACES.
AH HAH HAH HAH!!
WHAT?! I'M SERIOUS!
STEVE, YOU WANTED TO FORM A DUO WITH ME CALLED DAVY AND GOLIATH. "I'LL BE GOLIATH!" YOU SAID.
YOU'RE SUCH A TICKET.
SHUT IT.
THAT IDEA WAS BRILLIANT TOO, BUT THIS ONE'S BETTER.
I'VE ALREADY TALKED TO ME MATES LANE, KENNY, AND JIMMY.
GOOD LUCK, STEVE.
WE'RE ALL ON THE VERGE OF SOMETHING.
I CAN FEEL IT.
YEAH. MAYBE IF YOU BOTH DIDN'T SING LIKE RUBBISH.

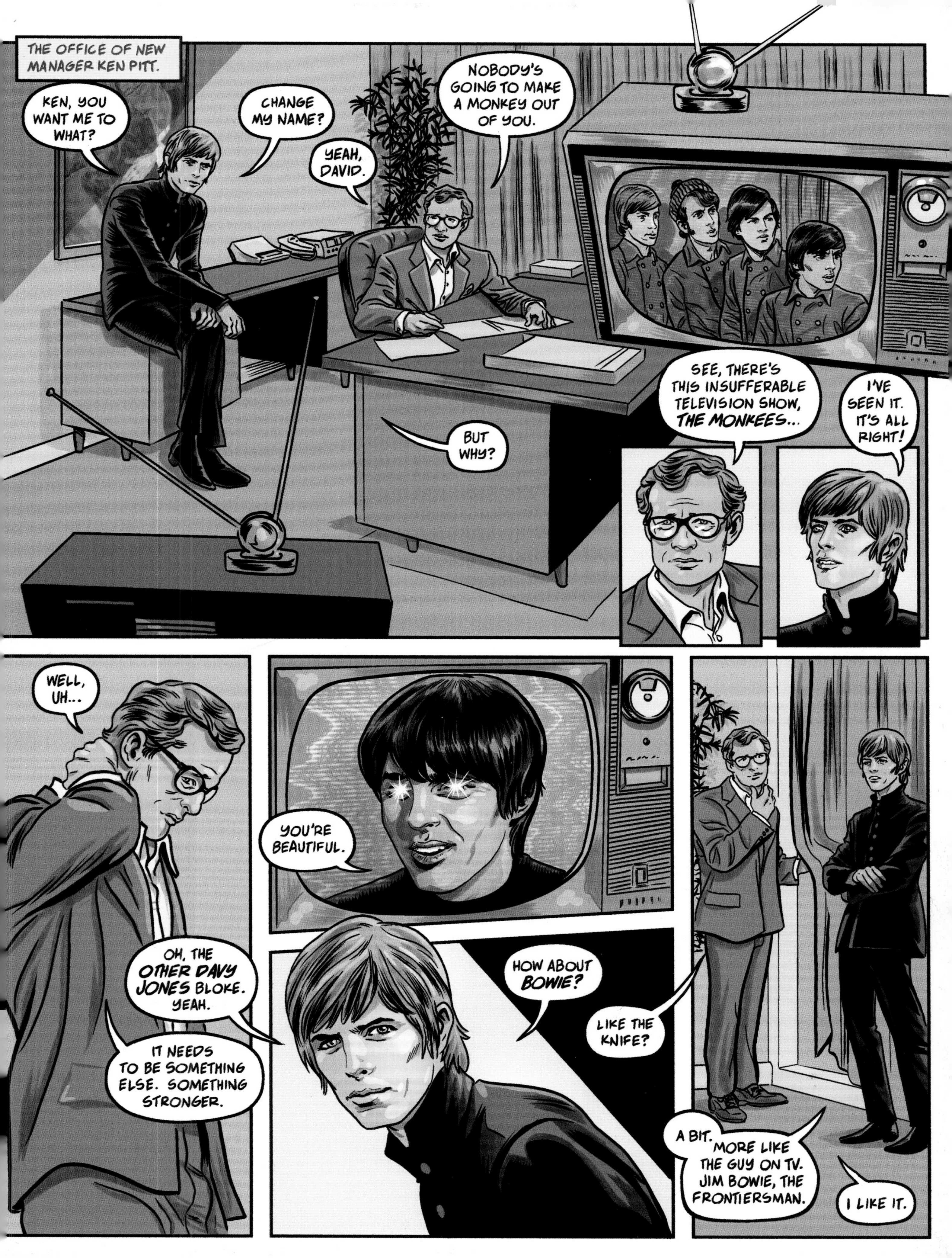
THE OFFICE OF NEW MANAGER KEN PITT.
KEN, YOU WANT ME TO WHAT?
CHANGE MY NAME?
YEAH, DAVID.
NOBODY'S GOING TO MAKE A MONKEY OUT OF YOU.
BUT WHY?
SEE, THERE'S THIS INSUFFERABLE TELEVISION SHOW, THE MONKEES...
I'VE SEEN IT. IT'S ALL RIGHT!
WELL, UH...
YOU'RE BEAUTIFUL.
OH, THE OTHER DAVY JONES BLOKE. YEAH.
IT NEEDS TO BE SOMETHING ELSE. SOMETHING STRONGER.
HOW ABOUT BOWIE?
LIKE THE KNIFE?
A BIT.
MORE LIKE THE GUY ON TV. JIM BOWIE, THE FRONTIERSMAN.
I LIKE IT.

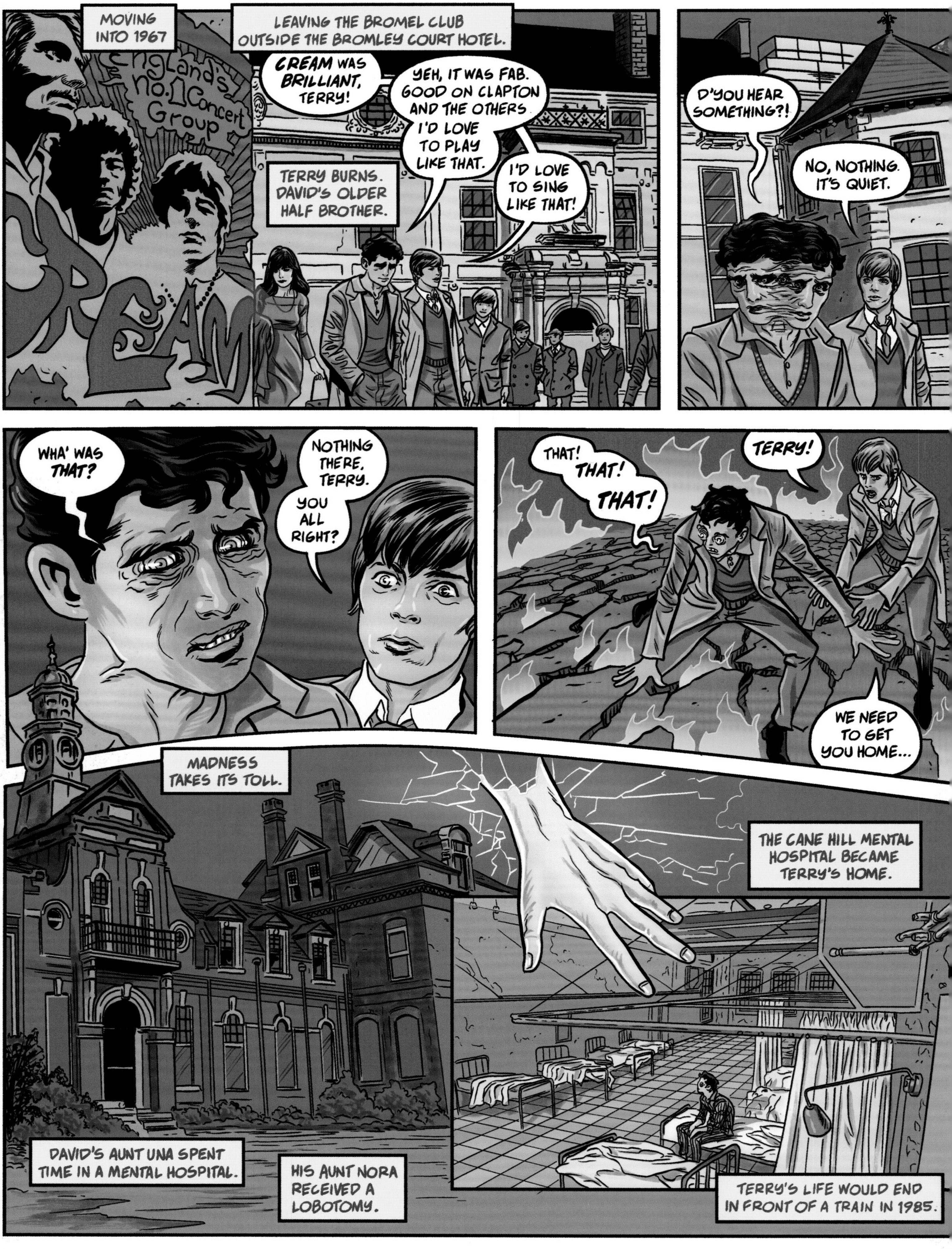
MOVING INTO 1967
England's No.1 Concert Group
CREAM
LEAVING THE BROMEL CLUB OUTSIDE THE BROMLEY COURT HOTEL.
CREAM WAS BRILLIANT, TERRY!
YEH, IT WAS FAB. GOOD ON CLAPTON AND THE OTHERS
I'D LOVE TO PLAY LIKE THAT.
TERRY BURNS. DAVID'S OLDER HALF BROTHER.
I'D LOVE TO SING LIKE THAT!
D'YOU HEAR SOMETHING?!
NO, NOTHING. IT'S QUIET.
WHA' WAS THAT?
NOTHING THERE, TERRY.
YOU ALL RIGHT?
THAT! THAT! THAT!
TERRY!
WE NEED TO GET YOU HOME...
MADNESS TAKES ITS TOLL.
THE CANE HILL MENTAL HOSPITAL BECAME TERRY'S HOME.
DAVID'S AUNT UNA SPENT TIME IN A MENTAL HOSPITAL.
HIS AUNT NORA RECEIVED A LOBOTOMY.
TERRY'S LIFE WOULD END IN FRONT OF A TRAIN IN 1985.

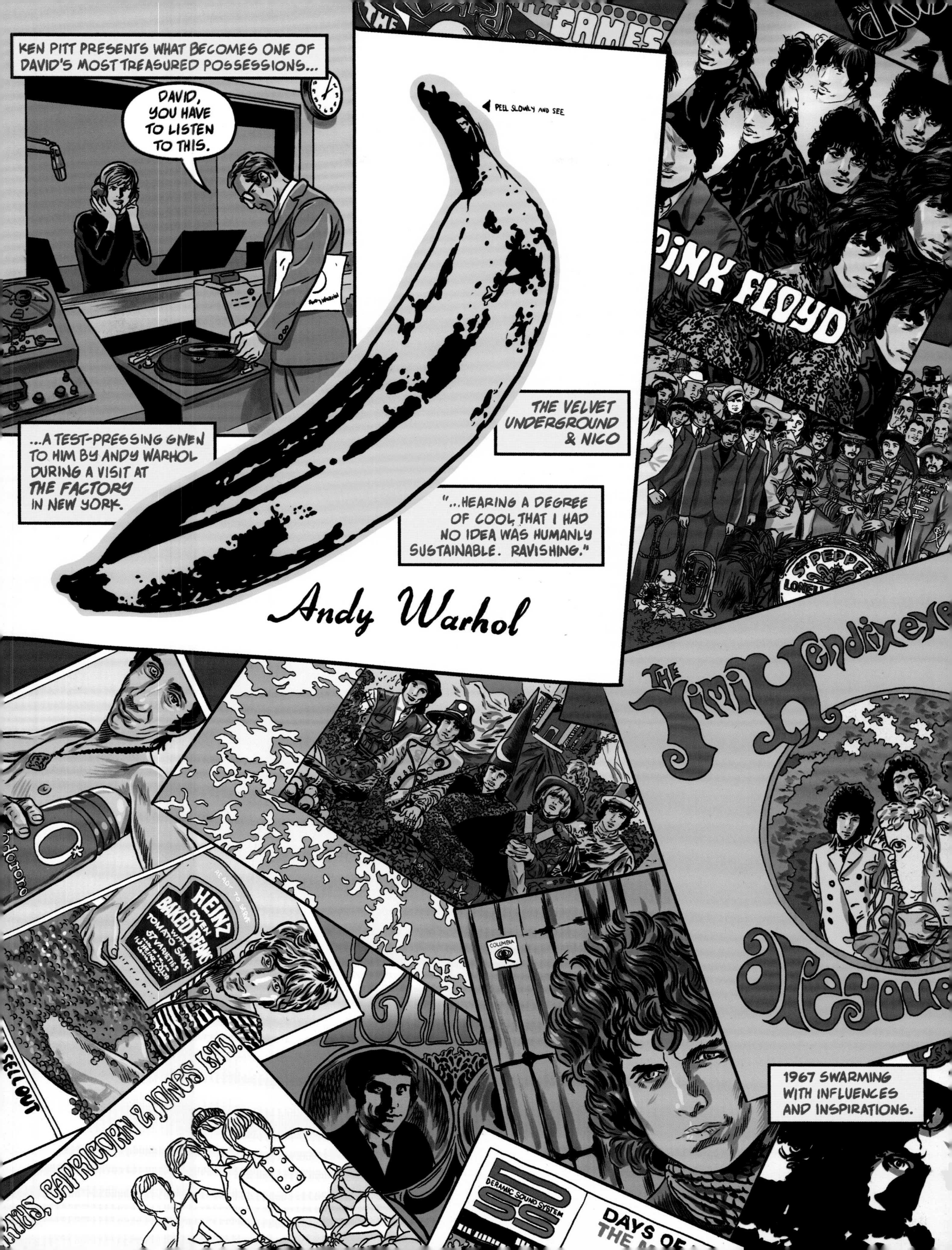

KEN PITT PRESENTS WHAT BECOMES ONE OF DAVID'S MOST TREASURED POSSESSIONS...
DAVID, YOU HAVE TO LISTEN TO THIS.
...A TEST-PRESSING GIVEN TO HIM BY ANDY WARHOL DURING A VISIT AT THE FACTORY IN NEW YORK.
PEEL SLOWLY AND SEE
THE VELVET UNDERGROUND & NICO
"...HEARING A DEGREE OF COOL THAT I HAD NO IDEA WAS HUMANLY SUSTAINABLE. RAVISHING."
Andy Warhol
PINK FLOYD
THE JIMI HENDRIX EXPERIENCE
HEINZ OVEN BAKED BEANS WITH TOMATO SAUCE
COLUMBIA
DERAMIC SOUND SYSTEM
1967 SWARMING WITH INFLUENCES AND INSPIRATIONS.

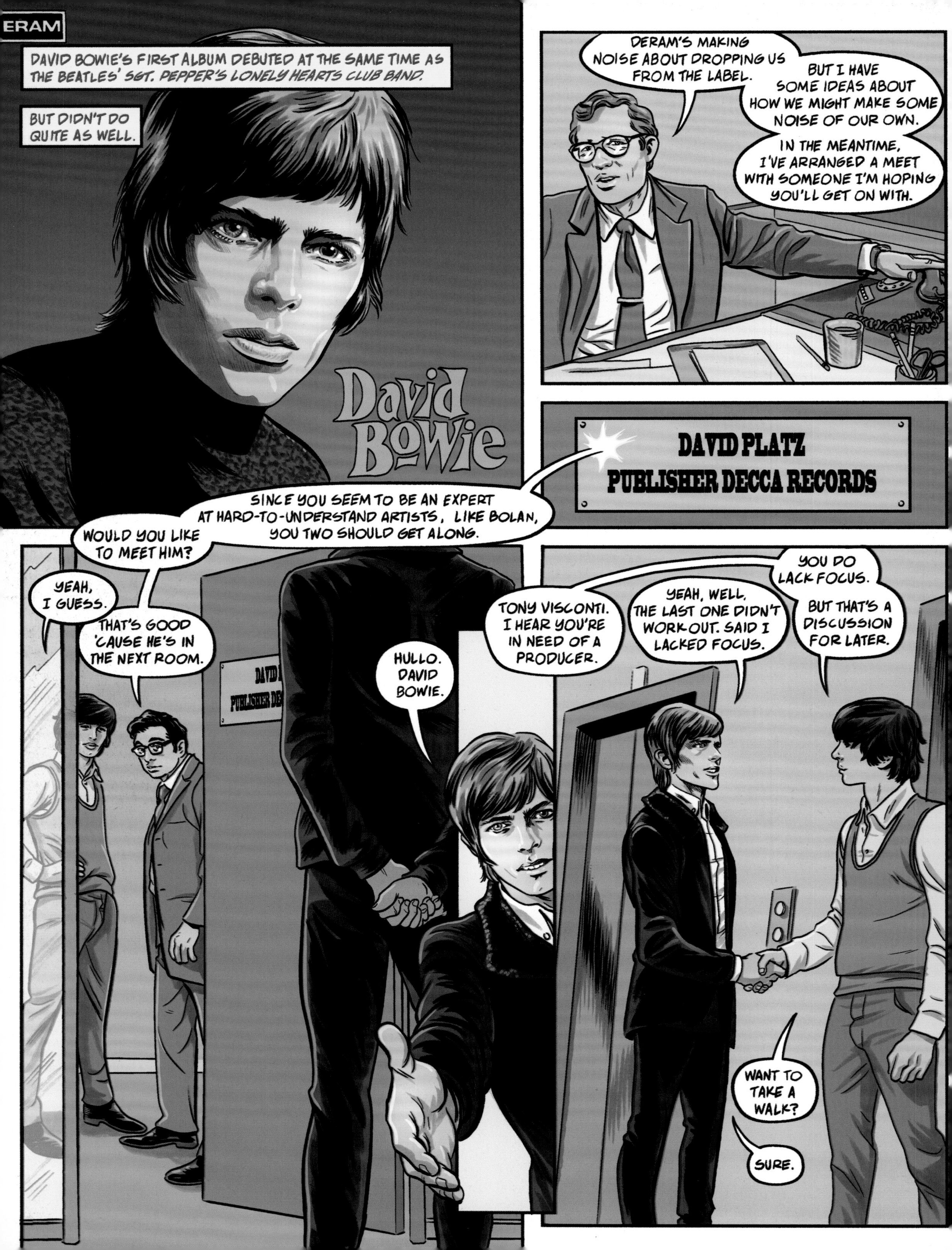
ERAM
DAVID BOWIE'S FIRST ALBUM DEBUTED AT THE SAME TIME AS THE BEATLES' SGT. PEPPER'S LONELY HEARTS CLUB BAND.
BUT DIDN'T DO QUITE AS WELL.
David Bowie
DERAM'S MAKING NOISE ABOUT DROPPING US FROM THE LABEL.
BUT I HAVE SOME IDEAS ABOUT HOW WE MIGHT MAKE SOME NOISE OF OUR OWN.
IN THE MEANTIME, I'VE ARRANGED A MEET WITH SOMEONE I'M HOPING YOU'LL GET ON WITH.
DAVID PLATZ
PUBLISHER DECCA RECORDS
SINCE YOU SEEM TO BE AN EXPERT AT HARD-TO-UNDERSTAND ARTISTS, LIKE BOLAN, YOU TWO SHOULD GET ALONG.
WOULD YOU LIKE TO MEET HIM?
YEAH, I GUESS.
THAT'S GOOD 'CAUSE HE'S IN THE NEXT ROOM.
HULLO. DAVID BOWIE.
TONY VISCONTI. I HEAR YOU'RE IN NEED OF A PRODUCER.
YEAH, WELL, THE LAST ONE DIDN'T WORK OUT. SAID I LACKED FOCUS.
YOU DO LACK FOCUS.
BUT THAT'S A DISCUSSION FOR LATER.
WANT TO TAKE A WALK?
SURE.

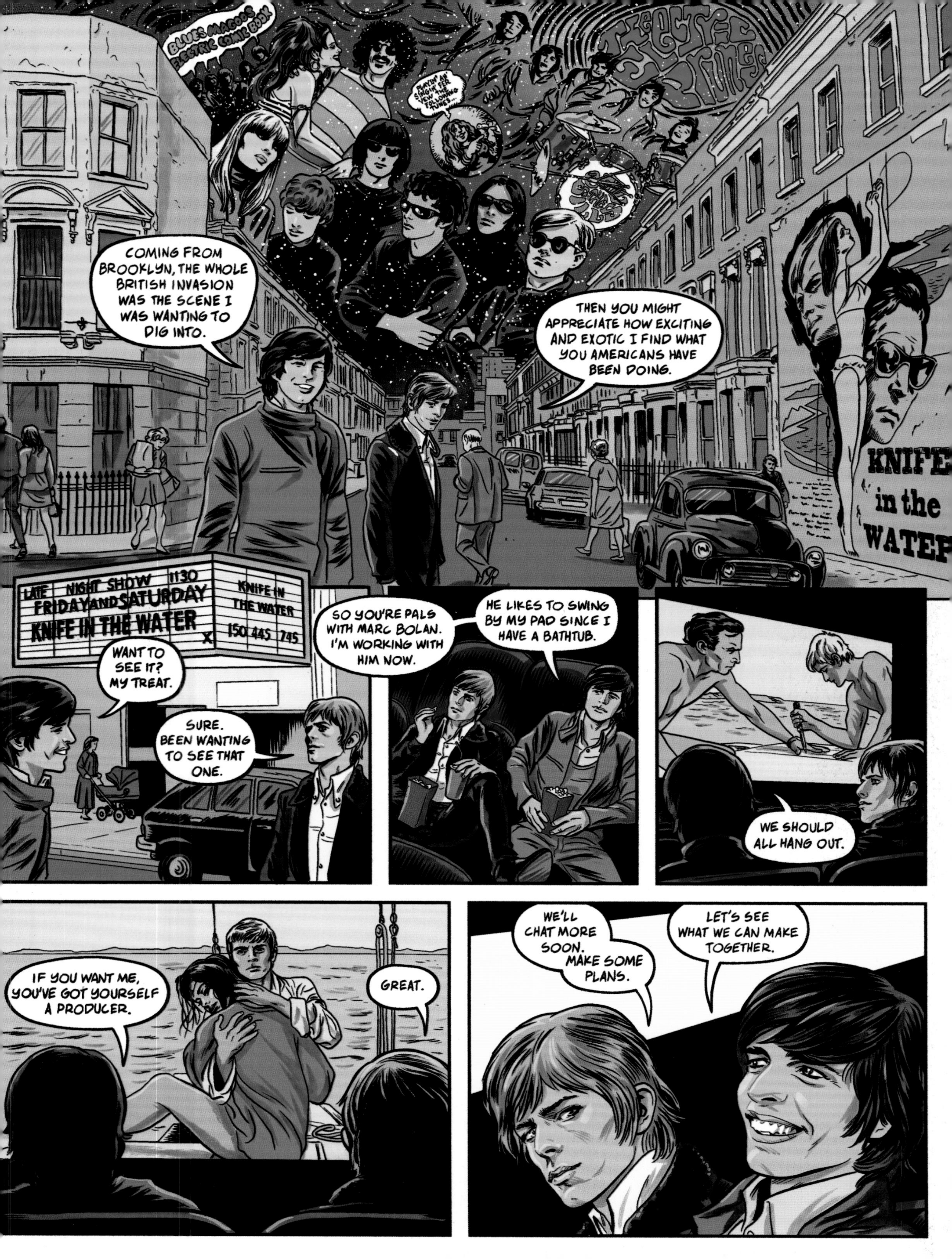
BLUES MAGOOS ELECTRIC COMIC BOOK
COMING FROM BROOKLYN, THE WHOLE BRITISH INVASION WAS THE SCENE I WAS WANTING TO DIG INTO.
THEN YOU MIGHT APPRECIATE HOW EXCITING AND EXOTIC I FIND WHAT YOU AMERICANS HAVE BEEN DOING.
KNIFE in the WATER
LATE NIGHT SHOW 1130
FRIDAY AND SATURDAY
KNIFE IN THE WATER
KNIFE IN THE WATER
150 445 745
WANT TO SEE IT? MY TREAT.
SURE. BEEN WANTING TO SEE THAT ONE.
SO YOU'RE PALS WITH MARC BOLAN. I'M WORKING WITH HIM NOW.
HE LIKES TO SWING BY MY PAD SINCE I HAVE A BATHTUB.
WE SHOULD ALL HANG OUT.
IF YOU WANT ME, YOU'VE GOT YOURSELF A PRODUCER.
GREAT.
WE'LL CHAT MORE SOON.
MAKE SOME PLANS.
LET'S SEE WHAT WE CAN MAKE TOGETHER.

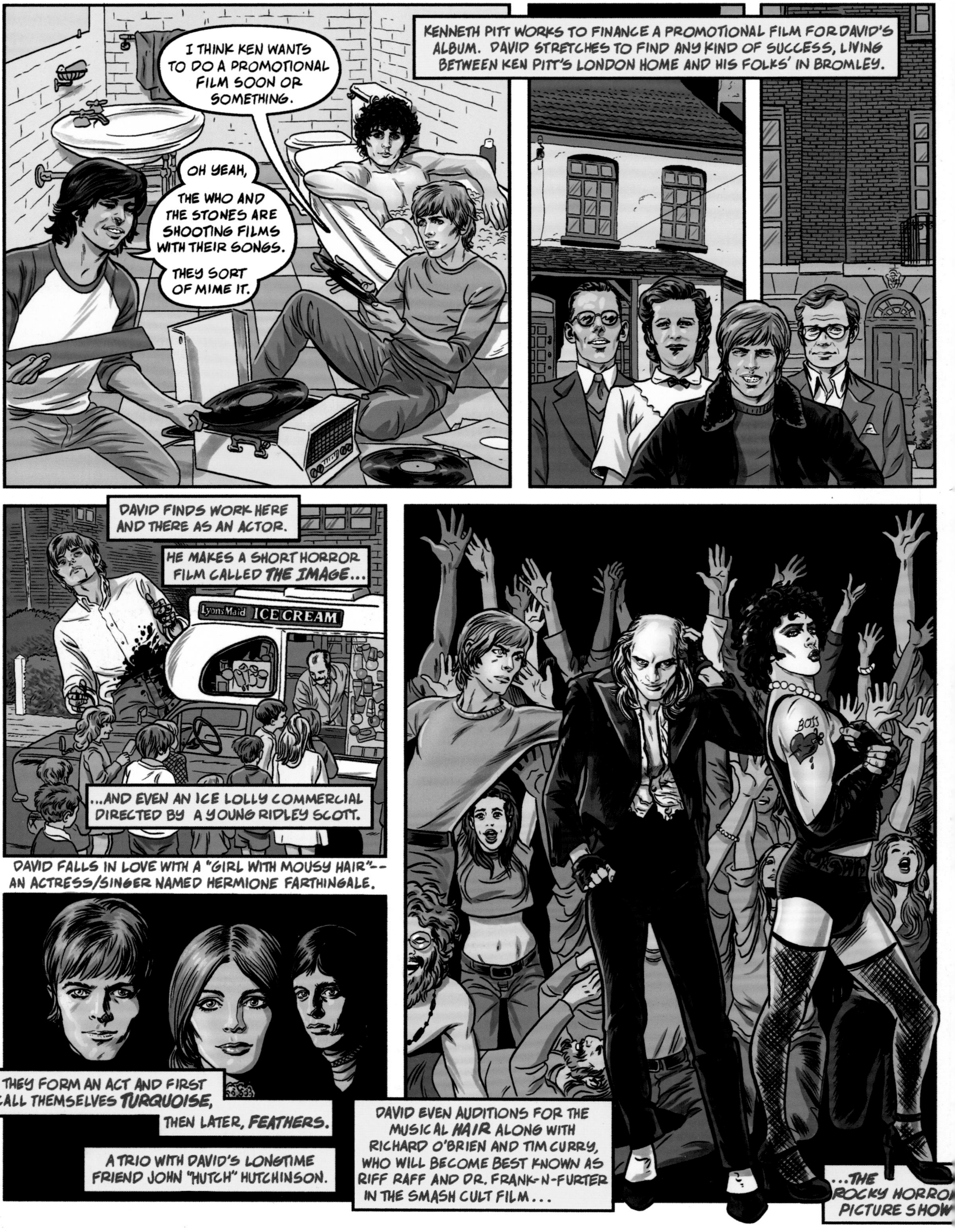

I THINK KEN WANTS TO DO A PROMOTIONAL FILM SOON OR SOMETHING.
OH YEAH,
THE WHO AND THE STONES ARE SHOOTING FILMS WITH THEIR SONGS.
THEY SORT OF MIME IT.
KENNETH PITT WORKS TO FINANCE A PROMOTIONAL FILM FOR DAVID'S ALBUM. DAVID STRETCHES TO FIND ANY KIND OF SUCCESS, LIVING BETWEEN KEN PITT'S LONDON HOME AND HIS FOLKS' IN BROMLEY.
DAVID FINDS WORK HERE AND THERE AS AN ACTOR.
HE MAKES A SHORT HORROR FILM CALLED THE IMAGE...
Lyons Maid ICE CREAM
...AND EVEN AN ICE LOLLY COMMERCIAL DIRECTED BY A YOUNG RIDLEY SCOTT.
DAVID FALLS IN LOVE WITH A "GIRL WITH MOUSY HAIR"-- AN ACTRESS/SINGER NAMED HERMIONE FARTHINGALE.
THEY FORM AN ACT AND FIRST CALL THEMSELVES TURQUOISE,
THEN LATER, FEATHERS.
A TRIO WITH DAVID'S LONGTIME FRIEND JOHN "HUTCH" HUTCHINSON.
BOSS
DAVID EVEN AUDITIONS FOR THE MUSICAL HAIR ALONG WITH RICHARD O'BRIEN AND TIM CURRY, WHO WILL BECOME BEST KNOWN AS RIFF RAFF AND DR. FRANK-N-FURTER IN THE SMASH CULT FILM...
...THE ROCKY HORROR PICTURE SHOW

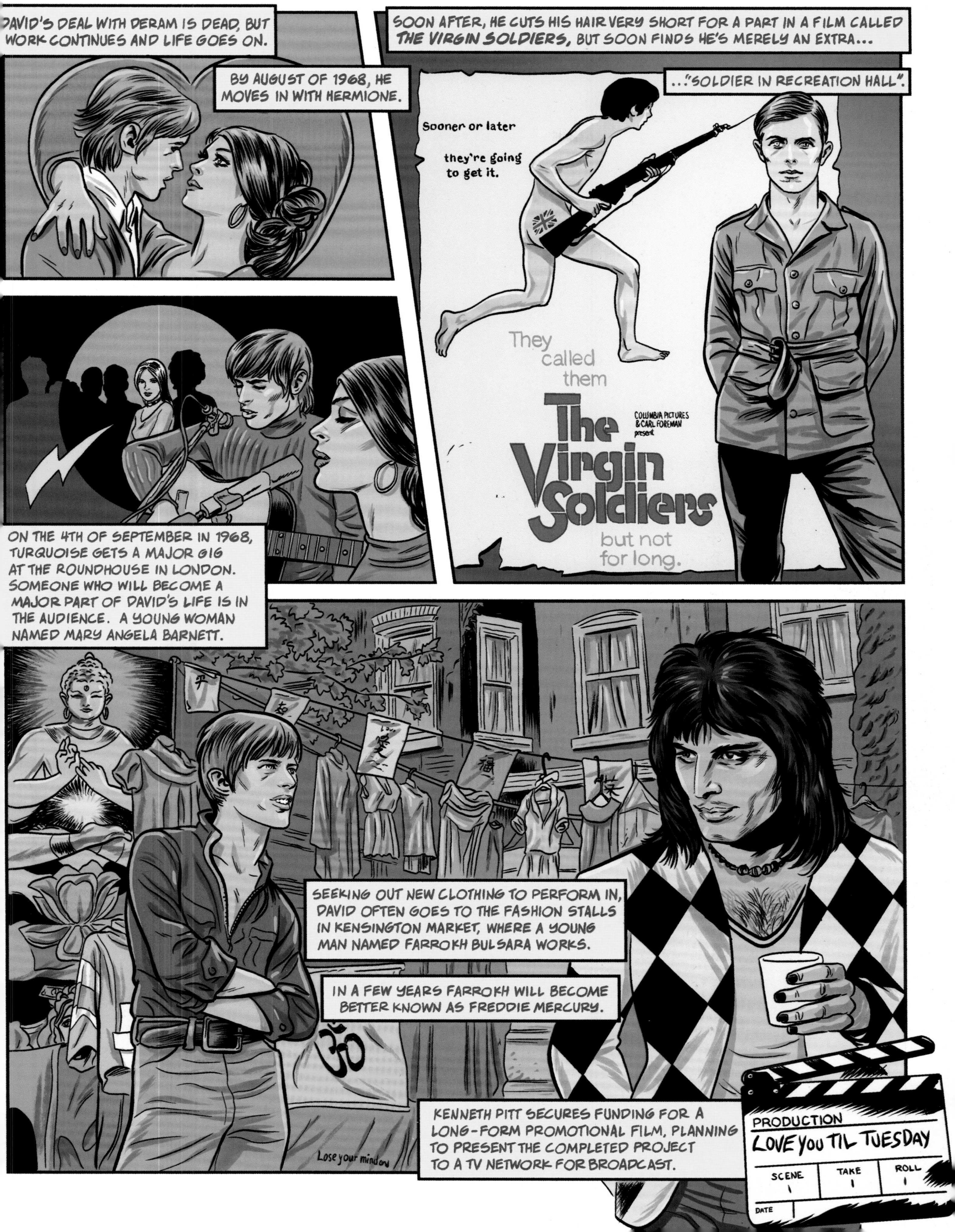
DAVID'S DEAL WITH DERAM IS DEAD, BUT WORK CONTINUES AND LIFE GOES ON.
BY AUGUST OF 1968, HE MOVES IN WITH HERMIONE.
SOON AFTER, HE CUTS HIS HAIR VERY SHORT FOR A PART IN A FILM CALLED THE VIRGIN SOLDIERS, BUT SOON FINDS HE'S MERELY AN EXTRA...
..."SOLDIER IN RECREATION HALL".
Sooner or later
they're going to get it.
They called them
COLUMBIA PICTURES & CARL FOREMAN present
The Virgin Soldiers
but not for long.
ON THE 4TH OF SEPTEMBER IN 1968, TURQUOISE GETS A MAJOR GIG AT THE ROUNDHOUSE IN LONDON. SOMEONE WHO WILL BECOME A MAJOR PART OF DAVID'S LIFE IS IN THE AUDIENCE. A YOUNG WOMAN NAMED MARY ANGELA BARNETT.
SEEKING OUT NEW CLOTHING TO PERFORM IN, DAVID OFTEN GOES TO THE FASHION STALLS IN KENSINGTON MARKET, WHERE A YOUNG MAN NAMED FARROKH BULSARA WORKS.
IN A FEW YEARS FARROKH WILL BECOME BETTER KNOWN AS FREDDIE MERCURY.
Lose your mind
KENNETH PITT SECURES FUNDING FOR A LONG-FORM PROMOTIONAL FILM, PLANNING TO PRESENT THE COMPLETED PROJECT TO A TV NETWORK FOR BROADCAST.
PRODUCTION
LOVE YOU TIL TUESDAY
SCENE
1
TAKE
1
ROLL
1
DATE

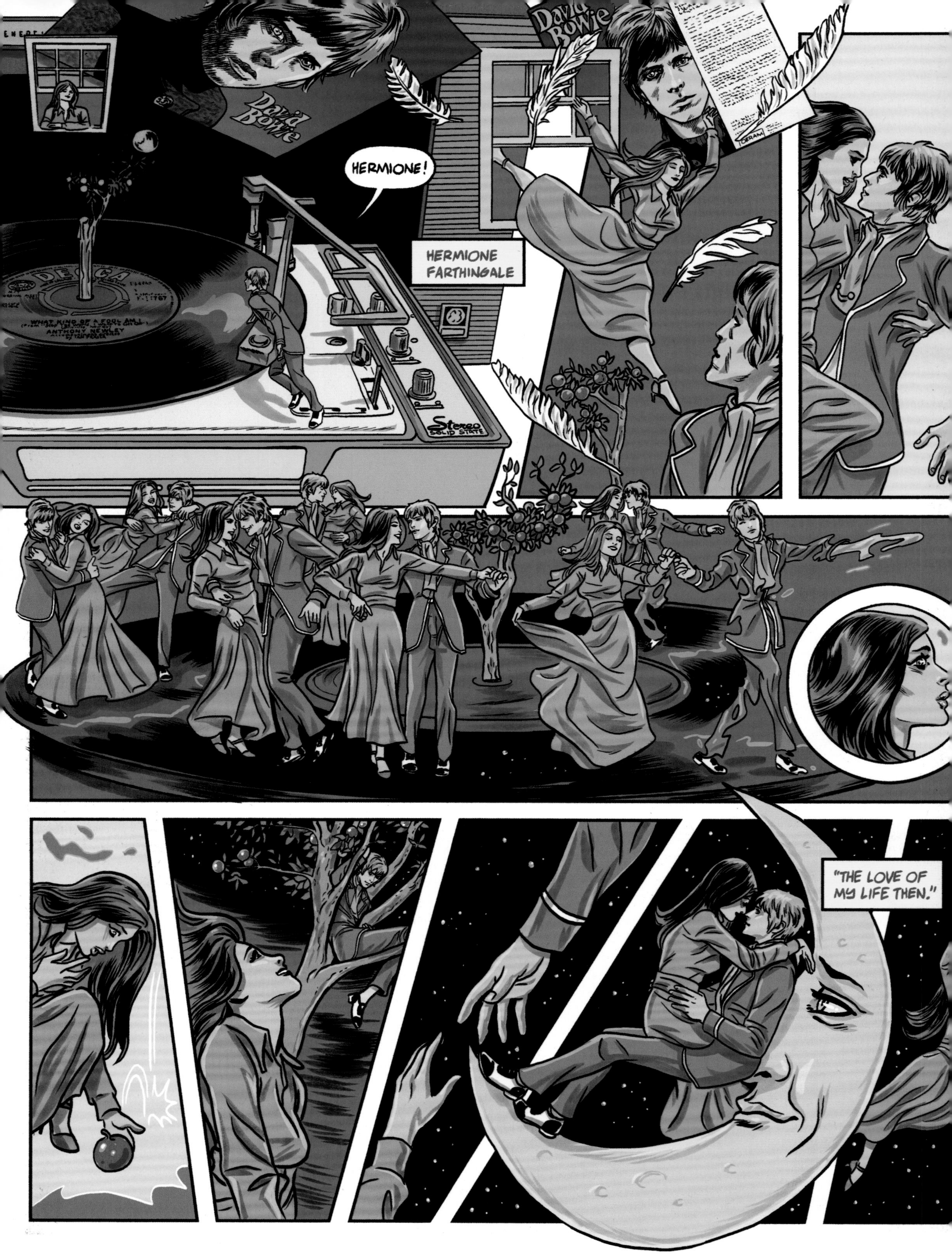

HERMIONE!
HERMIONE FARTHINGALE
David Bowie
DECCA
WHAT KIND OF A FOOL AM I
ANTHONY NEWLEY
Stereo
SOLID STATE
"THE LOVE OF MY LIFE THEN."

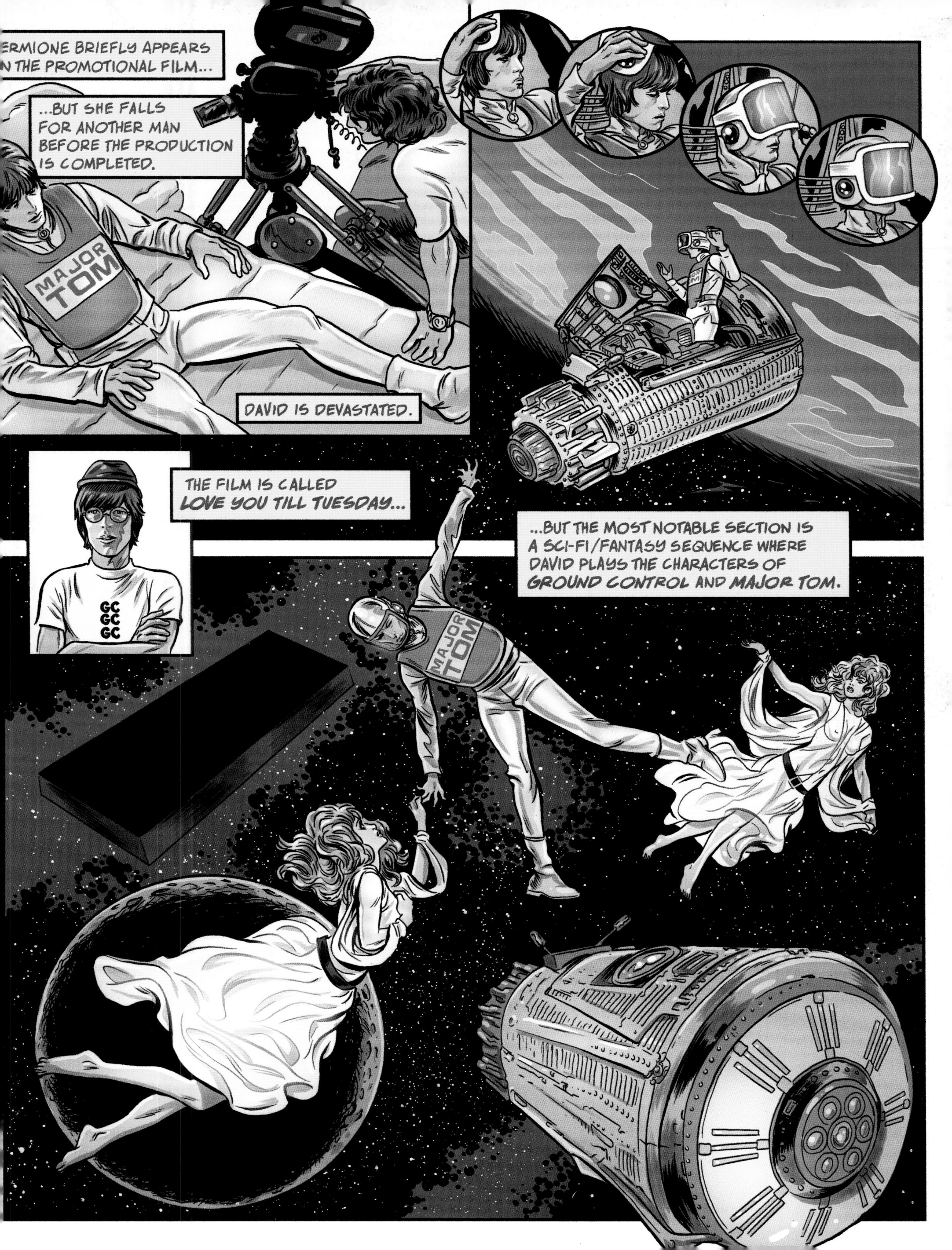

ERMIONE BRIEFLY APPEARS
N THE PROMOTIONAL FILM...
...BUT SHE FALLS FOR ANOTHER MAN BEFORE THE PRODUCTION IS COMPLETED.
MAJOR TOM
DAVID IS DEVASTATED.
THE FILM IS CALLED LOVE YOU TILL TUESDAY...
GC GC GC
...BUT THE MOST NOTABLE SECTION IS A SCI-FI/FANTASY SEQUENCE WHERE DAVID PLAYS THE CHARACTERS OF GROUND CONTROL AND MAJOR TOM.
MAJOR TOM

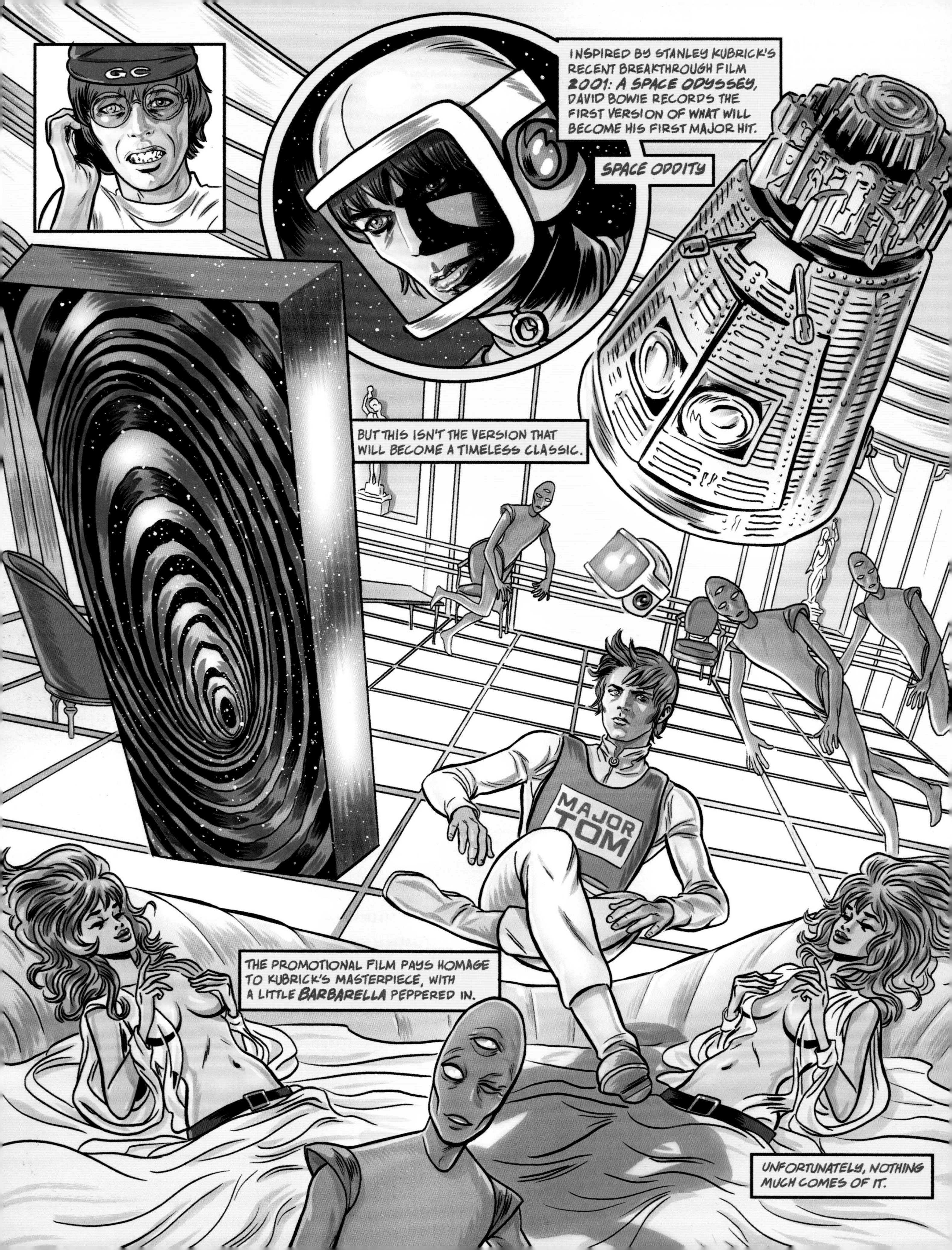
INSPIRED BY STANLEY KUBRICK'S RECENT BREAKTHROUGH FILM *2001: A SPACE ODYSSEY*, DAVID BOWIE RECORDS THE FIRST VERSION OF WHAT WILL BECOME HIS FIRST MAJOR HIT.
SPACE ODDITY
GC
BUT THIS ISN'T THE VERSION THAT WILL BECOME A TIMELESS CLASSIC.
MAJOR TOM
THE PROMOTIONAL FILM PAYS HOMAGE TO KUBRICK'S MASTERPIECE, WITH A LITTLE *BARBARELLA* PEPPERED IN.
UNFORTUNATELY, NOTHING MUCH COMES OF IT.

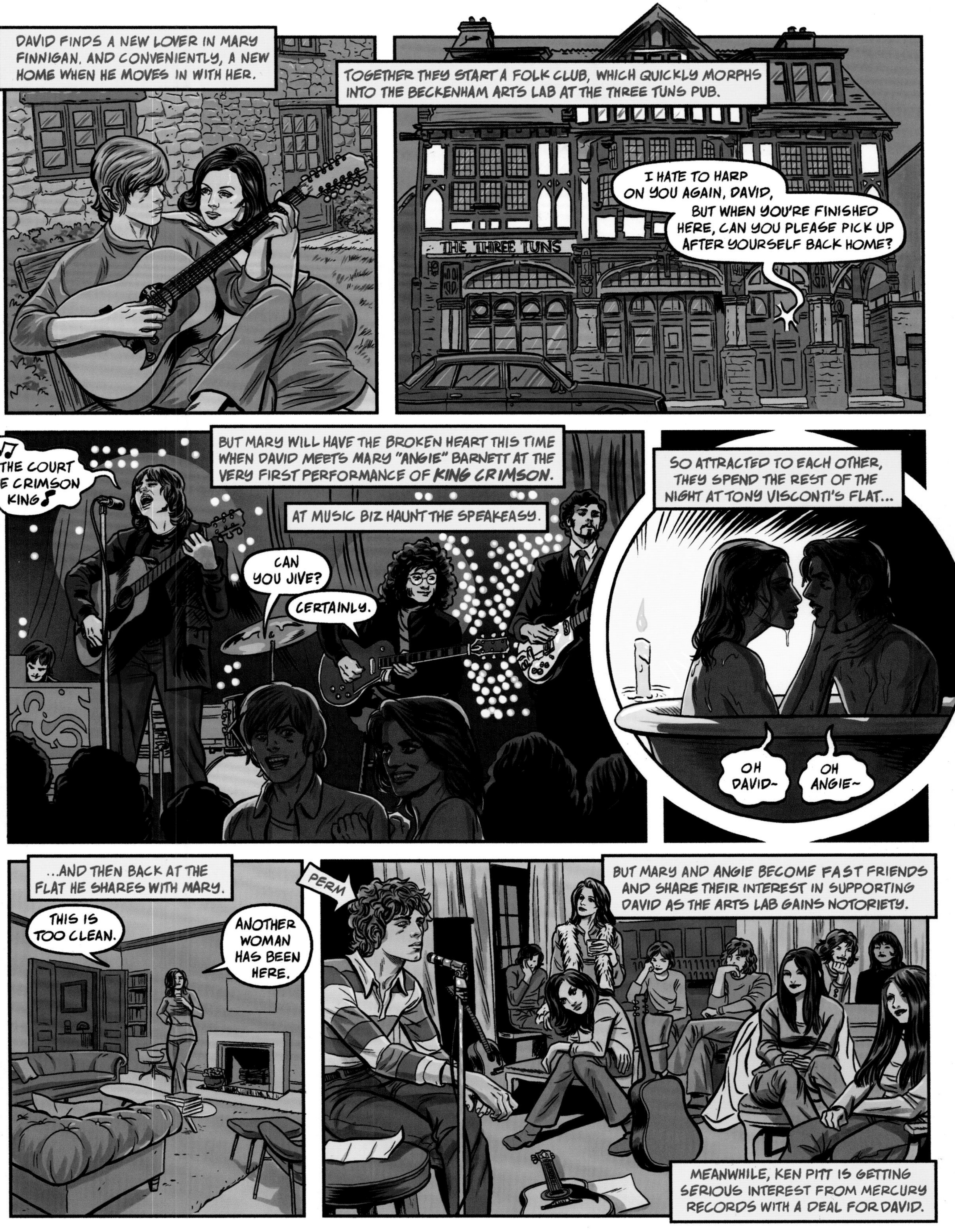

DAVID FINDS A NEW LOVER IN MARY FINNIGAN. AND CONVENIENTLY, A NEW HOME WHEN HE MOVES IN WITH HER.
TOGETHER THEY START A FOLK CLUB, WHICH QUICKLY MORPHS INTO THE BECKENHAM ARTS LAB AT THE THREE TUNS PUB.
THE THREE TUNS
I HATE TO HARP ON YOU AGAIN, DAVID,
BUT WHEN YOU'RE FINISHED HERE, CAN YOU PLEASE PICK UP AFTER YOURSELF BACK HOME?
BUT MARY WILL HAVE THE BROKEN HEART THIS TIME WHEN DAVID MEETS MARY "ANGIE" BARNETT AT THE VERY FIRST PERFORMANCE OF KING CRIMSON.
AT MUSIC BIZ HAUNT THE SPEAKEASY.
THE COURT HE CRIMSON KING
CAN YOU JIVE?
CERTAINLY.
SO ATTRACTED TO EACH OTHER, THEY SPEND THE REST OF THE NIGHT AT TONY VISCONTI'S FLAT...
OH DAVID~
OH ANGIE~
...AND THEN BACK AT THE FLAT HE SHARES WITH MARY.
THIS IS TOO CLEAN.
ANOTHER WOMAN HAS BEEN HERE.
PERM
BUT MARY AND ANGIE BECOME FAST FRIENDS AND SHARE THEIR INTEREST IN SUPPORTING DAVID AS THE ARTS LAB GAINS NOTORIETY.
MEANWHILE, KEN PITT IS GETTING SERIOUS INTEREST FROM MERCURY RECORDS WITH A DEAL FOR DAVID.

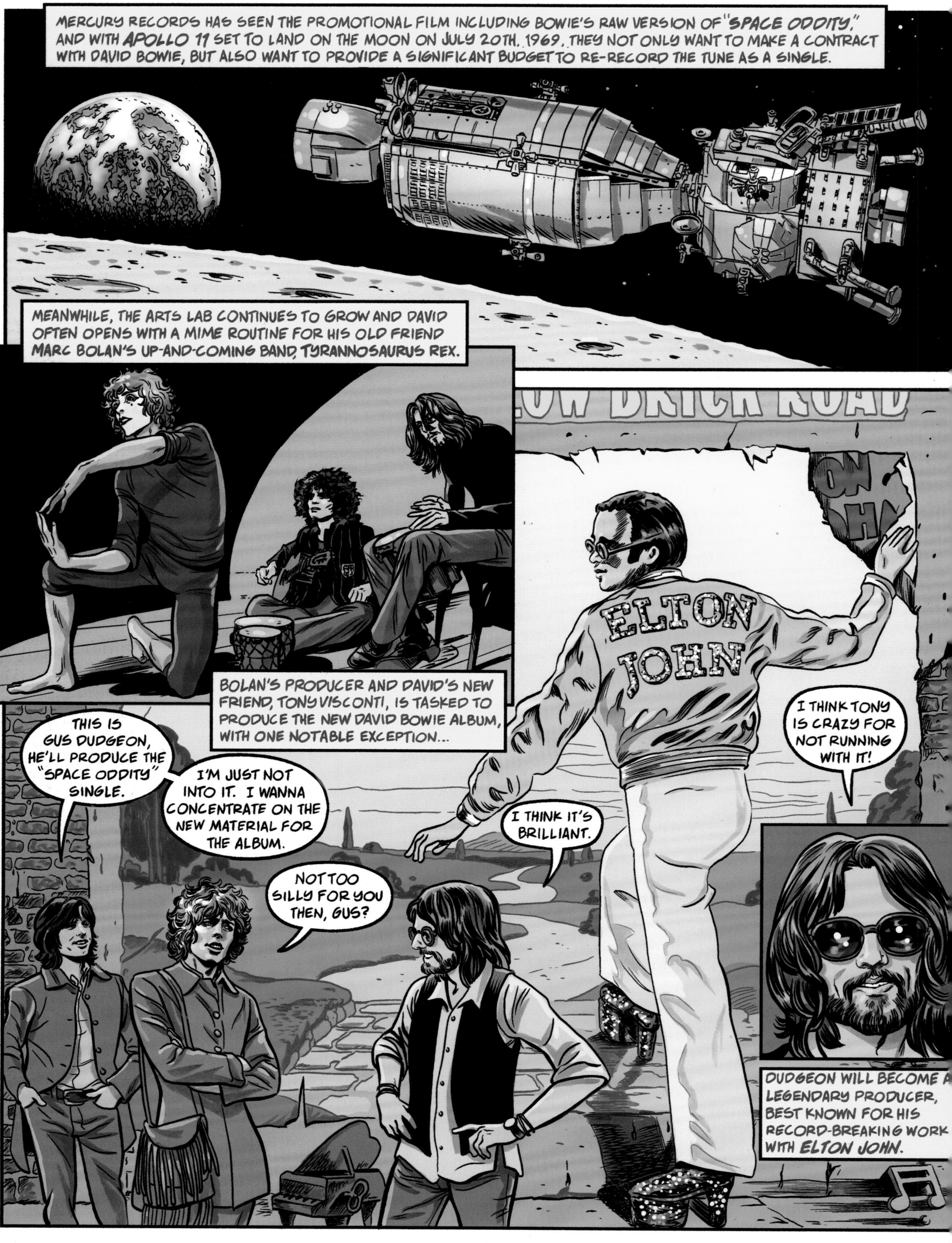

MERCURY RECORDS HAS SEEN THE PROMOTIONAL FILM INCLUDING BOWIE'S RAW VERSION OF "SPACE ODDITY," AND WITH APOLLO 11 SET TO LAND ON THE MOON ON JULY 20TH, 1969, THEY NOT ONLY WANT TO MAKE A CONTRACT WITH DAVID BOWIE, BUT ALSO WANT TO PROVIDE A SIGNIFICANT BUDGET TO RE-RECORD THE TUNE AS A SINGLE.
MEANWHILE, THE ARTS LAB CONTINUES TO GROW AND DAVID OFTEN OPENS WITH A MIME ROUTINE FOR HIS OLD FRIEND MARC BOLAN'S UP-AND-COMING BAND, TYRANNOSAURUS REX.
BOLAN'S PRODUCER AND DAVID'S NEW FRIEND, TONY VISCONTI, IS TASKED TO PRODUCE THE NEW DAVID BOWIE ALBUM, WITH ONE NOTABLE EXCEPTION...
ELTON JOHN
THIS IS GUS DUDGEON, HE'LL PRODUCE THE "SPACE ODDITY" SINGLE.
I'M JUST NOT INTO IT. I WANNA CONCENTRATE ON THE NEW MATERIAL FOR THE ALBUM.
NOT TOO SILLY FOR YOU THEN, GUS?
I THINK IT'S BRILLIANT.
I THINK TONY IS CRAZY FOR NOT RUNNING WITH IT!
DUDGEON WILL BECOME A LEGENDARY PRODUCER, BEST KNOWN FOR HIS RECORD-BREAKING WORK WITH ELTON JOHN.

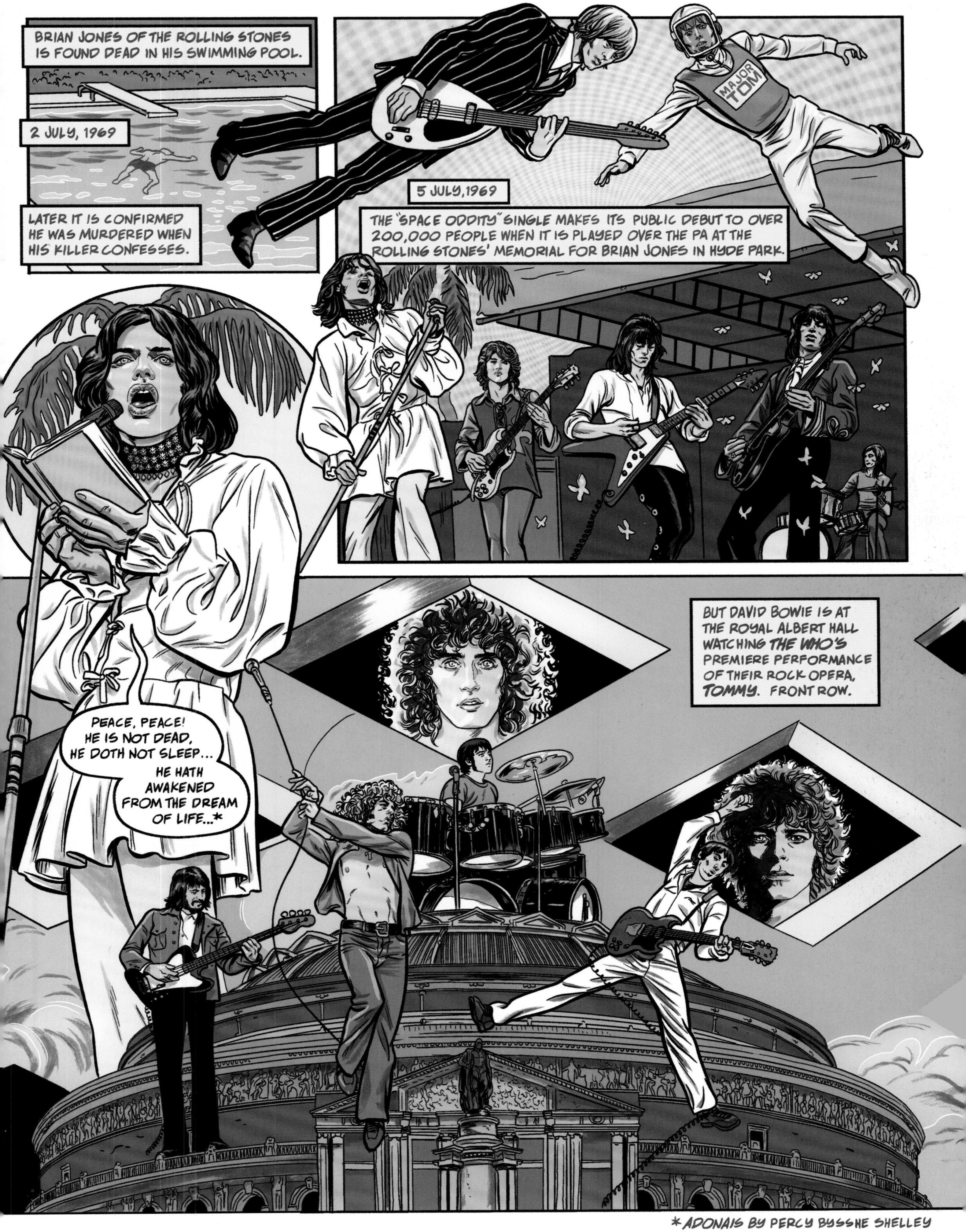
BRIAN JONES OF THE ROLLING STONES IS FOUND DEAD IN HIS SWIMMING POOL.
2 JULY, 1969
LATER IT IS CONFIRMED HE WAS MURDERED WHEN HIS KILLER CONFESSES.
MAJOR TOM
5 JULY, 1969
THE "SPACE ODDITY" SINGLE MAKES ITS PUBLIC DEBUT TO OVER 200,000 PEOPLE WHEN IT IS PLAYED OVER THE PA AT THE ROLLING STONES' MEMORIAL FOR BRIAN JONES IN HYDE PARK.
PEACE, PEACE! HE IS NOT DEAD, HE DOTH NOT SLEEP... HE HATH AWAKENED FROM THE DREAM OF LIFE...*
BUT DAVID BOWIE IS AT THE ROYAL ALBERT HALL WATCHING THE WHO'S PREMIERE PERFORMANCE OF THEIR ROCK OPERA, TOMMY. FRONT ROW.

*ADONAIS BY PERCY BYSSHE SHELLEY

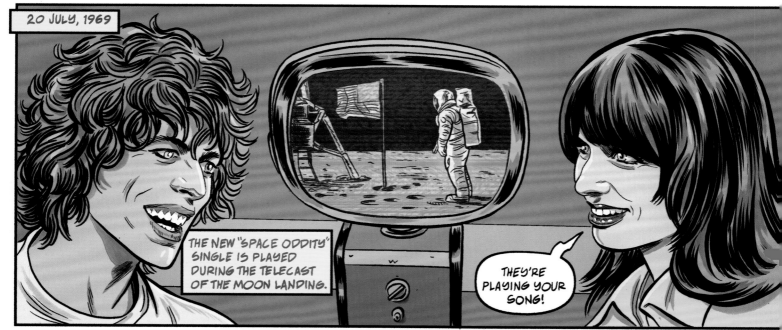

20 JULY, 1969

THE NEW "SPACE ODDITY" SINGLE IS PLAYED DURING THE TELECAST OF THE MOON LANDING.

THEY'RE PLAYING YOUR SONG!

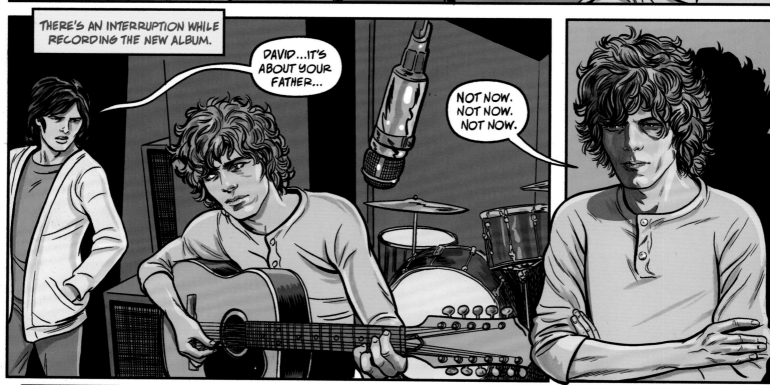

THERE'S AN INTERRUPTION WHILE RECORDING THE NEW ALBUM.

DAVID...IT'S ABOUT YOUR FATHER...

NOT NOW. NOT NOW. NOT NOW.

AUGUST 1969

HAYWOOD STENTON "JOHN" JONES.

DEAD AT 57 FROM PNEUMONIA.

IMMEDIATELY AFTER THE FUNERAL...

...DAVID AND ANGIE MOVE INTO HADDON HALL, WHAT WILL BECOME THEIR CREATIVE HEADQUARTERS FOR THE NEXT SEVERAL YEARS.

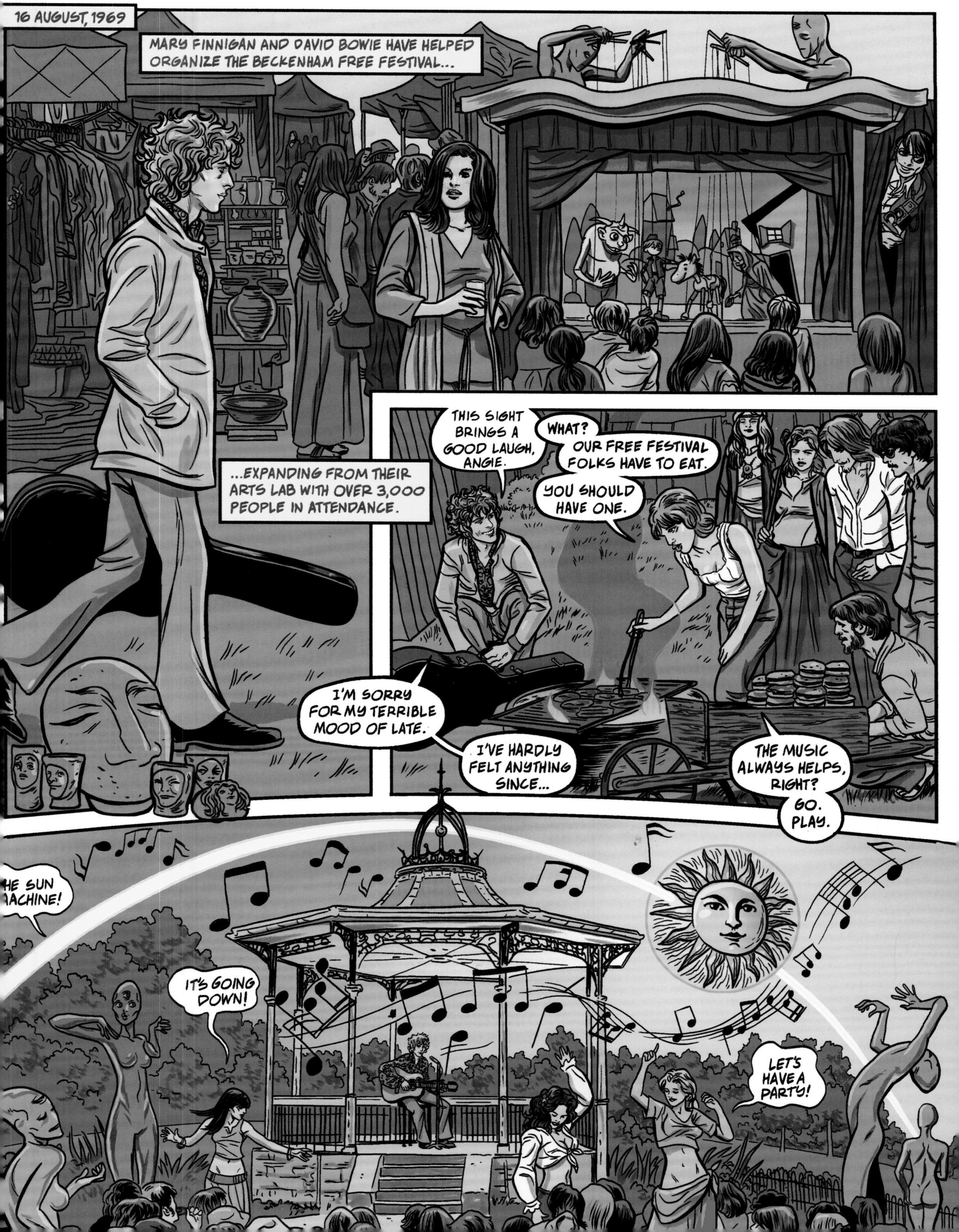

16 AUGUST, 1969
MARY FINNIGAN AND DAVID BOWIE HAVE HELPED ORGANIZE THE BECKENHAM FREE FESTIVAL...
...EXPANDING FROM THEIR ARTS LAB WITH OVER 3,000 PEOPLE IN ATTENDANCE.
THIS SIGHT BRINGS A GOOD LAUGH, ANGIE.
WHAT? OUR FREE FESTIVAL FOLKS HAVE TO EAT.
YOU SHOULD HAVE ONE.
I'M SORRY FOR MY TERRIBLE MOOD OF LATE.
I'VE HARDLY FELT ANYTHING SINCE...
THE MUSIC ALWAYS HELPS, RIGHT?
GO. PLAY.
HE SUN ACHINE!
IT'S GOING DOWN!
LET'S HAVE A PARTY!

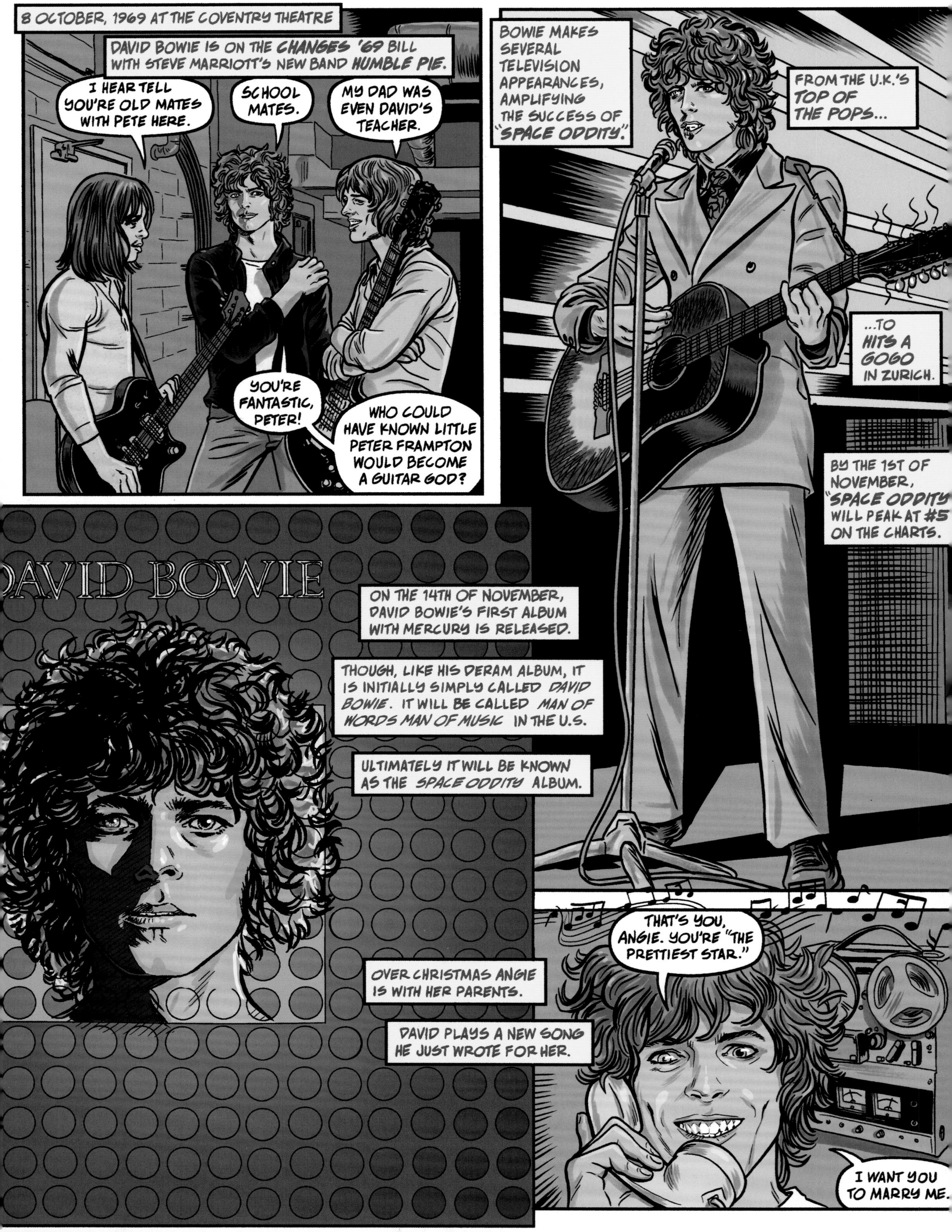
8 OCTOBER, 1969 AT THE COVENTRY THEATRE
DAVID BOWIE IS ON THE CHANGES '69 BILL WITH STEVE MARRIOTT'S NEW BAND HUMBLE PIE.
I HEAR TELL YOU'RE OLD MATES WITH PETE HERE.
SCHOOL MATES.
MY DAD WAS EVEN DAVID'S TEACHER.
YOU'RE FANTASTIC, PETER!
WHO COULD HAVE KNOWN LITTLE PETER FRAMPTON WOULD BECOME A GUITAR GOD?
BOWIE MAKES SEVERAL TELEVISION APPEARANCES, AMPLIFYING THE SUCCESS OF "SPACE ODDITY."
FROM THE U.K.'S TOP OF THE POPS...
...TO HITS A GOGO IN ZURICH.
BY THE 1ST OF NOVEMBER, "SPACE ODDITY" WILL PEAK AT #5 ON THE CHARTS.
DAVID BOWIE
ON THE 14TH OF NOVEMBER, DAVID BOWIE'S FIRST ALBUM WITH MERCURY IS RELEASED.
THOUGH, LIKE HIS DERAM ALBUM, IT IS INITIALLY SIMPLY CALLED DAVID BOWIE. IT WILL BE CALLED MAN OF WORDS MAN OF MUSIC IN THE U.S.
ULTIMATELY IT WILL BE KNOWN AS THE SPACE ODDITY ALBUM.
OVER CHRISTMAS ANGIE IS WITH HER PARENTS.
DAVID PLAYS A NEW SONG HE JUST WROTE FOR HER.
THAT'S YOU, ANGIE. YOU'RE "THE PRETTIEST STAR."
I WANT YOU TO MARRY ME.

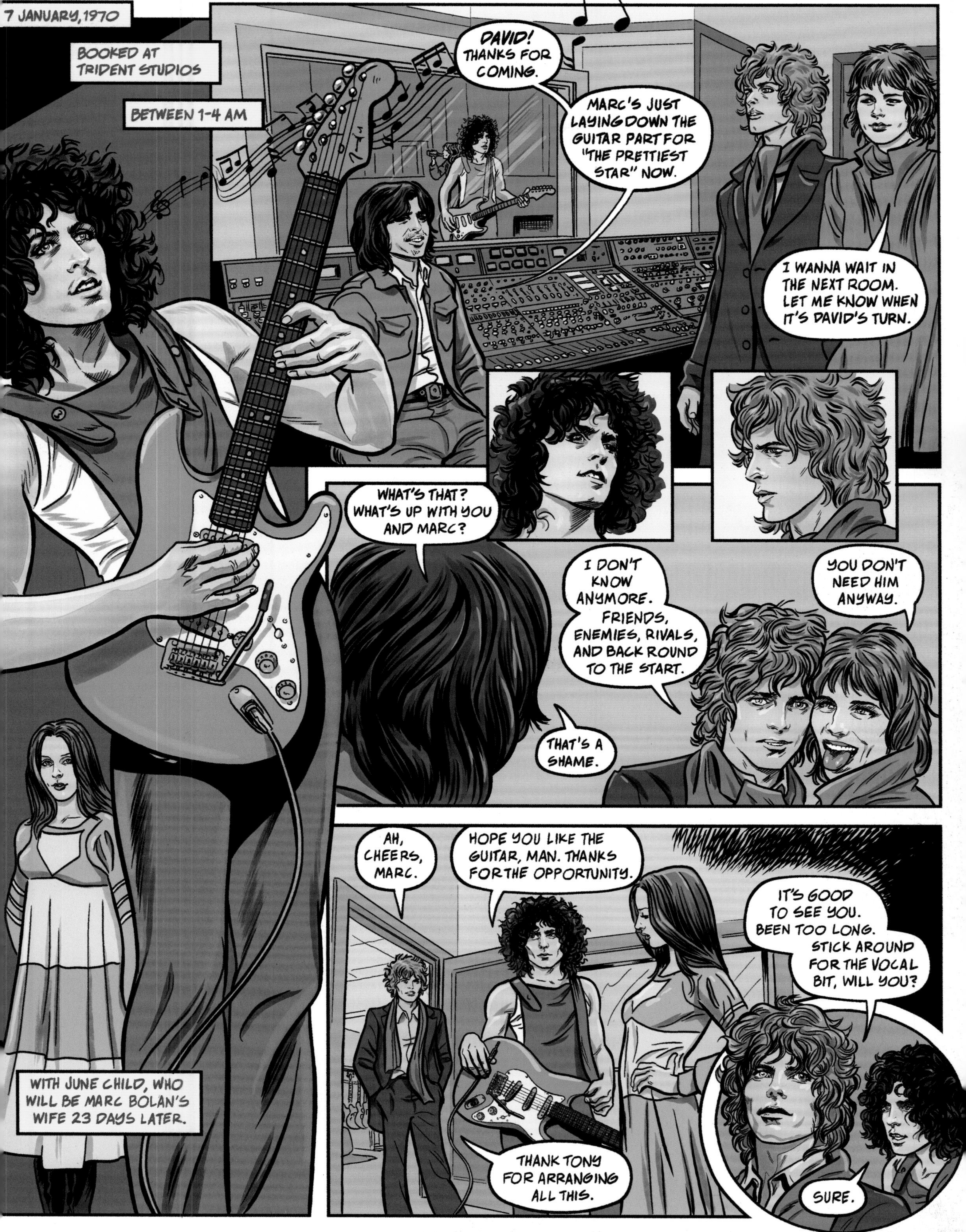

7 JANUARY, 1970
BOOKED AT TRIDENT STUDIOS
BETWEEN 1-4 AM
DAVID! THANKS FOR COMING.
MARC'S JUST LAYING DOWN THE GUITAR PART FOR "THE PRETTIEST STAR" NOW.
I WANNA WAIT IN THE NEXT ROOM. LET ME KNOW WHEN IT'S DAVID'S TURN.
WHAT'S THAT? WHAT'S UP WITH YOU AND MARC?
I DON'T KNOW ANYMORE. FRIENDS, ENEMIES, RIVALS, AND BACK ROUND TO THE START.
YOU DON'T NEED HIM ANYWAY.
THAT'S A SHAME.
WITH JUNE CHILD, WHO WILL BE MARC BOLAN'S WIFE 23 DAYS LATER.
AH, CHEERS, MARC.
HOPE YOU LIKE THE GUITAR, MAN. THANKS FOR THE OPPORTUNITY.
IT'S GOOD TO SEE YOU. BEEN TOO LONG. STICK AROUND FOR THE VOCAL BIT, WILL YOU?
THANK TONY FOR ARRANGING ALL THIS.
SURE.

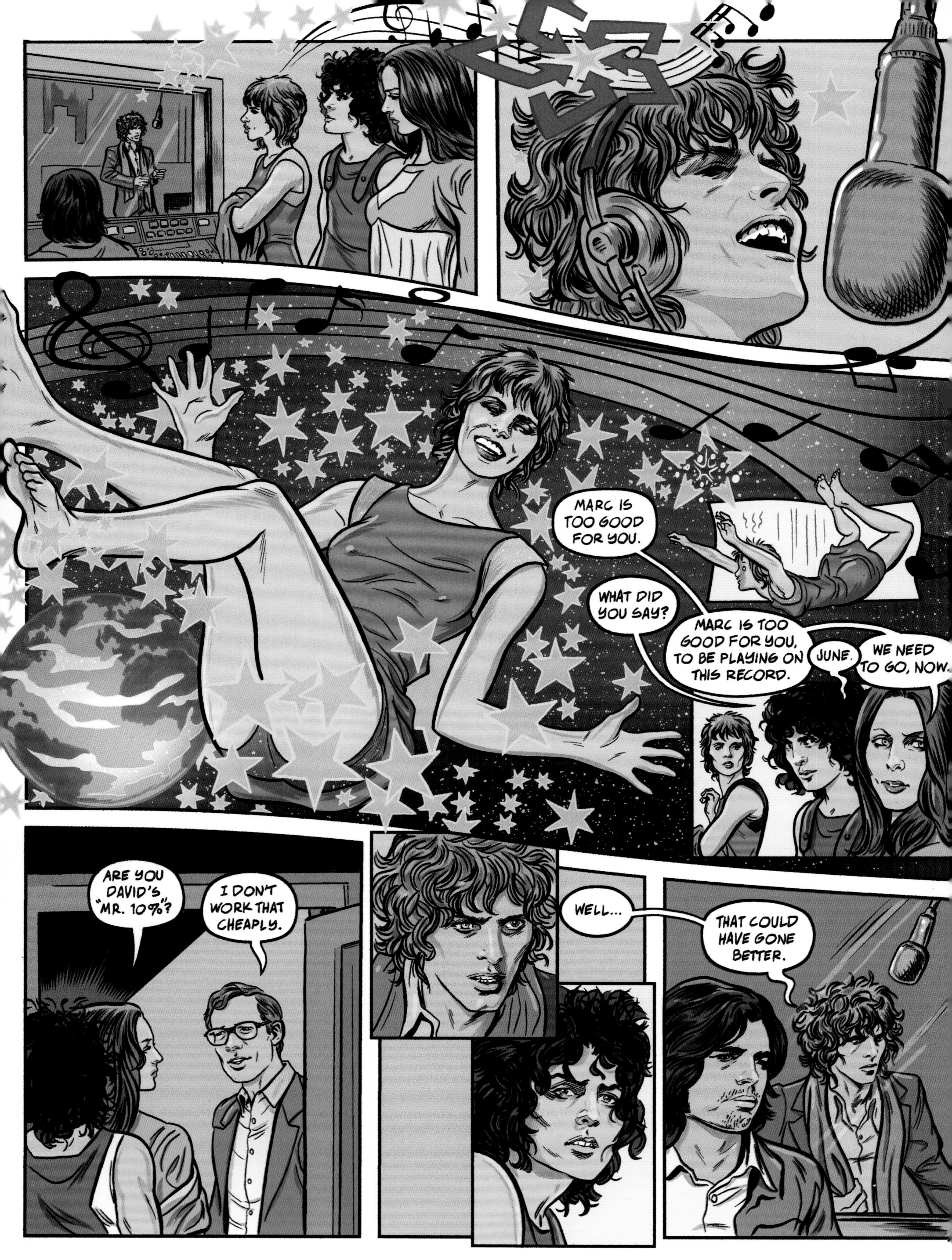
MARC IS TOO GOOD FOR YOU.
WHAT DID YOU SAY?
MARC IS TOO GOOD FOR YOU, TO BE PLAYING ON THIS RECORD.
JUNE.
WE NEED TO GO, NOW.
ARE YOU DAVID'S "MR. 10%"?
I DON'T WORK THAT CHEAPLY.
WELL...
THAT COULD HAVE GONE BETTER.

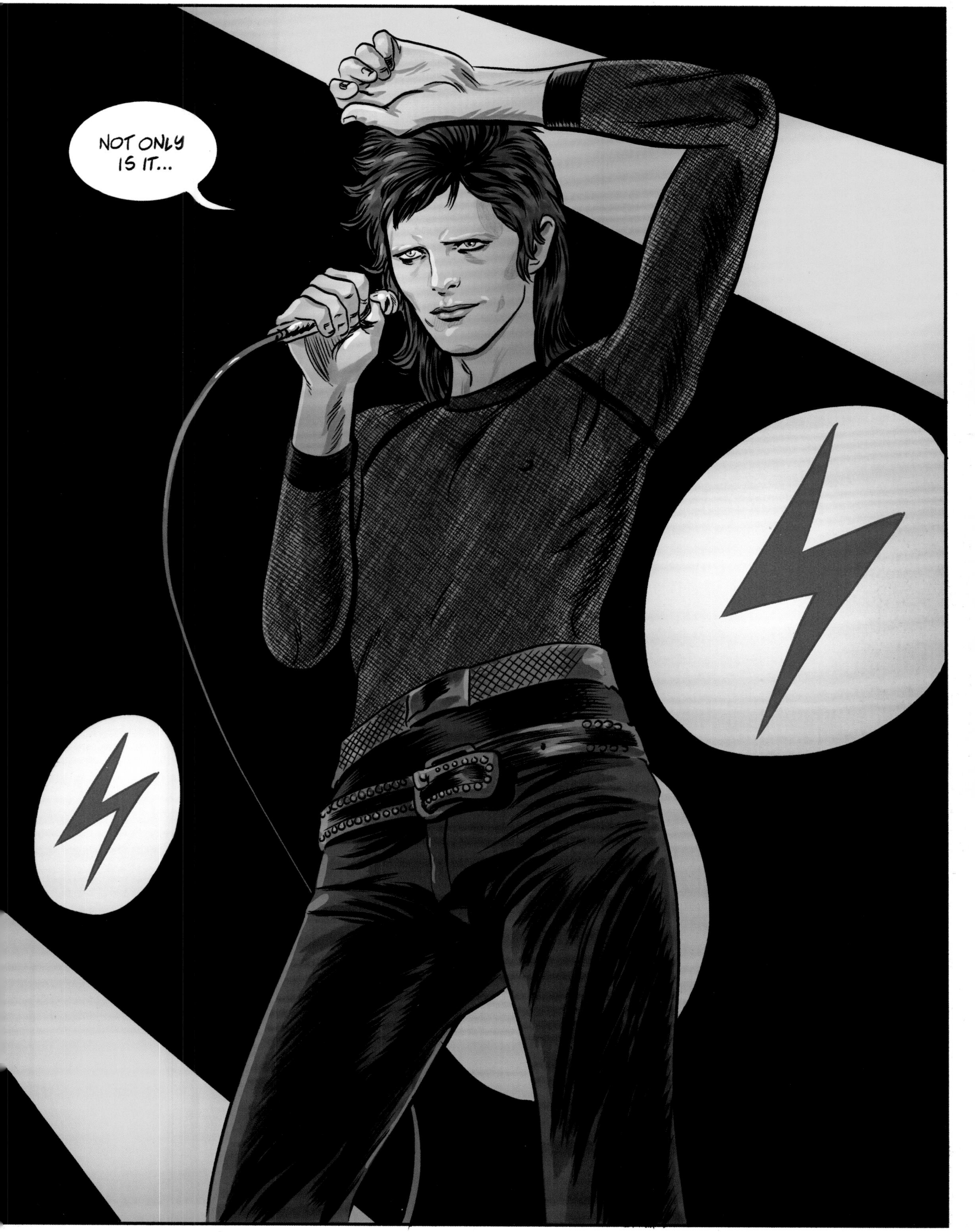
NOT ONLY IS IT...

TONY VISCONTI AND HIS GIRLFRIEND, LIZ HARTLEY, MOVE INTO HADDON HALL FOR THE SOLE PURPOSE OF MAKING DAVID BOWIE A BIG STAR.

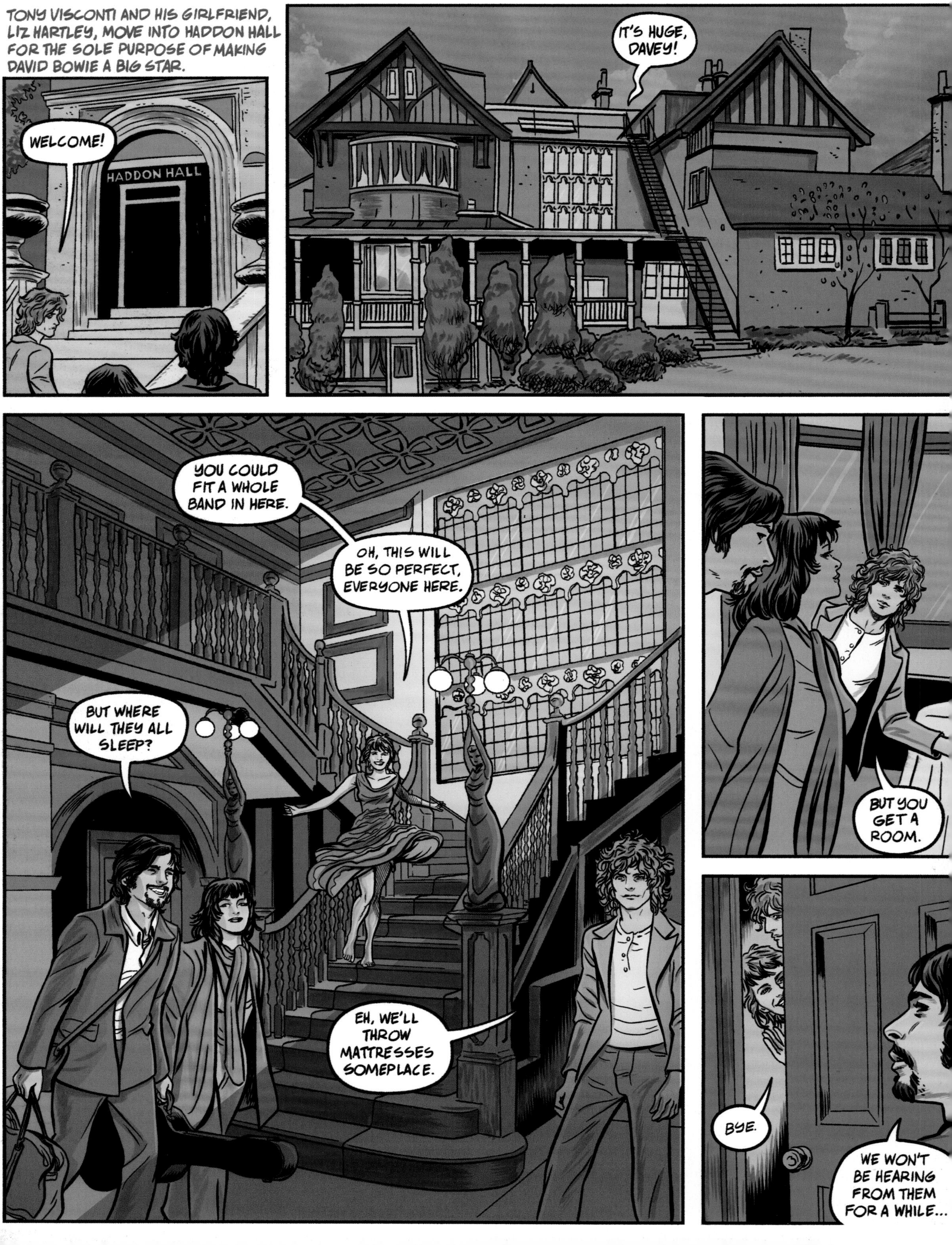

HADDON HALL
WELCOME!
IT'S HUGE, DAVEY!
YOU COULD FIT A WHOLE BAND IN HERE.
OH, THIS WILL BE SO PERFECT, EVERYONE HERE.
BUT WHERE WILL THEY ALL SLEEP?
EH, WE'LL THROW MATTRESSES SOMEPLACE.
BUT YOU GET A ROOM.
BYE.
WE WON'T BE HEARING FROM THEM FOR A WHILE...

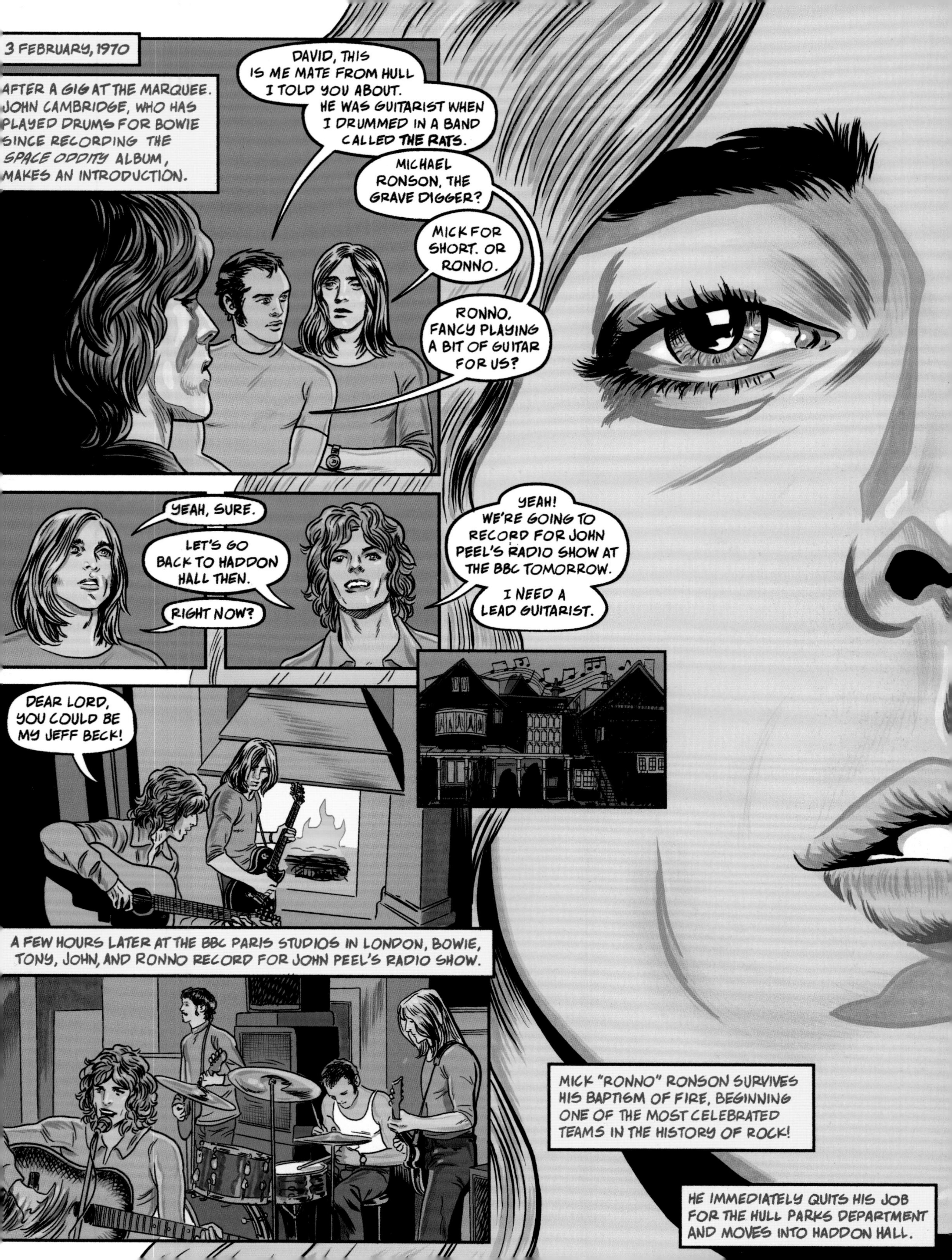
3 FEBRUARY, 1970
AFTER A GIG AT THE MARQUEE. JOHN CAMBRIDGE, WHO HAS PLAYED DRUMS FOR BOWIE SINCE RECORDING THE SPACE ODDITY ALBUM, MAKES AN INTRODUCTION.
DAVID, THIS IS ME MATE FROM HULL I TOLD YOU ABOUT.
HE WAS GUITARIST WHEN I DRUMMED IN A BAND CALLED THE RATS.
MICHAEL RONSON, THE GRAVE DIGGER?
MICK FOR SHORT. OR RONNO.
RONNO, FANCY PLAYING A BIT OF GUITAR FOR US?
YEAH, SURE.
LET'S GO BACK TO HADDON HALL THEN.
RIGHT NOW?
YEAH! WE'RE GOING TO RECORD FOR JOHN PEEL'S RADIO SHOW AT THE BBC TOMORROW.
I NEED A LEAD GUITARIST.
DEAR LORD, YOU COULD BE MY JEFF BECK!
A FEW HOURS LATER AT THE BBC PARIS STUDIOS IN LONDON, BOWIE, TONY, JOHN, AND RONNO RECORD FOR JOHN PEEL'S RADIO SHOW.
MICK "RONNO" RONSON SURVIVES HIS BAPTISM OF FIRE, BEGINNING ONE OF THE MOST CELEBRATED TEAMS IN THE HISTORY OF ROCK!
HE IMMEDIATELY QUITS HIS JOB FOR THE HULL PARKS DEPARTMENT AND MOVES INTO HADDON HALL.

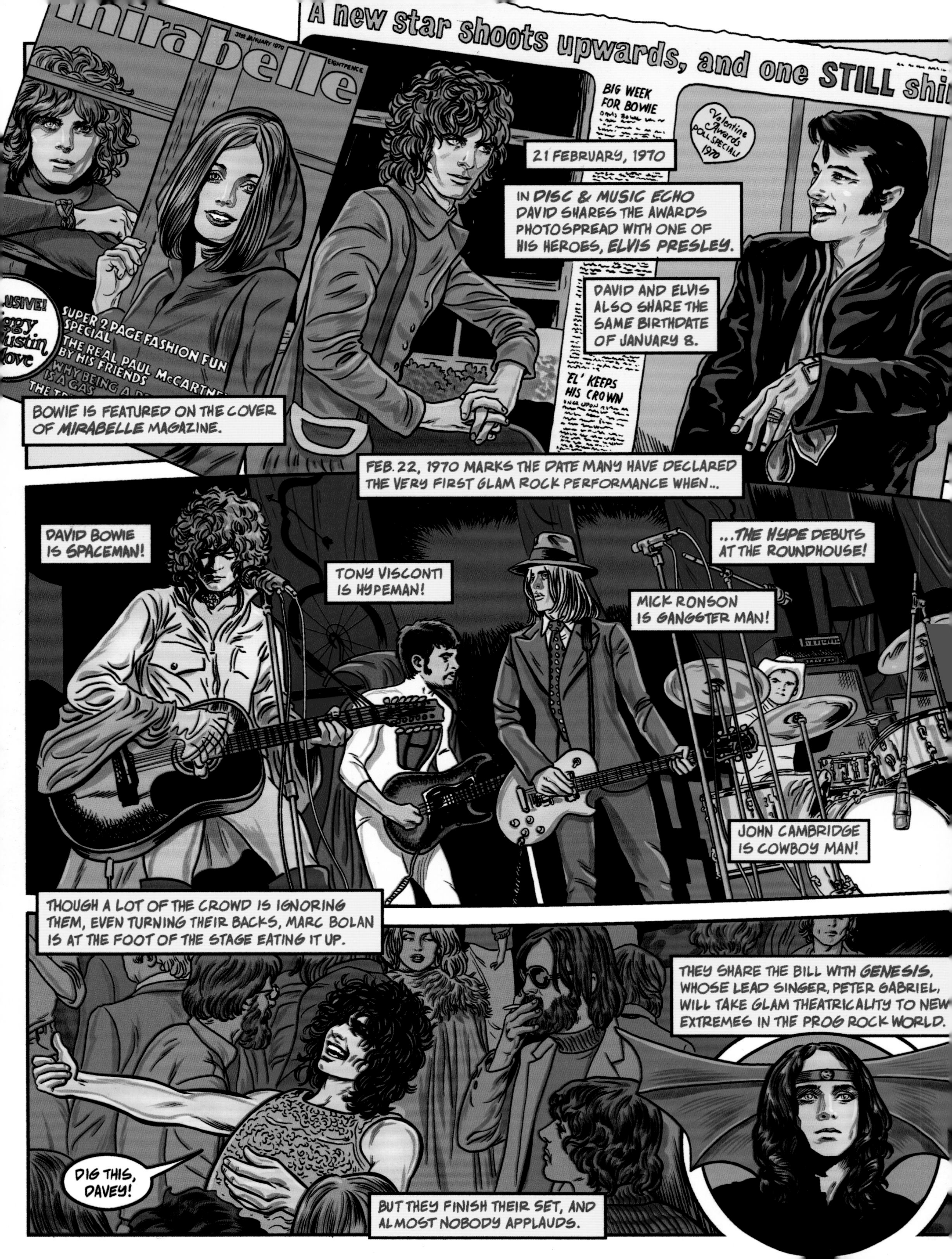
mirabelle
31st JANUARY 1970
EIGHTPENCE
SUPER 2 PAGE FASHION FUN SPECIAL
THE REAL PAUL McCARTNEY BY HIS FRIENDS
WHY BEING A
IS A GAS
BOWIE IS FEATURED ON THE COVER OF MIRABELLE MAGAZINE.
A new star shoots upwards, and one STILL shi
BIG WEEK FOR BOWIE
Valentine Awards POLL SPECIAL! 1970
'EL' KEEPS HIS CROWN
21 FEBRUARY, 1970
IN DISC & MUSIC ECHO DAVID SHARES THE AWARDS PHOTOSPREAD WITH ONE OF HIS HEROES, ELVIS PRESLEY.
DAVID AND ELVIS ALSO SHARE THE SAME BIRTHDATE OF JANUARY 8.
FEB. 22, 1970 MARKS THE DATE MANY HAVE DECLARED THE VERY FIRST GLAM ROCK PERFORMANCE WHEN...
...THE HYPE DEBUTS AT THE ROUNDHOUSE!
DAVID BOWIE IS SPACEMAN!
TONY VISCONTI IS HYPEMAN!
MICK RONSON IS GANGSTER MAN!
JOHN CAMBRIDGE IS COWBOY MAN!
THOUGH A LOT OF THE CROWD IS IGNORING THEM, EVEN TURNING THEIR BACKS, MARC BOLAN IS AT THE FOOT OF THE STAGE EATING IT UP.
DIG THIS, DAVEY!
THEY SHARE THE BILL WITH GENESIS, WHOSE LEAD SINGER, PETER GABRIEL, WILL TAKE GLAM THEATRICALITY TO NEW EXTREMES IN THE PROG ROCK WORLD.
BUT THEY FINISH THEIR SET, AND ALMOST NOBODY APPLAUDS.

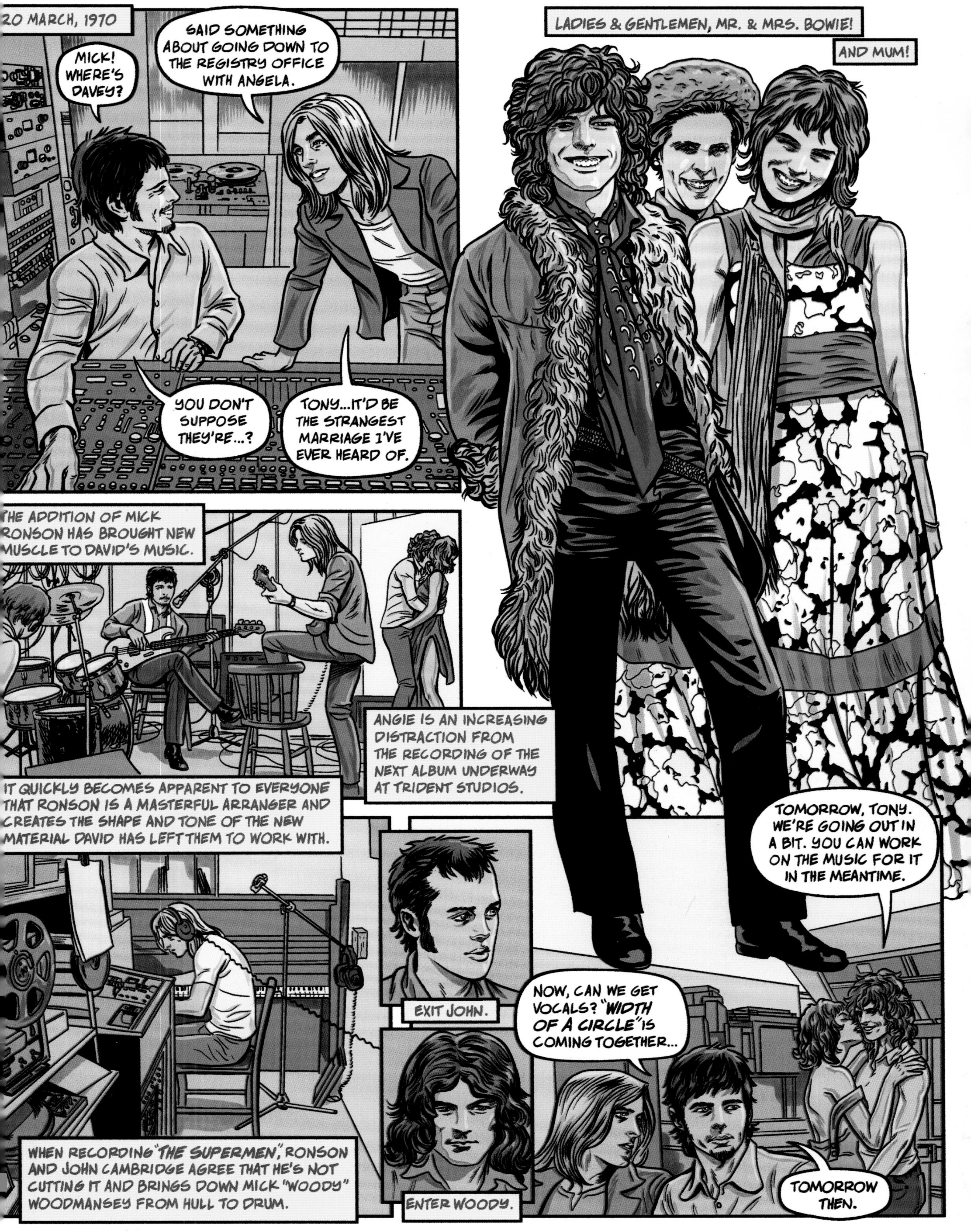
20 MARCH, 1970
MICK! WHERE'S DAVEY?
SAID SOMETHING ABOUT GOING DOWN TO THE REGISTRY OFFICE WITH ANGELA.
YOU DON'T SUPPOSE THEY'RE...?
TONY...IT'D BE THE STRANGEST MARRIAGE I'VE EVER HEARD OF.
LADIES & GENTLEMEN, MR. & MRS. BOWIE!
AND MUM!
THE ADDITION OF MICK RONSON HAS BROUGHT NEW MUSCLE TO DAVID'S MUSIC.
ANGIE IS AN INCREASING DISTRACTION FROM THE RECORDING OF THE NEXT ALBUM UNDERWAY AT TRIDENT STUDIOS.
IT QUICKLY BECOMES APPARENT TO EVERYONE THAT RONSON IS A MASTERFUL ARRANGER AND CREATES THE SHAPE AND TONE OF THE NEW MATERIAL DAVID HAS LEFT THEM TO WORK WITH.
TOMORROW, TONY. WE'RE GOING OUT IN A BIT. YOU CAN WORK ON THE MUSIC FOR IT IN THE MEANTIME.
EXIT JOHN.
NOW, CAN WE GET VOCALS? "WIDTH OF A CIRCLE" IS COMING TOGETHER...
WHEN RECORDING "THE SUPERMEN," RONSON AND JOHN CAMBRIDGE AGREE THAT HE'S NOT CUTTING IT AND BRINGS DOWN MICK "WOODY" WOODMANSEY FROM HULL TO DRUM.
ENTER WOODY.
TOMORROW THEN.

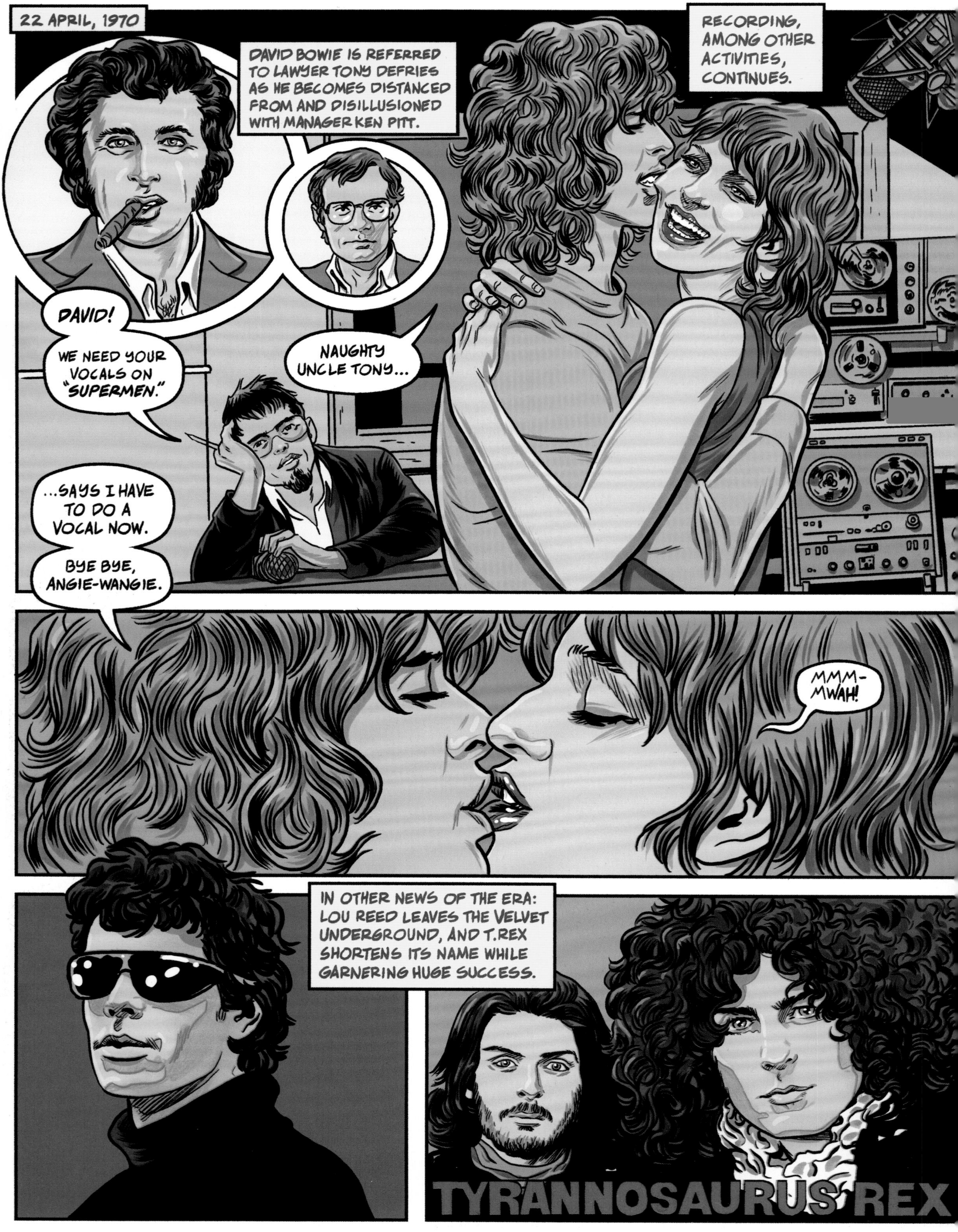

22 APRIL, 1970
DAVID BOWIE IS REFERRED TO LAWYER TONY DEFRIES AS HE BECOMES DISTANCED FROM AND DISILLUSIONED WITH MANAGER KEN PITT.
RECORDING, AMONG OTHER ACTIVITIES, CONTINUES.
DAVID!
WE NEED YOUR VOCALS ON "SUPERMEN."
NAUGHTY UNCLE TONY...
...SAYS I HAVE TO DO A VOCAL NOW.
BYE BYE, ANGIE-WANGIE.
MMM-MWAH!
IN OTHER NEWS OF THE ERA: LOU REED LEAVES THE VELVET UNDERGROUND, AND T.REX SHORTENS ITS NAME WHILE GARNERING HUGE SUCCESS.
TYRANNOSAURUS REX

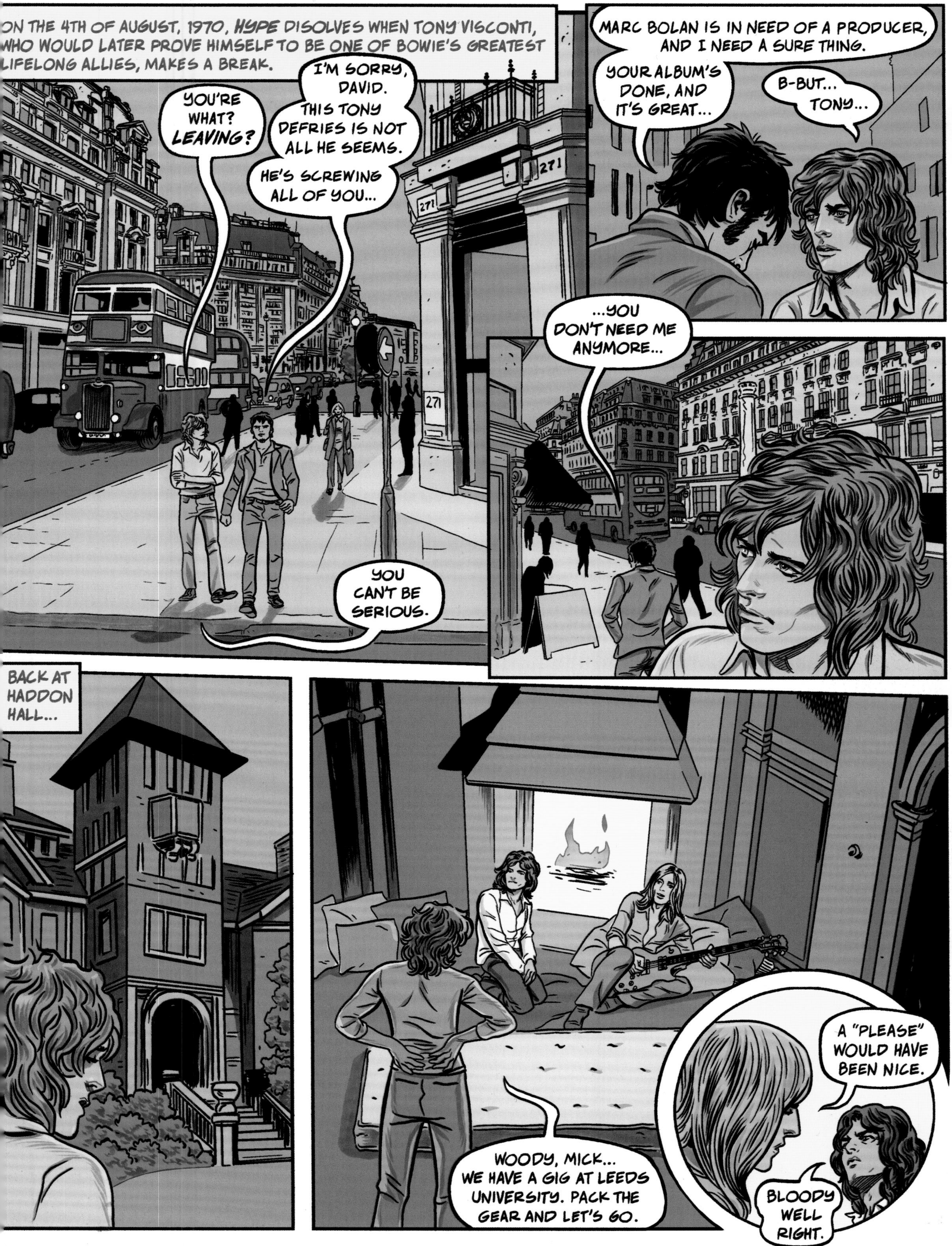

ON THE 4TH OF AUGUST, 1970, HYPE DISOLVES WHEN TONY VISCONTI, WHO WOULD LATER PROVE HIMSELF TO BE ONE OF BOWIE'S GREATEST LIFELONG ALLIES, MAKES A BREAK.
YOU'RE WHAT? LEAVING?
I'M SORRY, DAVID. THIS TONY DEFRIES IS NOT ALL HE SEEMS.
HE'S SCREWING ALL OF YOU...
271
YOU CAN'T BE SERIOUS.
MARC BOLAN IS IN NEED OF A PRODUCER, AND I NEED A SURE THING.
YOUR ALBUM'S DONE, AND IT'S GREAT...
B-BUT... TONY...
...YOU DON'T NEED ME ANYMORE...
BACK AT HADDON HALL...
WOODY, MICK... WE HAVE A GIG AT LEEDS UNIVERSITY. PACK THE GEAR AND LET'S GO.
A "PLEASE" WOULD HAVE BEEN NICE.
BLOODY WELL RIGHT.

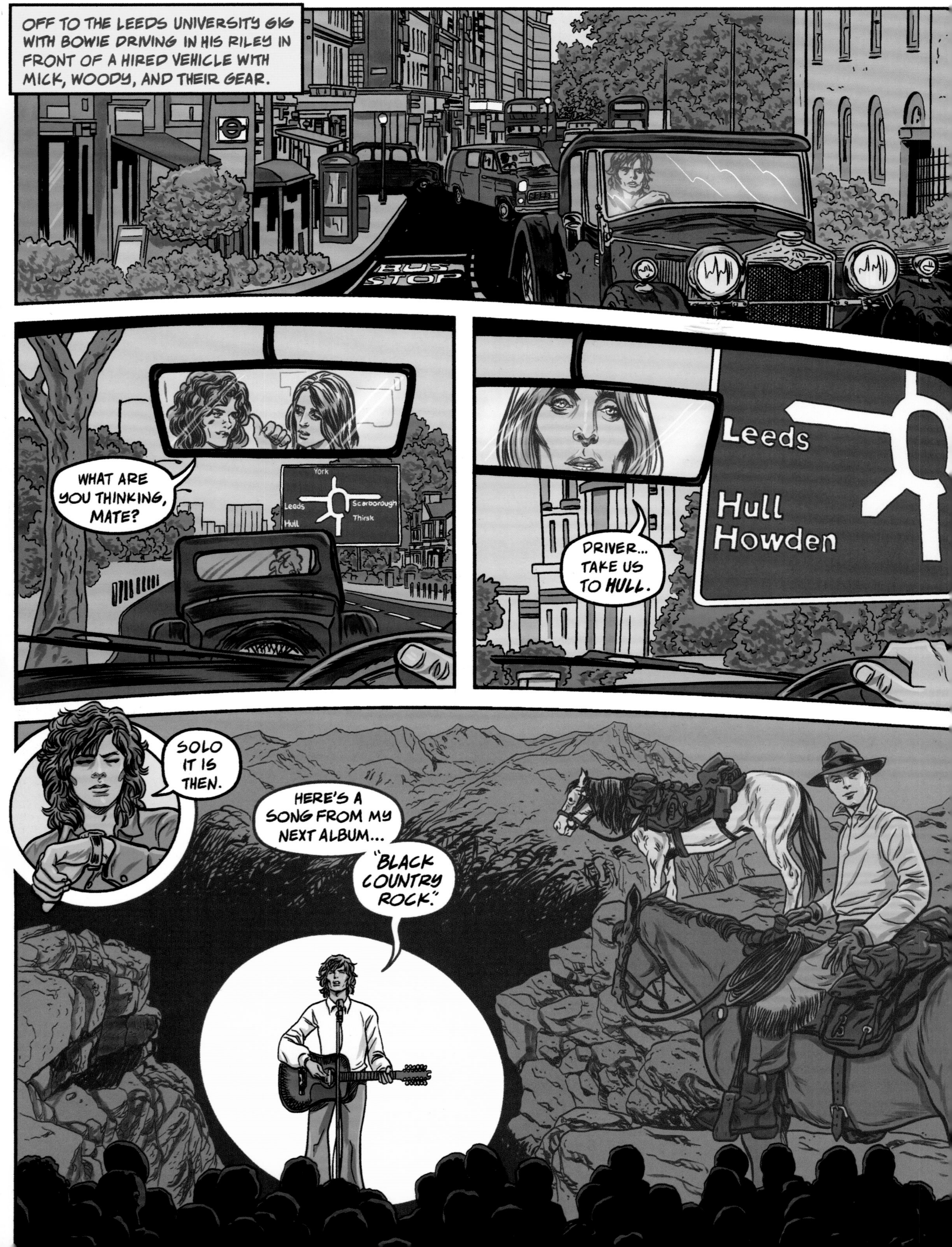
OFF TO THE LEEDS UNIVERSITY GIG WITH BOWIE DRIVING IN HIS RILEY IN FRONT OF A HIRED VEHICLE WITH MICK, WOODY, AND THEIR GEAR.
BUS STOP
WHAT ARE YOU THINKING, MATE?
York
Leeds
Scarborough
Hull
Thirsk
Leeds
Hull
Howden
DRIVER... TAKE US TO HULL.
SOLO IT IS THEN.
HERE'S A SONG FROM MY NEXT ALBUM...
"BLACK COUNTRY ROCK."

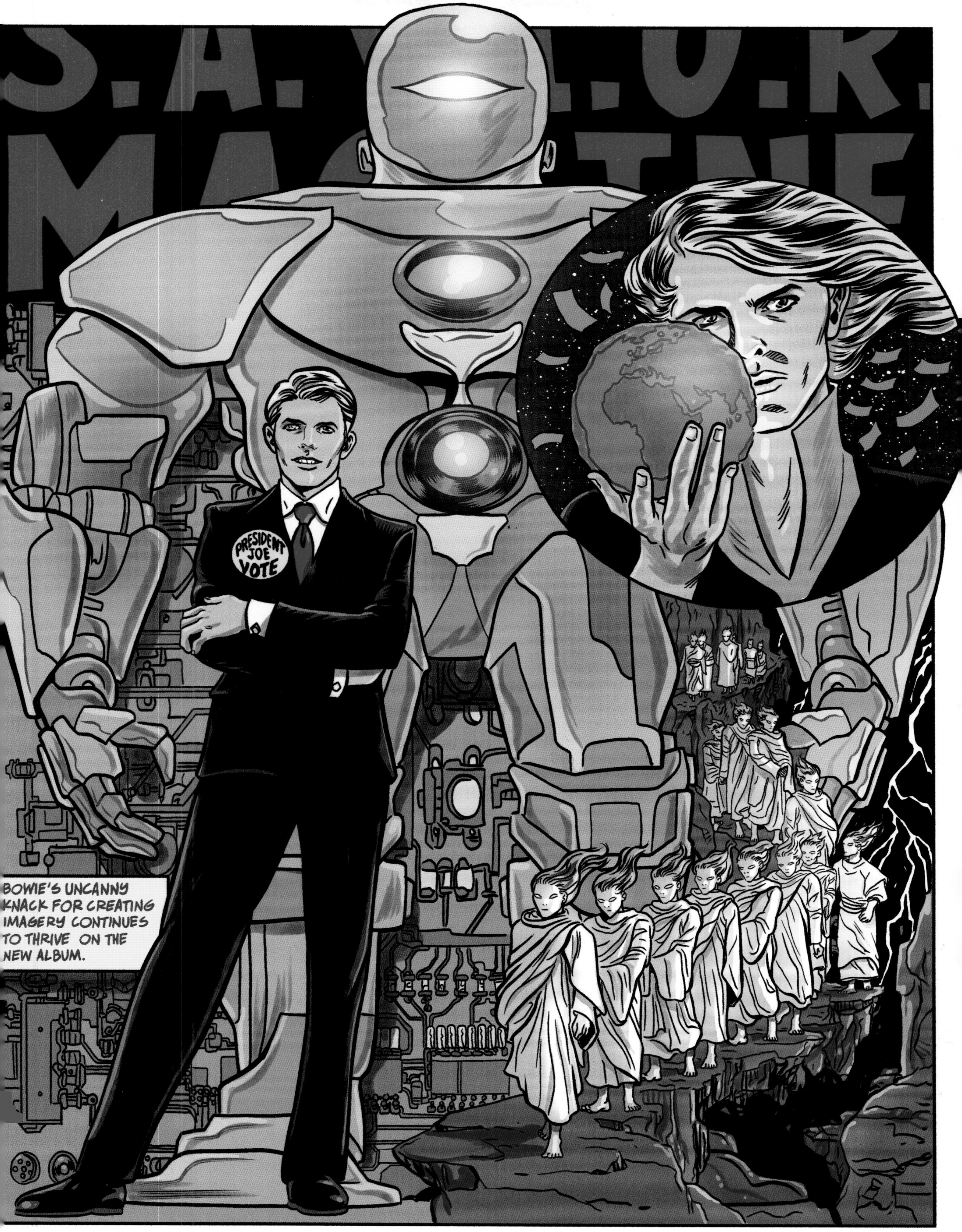
PRESIDENT JOE VOTE
BOWIE'S UNCANNY KNACK FOR CREATING IMAGERY CONTINUES TO THRIVE ON THE NEW ALBUM.

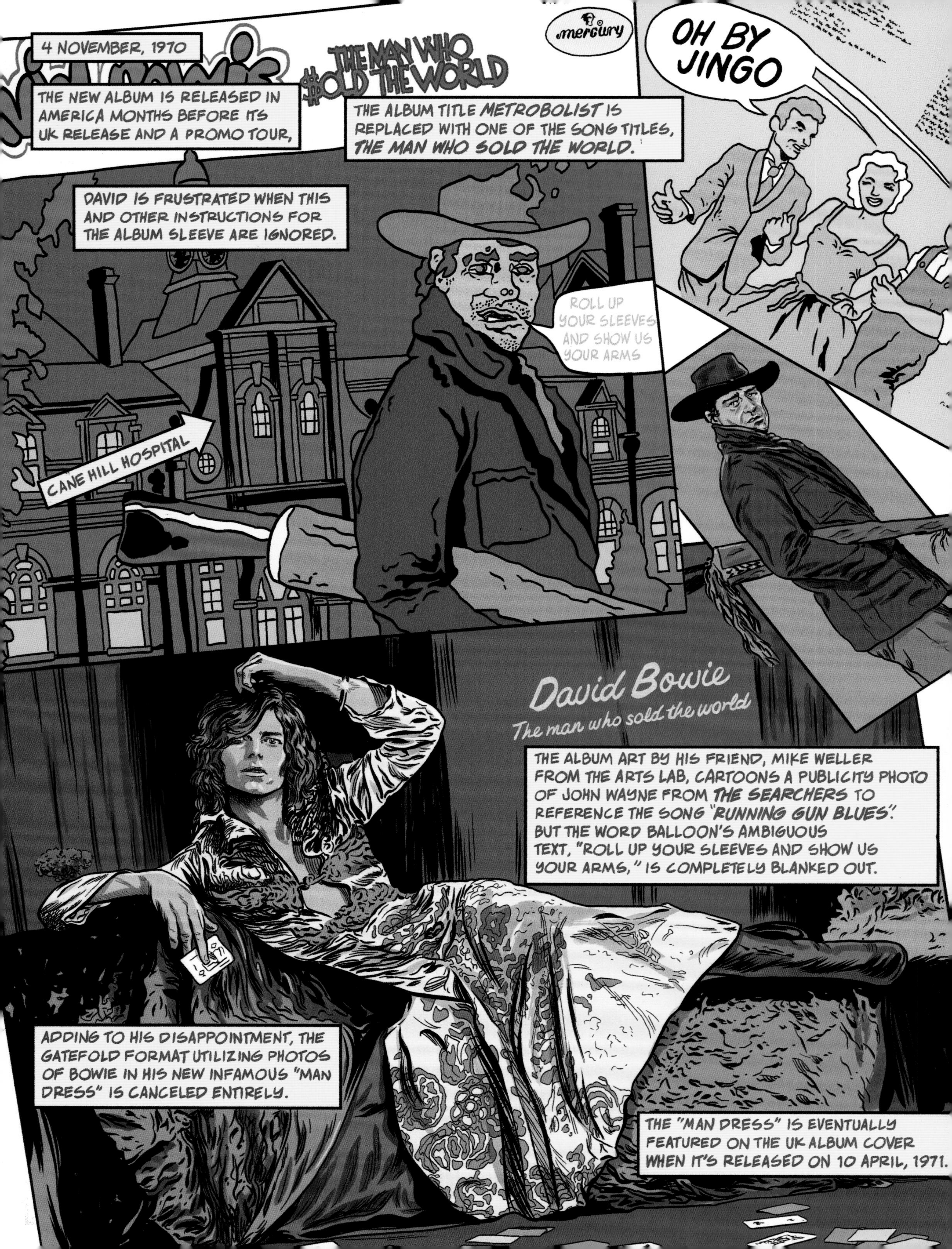

4 NOVEMBER, 1970
THE NEW ALBUM IS RELEASED IN AMERICA MONTHS BEFORE ITS UK RELEASE AND A PROMO TOUR,
THE MAN WHO $OLD THE WORLD
mercury
THE ALBUM TITLE METROBOLIST IS REPLACED WITH ONE OF THE SONG TITLES, THE MAN WHO SOLD THE WORLD.
OH BY JINGO
DAVID IS FRUSTRATED WHEN THIS AND OTHER INSTRUCTIONS FOR THE ALBUM SLEEVE ARE IGNORED.
ROLL UP YOUR SLEEVES AND SHOW US YOUR ARMS
CANE HILL HOSPITAL
David Bowie
The man who sold the world
THE ALBUM ART BY HIS FRIEND, MIKE WELLER FROM THE ARTS LAB, CARTOONS A PUBLICITY PHOTO OF JOHN WAYNE FROM THE SEARCHERS TO REFERENCE THE SONG "RUNNING GUN BLUES". BUT THE WORD BALLOON'S AMBIGUOUS TEXT, "ROLL UP YOUR SLEEVES AND SHOW US YOUR ARMS," IS COMPLETELY BLANKED OUT.
ADDING TO HIS DISAPPOINTMENT, THE GATEFOLD FORMAT UTILIZING PHOTOS OF BOWIE IN HIS NEW INFAMOUS "MAN DRESS" IS CANCELED ENTIRELY.
THE "MAN DRESS" IS EVENTUALLY FEATURED ON THE UK ALBUM COVER WHEN IT'S RELEASED ON 10 APRIL, 1971.

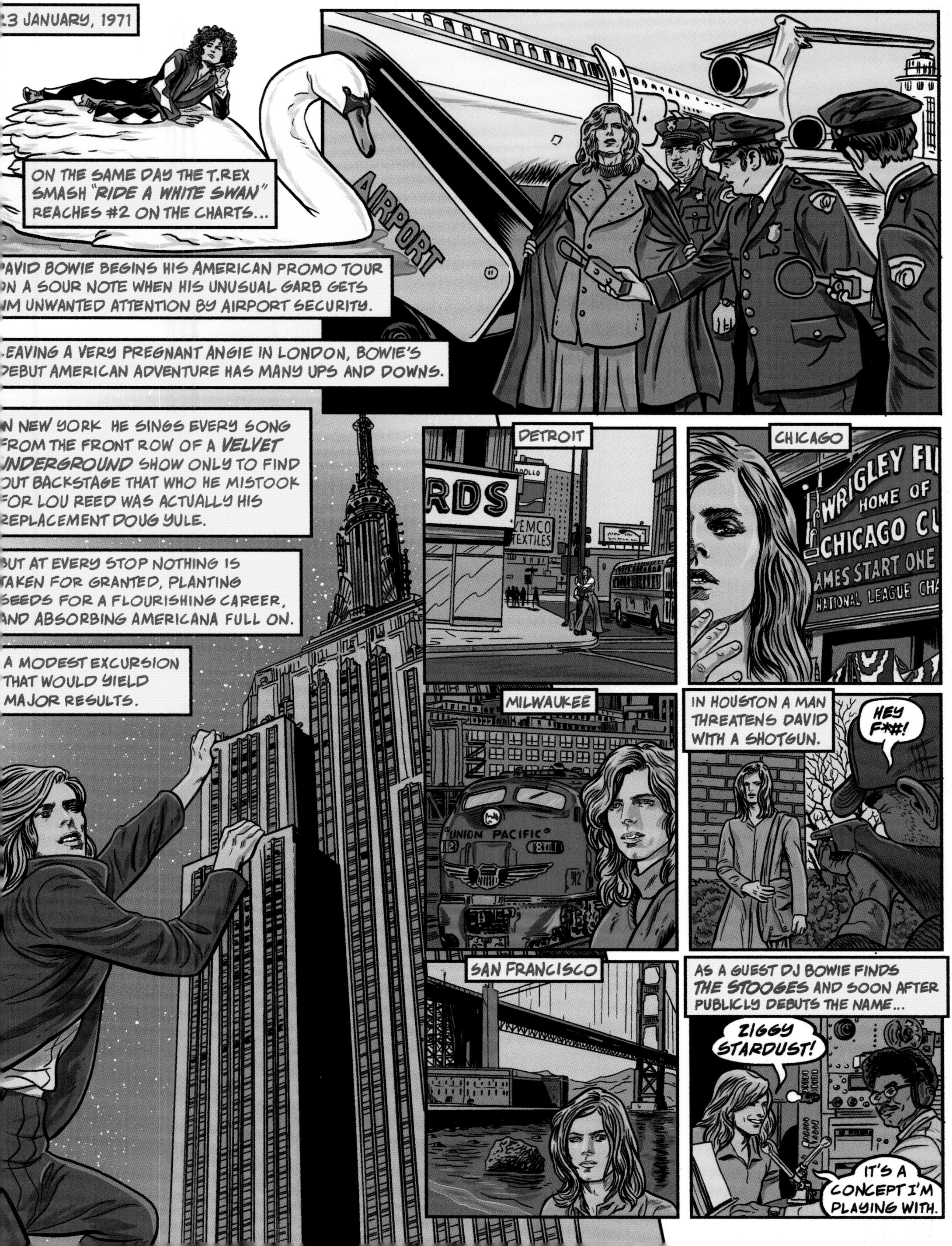

23 JANUARY, 1971
ON THE SAME DAY THE T.REX SMASH "RIDE A WHITE SWAN" REACHES #2 ON THE CHARTS...
AIRPORT
DAVID BOWIE BEGINS HIS AMERICAN PROMO TOUR ON A SOUR NOTE WHEN HIS UNUSUAL GARB GETS HIM UNWANTED ATTENTION BY AIRPORT SECURITY.
LEAVING A VERY PREGNANT ANGIE IN LONDON, BOWIE'S DEBUT AMERICAN ADVENTURE HAS MANY UPS AND DOWNS.
IN NEW YORK HE SINGS EVERY SONG FROM THE FRONT ROW OF A VELVET UNDERGROUND SHOW ONLY TO FIND OUT BACKSTAGE THAT WHO HE MISTOOK FOR LOU REED WAS ACTUALLY HIS REPLACEMENT DOUG YULE.
BUT AT EVERY STOP NOTHING IS TAKEN FOR GRANTED, PLANTING SEEDS FOR A FLOURISHING CAREER, AND ABSORBING AMERICANA FULL ON.
A MODEST EXCURSION THAT WOULD YIELD MAJOR RESULTS.
DETROIT
RDS
APOLLO
VEMCO TEXTILES
CHICAGO
WRIGLEY FI
HOME OF
CHICAGO CU
AMES START ONE
NATIONAL LEAGUE CHA
MILWAUKEE
UNION PACIFIC
IN HOUSTON A MAN THREATENS DAVID WITH A SHOTGUN.
HEY F*#!
SAN FRANCISCO
AS A GUEST DJ BOWIE FINDS THE STOOGES AND SOON AFTER PUBLICLY DEBUTS THE NAME...
ZIGGY STARDUST!
IT'S A CONCEPT I'M PLAYING WITH.

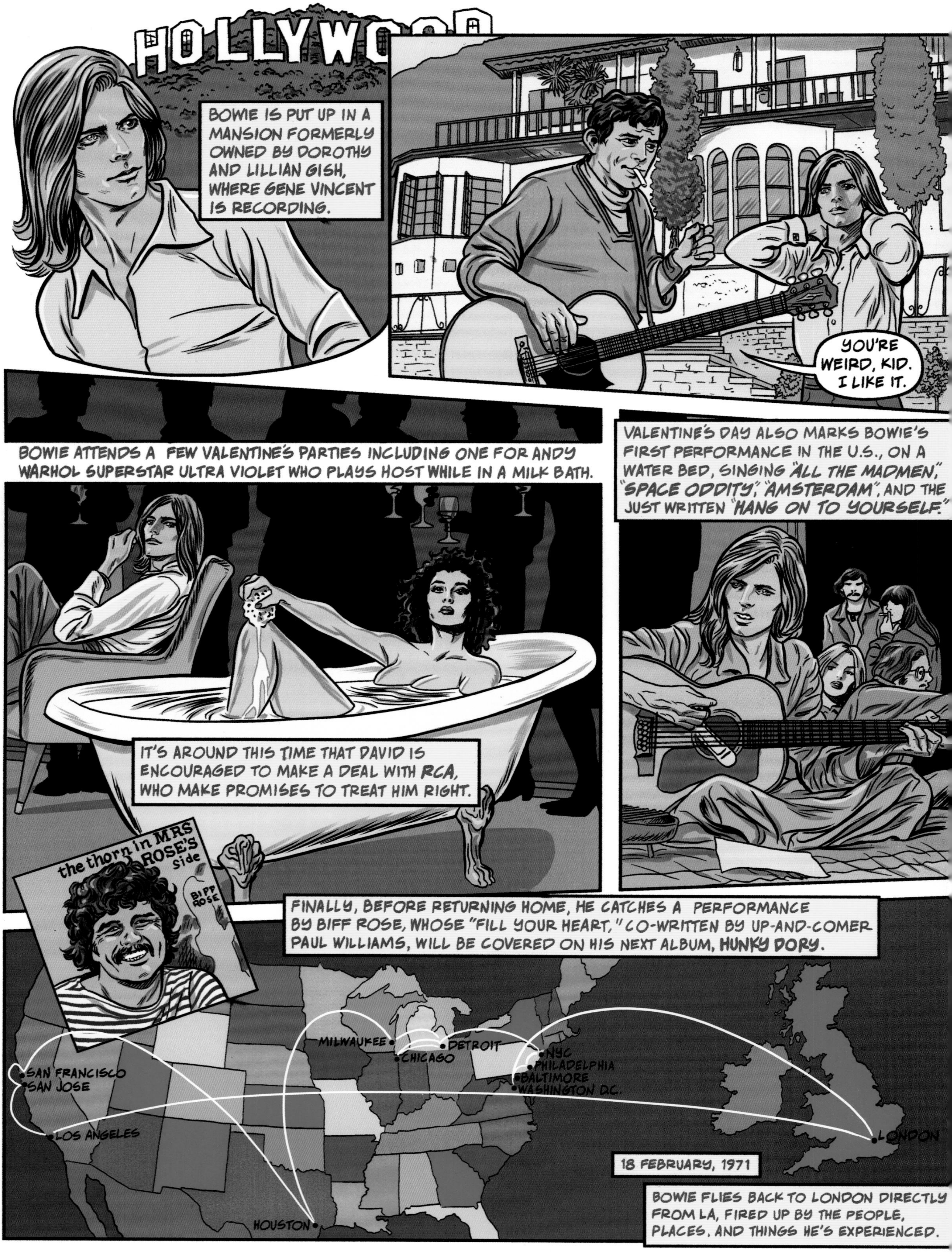
HOLLYWOOD
BOWIE IS PUT UP IN A MANSION FORMERLY OWNED BY DOROTHY AND LILLIAN GISH, WHERE GENE VINCENT IS RECORDING.
YOU'RE WEIRD, KID. I LIKE IT.
BOWIE ATTENDS A FEW VALENTINE'S PARTIES INCLUDING ONE FOR ANDY WARHOL SUPERSTAR ULTRA VIOLET WHO PLAYS HOST WHILE IN A MILK BATH.
VALENTINE'S DAY ALSO MARKS BOWIE'S FIRST PERFORMANCE IN THE U.S., ON A WATER BED, SINGING "ALL THE MADMEN," "SPACE ODDITY," "AMSTERDAM", AND THE JUST WRITTEN "HANG ON TO YOURSELF."
IT'S AROUND THIS TIME THAT DAVID IS ENCOURAGED TO MAKE A DEAL WITH RCA, WHO MAKE PROMISES TO TREAT HIM RIGHT.
the thorn in MRS ROSE'S side
BIFF ROSE
FINALLY, BEFORE RETURNING HOME, HE CATCHES A PERFORMANCE BY BIFF ROSE, WHOSE "FILL YOUR HEART," CO-WRITTEN BY UP-AND-COMER PAUL WILLIAMS, WILL BE COVERED ON HIS NEXT ALBUM, HUNKY DORY.
MILWAUKEE
DETROIT
CHICAGO
NYC
PHILADELPHIA
BALTIMORE
WASHINGTON D.C.
SAN FRANCISCO
SAN JOSE
LOS ANGELES
HOUSTON
LONDON
18 FEBRUARY, 1971
BOWIE FLIES BACK TO LONDON DIRECTLY FROM LA, FIRED UP BY THE PEOPLE, PLACES, AND THINGS HE'S EXPERIENCED.

HOT LOVE

25 FEB, 1971

BOWIE CREATES A SIDE PROJECT, *THE ARNOLD CORNS,* TO HELP FRIEND AND FASHION DESIGNER FREDDIE BRUNETTI AS A BRIEF OUTLET FOR THE BURST OF CREATIVITY HE'S EXPERIENCING.

20 MARCH, 1971

HOT LOVE BY T.REX REACHES #1 ON THE CHARTS!

FORMER HERMAN'S HERMIT, PETER NOONE RECORDS A COVER OF *OH! YOU PRETTY THINGS.* IT WILL REACH #12 ON THE SINGLES CHART, FURTHER SEEDING BOWIE'S PROFILE AS A MOVER & SHAKER.

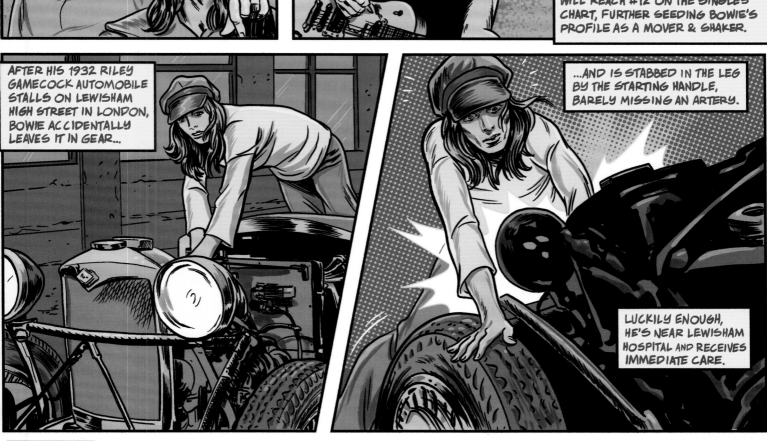

AFTER HIS 1932 RILEY GAMECOCK AUTOMOBILE STALLS ON LEWISHAM HIGH STREET IN LONDON, BOWIE ACCIDENTALLY LEAVES IT IN GEAR...

...AND IS STABBED IN THE LEG BY THE STARTING HANDLE, BARELY MISSING AN ARTERY.

LUCKILY ENOUGH, HE'S NEAR LEWISHAM HOSPITAL AND RECEIVES IMMEDIATE CARE.

12 MAY, 1971

THERE'S A NEW APPRECIATION FOR LIFE AND WHAT'S TO COME.

DAVID AND ANGIE ATTEND GEORGE UNDERWOOD'S WEDDING TO BERGIT GRAVERSON...

MAY, 1971

AND *ZOWIE BOWIE** IS BORN!

I GOT THE NAME FROM A *BATMAN* COMIC. IF HE DOESN'T LIKE IT, HE CAN CALL HIMSELF ANYTHING HE WANTS.

*AKA DUNCAN ZOWIE HAYWOOD JONES

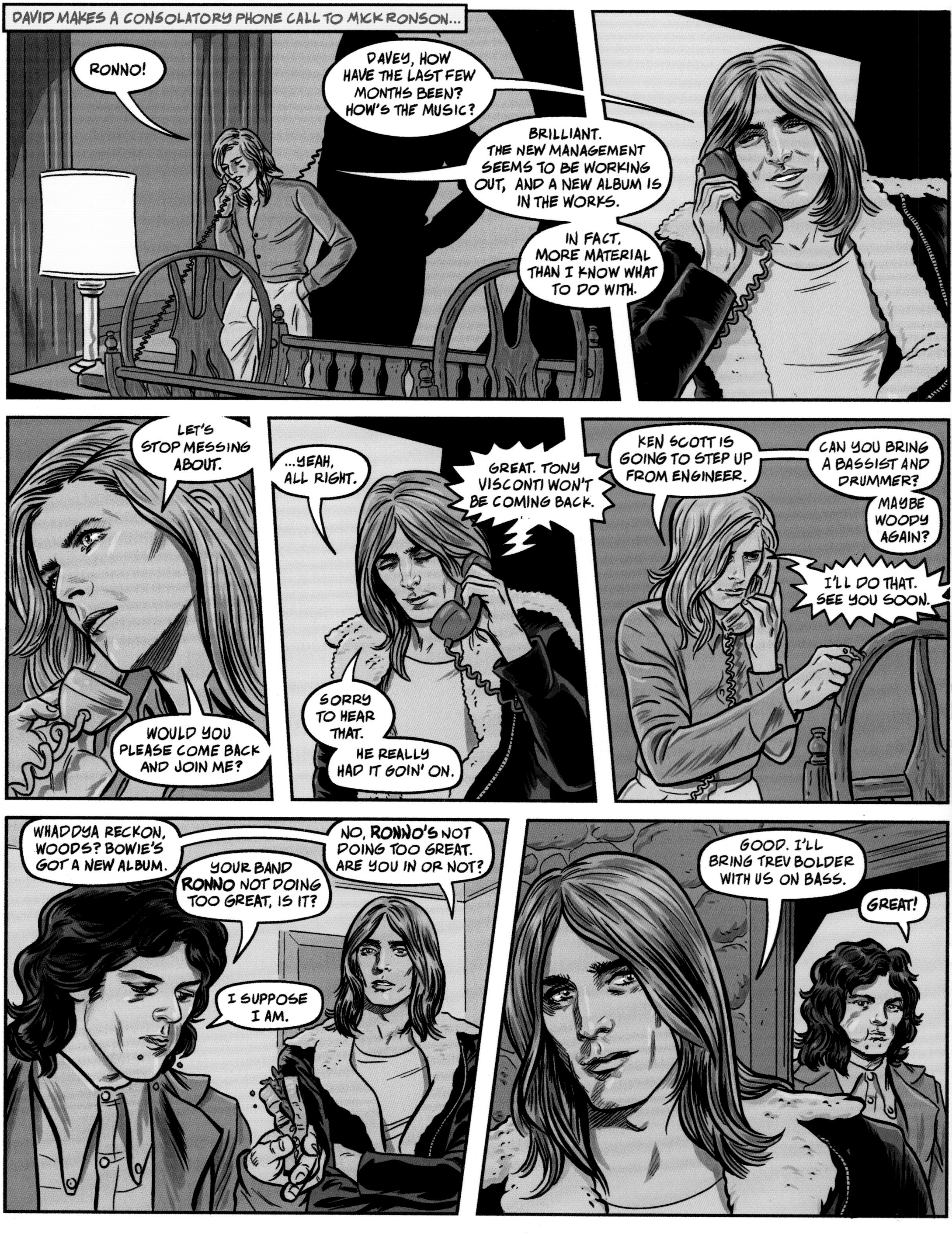
DAVID MAKES A CONSOLATORY PHONE CALL TO MICK RONSON...
RONNO!
DAVEY, HOW HAVE THE LAST FEW MONTHS BEEN? HOW'S THE MUSIC?
BRILLIANT. THE NEW MANAGEMENT SEEMS TO BE WORKING OUT, AND A NEW ALBUM IS IN THE WORKS.
IN FACT, MORE MATERIAL THAN I KNOW WHAT TO DO WITH.
LET'S STOP MESSING ABOUT.
WOULD YOU PLEASE COME BACK AND JOIN ME?
...YEAH, ALL RIGHT.
SORRY TO HEAR THAT.
HE REALLY HAD IT GOIN' ON.
GREAT. TONY VISCONTI WON'T BE COMING BACK.
KEN SCOTT IS GOING TO STEP UP FROM ENGINEER.
CAN YOU BRING A BASSIST AND DRUMMER?
MAYBE WOODY AGAIN?
I'LL DO THAT. SEE YOU SOON.
WHADDYA RECKON, WOODS? BOWIE'S GOT A NEW ALBUM.
YOUR BAND RONNO NOT DOING TOO GREAT, IS IT?
NO, RONNO'S NOT DOING TOO GREAT. ARE YOU IN OR NOT?
I SUPPOSE I AM.
GOOD. I'LL BRING TREV BOLDER WITH US ON BASS.
GREAT!

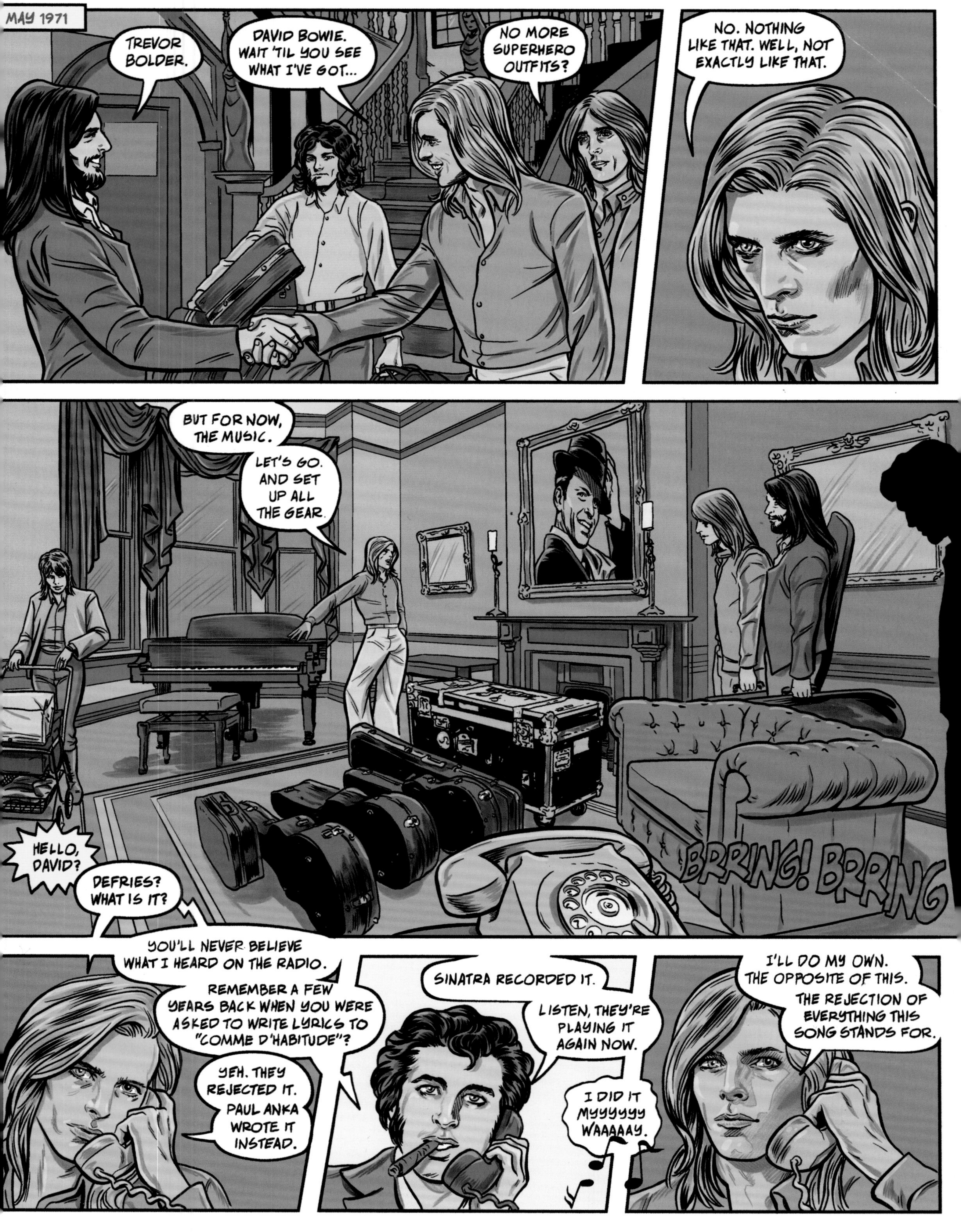
MAY 1971
TREVOR BOLDER.
DAVID BOWIE. WAIT 'TIL YOU SEE WHAT I'VE GOT...
NO MORE SUPERHERO OUTFITS?
NO. NOTHING LIKE THAT. WELL, NOT EXACTLY LIKE THAT.
BUT FOR NOW, THE MUSIC.
LET'S GO. AND SET UP ALL THE GEAR.
BRRING! BRRING
HELLO, DAVID?
DEFRIES? WHAT IS IT?
YOU'LL NEVER BELIEVE WHAT I HEARD ON THE RADIO.
REMEMBER A FEW YEARS BACK WHEN YOU WERE ASKED TO WRITE LYRICS TO "COMME D'HABITUDE"?
YEH. THEY REJECTED IT. PAUL ANKA WROTE IT INSTEAD.
SINATRA RECORDED IT.
LISTEN, THEY'RE PLAYING IT AGAIN NOW.
I DID IT MYYYYYY WAAAAAY.
I'LL DO MY OWN. THE OPPOSITE OF THIS.
THE REJECTION OF EVERYTHING THIS SONG STANDS FOR.

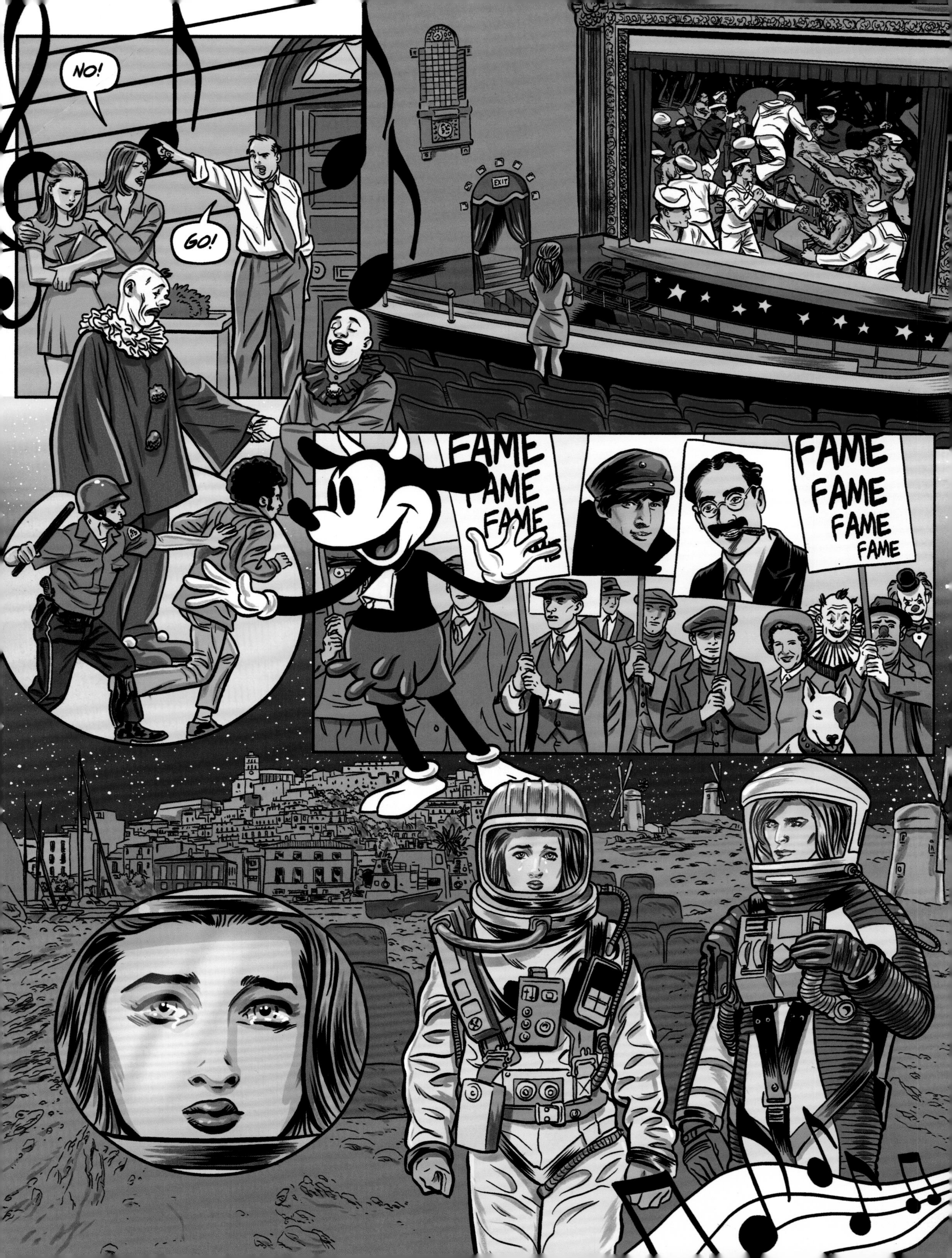
NO!
GO!
EXIT
FAME
FAME
FAME
FAME
FAME
FAME
FAME

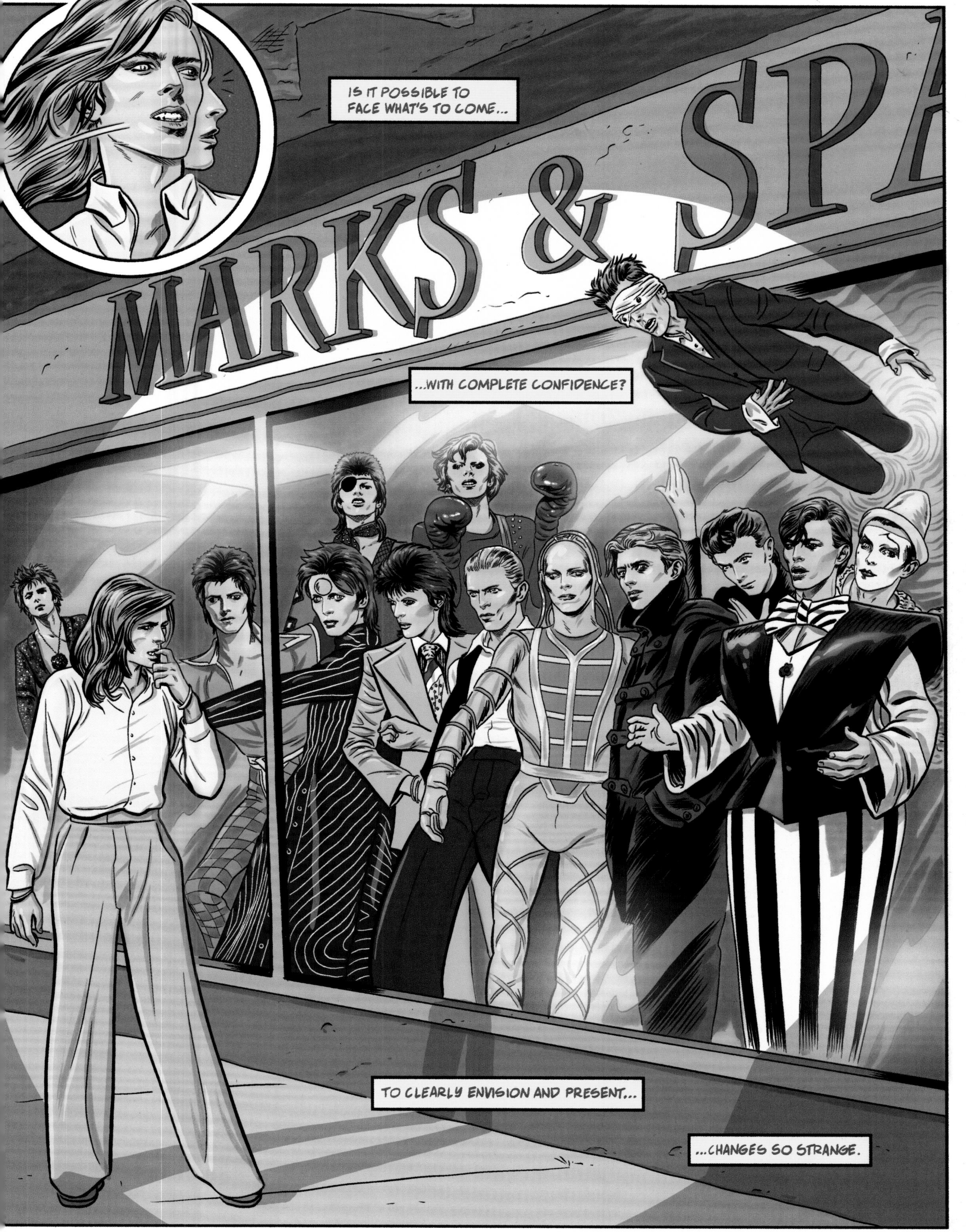

IS IT POSSIBLE TO FACE WHAT'S TO COME...
MARKS & SPA
...WITH COMPLETE CONFIDENCE?
TO CLEARLY ENVISION AND PRESENT...
...CHANGES SO STRANGE.

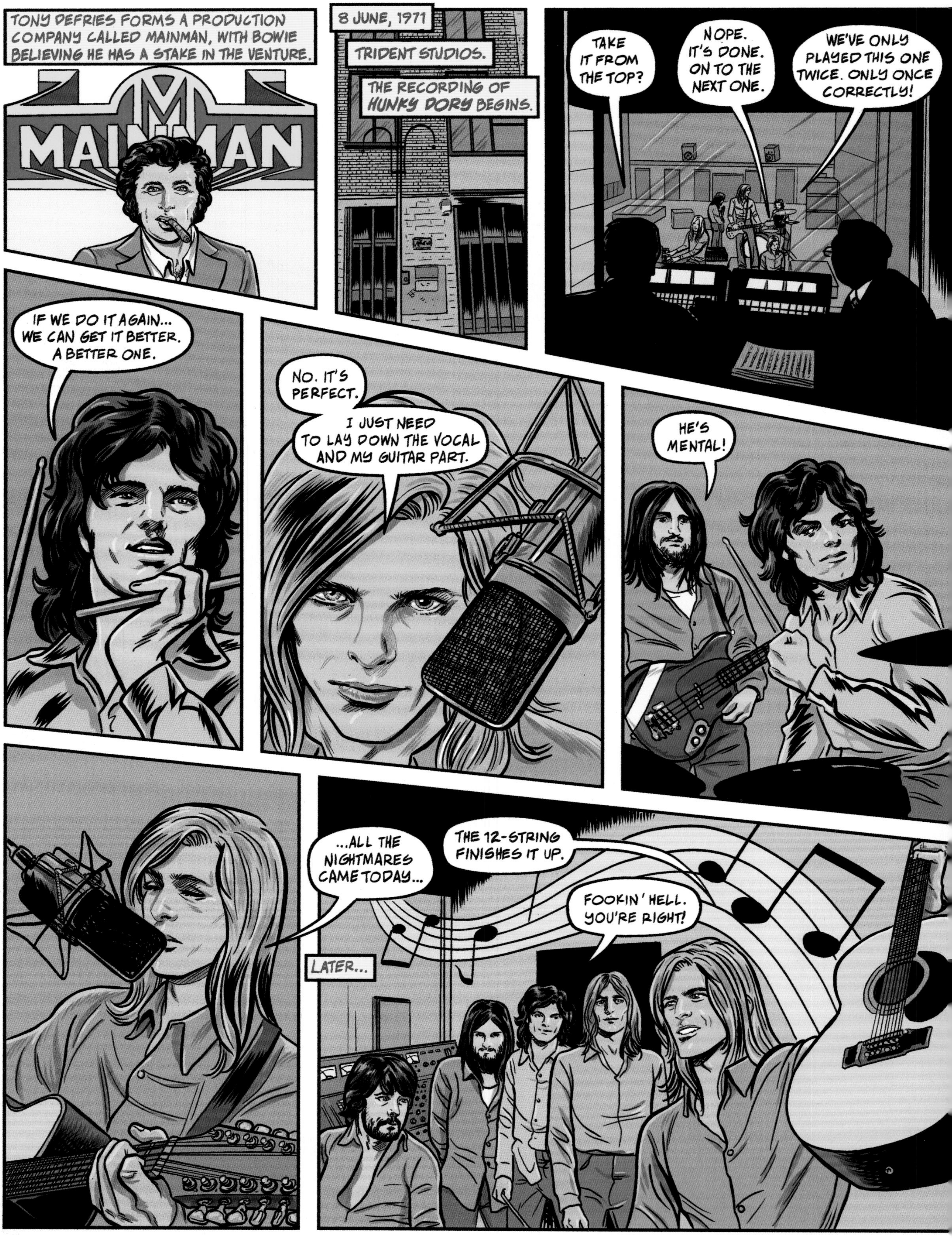
TONY DEFRIES FORMS A PRODUCTION COMPANY CALLED MAINMAN, WITH BOWIE BELIEVING HE HAS A STAKE IN THE VENTURE.
MAINMAN
8 JUNE, 1971
TRIDENT STUDIOS.
THE RECORDING OF HUNKY DORY BEGINS.
TAKE IT FROM THE TOP?
NOPE. IT'S DONE. ON TO THE NEXT ONE.
WE'VE ONLY PLAYED THIS ONE TWICE. ONLY ONCE CORRECTLY!
IF WE DO IT AGAIN... WE CAN GET IT BETTER. A BETTER ONE.
NO. IT'S PERFECT.
I JUST NEED TO LAY DOWN THE VOCAL AND MY GUITAR PART.
HE'S MENTAL!
...ALL THE NIGHTMARES CAME TODAY...
LATER...
THE 12-STRING FINISHES IT UP.
FOOKIN' HELL. YOU'RE RIGHT!

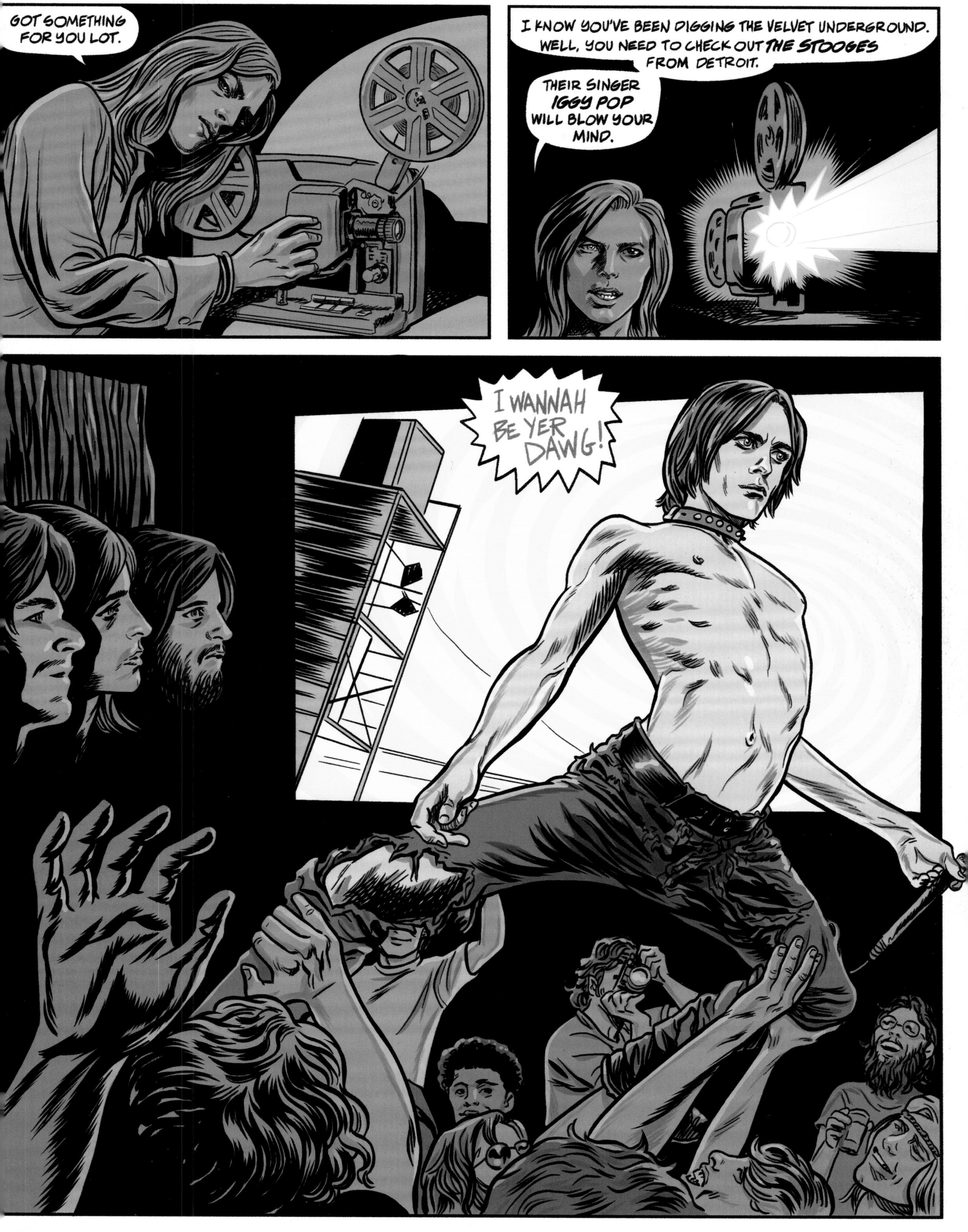
GOT SOMETHING FOR YOU LOT.
I KNOW YOU'VE BEEN DIGGING THE VELVET UNDERGROUND. WELL, YOU NEED TO CHECK OUT THE STOOGES FROM DETROIT.
THEIR SINGER IGGY POP WILL BLOW YOUR MIND.
I WANNAH BE YER DAWG!

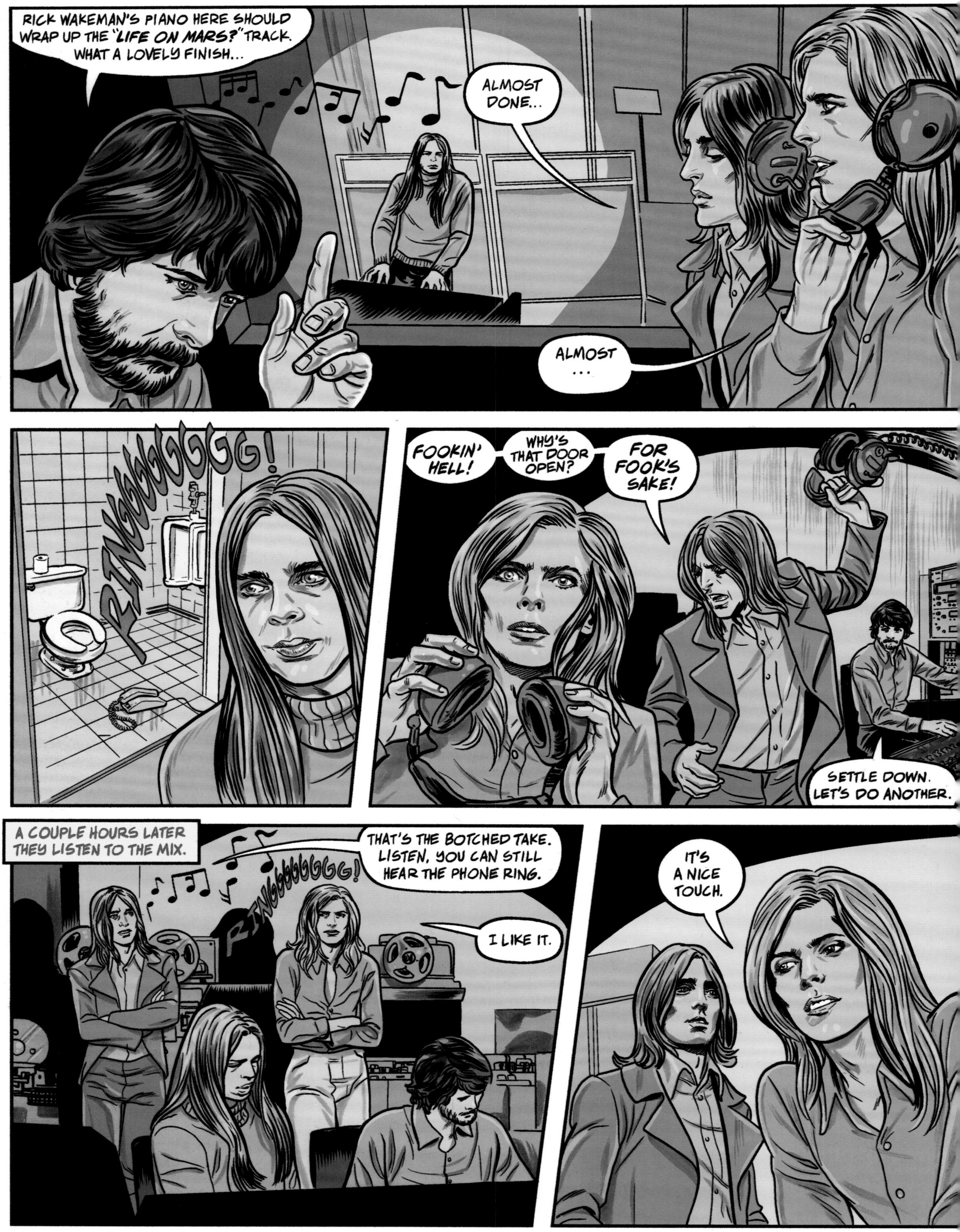
RICK WAKEMAN'S PIANO HERE SHOULD WRAP UP THE "LIFE ON MARS?" TRACK. WHAT A LOVELY FINISH...
ALMOST DONE...
ALMOST ...
RINGGGGGGG!
FOOKIN' HELL!
WHY'S THAT DOOR OPEN?
FOR FOOK'S SAKE!
SETTLE DOWN. LET'S DO ANOTHER.
A COUPLE HOURS LATER THEY LISTEN TO THE MIX.
THAT'S THE BOTCHED TAKE. LISTEN, YOU CAN STILL HEAR THE PHONE RING.
RINGGGGGGGG!
I LIKE IT.
IT'S A NICE TOUCH.

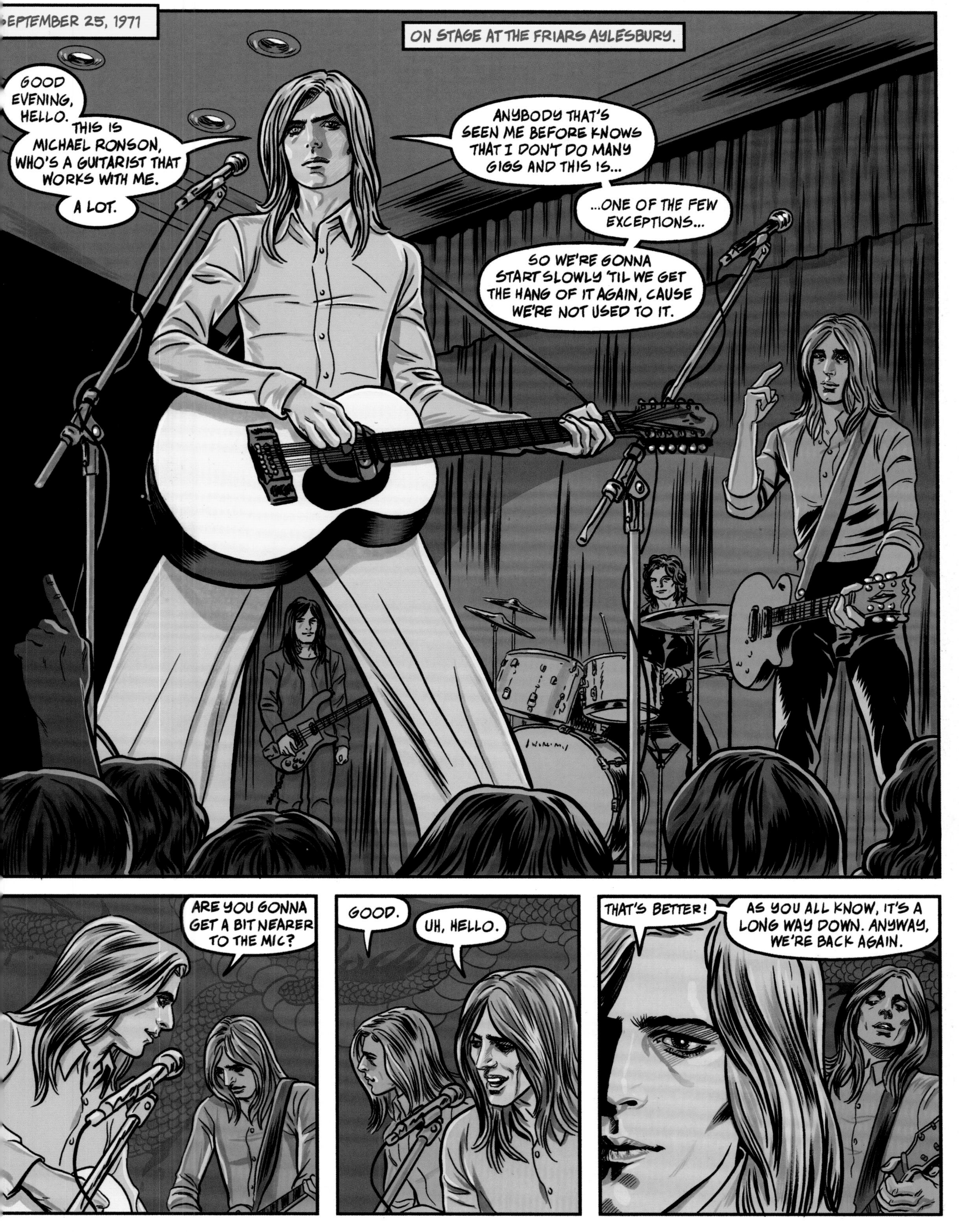
EPTEMBER 25, 1971
ON STAGE AT THE FRIARS AYLESBURY.
GOOD EVENING, HELLO.
THIS IS MICHAEL RONSON, WHO'S A GUITARIST THAT WORKS WITH ME.
A LOT.
ANYBODY THAT'S SEEN ME BEFORE KNOWS THAT I DON'T DO MANY GIGS AND THIS IS...
...ONE OF THE FEW EXCEPTIONS...
SO WE'RE GONNA START SLOWLY 'TIL WE GET THE HANG OF IT AGAIN, CAUSE WE'RE NOT USED TO IT.
ARE YOU GONNA GET A BIT NEARER TO THE MIC?
GOOD.
UH, HELLO.
THAT'S BETTER!
AS YOU ALL KNOW, IT'S A LONG WAY DOWN. ANYWAY, WE'RE BACK AGAIN.

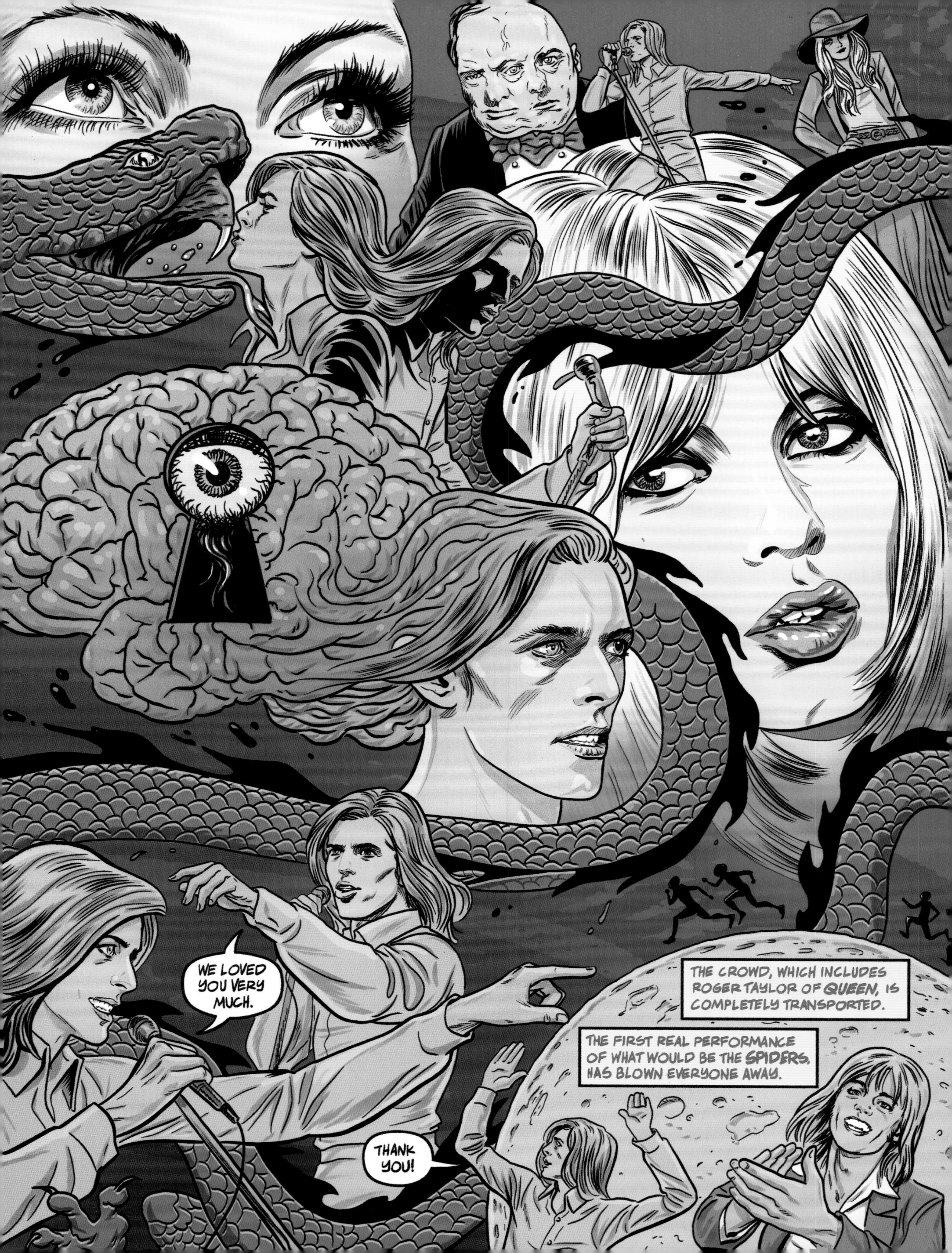

WE LOVED YOU VERY MUCH.
THE CROWD, WHICH INCLUDES ROGER TAYLOR OF QUEEN, IS COMPLETELY TRANSPORTED.
THE FIRST REAL PERFORMANCE OF WHAT WOULD BE THE SPIDERS, HAS BLOWN EVERYONE AWAY.
THANK YOU!

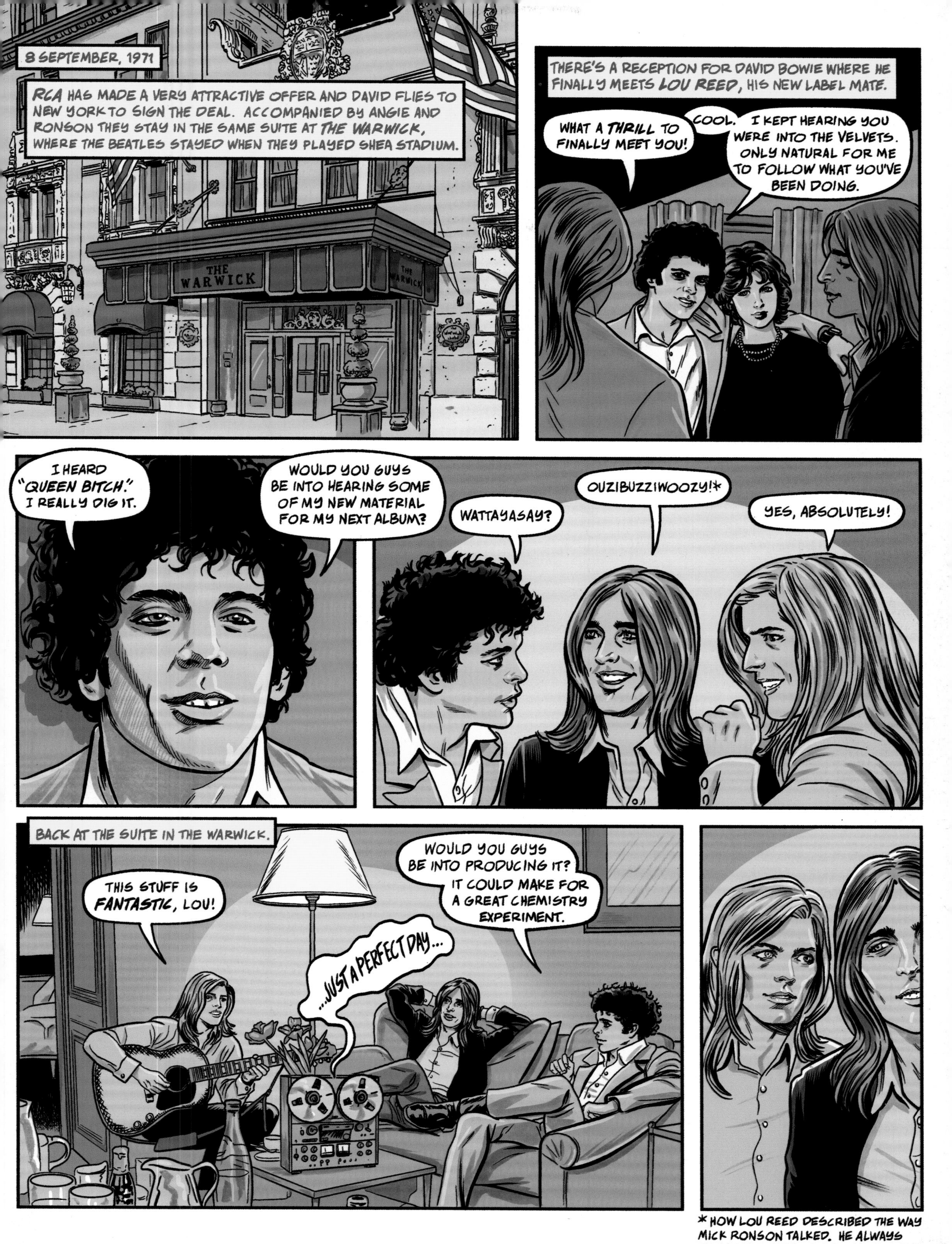
8 SEPTEMBER, 1971
RCA HAS MADE A VERY ATTRACTIVE OFFER AND DAVID FLIES TO NEW YORK TO SIGN THE DEAL. ACCOMPANIED BY ANGIE AND RONSON THEY STAY IN THE SAME SUITE AT THE WARWICK, WHERE THE BEATLES STAYED WHEN THEY PLAYED SHEA STADIUM.
THE WARWICK
THERE'S A RECEPTION FOR DAVID BOWIE WHERE HE FINALLY MEETS LOU REED, HIS NEW LABEL MATE.
WHAT A THRILL TO FINALLY MEET YOU!
COOL.
I KEPT HEARING YOU WERE INTO THE VELVETS. ONLY NATURAL FOR ME TO FOLLOW WHAT YOU'VE BEEN DOING.
I HEARD "QUEEN BITCH." I REALLY DIG IT.
WOULD YOU GUYS BE INTO HEARING SOME OF MY NEW MATERIAL FOR MY NEXT ALBUM?
WATTAYASAY?
OUZIBUZZIWOOZY!*
YES, ABSOLUTELY!
BACK AT THE SUITE IN THE WARWICK.
THIS STUFF IS FANTASTIC, LOU!
...JUST A PERFECT DAY...
WOULD YOU GUYS BE INTO PRODUCING IT?
IT COULD MAKE FOR A GREAT CHEMISTRY EXPERIMENT.

* HOW LOU REED DESCRIBED THE WAY MICK RONSON TALKED. HE ALWAYS FOUND HIM DIFFICULT TO UNDERSTAND.

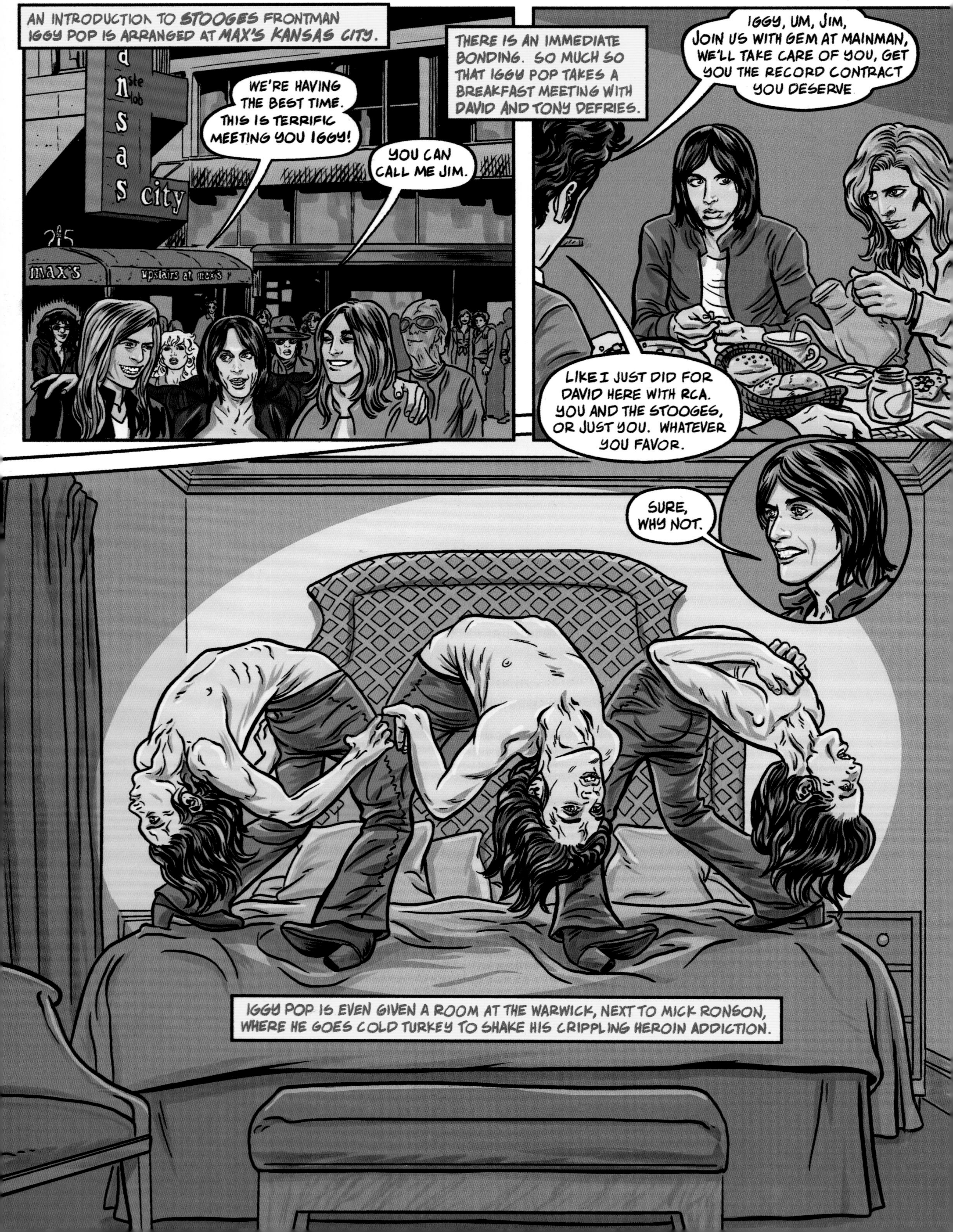

AN INTRODUCTION TO STOOGES FRONTMAN IGGY POP IS ARRANGED AT MAX'S KANSAS CITY.
WE'RE HAVING THE BEST TIME. THIS IS TERRIFIC MEETING YOU IGGY!
YOU CAN CALL ME JIM.
max's
upstairs at max's
city
THERE IS AN IMMEDIATE BONDING. SO MUCH SO THAT IGGY POP TAKES A BREAKFAST MEETING WITH DAVID AND TONY DEFRIES.
IGGY, UM, JIM, JOIN US WITH GEM AT MAINMAN, WE'LL TAKE CARE OF YOU, GET YOU THE RECORD CONTRACT YOU DESERVE.
LIKE I JUST DID FOR DAVID HERE WITH RCA. YOU AND THE STOOGES, OR JUST YOU. WHATEVER YOU FAVOR.
SURE, WHY NOT.
IGGY POP IS EVEN GIVEN A ROOM AT THE WARWICK, NEXT TO MICK RONSON, WHERE HE GOES COLD TURKEY TO SHAKE HIS CRIPPLING HEROIN ADDICTION.

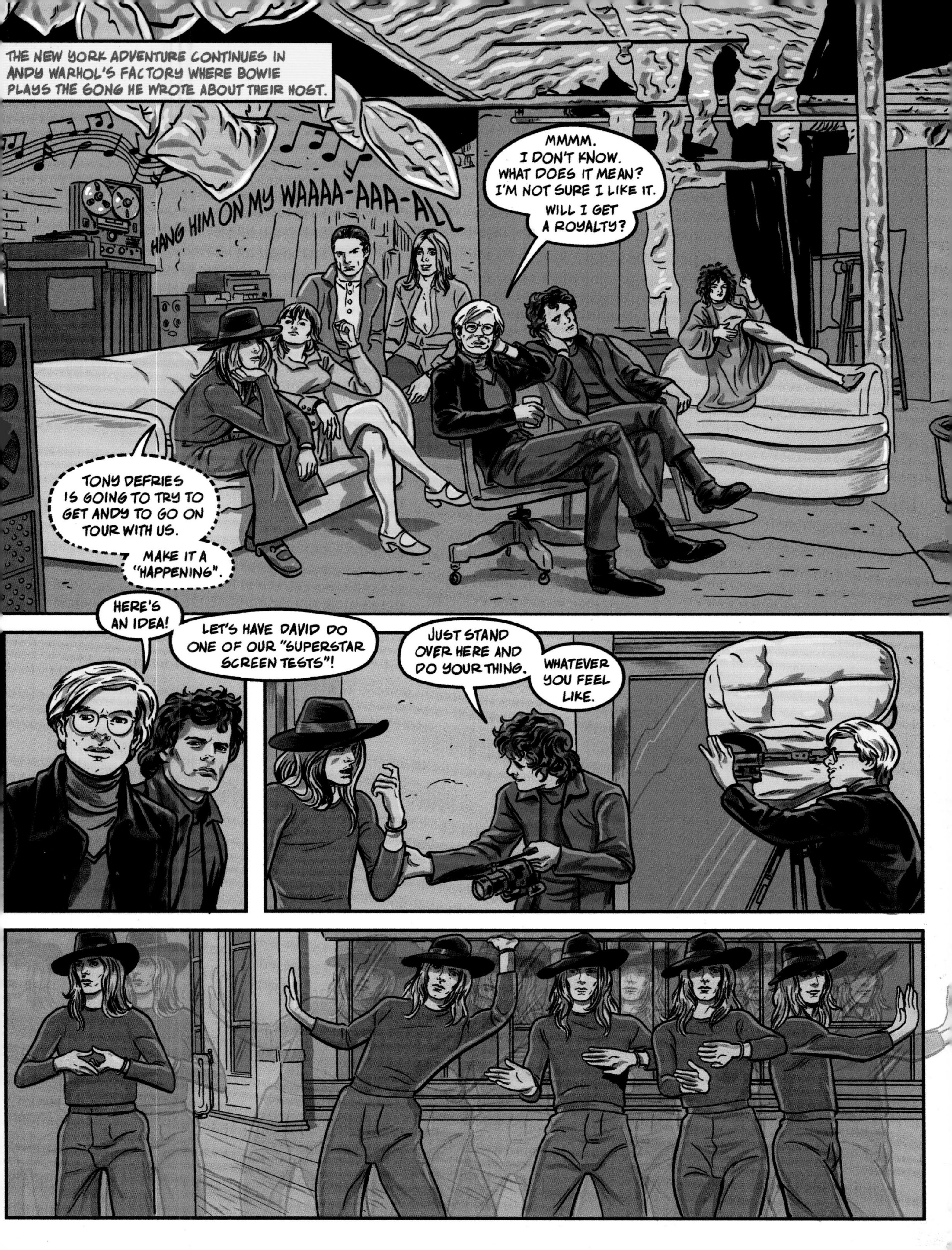
THE NEW YORK ADVENTURE CONTINUES IN ANDY WARHOL'S FACTORY WHERE BOWIE PLAYS THE SONG HE WROTE ABOUT THEIR HOST.
HANG HIM ON MY WAAAA-AAA-ALL
MMMM. I DON'T KNOW. WHAT DOES IT MEAN? I'M NOT SURE I LIKE IT.
WILL I GET A ROYALTY?
TONY DEFRIES IS GOING TO TRY TO GET ANDY TO GO ON TOUR WITH US.
MAKE IT A "HAPPENING".
HERE'S AN IDEA!
LET'S HAVE DAVID DO ONE OF OUR "SUPERSTAR SCREEN TESTS"!
JUST STAND OVER HERE AND DO YOUR THING.
WHATEVER YOU FEEL LIKE.

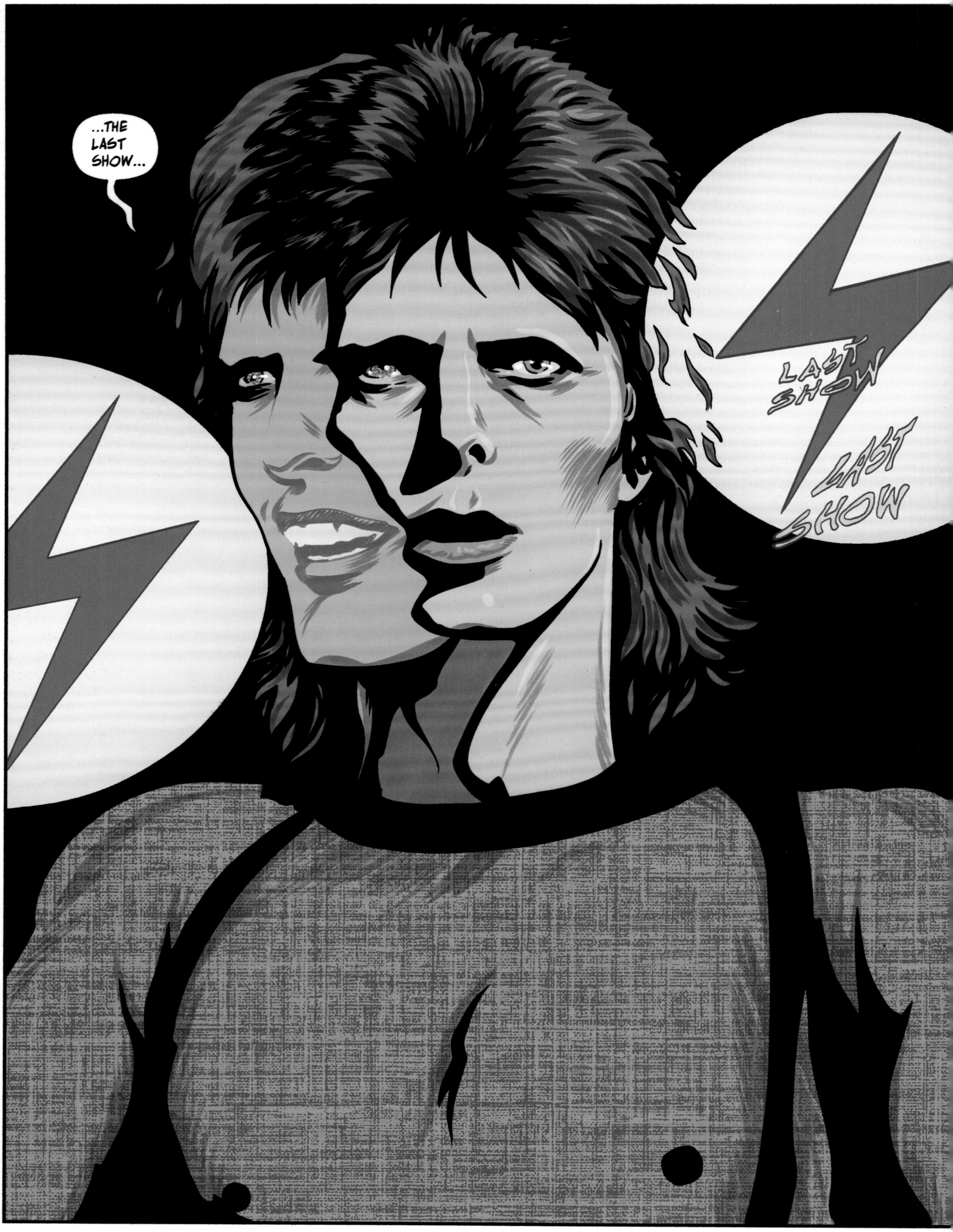

...THE LAST SHOW...
LAST SHOW
LAST SHOW

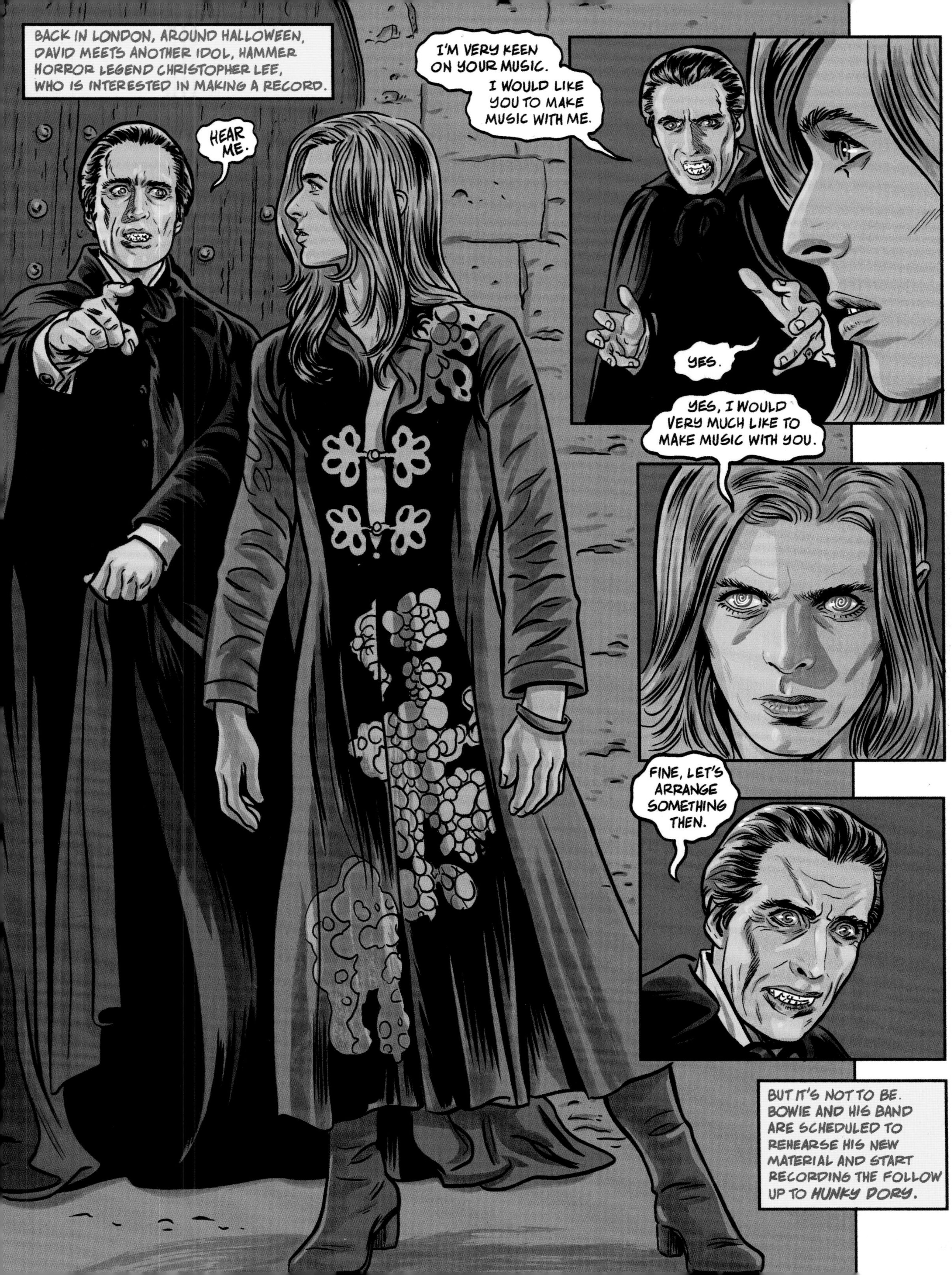

BACK IN LONDON, AROUND HALLOWEEN, DAVID MEETS ANOTHER IDOL, HAMMER HORROR LEGEND CHRISTOPHER LEE, WHO IS INTERESTED IN MAKING A RECORD.
HEAR ME.
I'M VERY KEEN ON YOUR MUSIC.
I WOULD LIKE YOU TO MAKE MUSIC WITH ME.
YES.
YES, I WOULD VERY MUCH LIKE TO MAKE MUSIC WITH YOU.
FINE, LET'S ARRANGE SOMETHING THEN.
BUT IT'S NOT TO BE. BOWIE AND HIS BAND ARE SCHEDULED TO REHEARSE HIS NEW MATERIAL AND START RECORDING THE FOLLOW UP TO *HUNKY DORY*.

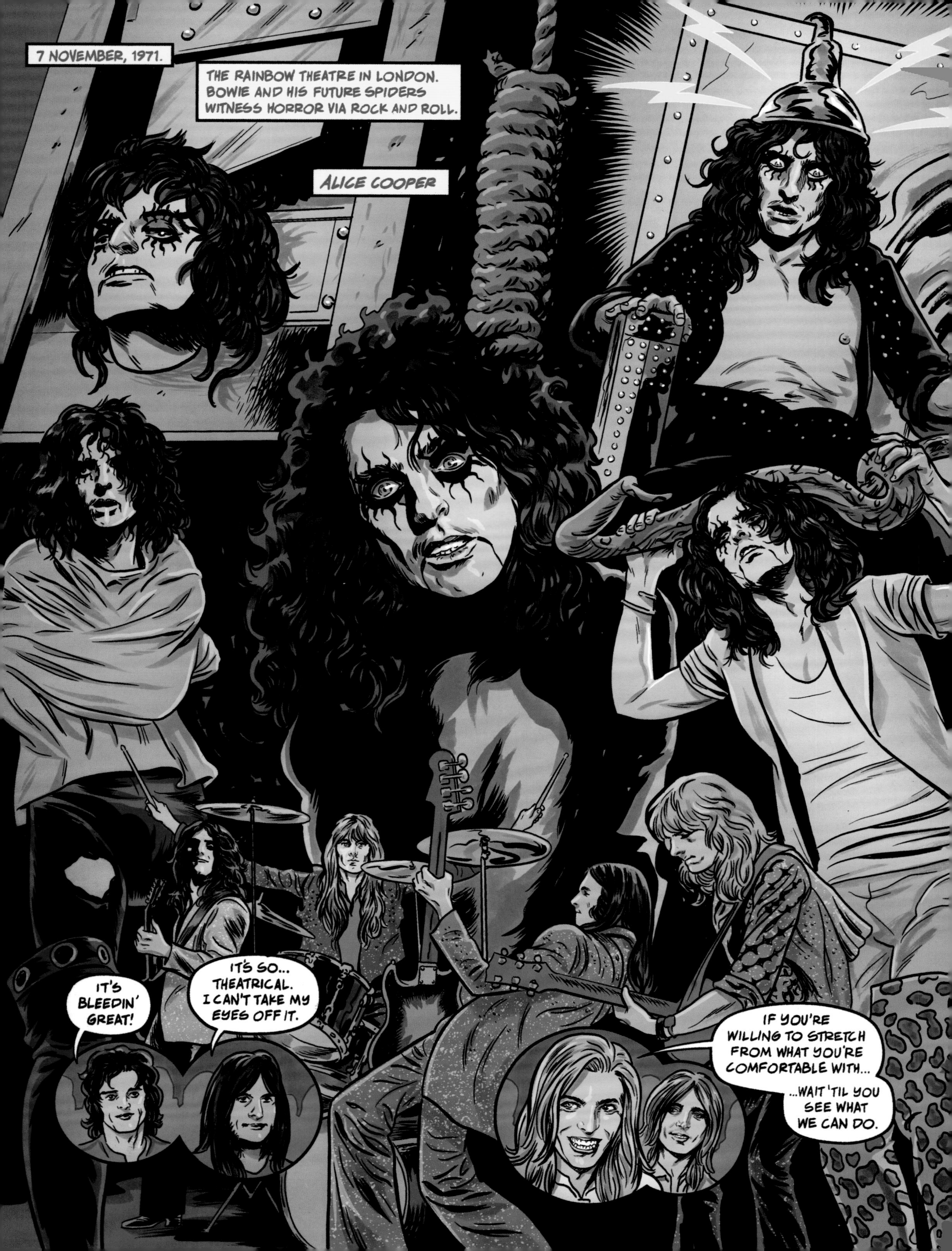
7 NOVEMBER, 1971.
THE RAINBOW THEATRE IN LONDON. BOWIE AND HIS FUTURE SPIDERS WITNESS HORROR VIA ROCK AND ROLL.
ALICE COOPER
IT'S BLEEDIN' GREAT!
IT'S SO... THEATRICAL. I CAN'T TAKE MY EYES OFF IT.
IF YOU'RE WILLING TO STRETCH FROM WHAT YOU'RE COMFORTABLE WITH...
...WAIT 'TIL YOU SEE WHAT WE CAN DO.

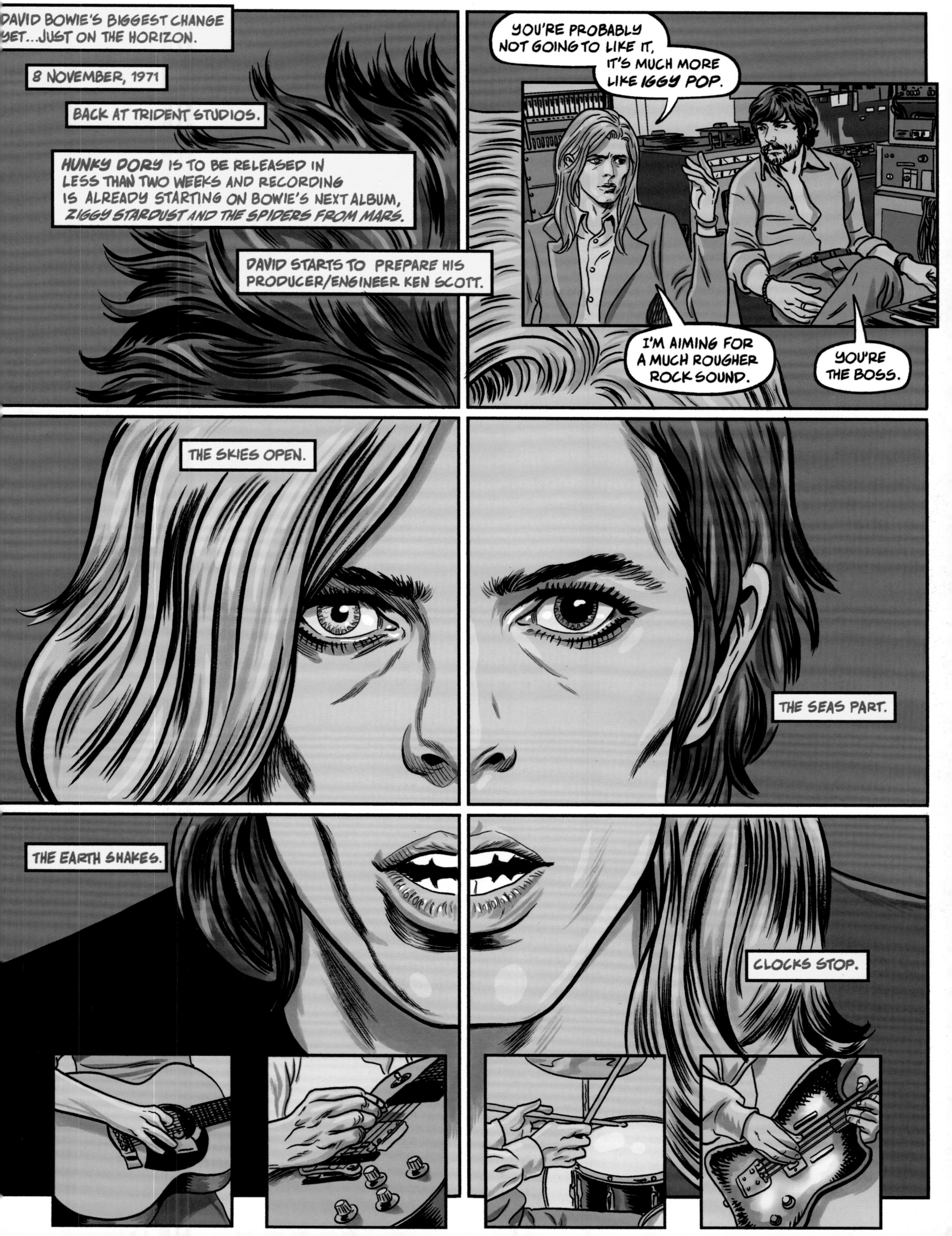
DAVID BOWIE'S BIGGEST CHANGE YET...JUST ON THE HORIZON.
8 NOVEMBER, 1971
BACK AT TRIDENT STUDIOS.
HUNKY DORY IS TO BE RELEASED IN LESS THAN TWO WEEKS AND RECORDING IS ALREADY STARTING ON BOWIE'S NEXT ALBUM, ZIGGY STARDUST AND THE SPIDERS FROM MARS.
DAVID STARTS TO PREPARE HIS PRODUCER/ENGINEER KEN SCOTT.
YOU'RE PROBABLY NOT GOING TO LIKE IT, IT'S MUCH MORE LIKE IGGY POP.
I'M AIMING FOR A MUCH ROUGHER ROCK SOUND.
YOU'RE THE BOSS.
THE SKIES OPEN.
THE SEAS PART.
THE EARTH SHAKES.
CLOCKS STOP.

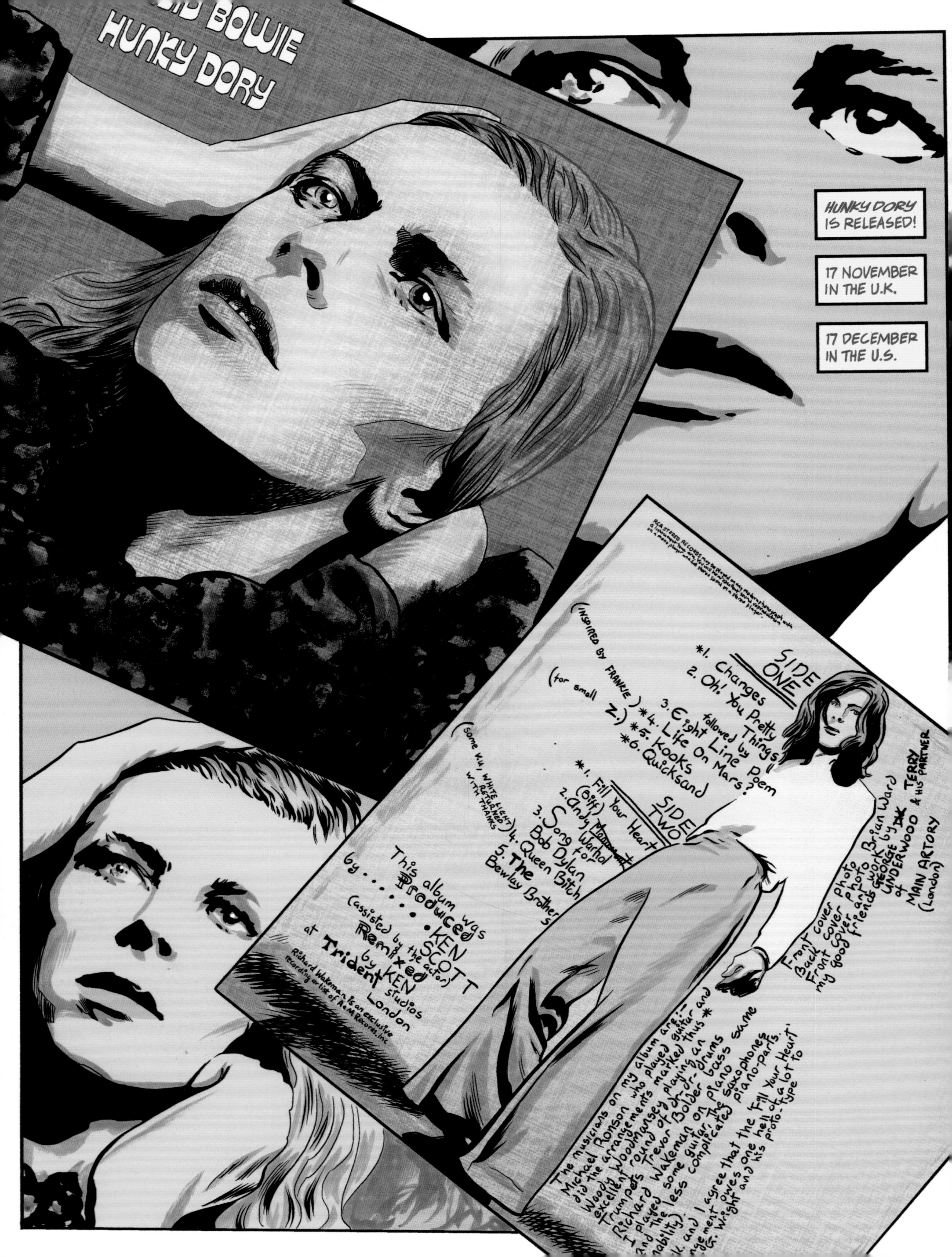

BOWIE
HUNKY DORY
HUNKY DORY IS RELEASED!
17 NOVEMBER IN THE U.K.
17 DECEMBER IN THE U.S.
SIDE ONE
*1. Changes
2. Oh! You Pretty Things
followed by
3. Eight Line Poem
*4. Life On Mars?
*5. Kooks
*6. Quicksand
(INSPIRED BY FRANKIE)
(for small Z.)
SIDE TWO
*1. Fill Your Heart
2. Andy Warhol
3. Song for Bob Dylan
4. Queen Bitch
5. The Bewlay Brothers
(SOME V.U., WHITE LIGHT RETURNED WITH THANKS)
This album was Produced by . . . . . . KEN SCOTT (assisted by the actor) Remixed by KEN at Trident studios London
Richard Wakeman is an exclusive recording artist of A&M Records, Inc
Front cover photo Brian Ward
Back cover photo
Front cover artwork by GEORGE UNDERWOOD & TERRY & HIS PARTNER at MAIN ARTORY (London)
my good friends
The musicians on my album are:-
Michael Ronson who played guitar and did the arrangements marked thus *
Woody Woodmansey playing an excellent round of dr-dr-drums
Trumpets Trevor Bolder bass
Richard Wakeman on piano
I played some guitar, the saxophones and the less complicated piano-parts.

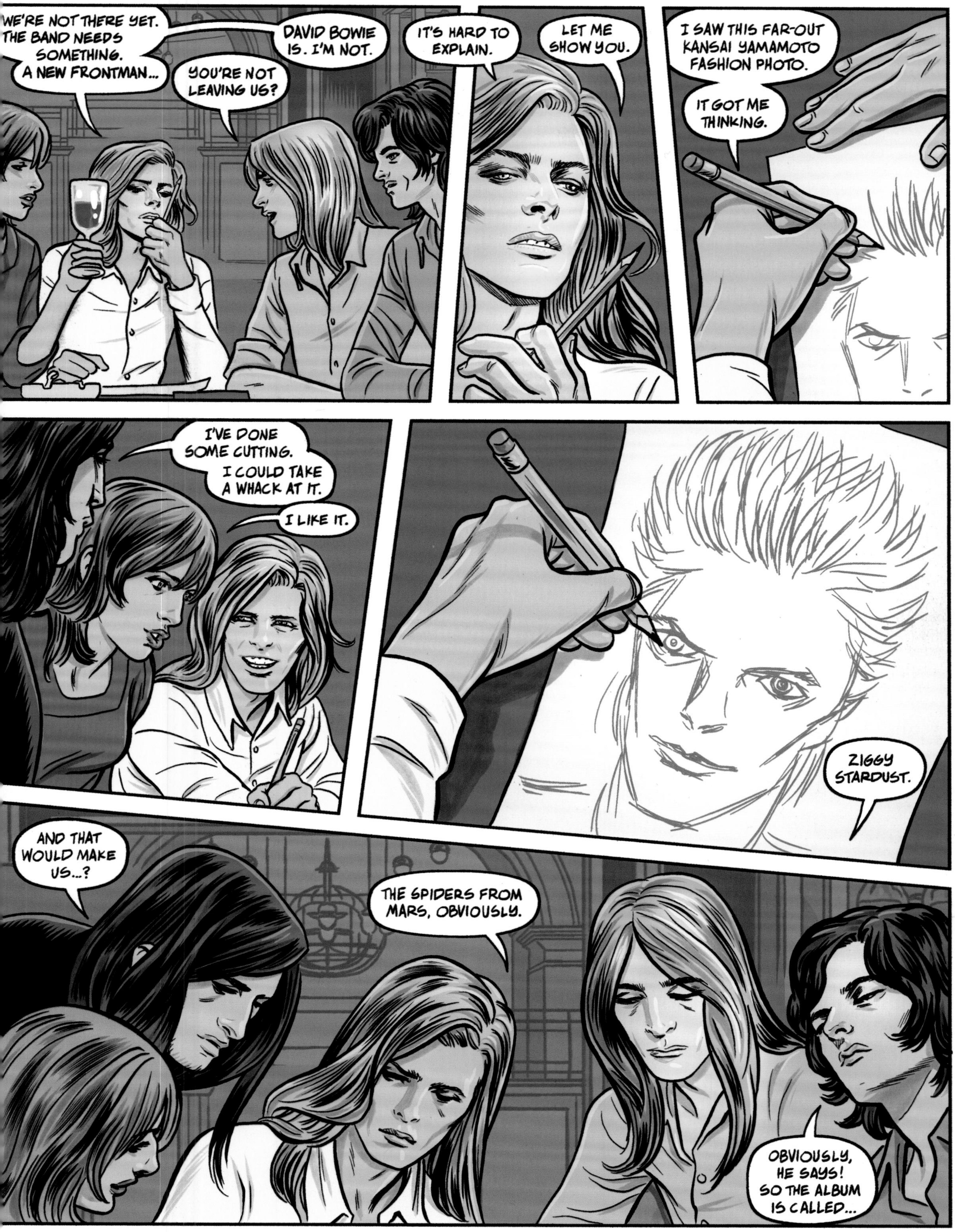
WE'RE NOT THERE YET. THE BAND NEEDS SOMETHING. A NEW FRONTMAN...
DAVID BOWIE IS. I'M NOT.
YOU'RE NOT LEAVING US?
IT'S HARD TO EXPLAIN.
LET ME SHOW YOU.
I SAW THIS FAR-OUT KANSAI YAMAMOTO FASHION PHOTO.
IT GOT ME THINKING.
I'VE DONE SOME CUTTING.
I COULD TAKE A WHACK AT IT.
I LIKE IT.
ZIGGY STARDUST.
AND THAT WOULD MAKE US...?
THE SPIDERS FROM MARS, OBVIOUSLY.
OBVIOUSLY, HE SAYS! SO THE ALBUM IS CALLED...

THE RISE AND FALL OF *ZIGGY STARDUST* AND THE *SPIDERS FROM MARS.*

FOOK ME, THAT'S A LONG NAME.

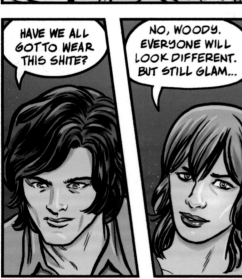

HAVE WE ALL GOT TO WEAR THIS SHITE?

NO, WOODY. EVERYONE WILL LOOK DIFFERENT. BUT STILL GLAM...

GLAM, LIKE MARC BOLAN GLAM. LIKE WITH THE GLITTER UNDER HIS EYES.

NO, NOT LIKE MARC. WE'RE NOT DOING ANYTHING LIKE WHAT HE'S DOING. WE'RE DOING MY THING.

SORRY, SORRY. YOU'RE RIGHT. THIS IS UNLIKE ANYTHING I'VE EVER SEEN.

REMINDS ME OF THAT SONG "MOONAGE DAYDREAM" THAT YOU WROTE A WHILE BACK.

SHARP AS EVER. I'M RE-RECORDING IT.

ALWAYS DID LIKE THE FILLS ON THAT.

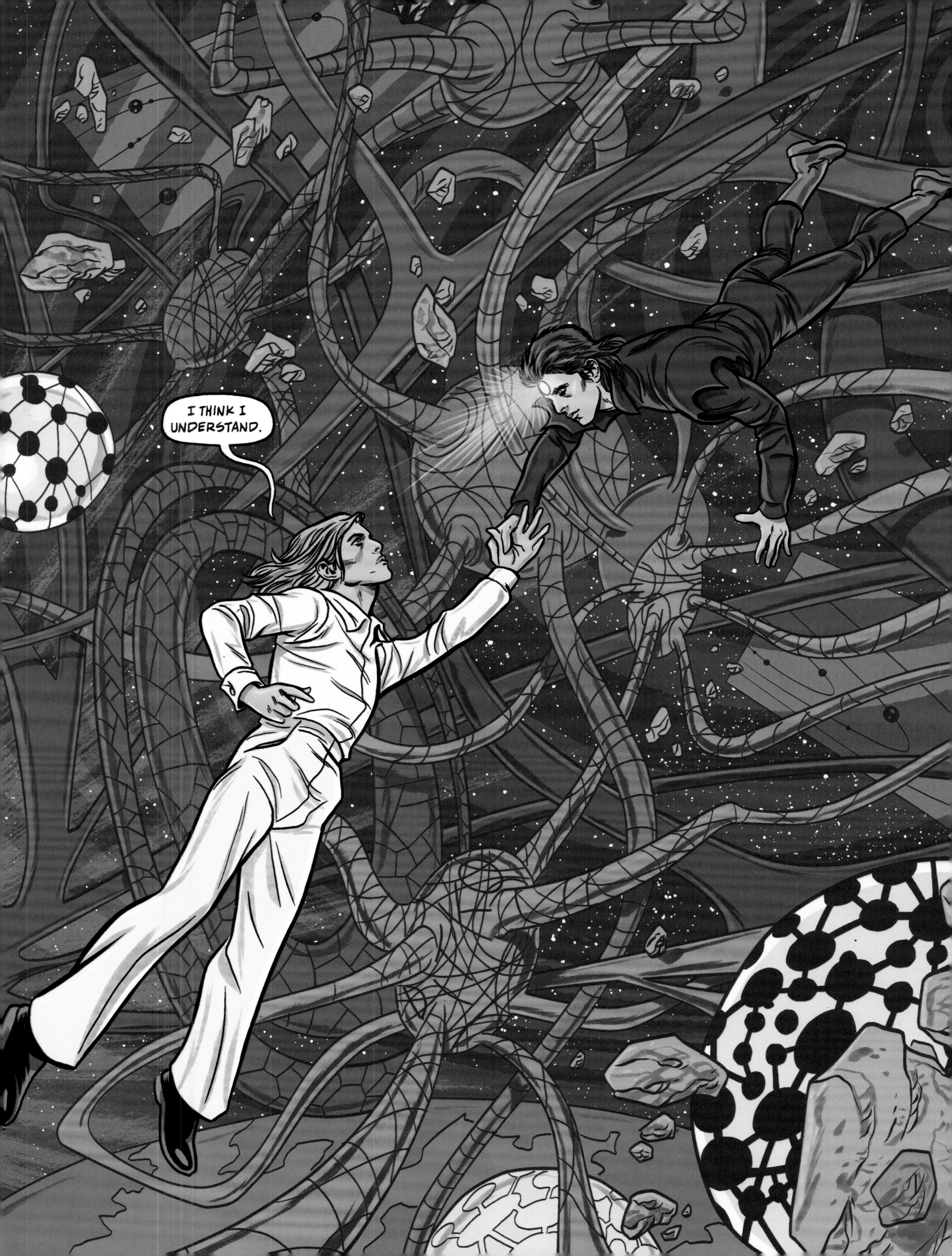
I THINK I UNDERSTAND.

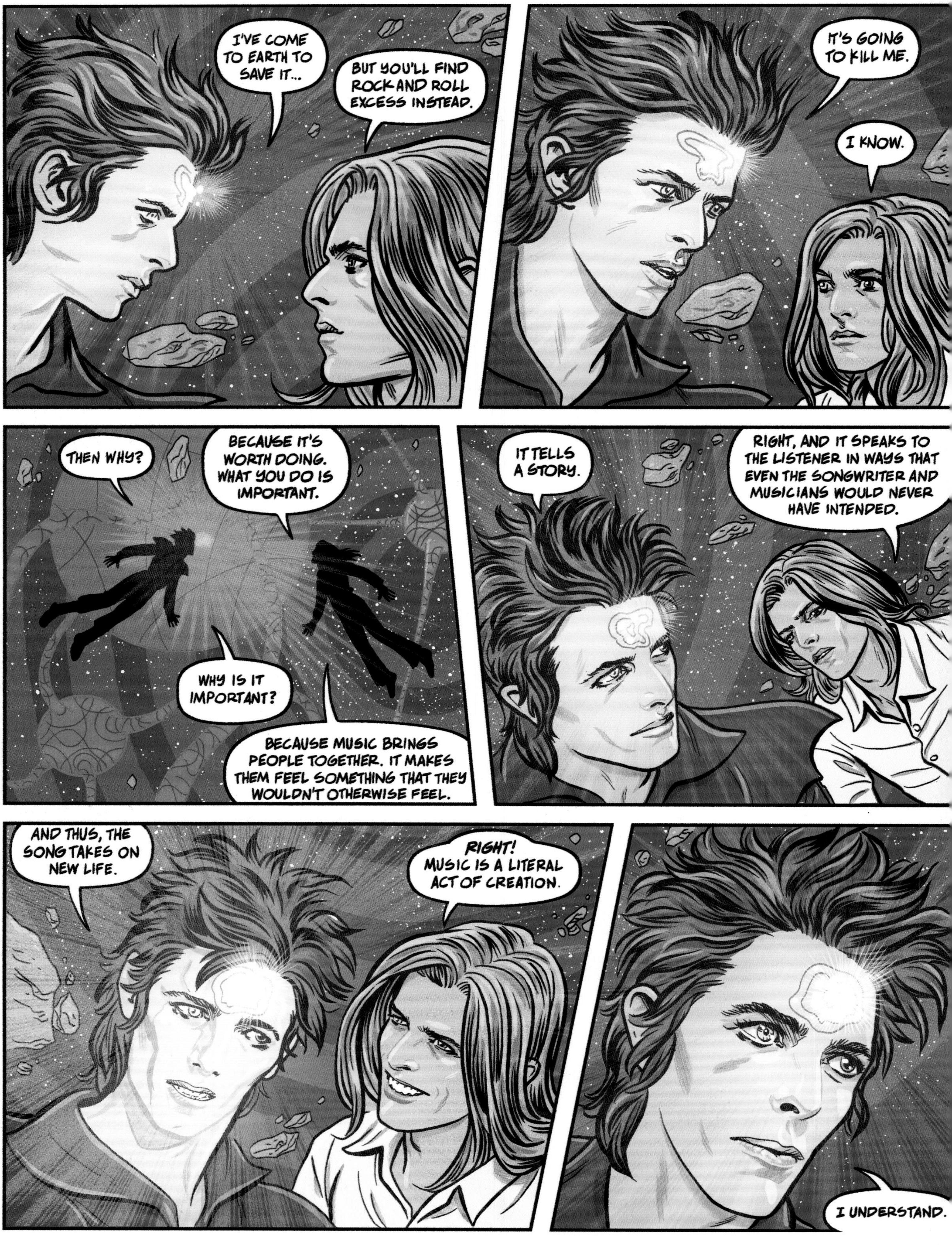
I'VE COME TO EARTH TO SAVE IT...
BUT YOU'LL FIND ROCK AND ROLL EXCESS INSTEAD.
IT'S GOING TO KILL ME.
I KNOW.
THEN WHY?
BECAUSE IT'S WORTH DOING. WHAT YOU DO IS IMPORTANT.
WHY IS IT IMPORTANT?
BECAUSE MUSIC BRINGS PEOPLE TOGETHER. IT MAKES THEM FEEL SOMETHING THAT THEY WOULDN'T OTHERWISE FEEL.
IT TELLS A STORY.
RIGHT, AND IT SPEAKS TO THE LISTENER IN WAYS THAT EVEN THE SONGWRITER AND MUSICIANS WOULD NEVER HAVE INTENDED.
AND THUS, THE SONG TAKES ON NEW LIFE.
RIGHT! MUSIC IS A LITERAL ACT OF CREATION.
I UNDERSTAND.

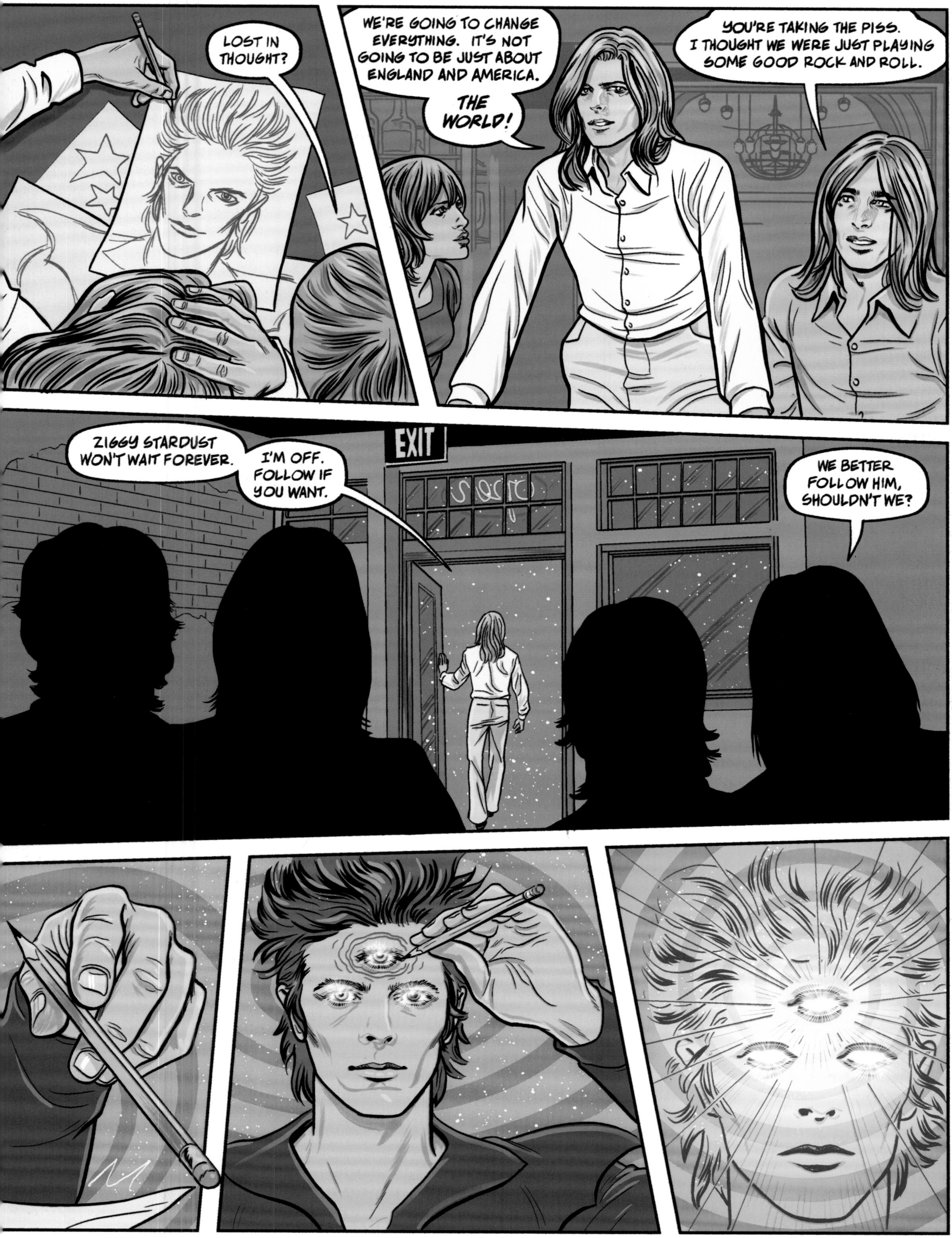
LOST IN THOUGHT?
WE'RE GOING TO CHANGE EVERYTHING. IT'S NOT GOING TO BE JUST ABOUT ENGLAND AND AMERICA.
THE WORLD!
YOU'RE TAKING THE PISS. I THOUGHT WE WERE JUST PLAYING SOME GOOD ROCK AND ROLL.
ZIGGY STARDUST WON'T WAIT FOREVER.
I'M OFF. FOLLOW IF YOU WANT.
EXIT
WE BETTER FOLLOW HIM, SHOULDN'T WE?

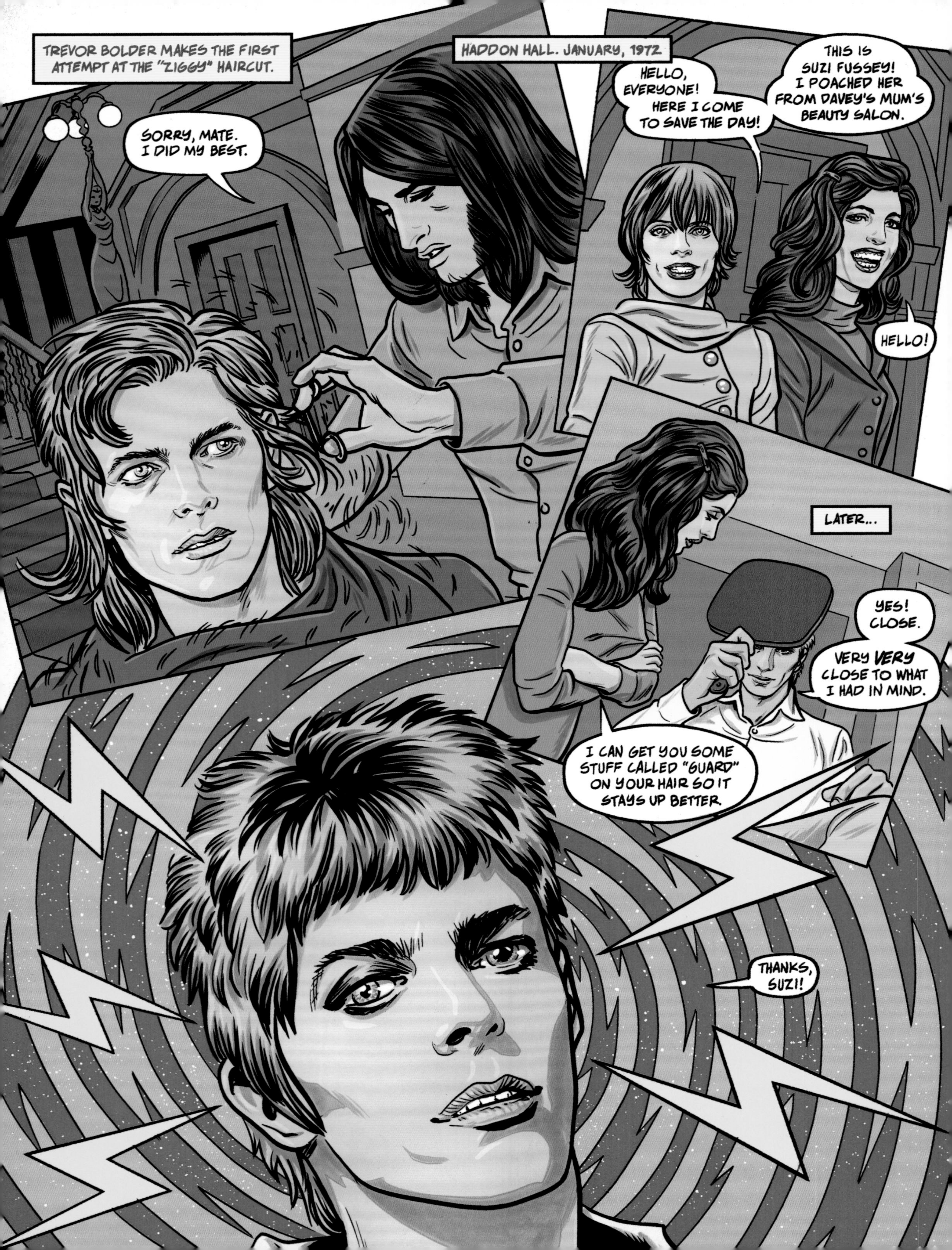
TREVOR BOLDER MAKES THE FIRST ATTEMPT AT THE "ZIGGY" HAIRCUT.
SORRY, MATE. I DID MY BEST.
HADDON HALL. JANUARY, 1972
HELLO, EVERYONE! HERE I COME TO SAVE THE DAY!
THIS IS SUZI FUSSEY! I POACHED HER FROM DAVEY'S MUM'S BEAUTY SALON.
HELLO!
LATER...
YES! CLOSE.
VERY VERY CLOSE TO WHAT I HAD IN MIND.
I CAN GET YOU SOME STUFF CALLED "GUARD" ON YOUR HAIR SO IT STAYS UP BETTER.
THANKS, SUZI!

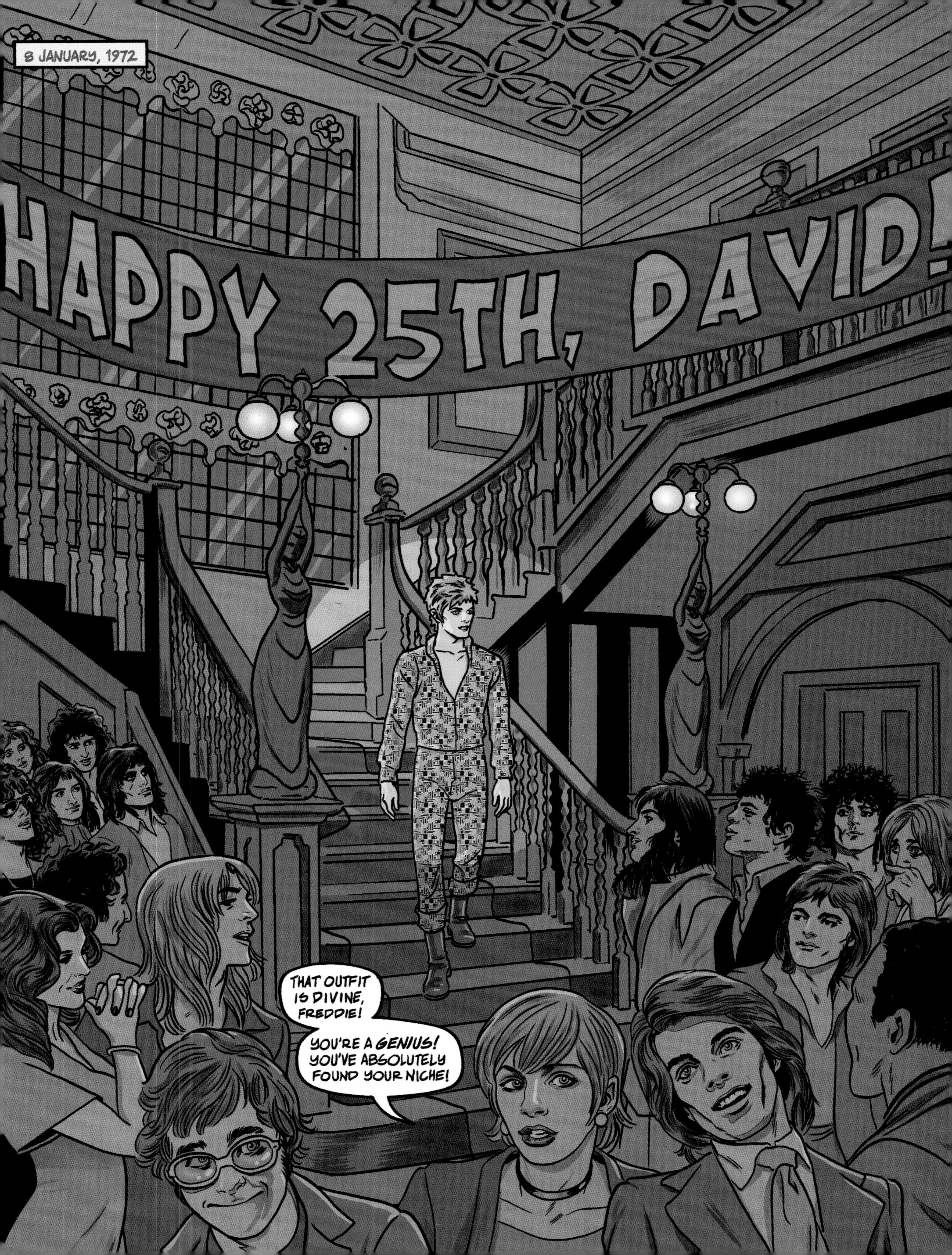
8 JANUARY, 1972
HAPPY 25TH, DAVID!
THAT OUTFIT IS DIVINE, FREDDIE!
YOU'RE A GENIUS! YOU'VE ABSOLUTELY FOUND YOUR NICHE!

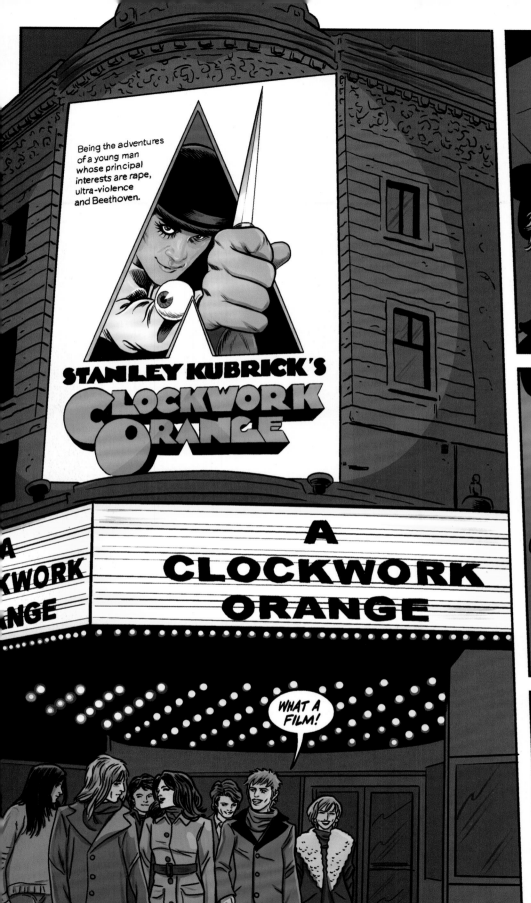

Being the adventures of a young man whose principal interests are rape, ultra-violence and Beethoven.

STANLEY KUBRICK'S
CLOCKWORK ORANGE

A CLOCKWORK ORANGE

WHAT A FILM!

I WANT TO REALLY INCORPORATE THE STYLE OF *THE DROOGS* IN OUR COSTUMING. CAN YOU DO MORE OF THAT, FREDDIE?

WHAT YOU'VE BEEN DOING LATELY WAS PRACTICALLY ALREADY UP THERE RIGHT ON THE SCREEN!

CERTAINLY! BUT WITH MORE GLAM, YEAH?

AT MAXIMUM VOLUME!

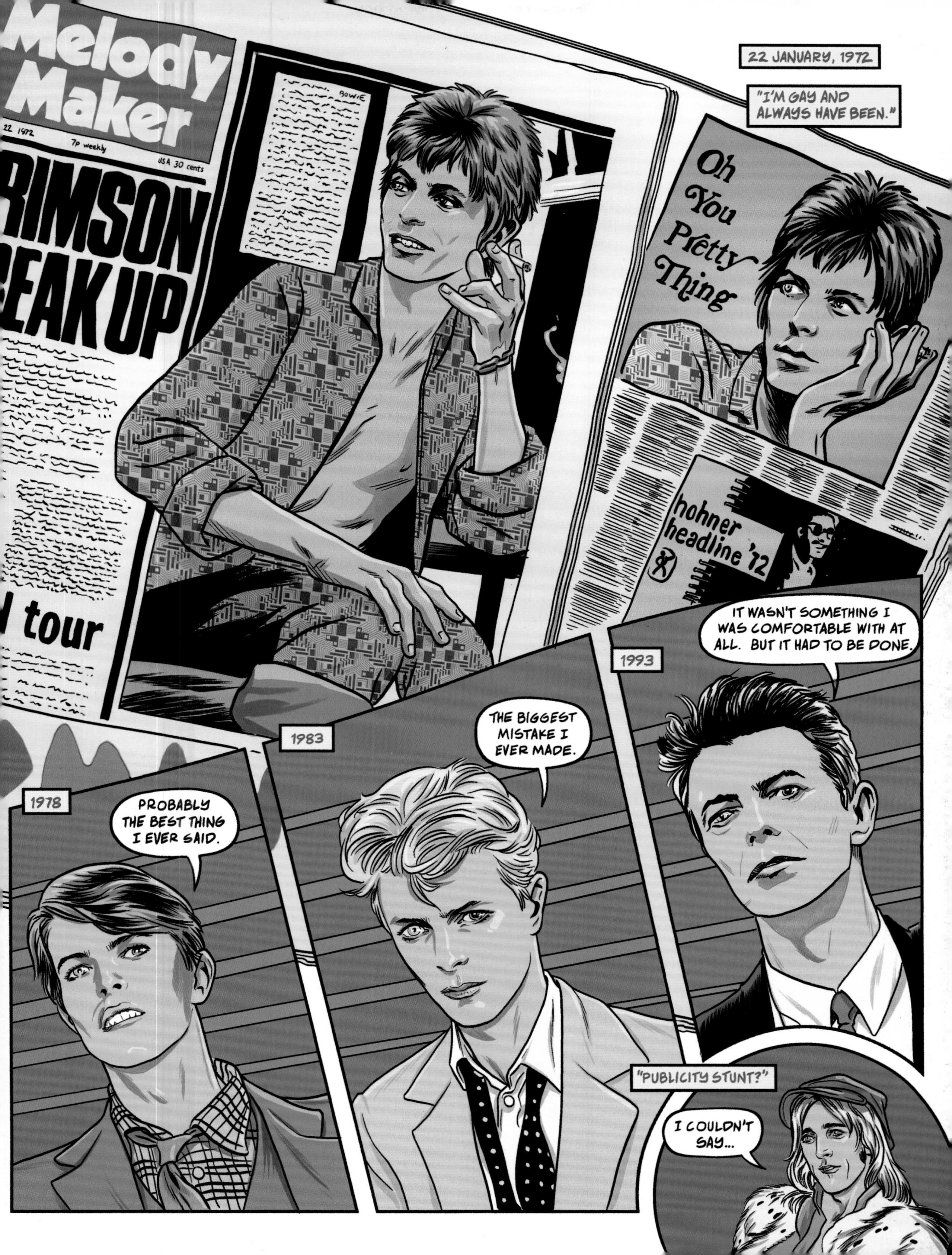
Melody Maker
22 1972
7p weekly
USA 30 cents
RIMSON
EAK UP
tour
BOWIE
22 JANUARY, 1972
"I'M GAY AND ALWAYS HAVE BEEN."
Oh You Pretty Thing
hohner headline '72
1978
PROBABLY THE BEST THING I EVER SAID.
1983
THE BIGGEST MISTAKE I EVER MADE.
1993
IT WASN'T SOMETHING I WAS COMFORTABLE WITH AT ALL. BUT IT HAD TO BE DONE.
"PUBLICITY STUNT?"
I COULDN'T SAY...

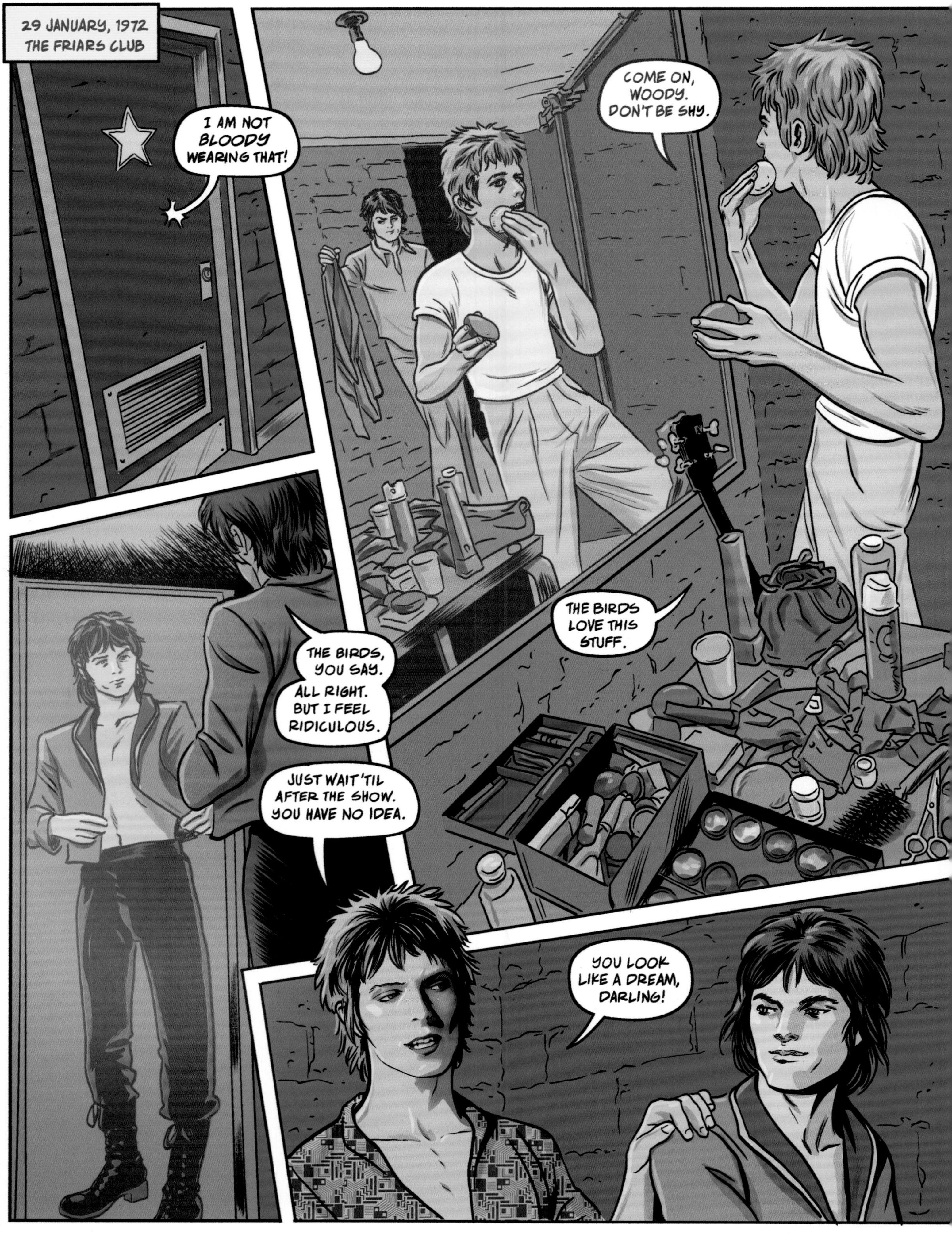
29 JANUARY, 1972
THE FRIARS CLUB
I AM NOT BLOODY WEARING THAT!
COME ON, WOODY. DON'T BE SHY.
THE BIRDS LOVE THIS STUFF.
THE BIRDS, YOU SAY.
ALL RIGHT. BUT I FEEL RIDICULOUS.
JUST WAIT 'TIL AFTER THE SHOW. YOU HAVE NO IDEA.
YOU LOOK LIKE A DREAM, DARLING!

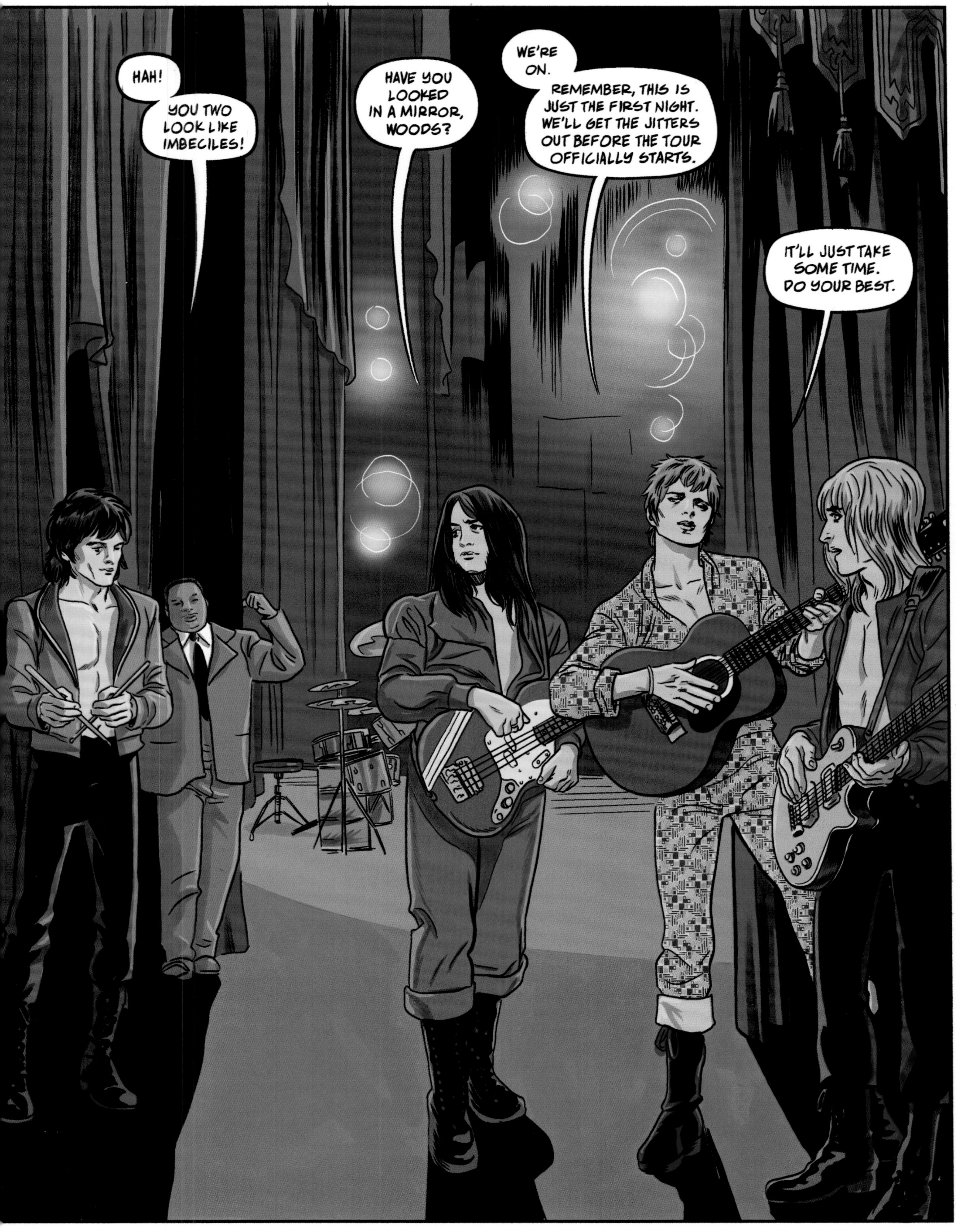
HAH!
YOU TWO LOOK LIKE IMBECILES!
HAVE YOU LOOKED IN A MIRROR, WOODS?
WE'RE ON.
REMEMBER, THIS IS JUST THE FIRST NIGHT. WE'LL GET THE JITTERS OUT BEFORE THE TOUR OFFICIALLY STARTS.
IT'LL JUST TAKE SOME TIME. DO YOUR BEST.

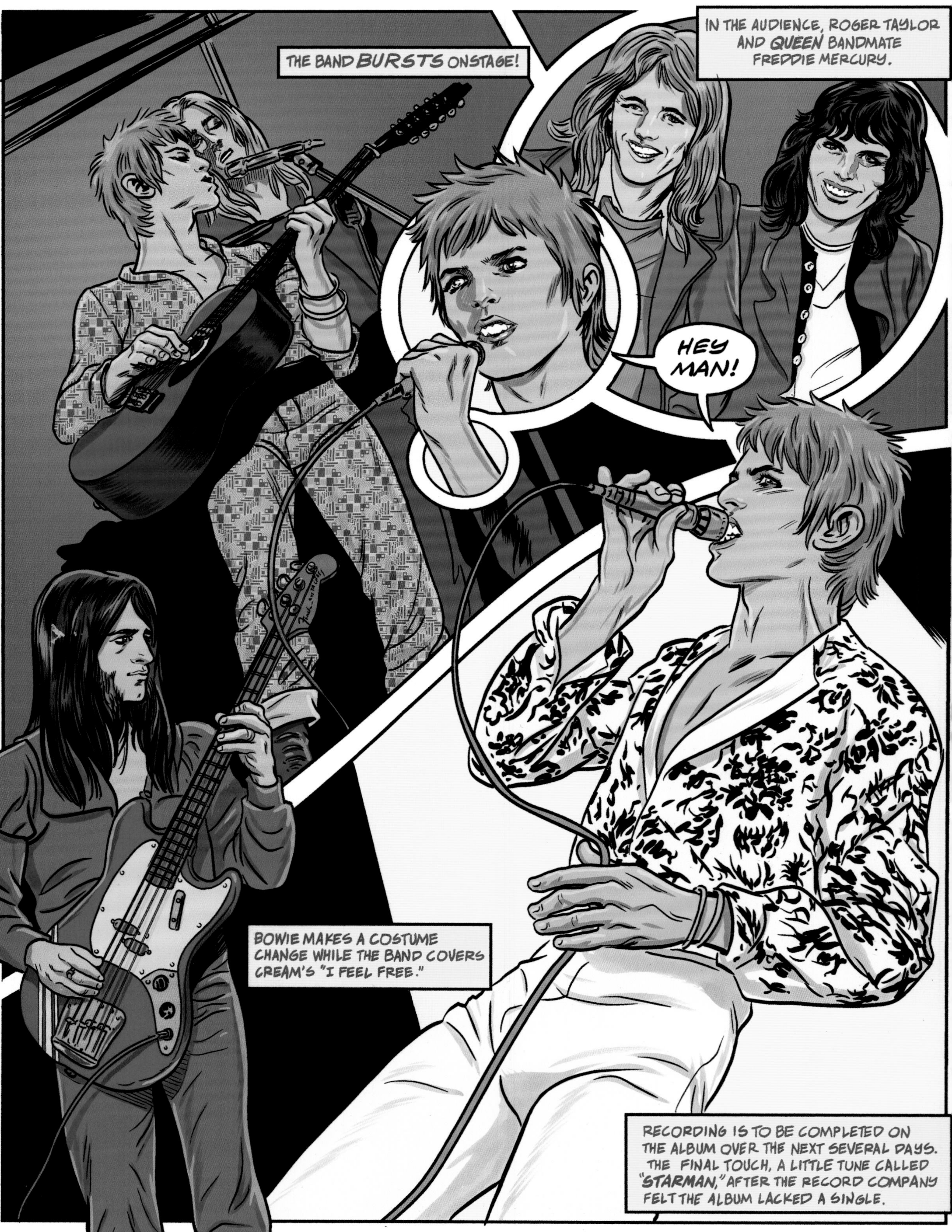
THE BAND BURSTS ONSTAGE!
IN THE AUDIENCE, ROGER TAYLOR AND QUEEN BANDMATE FREDDIE MERCURY.
HEY MAN!
BOWIE MAKES A COSTUME CHANGE WHILE THE BAND COVERS CREAM'S "I FEEL FREE."
RECORDING IS TO BE COMPLETED ON THE ALBUM OVER THE NEXT SEVERAL DAYS. THE FINAL TOUCH, A LITTLE TUNE CALLED "STARMAN," AFTER THE RECORD COMPANY FELT THE ALBUM LACKED A SINGLE.

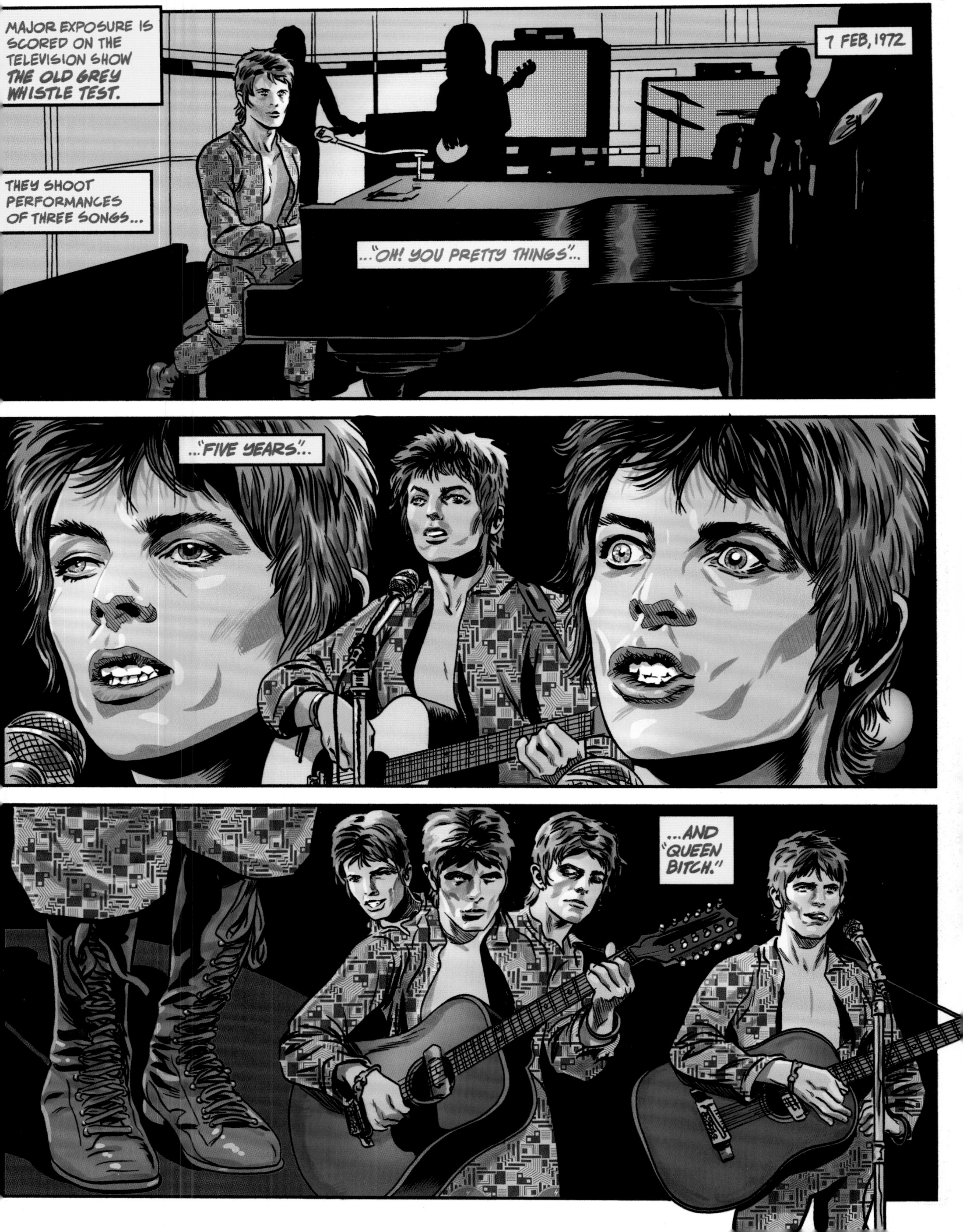
MAJOR EXPOSURE IS SCORED ON THE TELEVISION SHOW *THE OLD GREY WHISTLE TEST.*
7 FEB, 1972
THEY SHOOT PERFORMANCES OF THREE SONGS...
..."OH! YOU PRETTY THINGS"...
..."FIVE YEARS"...
...AND "QUEEN BITCH."

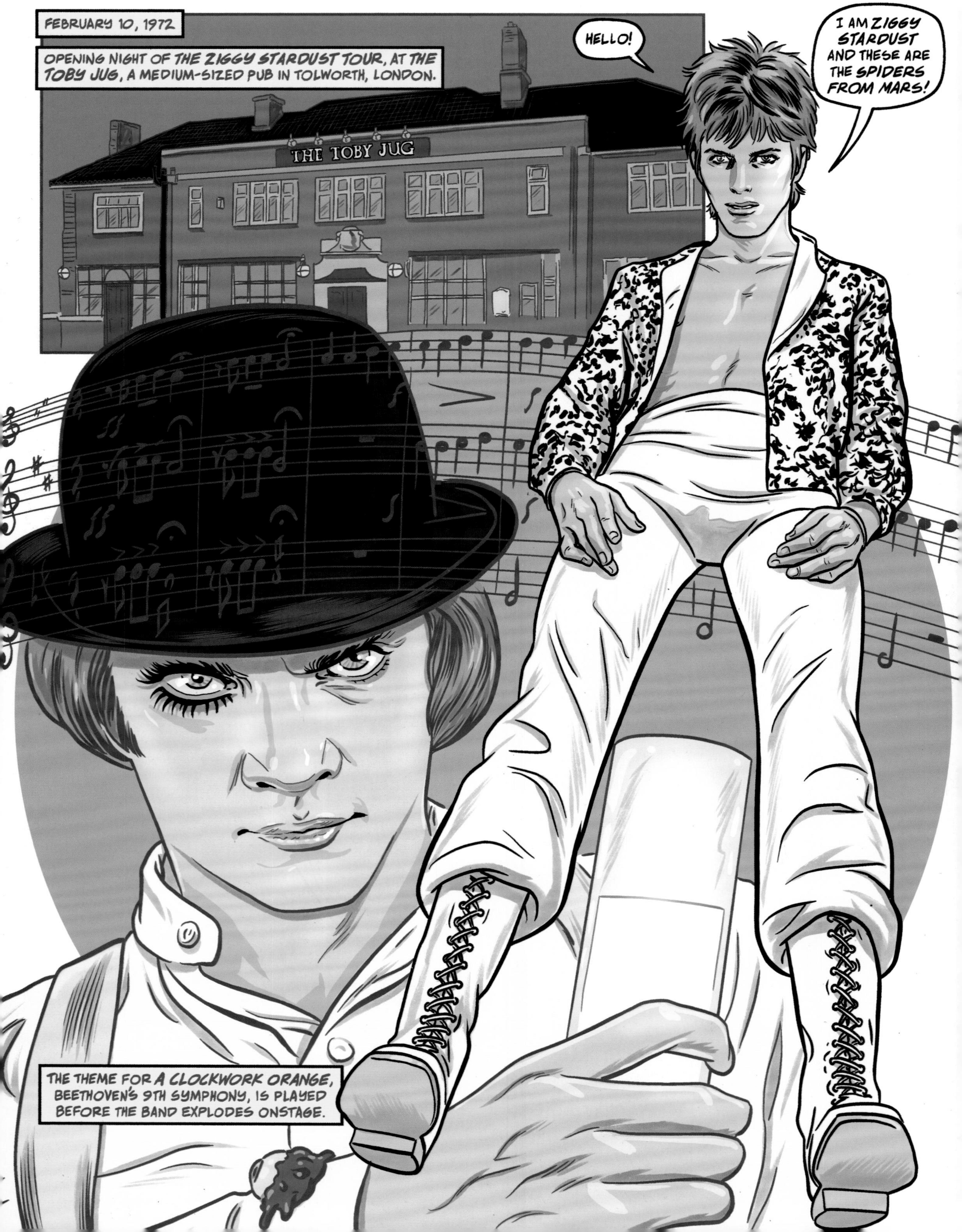
FEBRUARY 10, 1972
OPENING NIGHT OF THE ZIGGY STARDUST TOUR, AT THE TOBY JUG, A MEDIUM-SIZED PUB IN TOLWORTH, LONDON.
THE TOBY JUG
HELLO!
I AM ZIGGY STARDUST AND THESE ARE THE SPIDERS FROM MARS!
THE THEME FOR A CLOCKWORK ORANGE, BEETHOVEN'S 9TH SYMPHONY, IS PLAYED BEFORE THE BAND EXPLODES ONSTAGE.

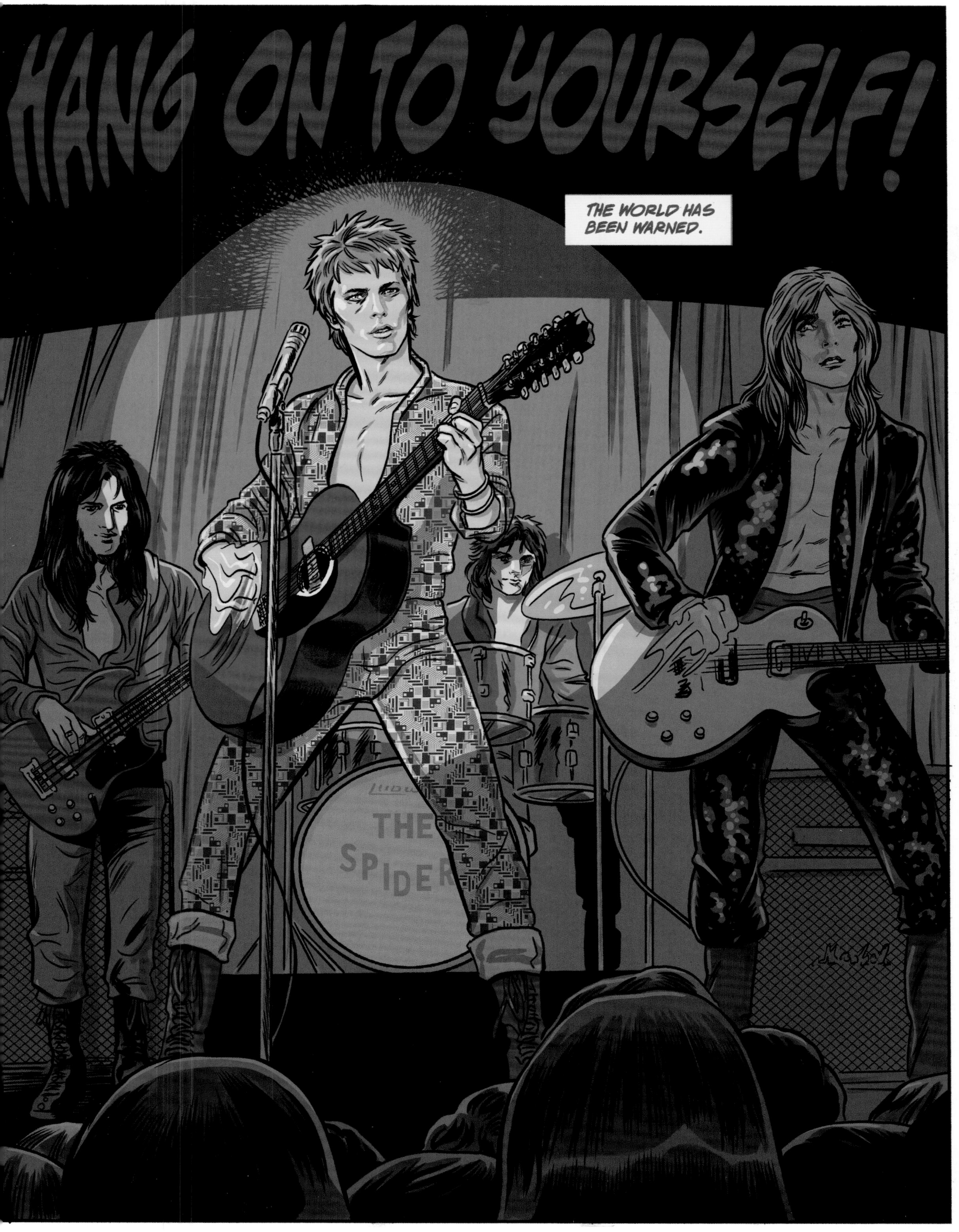
HANG ON TO YOURSELF!
THE WORLD HAS BEEN WARNED.
THE SPIDER

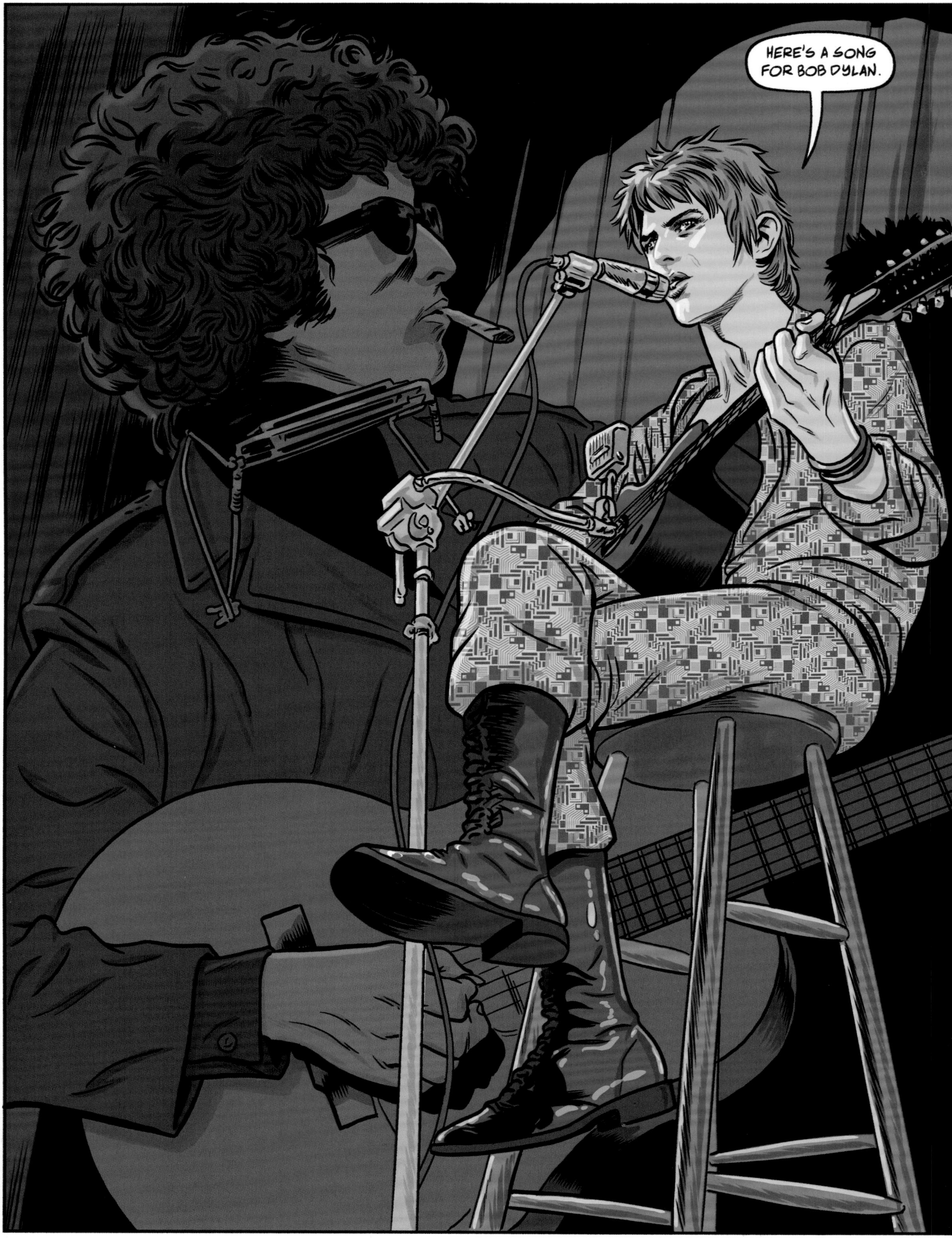
HERE'S A SONG FOR BOB DYLAN.

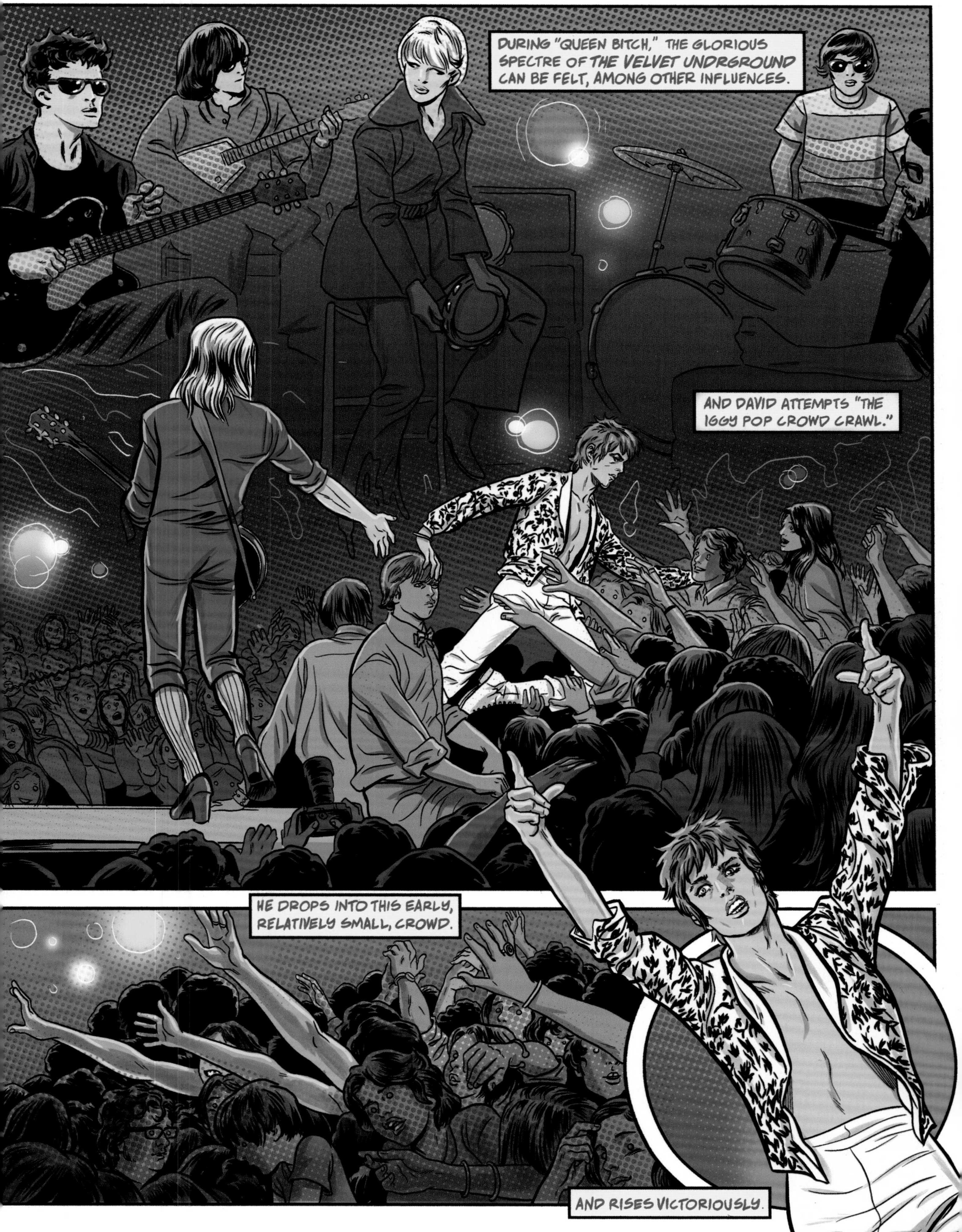
DURING "QUEEN BITCH," THE GLORIOUS SPECTRE OF THE VELVET UNDRGROUND CAN BE FELT, AMONG OTHER INFLUENCES.
AND DAVID ATTEMPTS "THE IGGY POP CROWD CRAWL."
HE DROPS INTO THIS EARLY, RELATIVELY SMALL, CROWD.
AND RISES VICTORIOUSLY.

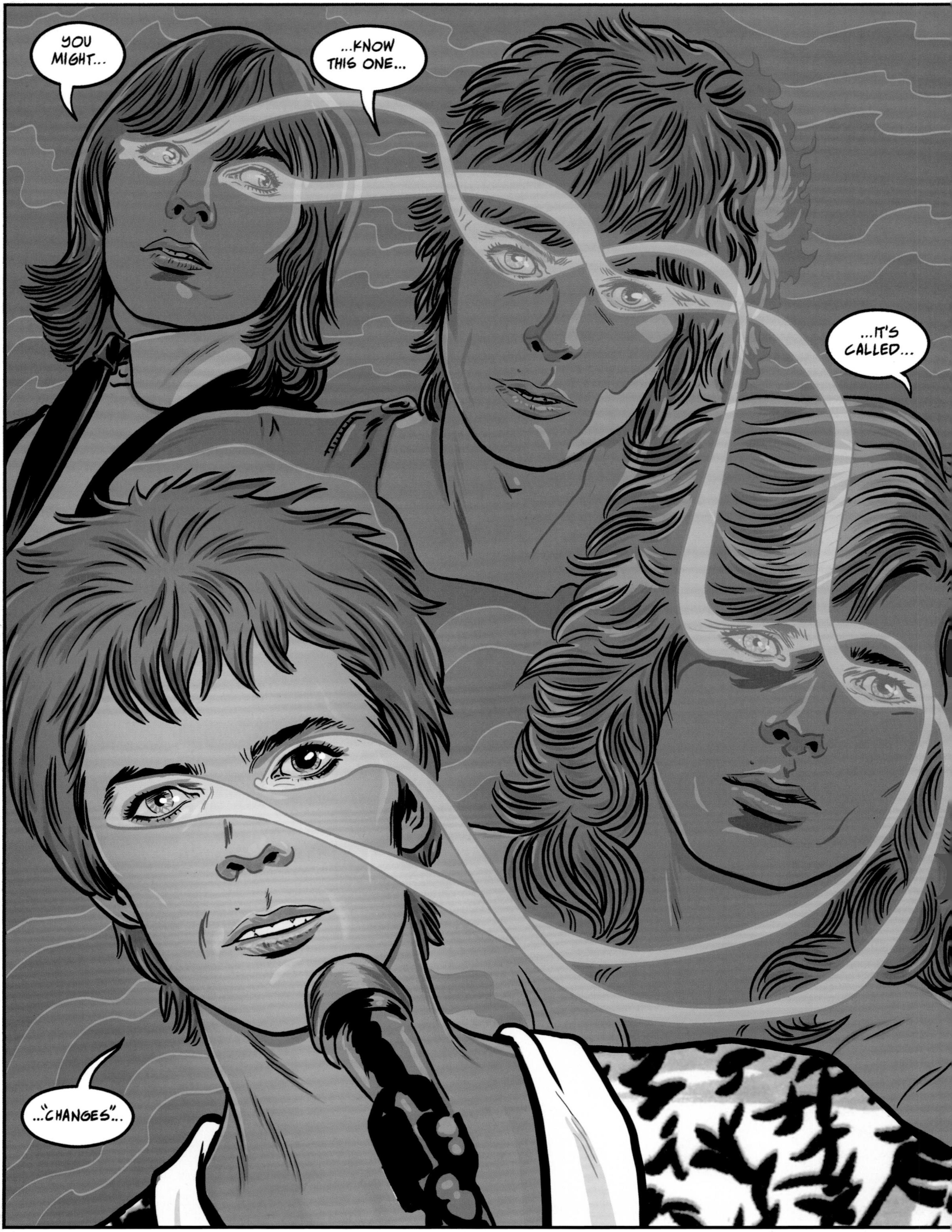
YOU MIGHT...
...KNOW THIS ONE...
...IT'S CALLED...
..."CHANGES"...

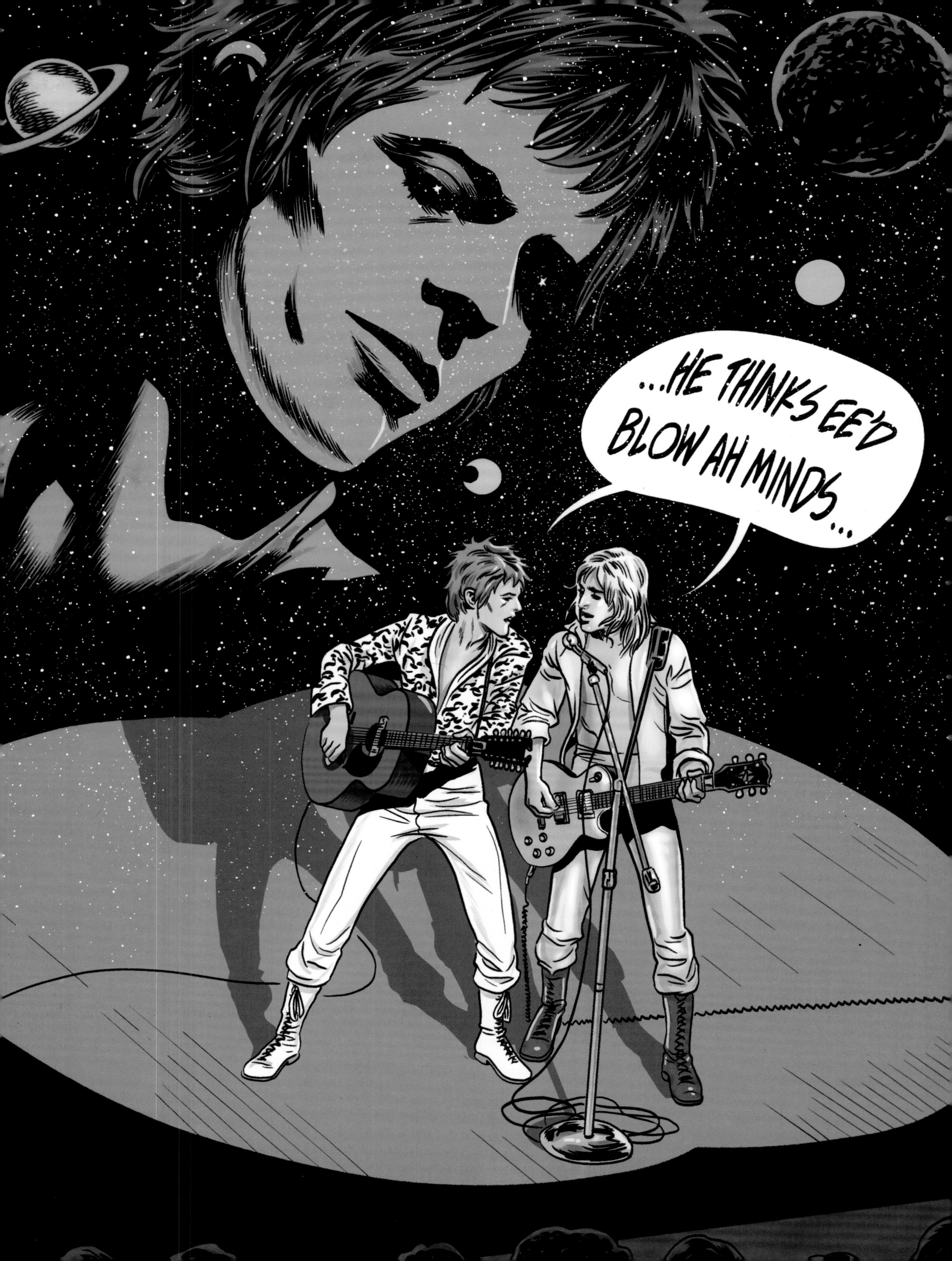
...HE THINKS EE'D BLOW AH MINDS...

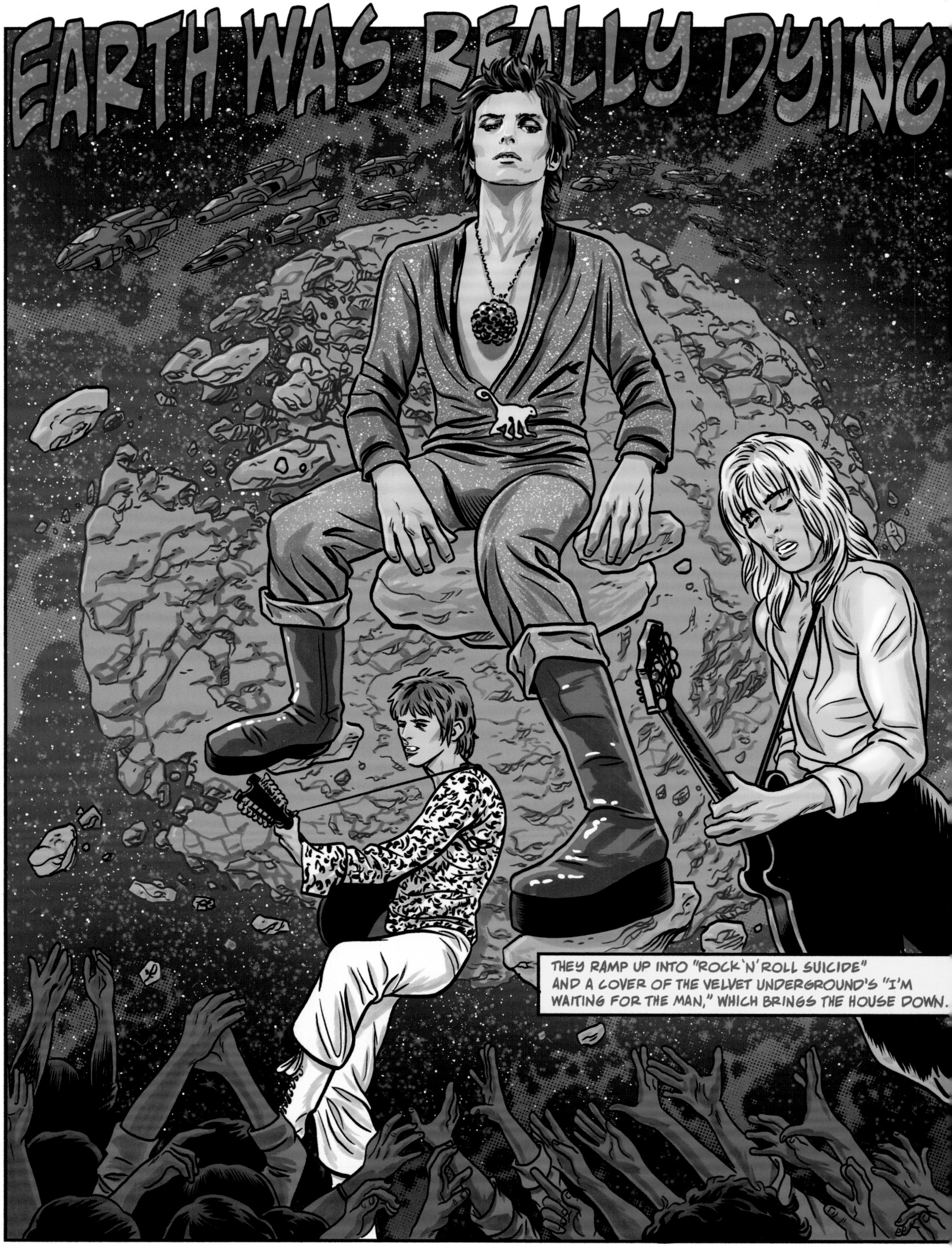
EARTH WAS REALLY DYING
THEY RAMP UP INTO "ROCK'N'ROLL SUICIDE" AND A COVER OF THE VELVET UNDERGROUND'S "I'M WAITING FOR THE MAN," WHICH BRINGS THE HOUSE DOWN.

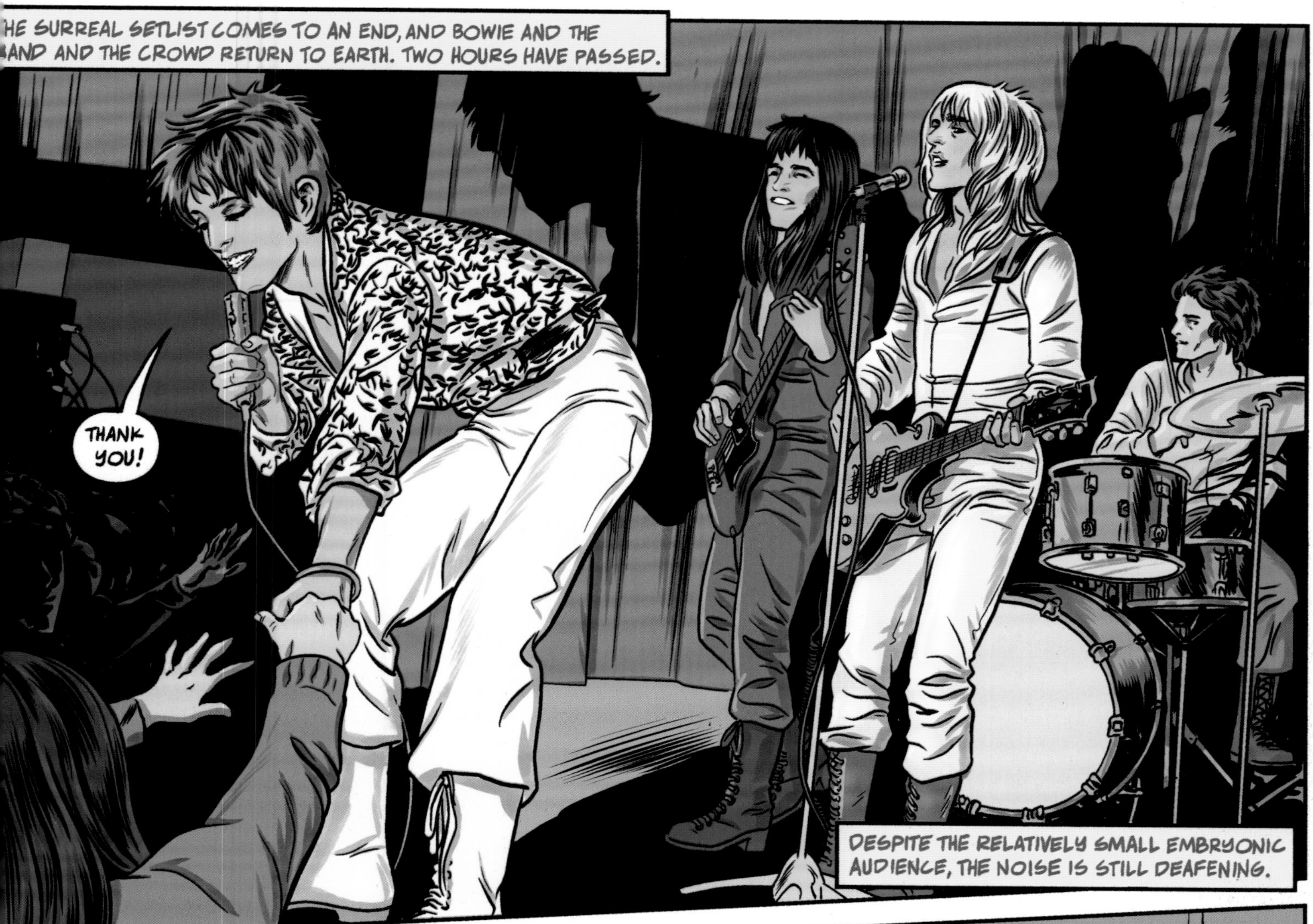
HE SURREAL SETLIST COMES TO AN END, AND BOWIE AND THE
AND AND THE CROWD RETURN TO EARTH. TWO HOURS HAVE PASSED.
THANK YOU!
DESPITE THE RELATIVELY SMALL EMBRYONIC AUDIENCE, THE NOISE IS STILL DEAFENING.

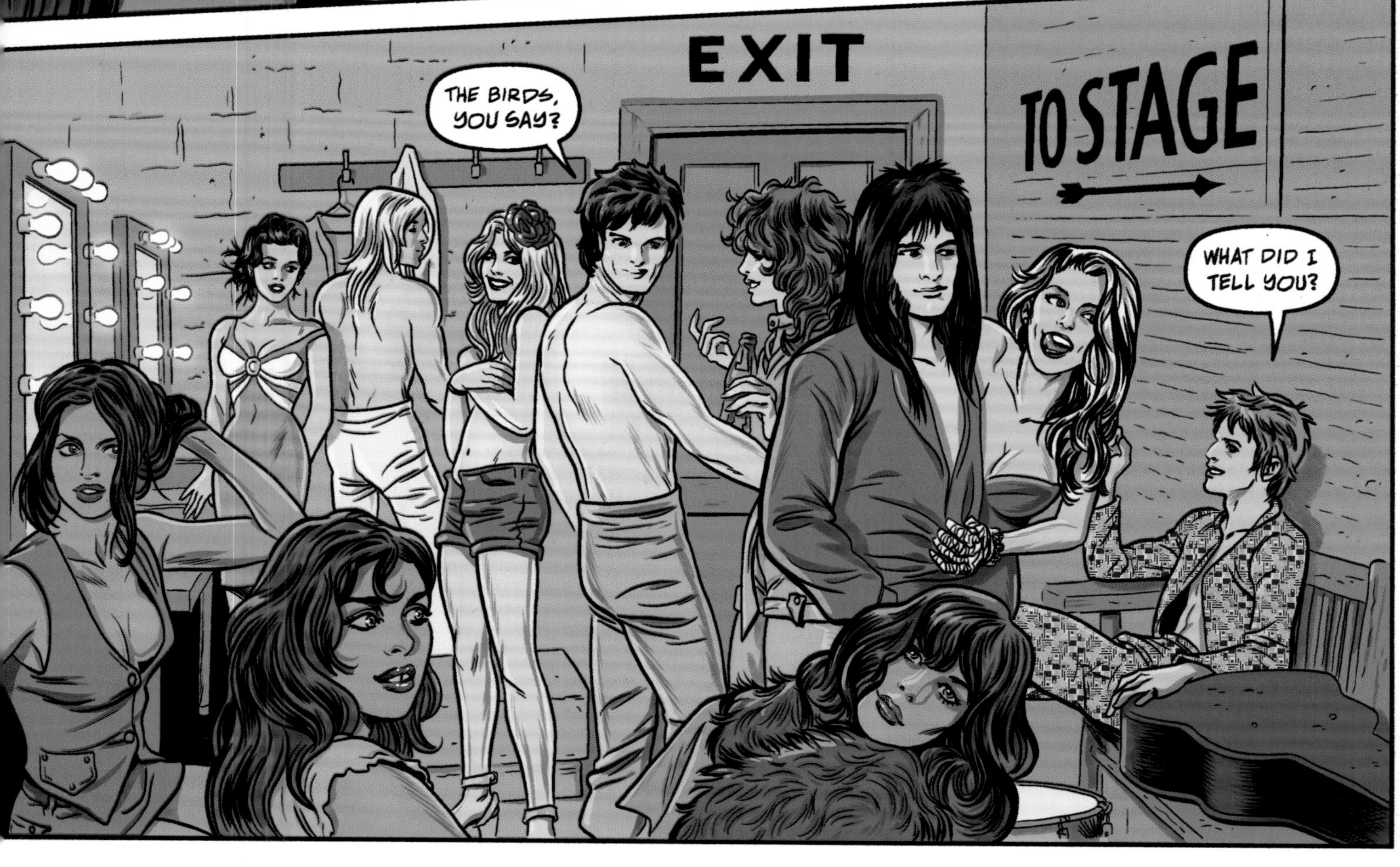
EXIT
THE BIRDS, YOU SAY?
TO STAGE
WHAT DID I TELL YOU?

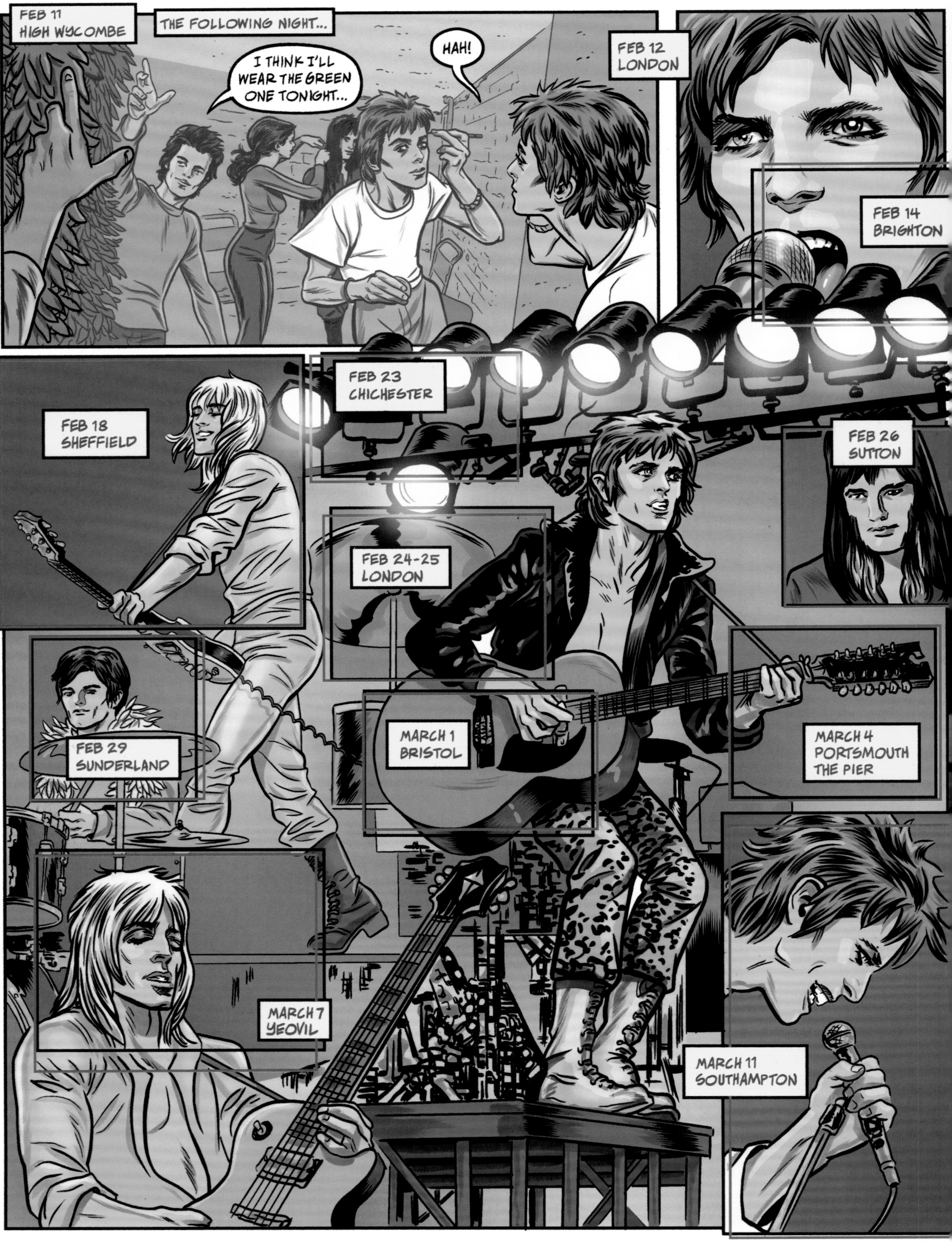
FEB 11
HIGH WYCOMBE
THE FOLLOWING NIGHT...
I THINK I'LL WEAR THE GREEN ONE TONIGHT...
HAH!
FEB 12
LONDON
FEB 14
BRIGHTON
FEB 18
SHEFFIELD
FEB 23
CHICHESTER
FEB 24-25
LONDON
FEB 26
SUTTON
FEB 29
SUNDERLAND
MARCH 1
BRISTOL
MARCH 4
PORTSMOUTH
THE PIER
MARCH 7
YEOVIL
MARCH 11
SOUTHAMPTON

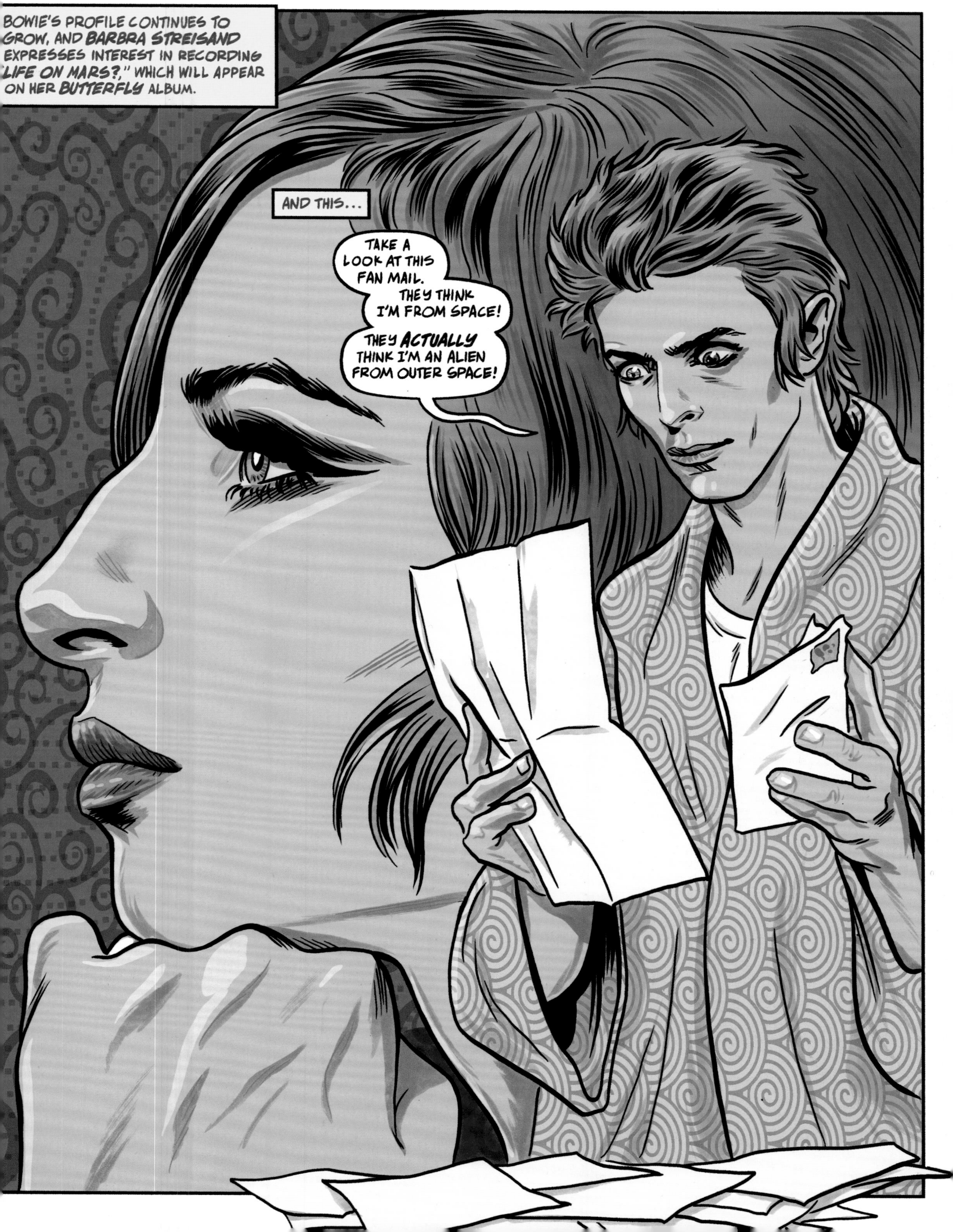
BOWIE'S PROFILE CONTINUES TO GROW, AND BARBRA STREISAND EXPRESSES INTEREST IN RECORDING "LIFE ON MARS?," WHICH WILL APPEAR ON HER BUTTERFLY ALBUM.
AND THIS...
TAKE A LOOK AT THIS FAN MAIL. THEY THINK I'M FROM SPACE!
THEY ACTUALLY THINK I'M AN ALIEN FROM OUTER SPACE!

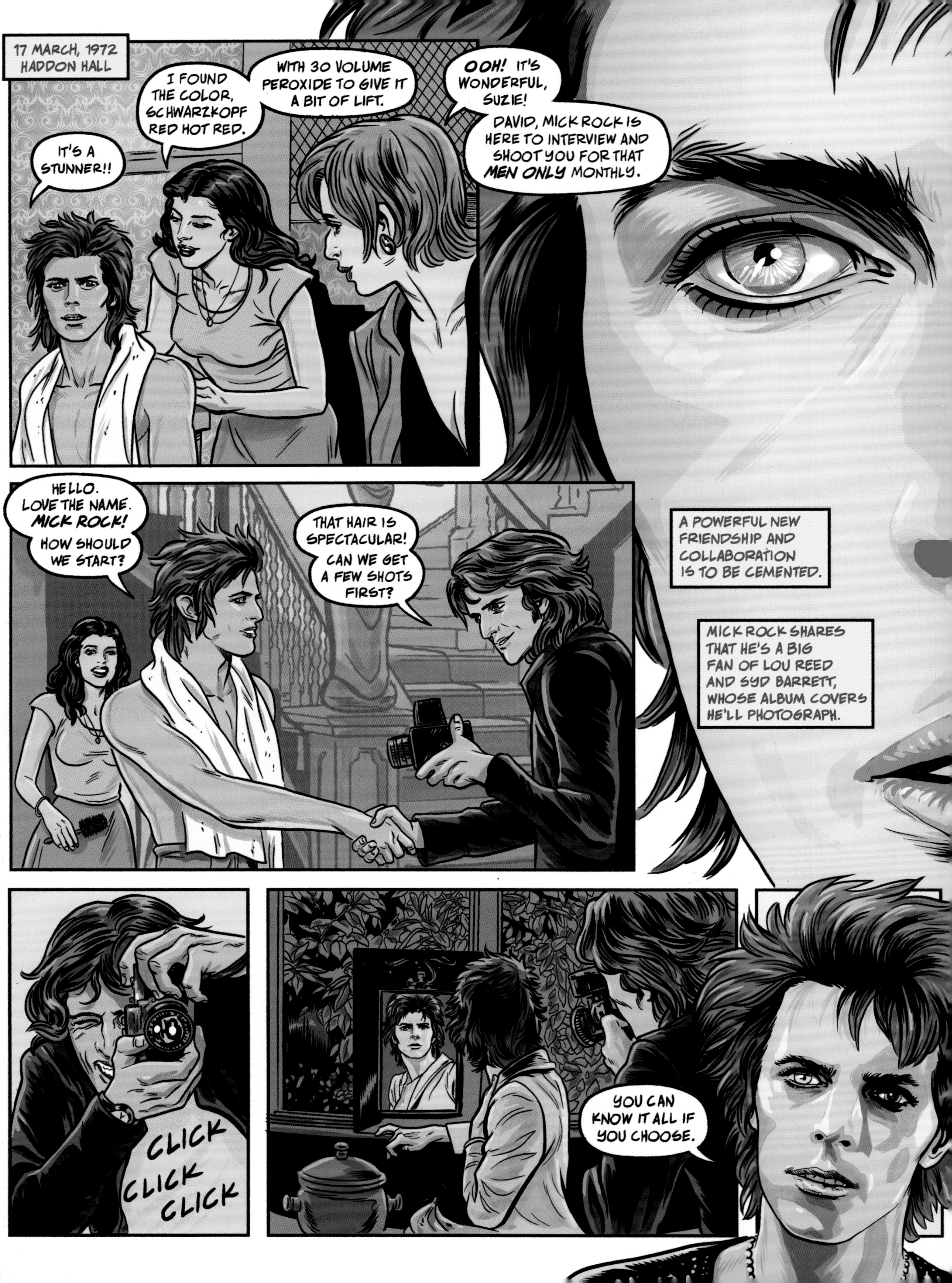

17 MARCH, 1972
HADDON HALL
IT'S A STUNNER!!
I FOUND THE COLOR, SCHWARZKOPF RED HOT RED.
WITH 30 VOLUME PEROXIDE TO GIVE IT A BIT OF LIFT.
OOH! IT'S WONDERFUL, SUZIE!
DAVID, MICK ROCK IS HERE TO INTERVIEW AND SHOOT YOU FOR THAT MEN ONLY MONTHLY.
HELLO. LOVE THE NAME. MICK ROCK!
HOW SHOULD WE START?
THAT HAIR IS SPECTACULAR!
CAN WE GET A FEW SHOTS FIRST?
A POWERFUL NEW FRIENDSHIP AND COLLABORATION IS TO BE CEMENTED.
MICK ROCK SHARES THAT HE'S A BIG FAN OF LOU REED AND SYD BARRETT, WHOSE ALBUM COVERS HE'LL PHOTOGRAPH.
CLICK
CLICK
CLICK
YOU CAN KNOW IT ALL IF YOU CHOOSE.

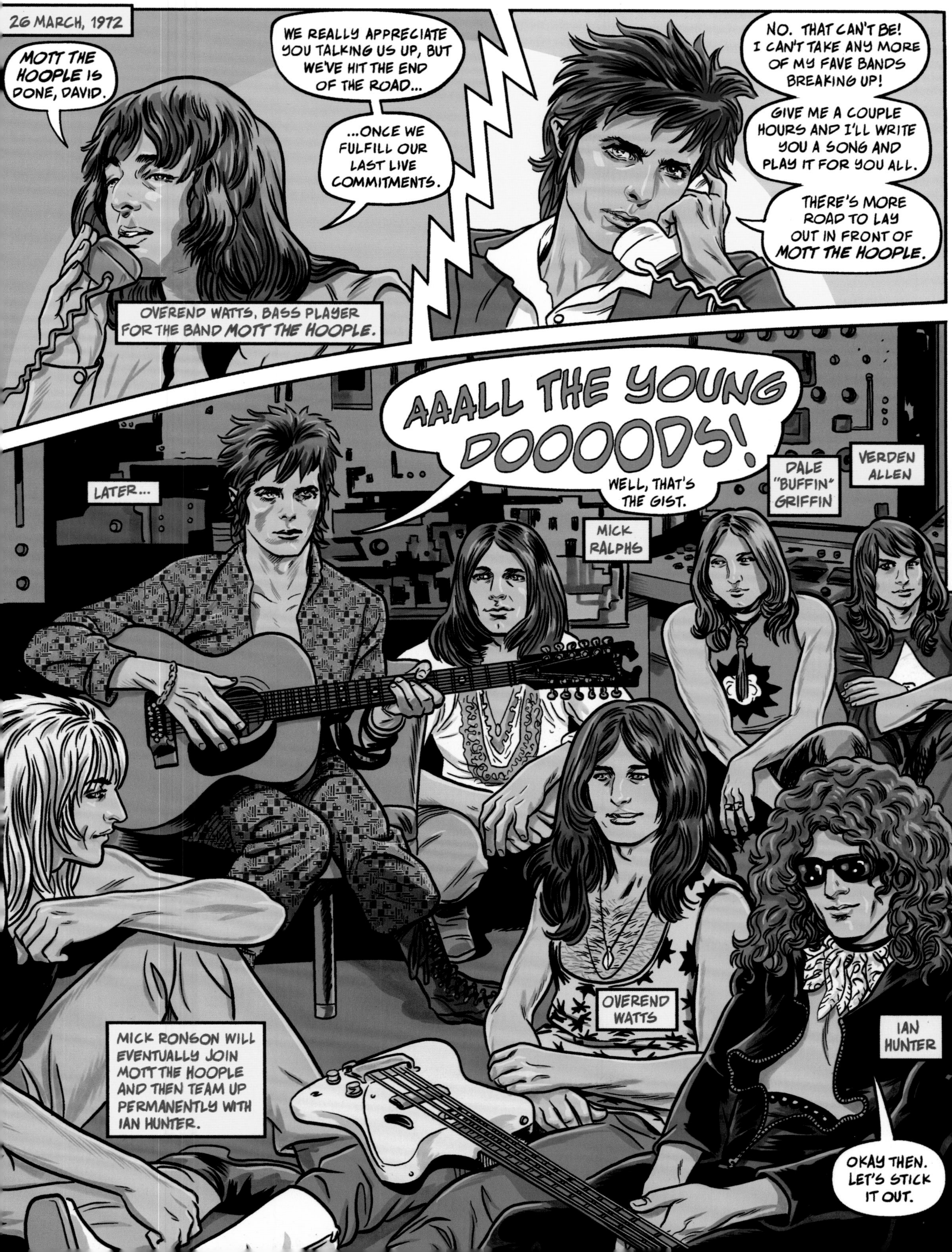

26 MARCH, 1972
MOTT THE HOOPLE IS DONE, DAVID.
WE REALLY APPRECIATE YOU TALKING US UP, BUT WE'VE HIT THE END OF THE ROAD...
...ONCE WE FULFILL OUR LAST LIVE COMMITMENTS.
OVEREND WATTS, BASS PLAYER FOR THE BAND MOTT THE HOOPLE.
NO. THAT CAN'T BE! I CAN'T TAKE ANY MORE OF MY FAVE BANDS BREAKING UP!
GIVE ME A COUPLE HOURS AND I'LL WRITE YOU A SONG AND PLAY IT FOR YOU ALL.
THERE'S MORE ROAD TO LAY OUT IN FRONT OF MOTT THE HOOPLE.
LATER...
AAALL THE YOUNG DOOOODS!
WELL, THAT'S THE GIST.
MICK RALPHS
DALE "BUFFIN" GRIFFIN
VERDEN ALLEN
OVEREND WATTS
IAN HUNTER
MICK RONSON WILL EVENTUALLY JOIN MOTT THE HOOPLE AND THEN TEAM UP PERMANENTLY WITH IAN HUNTER.
OKAY THEN. LET'S STICK IT OUT.

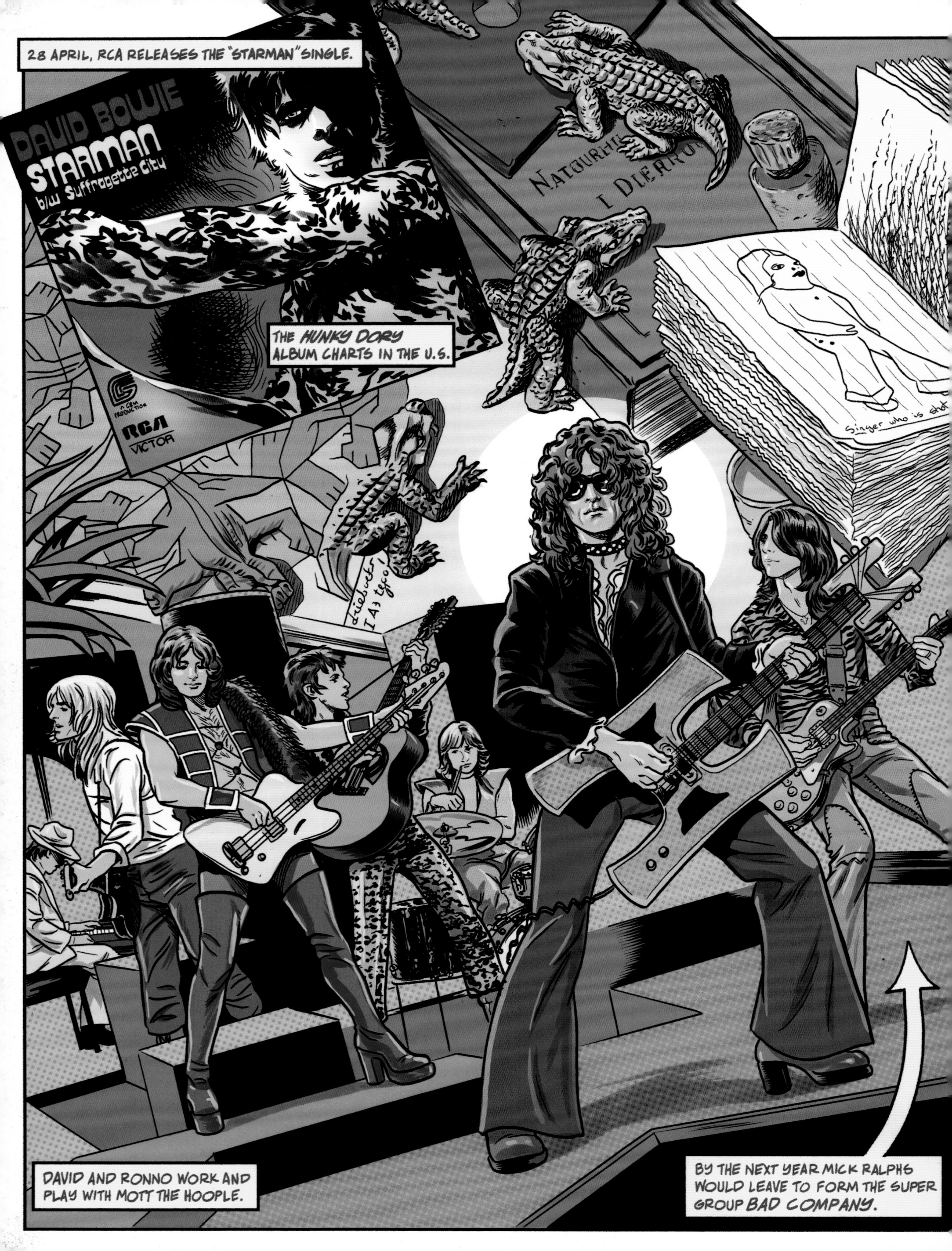

28 APRIL, RCA RELEASES THE "STARMAN" SINGLE.
DAVID BOWIE
STARMAN
b/w Suffragette City
RCA
VICTOR
THE HUNKY DORY ALBUM CHARTS IN THE U.S.
DAVID AND RONNO WORK AND PLAY WITH MOTT THE HOOPLE.
BY THE NEXT YEAR MICK RALPHS WOULD LEAVE TO FORM THE SUPER GROUP BAD COMPANY.

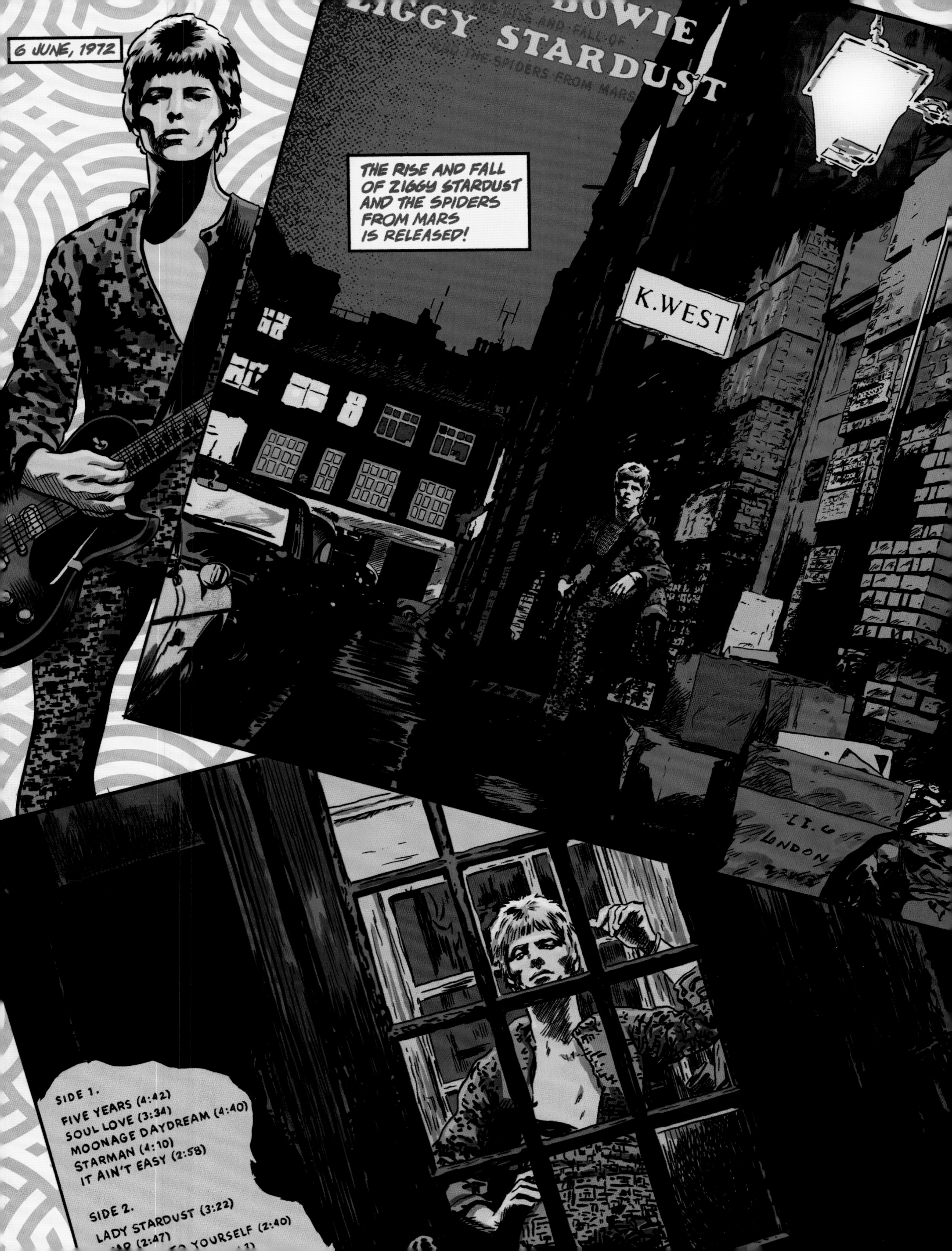

6 JUNE, 1972
BOWIE
STARDUST
THE RISE AND FALL OF ZIGGY STARDUST AND THE SPIDERS FROM MARS IS RELEASED!
K.WEST
LONDON
SIDE 1.
FIVE YEARS (4:42)
SOUL LOVE (3:34)
MOONAGE DAYDREAM (4:40)
STARMAN (4:10)
IT AIN'T EASY (2:58)
SIDE 2.
LADY STARDUST (3:22)
(2:47)
YOURSELF (2:40)

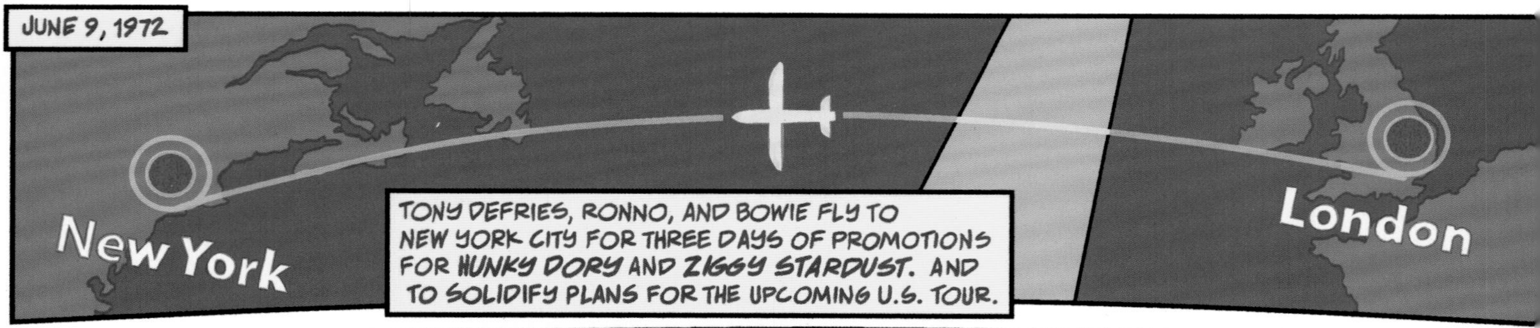
JUNE 9, 1972
New York
London
TONY DEFRIES, RONNO, AND BOWIE FLY TO NEW YORK CITY FOR THREE DAYS OF PROMOTIONS FOR HUNKY DORY AND ZIGGY STARDUST. AND TO SOLIDIFY PLANS FOR THE UPCOMING U.S. TOUR.

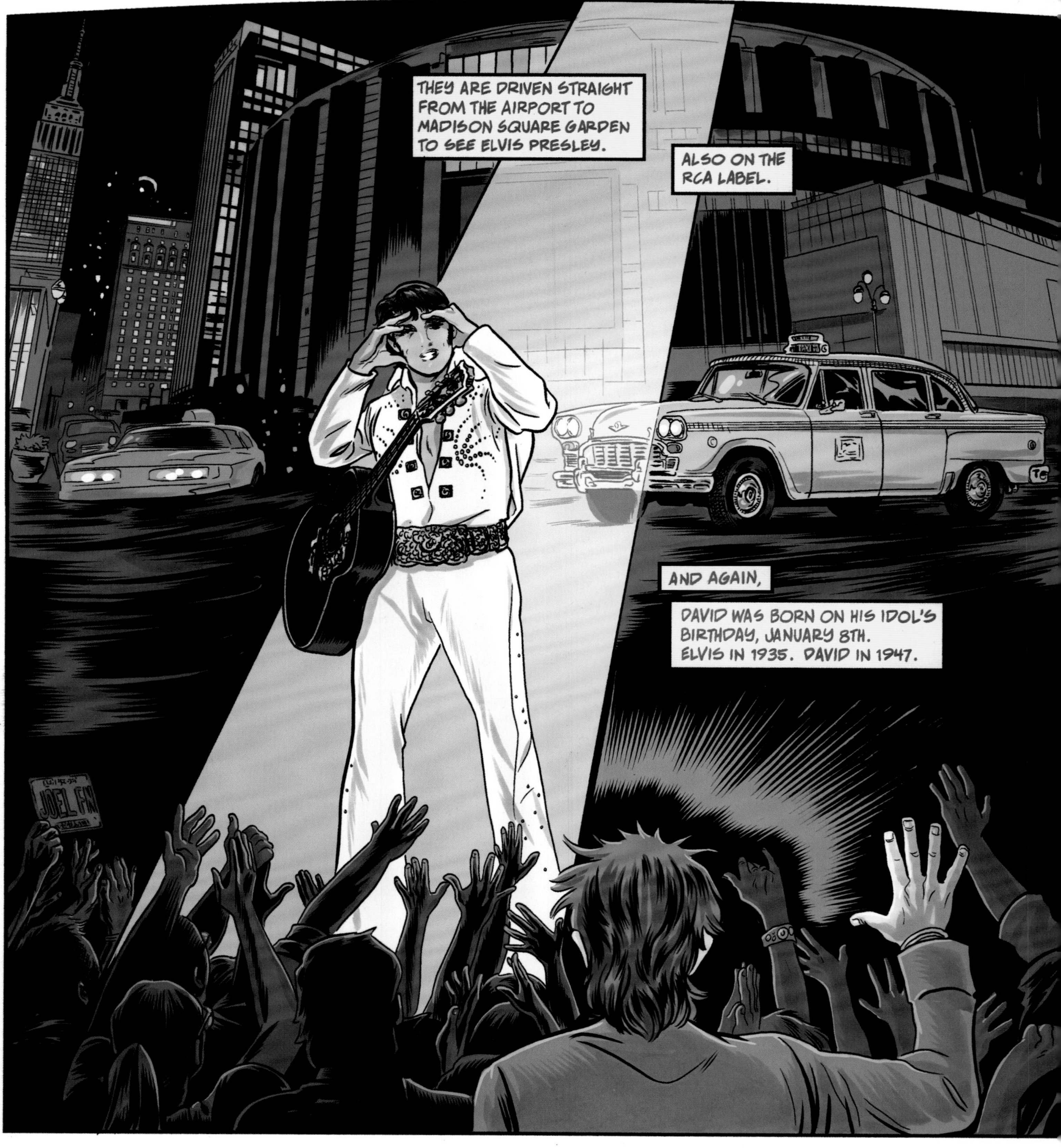
THEY ARE DRIVEN STRAIGHT FROM THE AIRPORT TO MADISON SQUARE GARDEN TO SEE ELVIS PRESLEY.
ALSO ON THE RCA LABEL.
AND AGAIN,
DAVID WAS BORN ON HIS IDOL'S BIRTHDAY, JANUARY 8TH. ELVIS IN 1935. DAVID IN 1947.
JOEL FM

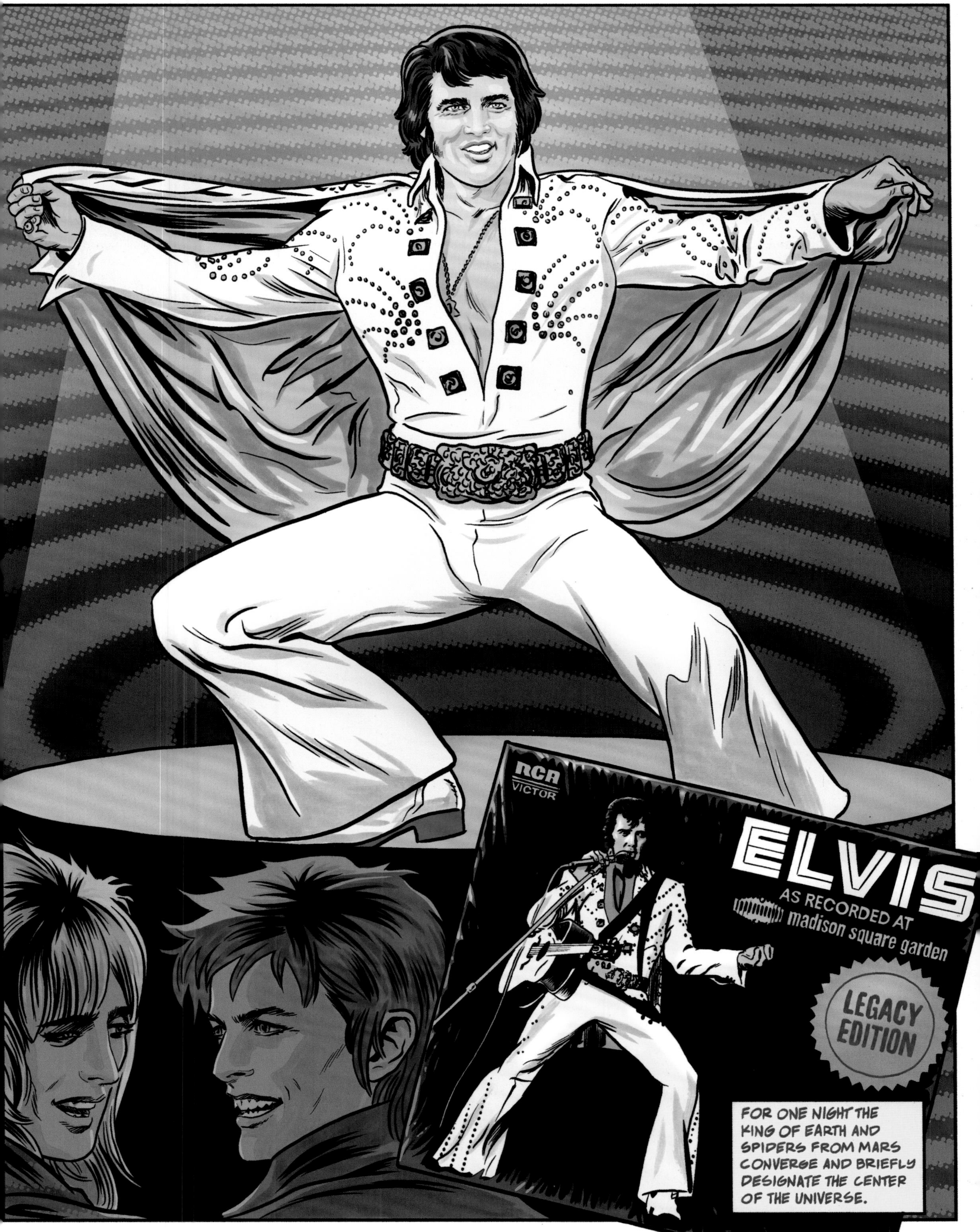
RCA
VICTOR
ELVIS
AS RECORDED AT
madison square garden
LEGACY EDITION
FOR ONE NIGHT THE KING OF EARTH AND SPIDERS FROM MARS CONVERGE AND BRIEFLY DESIGNATE THE CENTER OF THE UNIVERSE.

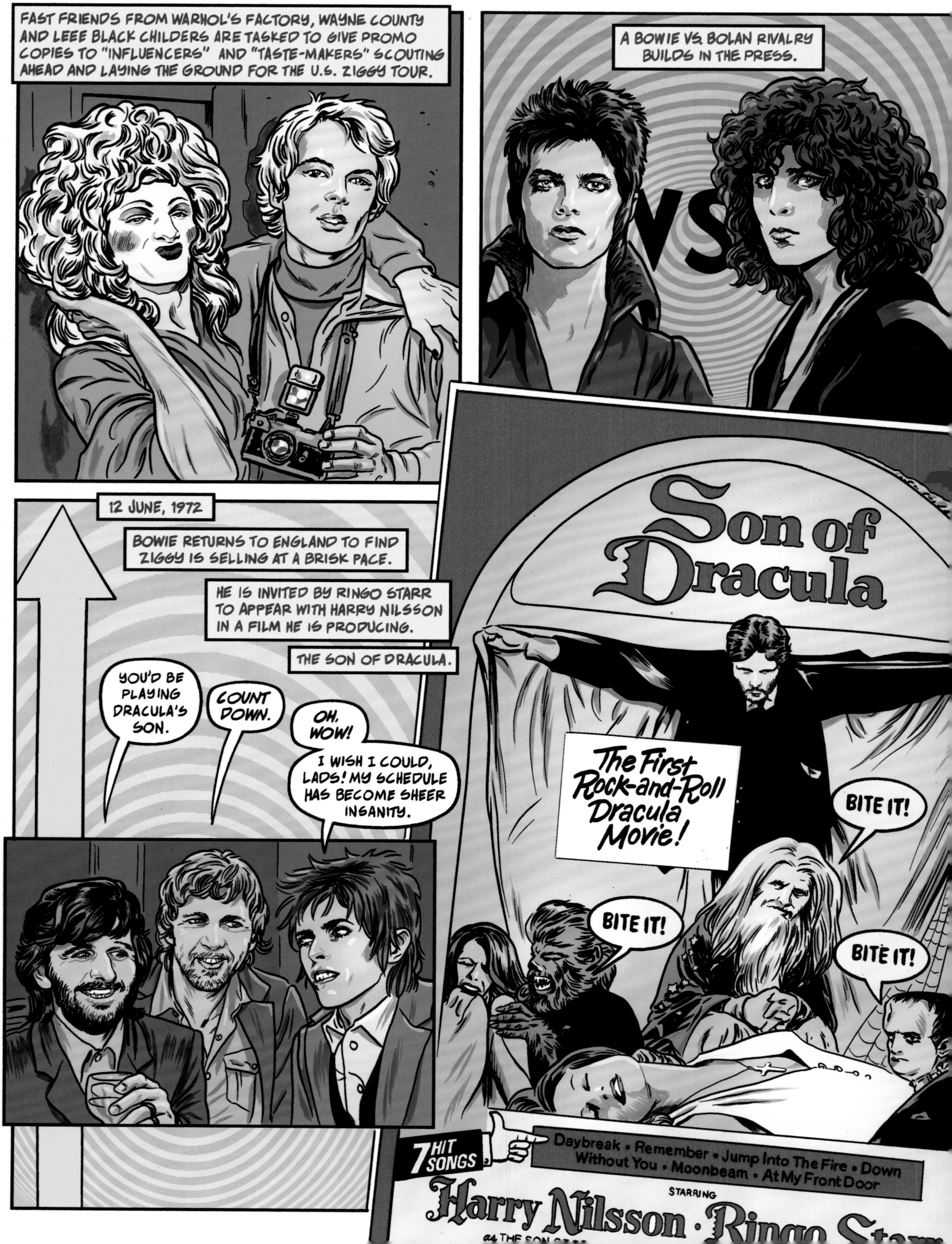

FAST FRIENDS FROM WARHOL'S FACTORY, WAYNE COUNTY AND LEEE BLACK CHILDERS ARE TASKED TO GIVE PROMO COPIES TO "INFLUENCERS" AND "TASTE-MAKERS" SCOUTING AHEAD AND LAYING THE GROUND FOR THE U.S. ZIGGY TOUR.
A BOWIE VS. BOLAN RIVALRY BUILDS IN THE PRESS.
VS
12 JUNE, 1972
BOWIE RETURNS TO ENGLAND TO FIND ZIGGY IS SELLING AT A BRISK PACE.
HE IS INVITED BY RINGO STARR TO APPEAR WITH HARRY NILSSON IN A FILM HE IS PRODUCING.
THE SON OF DRACULA.
YOU'D BE PLAYING DRACULA'S SON.
COUNT DOWN.
OH, WOW!
I WISH I COULD, LADS! MY SCHEDULE HAS BECOME SHEER INSANITY.
Son of Dracula
The First Rock-and-Roll Dracula Movie!
BITE IT!
BITE IT!
BITE IT!
7 HIT SONGS
Daybreak • Remember • Jump Into The Fire • Down
Without You • Moonbeam • At My Front Door
STARRING
Harry Nilsson · Ringo Sta

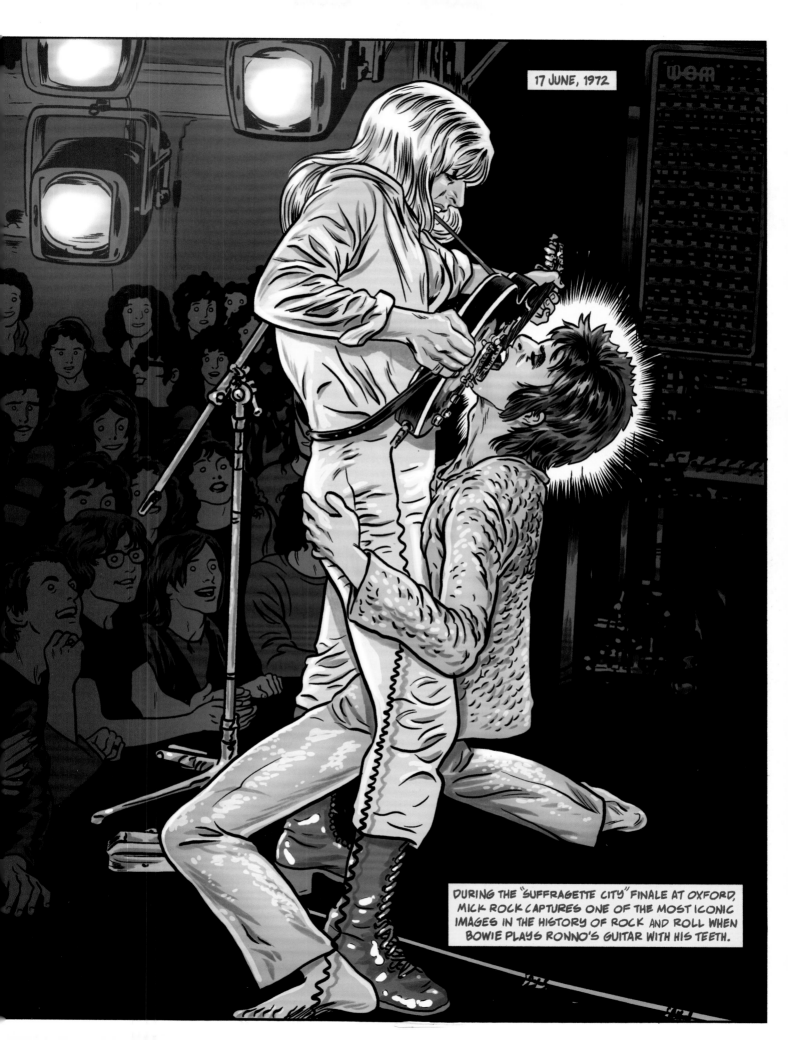

17 JUNE, 1972

DURING THE "SUFFRAGETTE CITY" FINALE AT OXFORD, MICK ROCK CAPTURES ONE OF THE MOST ICONIC IMAGES IN THE HISTORY OF ROCK AND ROLL WHEN BOWIE PLAYS RONNO'S GUITAR WITH HIS TEETH.

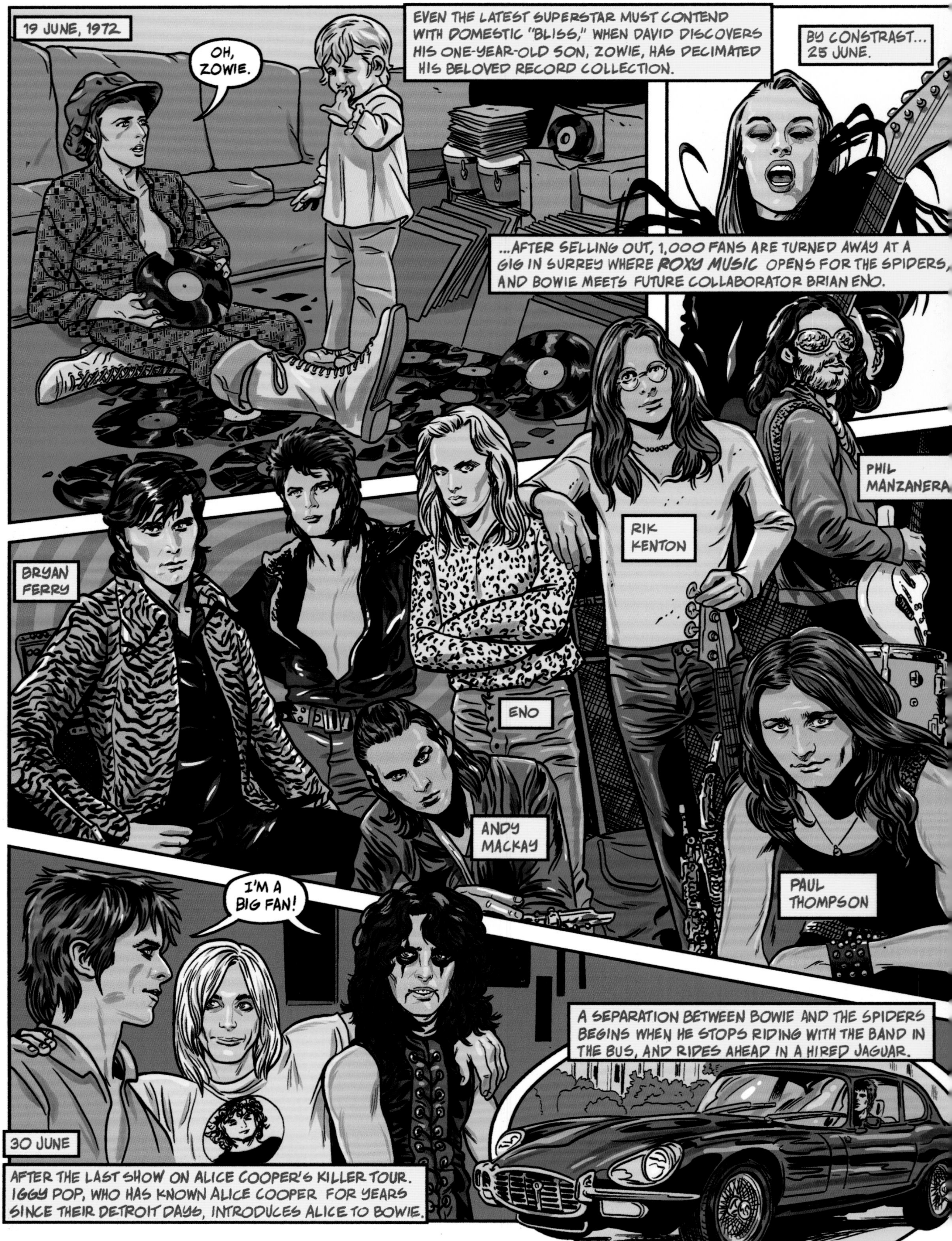
19 JUNE, 1972
EVEN THE LATEST SUPERSTAR MUST CONTEND WITH DOMESTIC "BLISS," WHEN DAVID DISCOVERS HIS ONE-YEAR-OLD SON, ZOWIE, HAS DECIMATED HIS BELOVED RECORD COLLECTION.
OH, ZOWIE.
BY CONSTRAST... 25 JUNE.
...AFTER SELLING OUT, 1,000 FANS ARE TURNED AWAY AT A GIG IN SURREY WHERE ROXY MUSIC OPENS FOR THE SPIDERS, AND BOWIE MEETS FUTURE COLLABORATOR BRIAN ENO.
PHIL MANZANERA
RIK KENTON
BRYAN FERRY
ENO
ANDY MACKAY
PAUL THOMPSON
30 JUNE
AFTER THE LAST SHOW ON ALICE COOPER'S KILLER TOUR. IGGY POP, WHO HAS KNOWN ALICE COOPER FOR YEARS SINCE THEIR DETROIT DAYS, INTRODUCES ALICE TO BOWIE.
I'M A BIG FAN!
A SEPARATION BETWEEN BOWIE AND THE SPIDERS BEGINS WHEN HE STOPS RIDING WITH THE BAND IN THE BUS, AND RIDES AHEAD IN A HIRED JAGUAR.

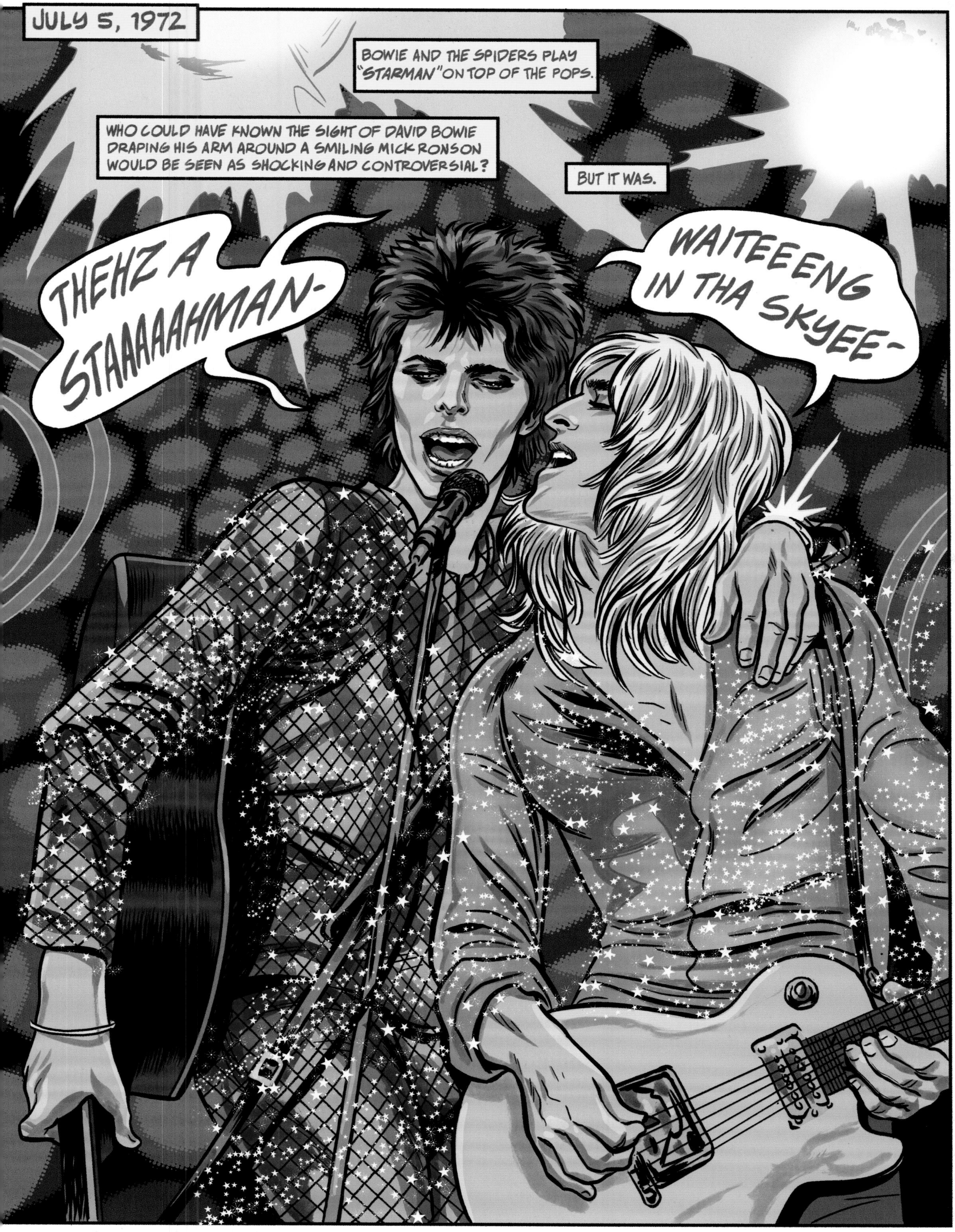
JULY 5, 1972
BOWIE AND THE SPIDERS PLAY "STARMAN" ON TOP OF THE POPS.
WHO COULD HAVE KNOWN THE SIGHT OF DAVID BOWIE DRAPING HIS ARM AROUND A SMILING MICK RONSON WOULD BE SEEN AS SHOCKING AND CONTROVERSIAL?
BUT IT WAS.
THEHZ A STAAAAAHMAN-
WAITEEENG IN THA SKYEE-

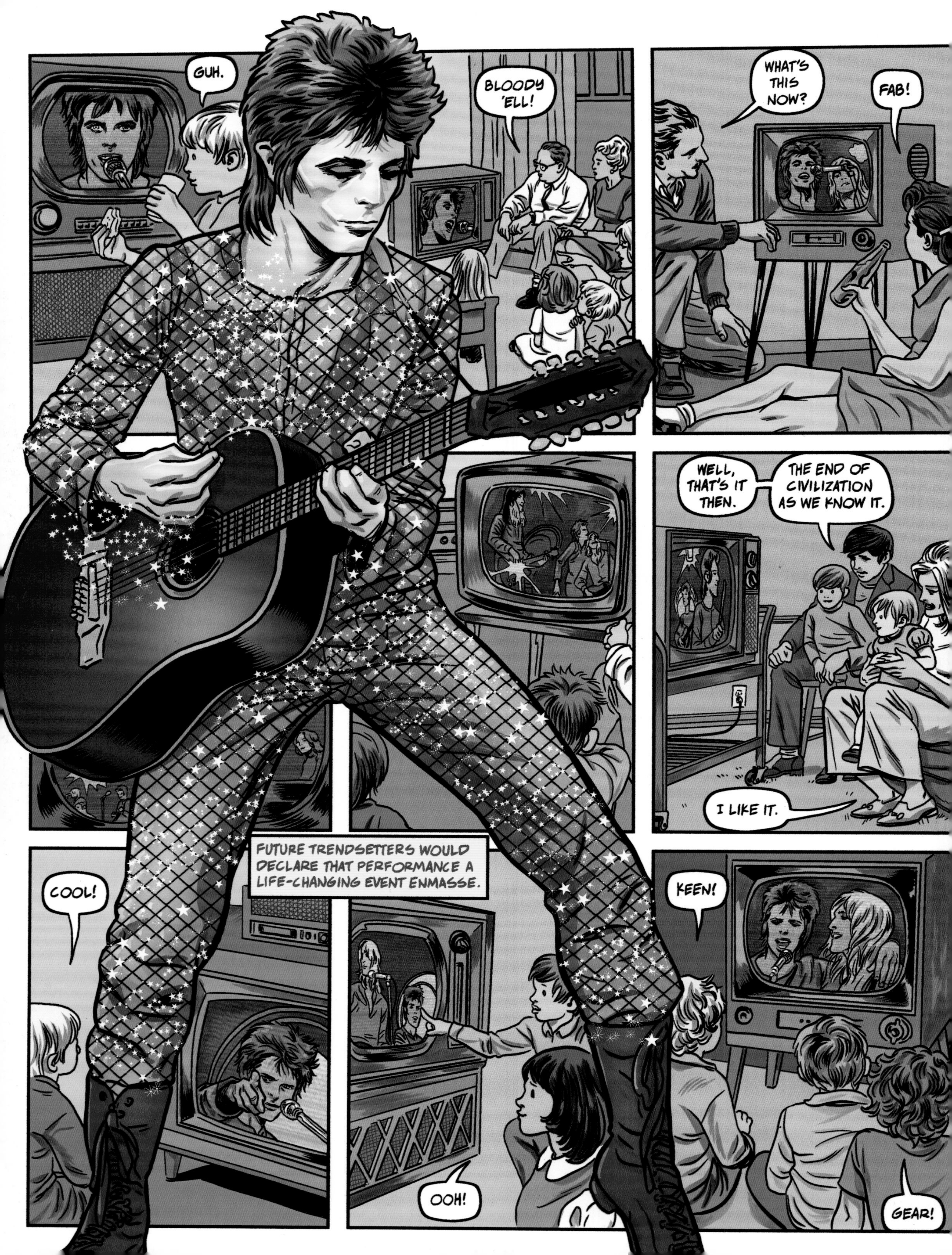
GUH.
BLOODY 'ELL!
WHAT'S THIS NOW?
FAB!
WELL, THAT'S IT THEN.
THE END OF CIVILIZATION AS WE KNOW IT.
I LIKE IT.
FUTURE TRENDSETTERS WOULD DECLARE THAT PERFORMANCE A LIFE-CHANGING EVENT ENMASSE.
COOL!
KEEN!
OOH!
GEAR!

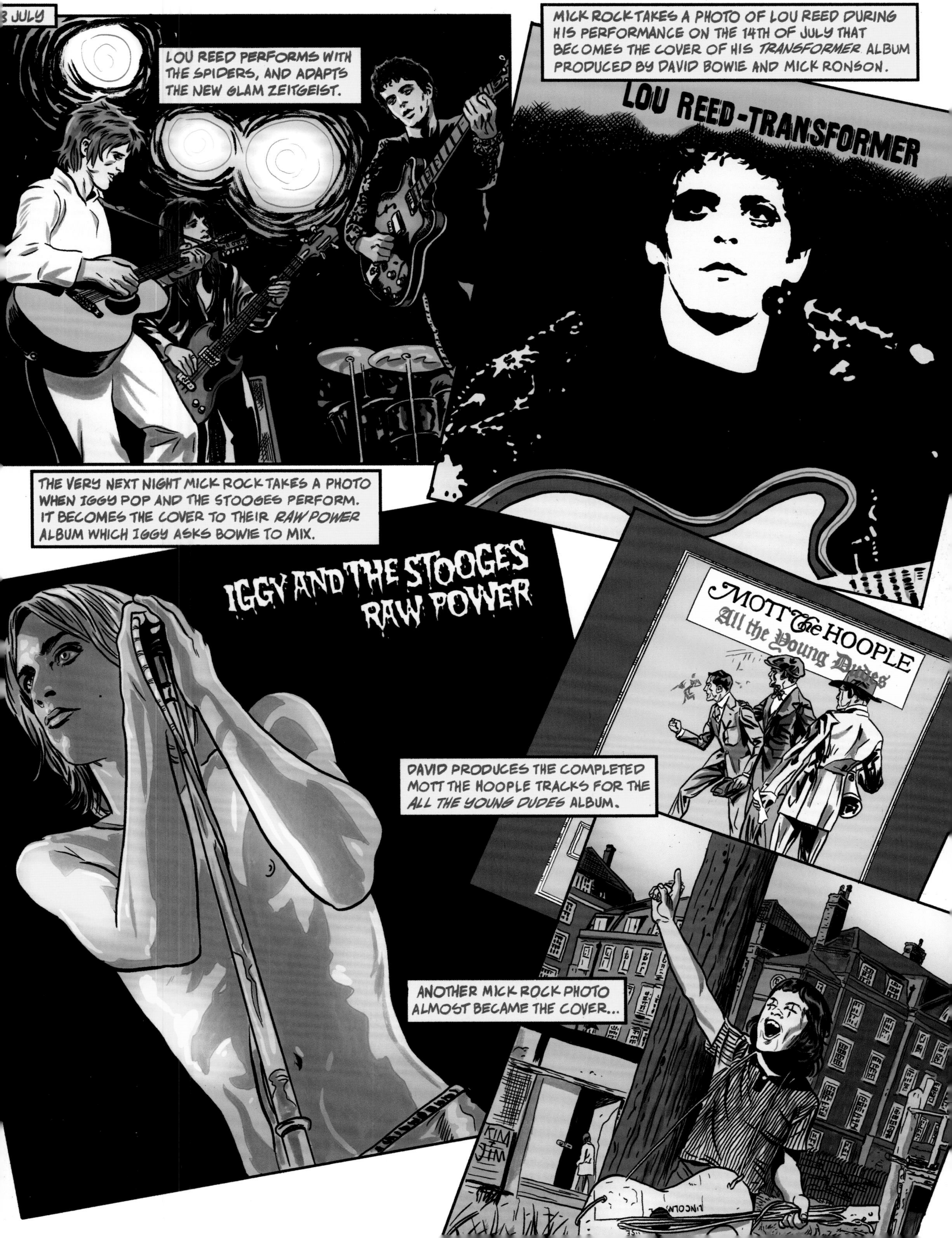

3 JULY
LOU REED PERFORMS WITH THE SPIDERS, AND ADAPTS THE NEW GLAM ZEITGEIST.
MICK ROCK TAKES A PHOTO OF LOU REED DURING HIS PERFORMANCE ON THE 14TH OF JULY THAT BECOMES THE COVER OF HIS TRANSFORMER ALBUM PRODUCED BY DAVID BOWIE AND MICK RONSON.
LOU REED-TRANSFORMER
THE VERY NEXT NIGHT MICK ROCK TAKES A PHOTO WHEN IGGY POP AND THE STOOGES PERFORM. IT BECOMES THE COVER TO THEIR RAW POWER ALBUM WHICH IGGY ASKS BOWIE TO MIX.
IGGY AND THE STOOGES
RAW POWER
MOTT The HOOPLE
All the Young Dudes
DAVID PRODUCES THE COMPLETED MOTT THE HOOPLE TRACKS FOR THE ALL THE YOUNG DUDES ALBUM.
ANOTHER MICK ROCK PHOTO ALMOST BECAME THE COVER...
KIM
JIM

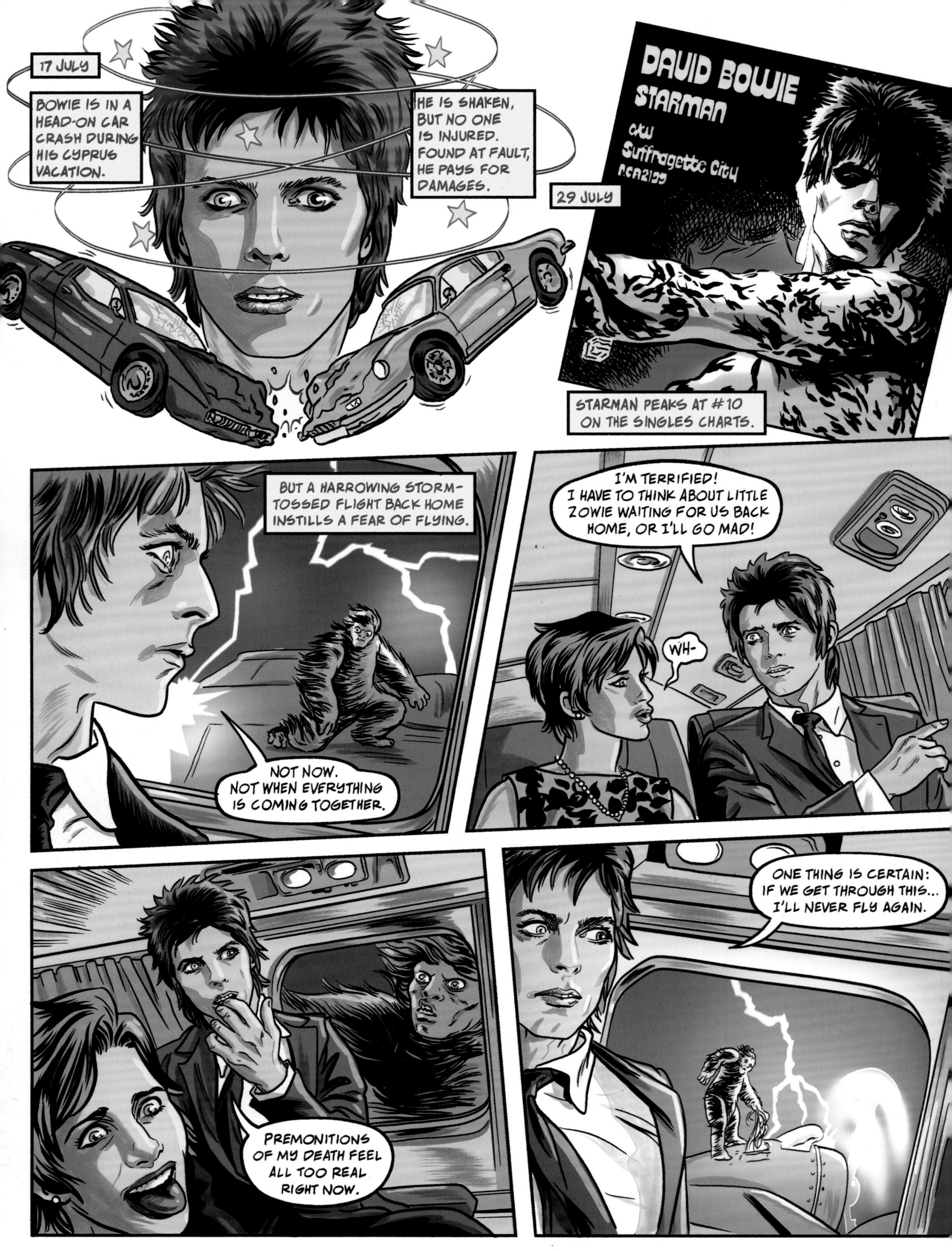
17 JULY
BOWIE IS IN A HEAD-ON CAR CRASH DURING HIS CYPRUS VACATION.
HE IS SHAKEN, BUT NO ONE IS INJURED. FOUND AT FAULT, HE PAYS FOR DAMAGES.
29 JULY
DAVID BOWIE
STARMAN
c/w
Suffragette City
RCA2199
STARMAN PEAKS AT #10 ON THE SINGLES CHARTS.
BUT A HARROWING STORM-TOSSED FLIGHT BACK HOME INSTILLS A FEAR OF FLYING.
NOT NOW. NOT WHEN EVERYTHING IS COMING TOGETHER.
I'M TERRIFIED! I HAVE TO THINK ABOUT LITTLE ZOWIE WAITING FOR US BACK HOME, OR I'LL GO MAD!
WH-
PREMONITIONS OF MY DEATH FEEL ALL TOO REAL RIGHT NOW.
ONE THING IS CERTAIN: IF WE GET THROUGH THIS... I'LL NEVER FLY AGAIN.

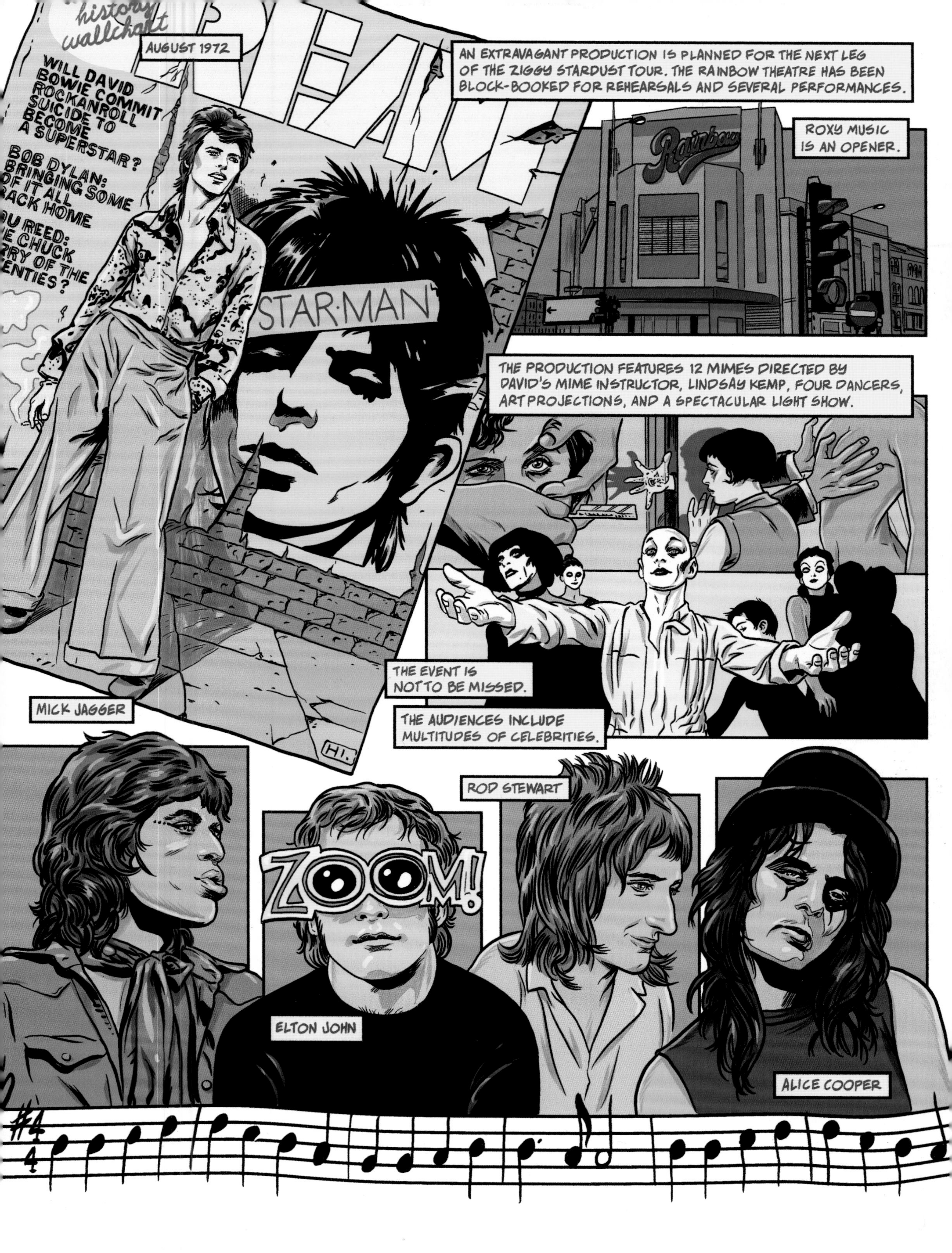

history wallchart
AUGUST 1972
WILL DAVID BOWIE COMMIT ROCKANROLL SUICIDE TO BECOME A SUPERSTAR?
BOB DYLAN: BRINGING SOME OF IT ALL BACK HOME
STAR·MAN
AN EXTRAVAGANT PRODUCTION IS PLANNED FOR THE NEXT LEG OF THE ZIGGY STARDUST TOUR. THE RAINBOW THEATRE HAS BEEN BLOCK-BOOKED FOR REHEARSALS AND SEVERAL PERFORMANCES.
Rainbow
ROXY MUSIC IS AN OPENER.
THE PRODUCTION FEATURES 12 MIMES DIRECTED BY DAVID'S MIME INSTRUCTOR, LINDSAY KEMP, FOUR DANCERS, ART PROJECTIONS, AND A SPECTACULAR LIGHT SHOW.
THE EVENT IS NOT TO BE MISSED.
THE AUDIENCES INCLUDE MULTITUDES OF CELEBRITIES.
MICK JAGGER
ZOOM!
ELTON JOHN
ROD STEWART
ALICE COOPER

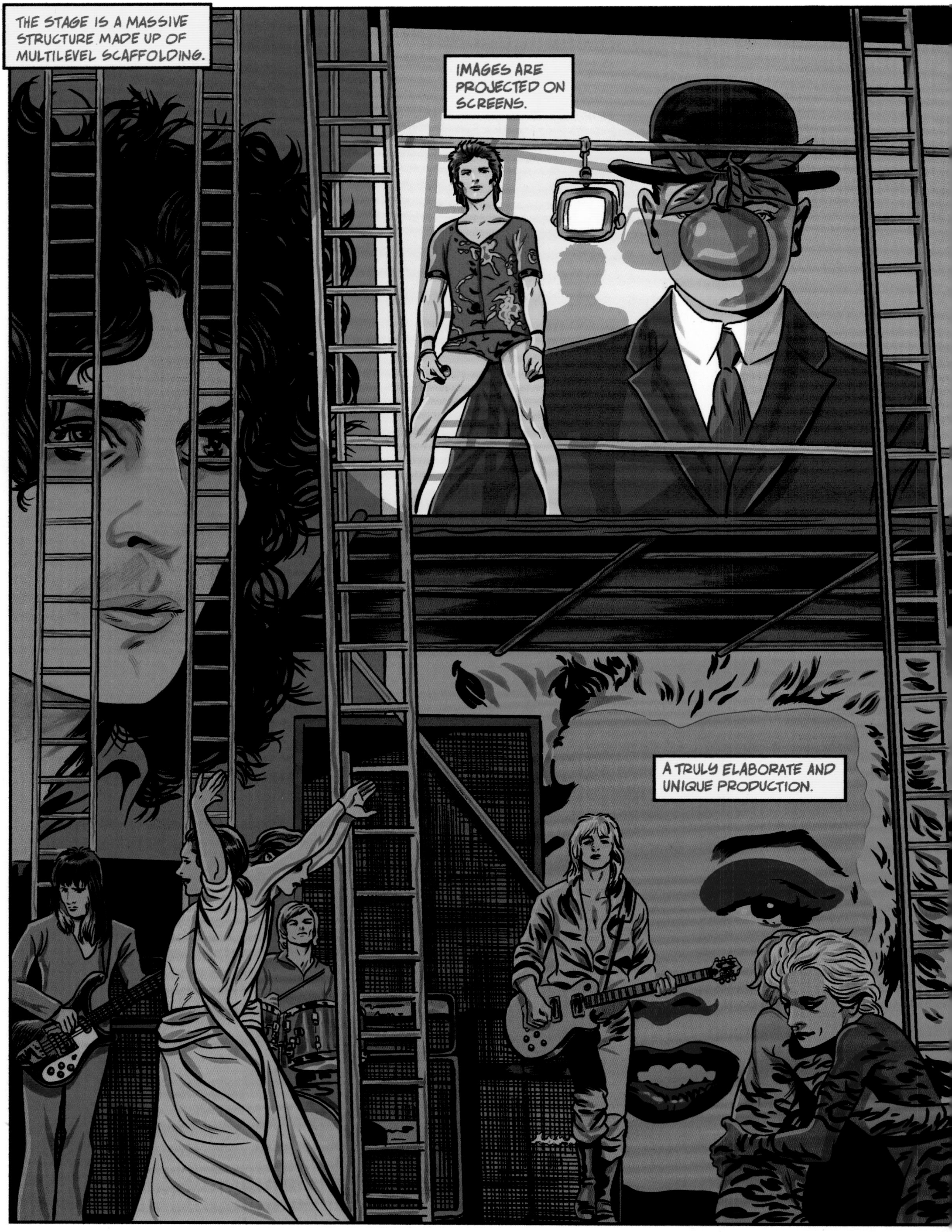
THE STAGE IS A MASSIVE STRUCTURE MADE UP OF MULTILEVEL SCAFFOLDING.
IMAGES ARE PROJECTED ON SCREENS.
A TRULY ELABORATE AND UNIQUE PRODUCTION.

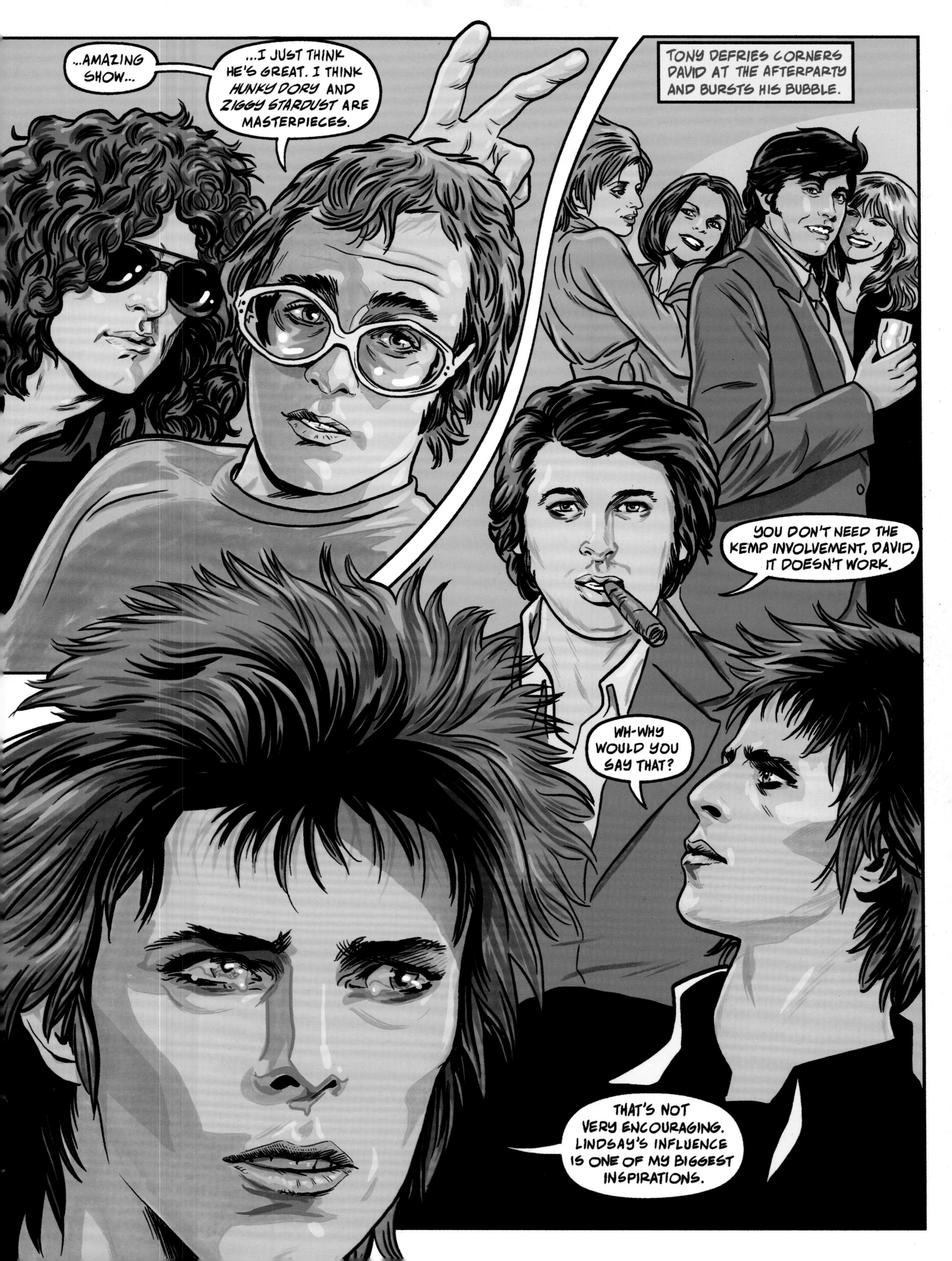
...AMAZING SHOW...
...I JUST THINK HE'S GREAT. I THINK *HUNKY DORY* AND *ZIGGY STARDUST* ARE MASTERPIECES.
TONY DEFRIES CORNERS DAVID AT THE AFTERPARTY AND BURSTS HIS BUBBLE.
YOU DON'T NEED THE KEMP INVOLVEMENT, DAVID. IT DOESN'T WORK.
WH-WHY WOULD YOU SAY THAT?
THAT'S NOT VERY ENCOURAGING. LINDSAY'S INFLUENCE IS ONE OF MY BIGGEST INSPIRATIONS.

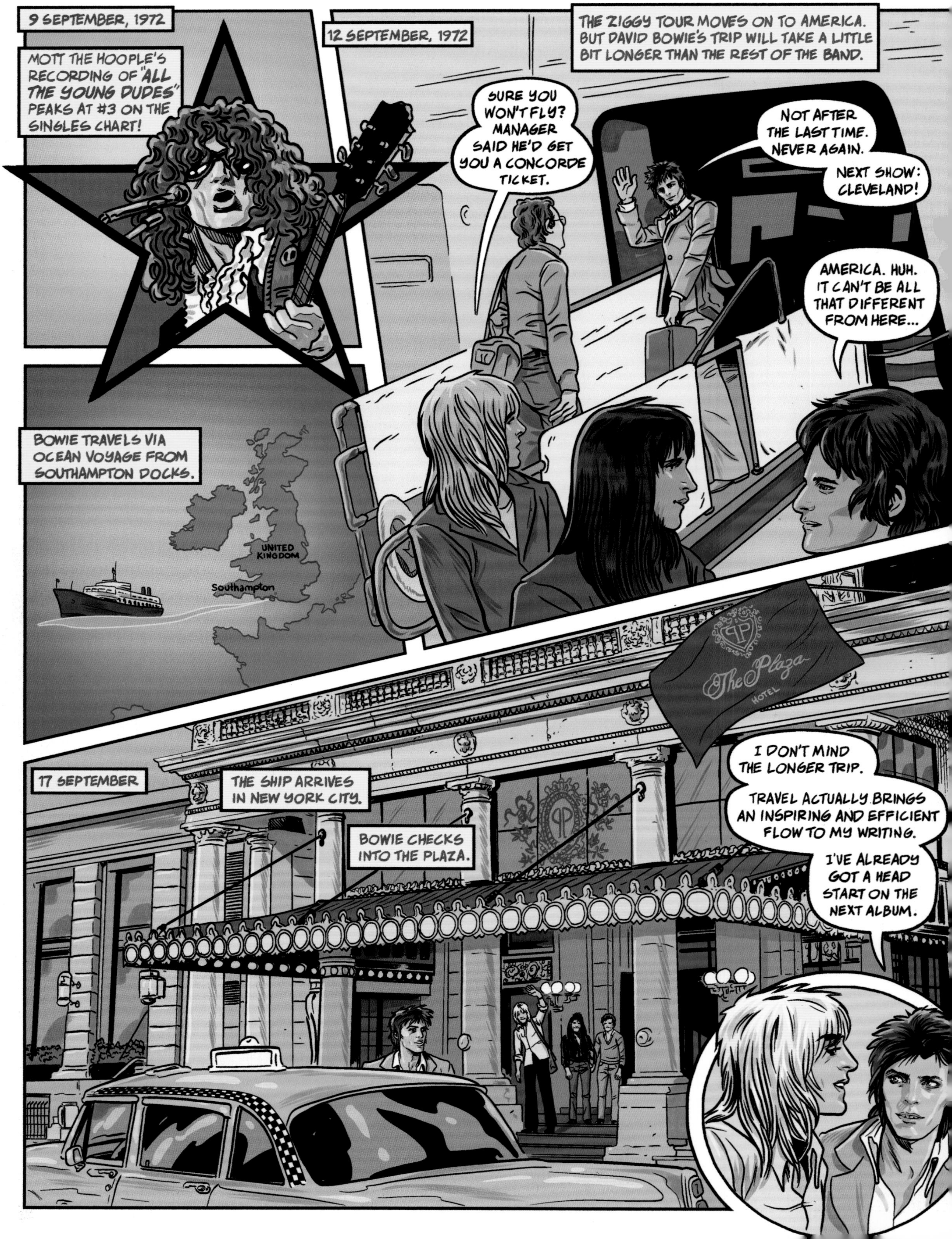
9 SEPTEMBER, 1972
MOTT THE HOOPLE'S RECORDING OF "ALL THE YOUNG DUDES" PEAKS AT #3 ON THE SINGLES CHART!
12 SEPTEMBER, 1972
THE ZIGGY TOUR MOVES ON TO AMERICA. BUT DAVID BOWIE'S TRIP WILL TAKE A LITTLE BIT LONGER THAN THE REST OF THE BAND.
SURE YOU WON'T FLY? MANAGER SAID HE'D GET YOU A CONCORDE TICKET.
NOT AFTER THE LAST TIME. NEVER AGAIN.
NEXT SHOW: CLEVELAND!
AMERICA. HUH. IT CAN'T BE ALL THAT DIFFERENT FROM HERE...
BOWIE TRAVELS VIA OCEAN VOYAGE FROM SOUTHAMPTON DOCKS.
UNITED KINGDOM
Southampton
The Plaza HOTEL
17 SEPTEMBER
THE SHIP ARRIVES IN NEW YORK CITY.
BOWIE CHECKS INTO THE PLAZA.
I DON'T MIND THE LONGER TRIP.
TRAVEL ACTUALLY BRINGS AN INSPIRING AND EFFICIENT FLOW TO MY WRITING.
I'VE ALREADY GOT A HEAD START ON THE NEXT ALBUM.

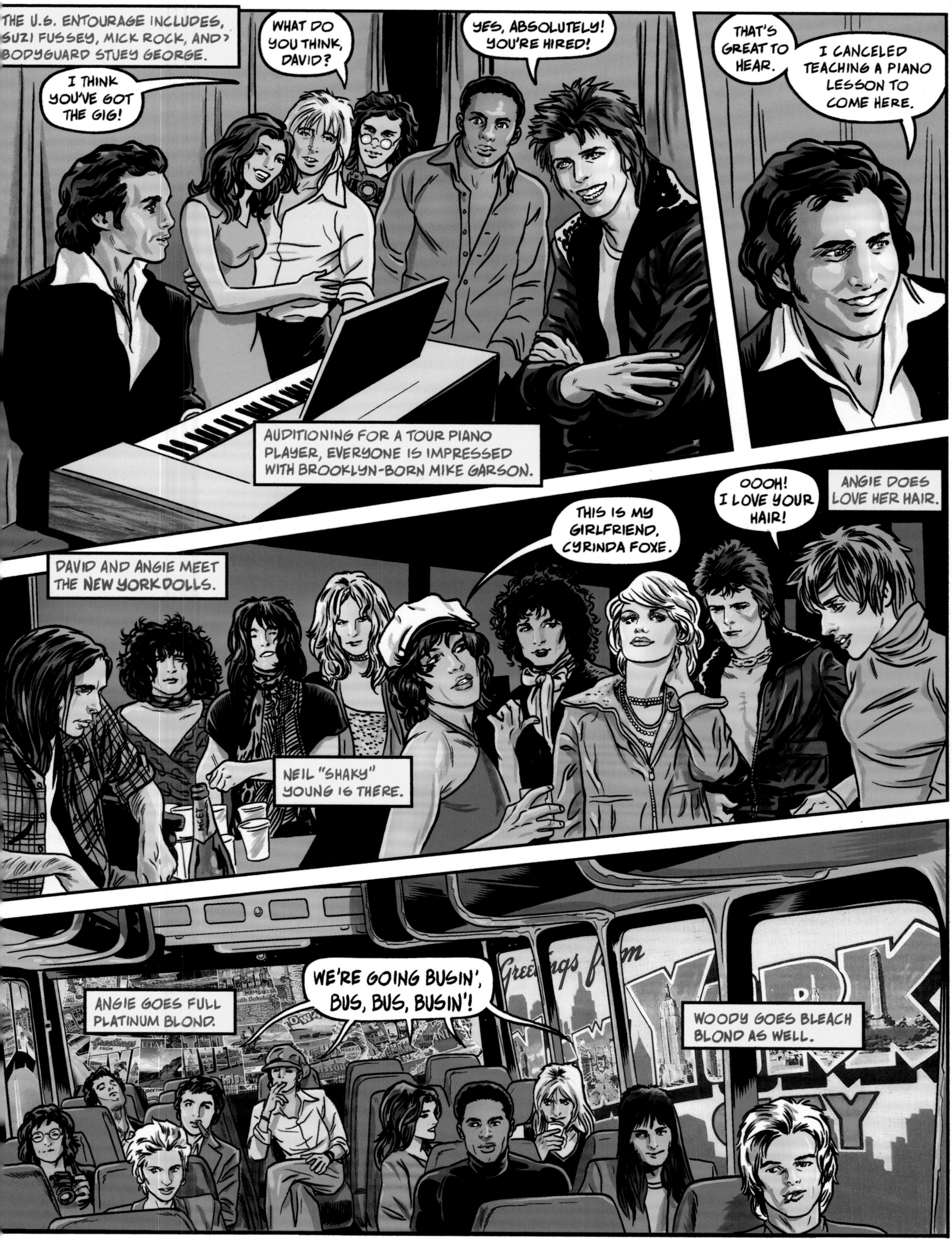
THE U.S. ENTOURAGE INCLUDES, SUZI FUSSEY, MICK ROCK, AND BODYGUARD STUEY GEORGE.
I THINK YOU'VE GOT THE GIG!
WHAT DO YOU THINK, DAVID?
YES, ABSOLUTELY! YOU'RE HIRED!
AUDITIONING FOR A TOUR PIANO PLAYER, EVERYONE IS IMPRESSED WITH BROOKLYN-BORN MIKE GARSON.
THAT'S GREAT TO HEAR.
I CANCELED TEACHING A PIANO LESSON TO COME HERE.
DAVID AND ANGIE MEET THE NEW YORK DOLLS.
THIS IS MY GIRLFRIEND, CYRINDA FOXE.
OOOH! I LOVE YOUR HAIR!
ANGIE DOES LOVE HER HAIR.
NEIL "SHAKY" YOUNG IS THERE.
ANGIE GOES FULL PLATINUM BLOND.
WE'RE GOING BUSIN', BUS, BUS, BUSIN'!
WOODY GOES BLEACH BLOND AS WELL.

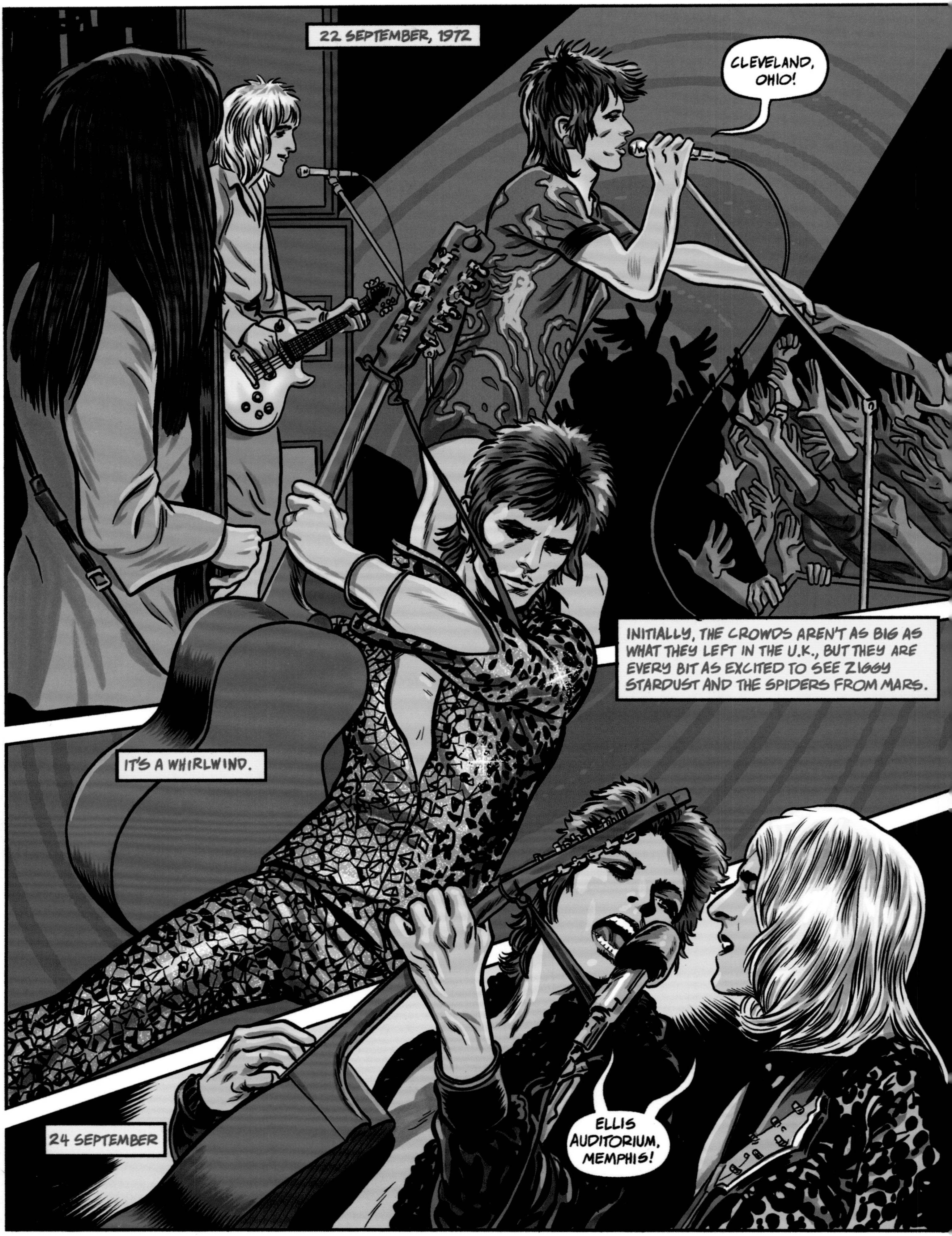
22 SEPTEMBER, 1972
CLEVELAND, OHIO!
INITIALLY, THE CROWDS AREN'T AS BIG AS WHAT THEY LEFT IN THE U.K., BUT THEY ARE EVERY BIT AS EXCITED TO SEE ZIGGY STARDUST AND THE SPIDERS FROM MARS.
IT'S A WHIRLWIND.
24 SEPTEMBER
ELLIS AUDITORIUM, MEMPHIS!

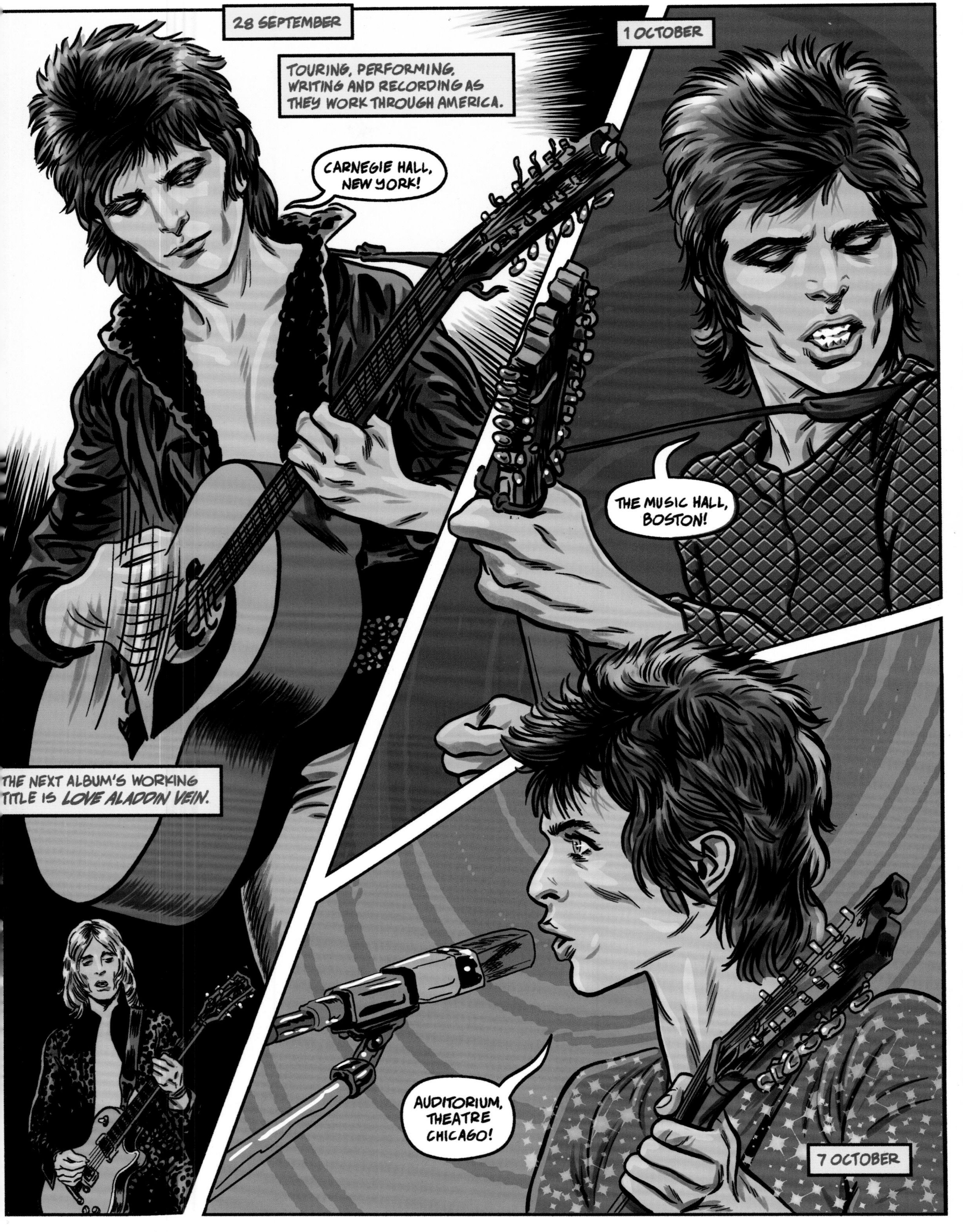
28 SEPTEMBER
TOURING, PERFORMING, WRITING AND RECORDING AS THEY WORK THROUGH AMERICA.
CARNEGIE HALL, NEW YORK!
THE NEXT ALBUM'S WORKING TITLE IS *LOVE ALADDIN VEIN*.
1 OCTOBER
THE MUSIC HALL, BOSTON!
AUDITORIUM, THEATRE CHICAGO!
7 OCTOBER

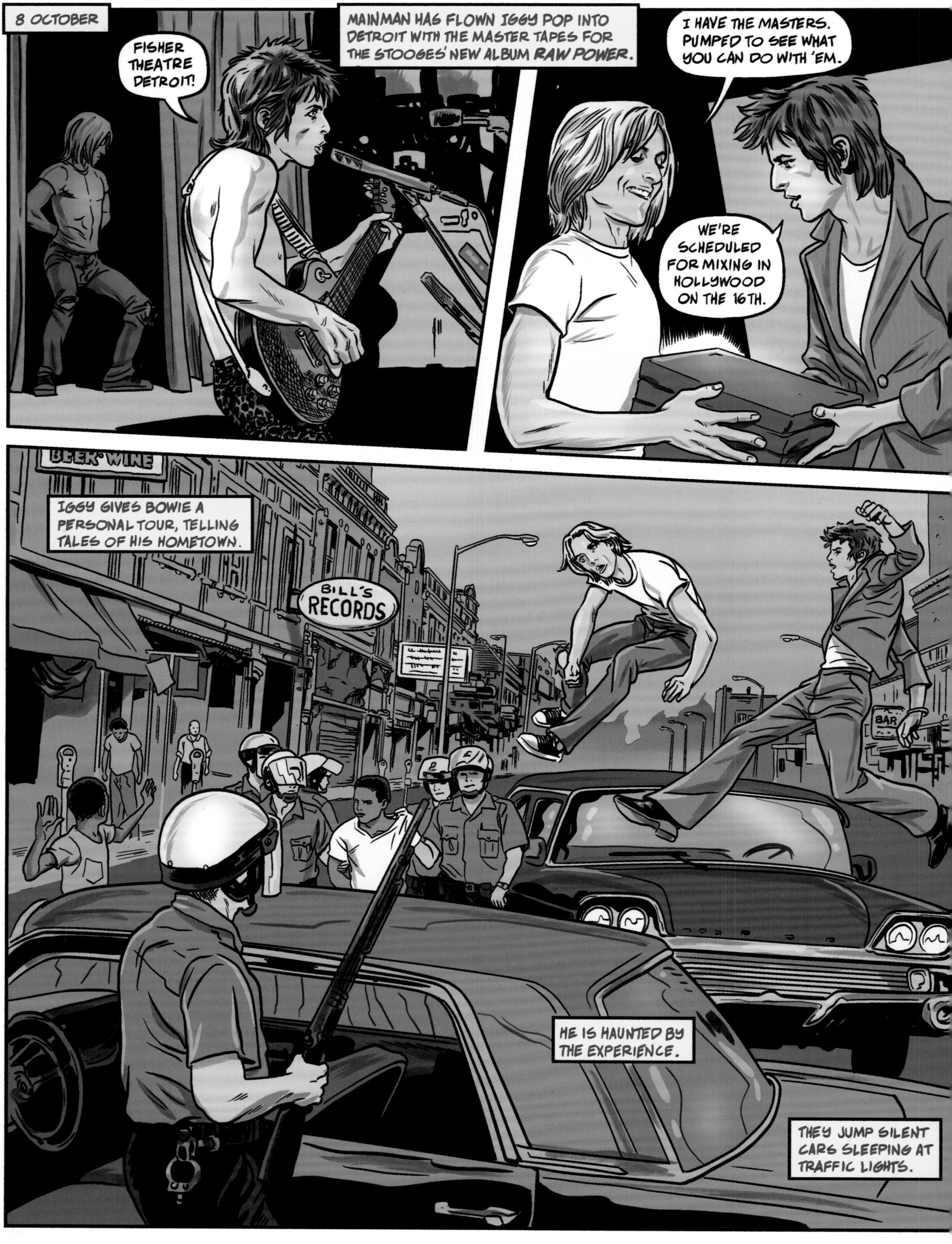
8 OCTOBER
FISHER THEATRE DETROIT!
MAINMAN HAS FLOWN IGGY POP INTO DETROIT WITH THE MASTER TAPES FOR THE STOOGES' NEW ALBUM RAW POWER.
I HAVE THE MASTERS. PUMPED TO SEE WHAT YOU CAN DO WITH 'EM.
WE'RE SCHEDULED FOR MIXING IN HOLLYWOOD ON THE 16TH.
BEER WINE
IGGY GIVES BOWIE A PERSONAL TOUR, TELLING TALES OF HIS HOMETOWN.
BILL'S RECORDS
BAR
HE IS HAUNTED BY THE EXPERIENCE.
THEY JUMP SILENT CARS SLEEPING AT TRAFFIC LIGHTS.

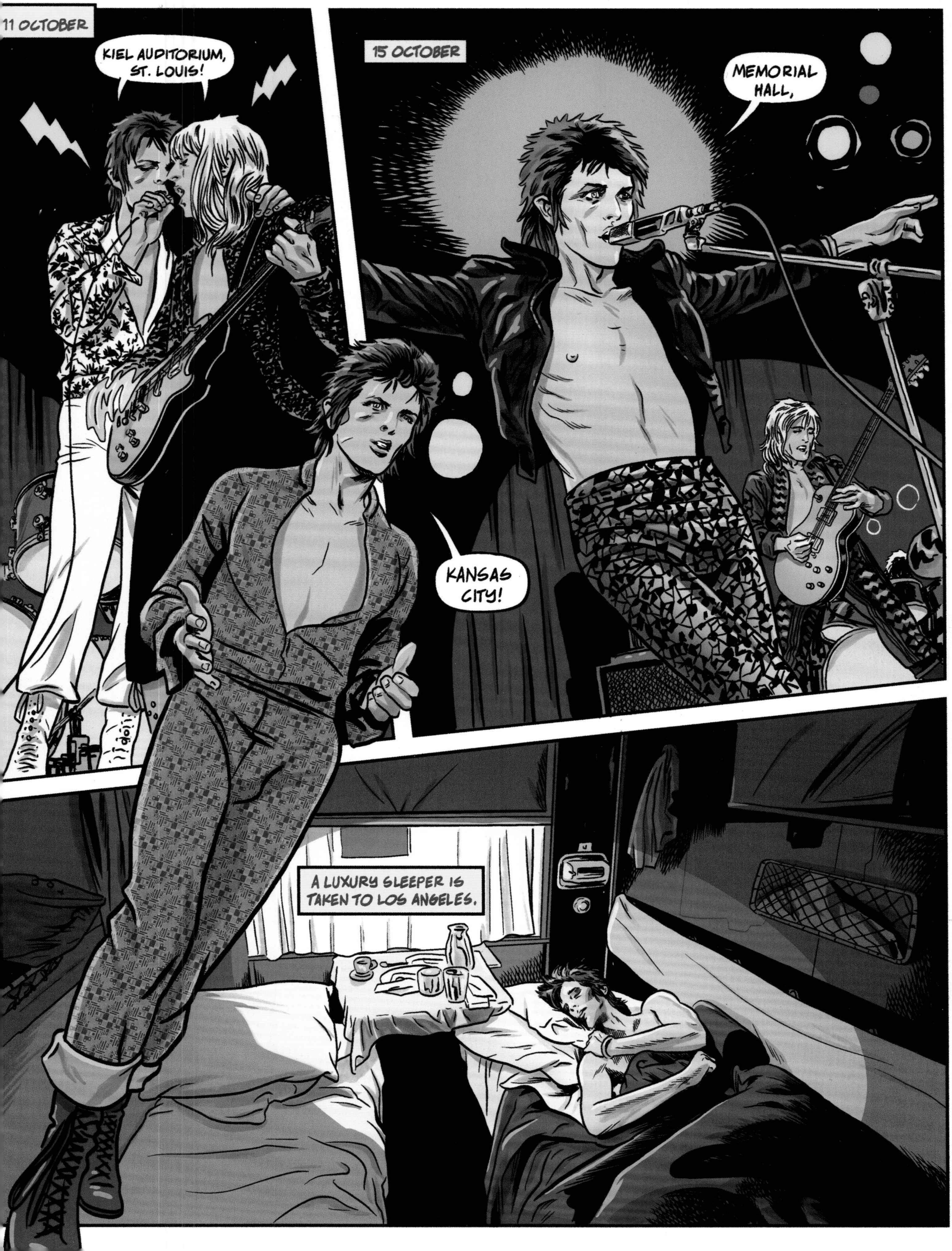
11 OCTOBER
KIEL AUDITORIUM, ST. LOUIS!
15 OCTOBER
MEMORIAL HALL,
KANSAS CITY!
A LUXURY SLEEPER IS TAKEN TO LOS ANGELES.

17 OCTOBER

TEA WITH ELTON JOHN AT THE BEVERLY HILLS HOTEL.

WE'RE ABOUT TO HEAD TO THE WINTERLAND IN SAN FRANCISCO.

RIGHT. WE'LL BE PERFORMING THERE ON THE 28TH.

OH, DEAR BOY, WHAT TRAGEDY HAS BEFALLEN YOU?

SUZI LIKES HER MEN LOBSTER RED WITH MOSS-COLORED HAIR.

THE GREEN HAIR FROM THE POOL? WE CAN FIX IT.

THAT IS, IF YOU'D LIKE ME TO.

YEAH, LET'S GET THE GREEN BACK TO GOLD.

BUT YOUR SUNBURN OFFERS A NICE CONTRAST WITH MY SNOW-WHITE TAN.

YOU PEOPLE ARE SO VERY WEIRD.

HOLLYWOOD IS WONDERFULLY WEIRD. LOOK BEHIND ME.

THERE'S A MOODGE WITH A CRACKED MOZG.

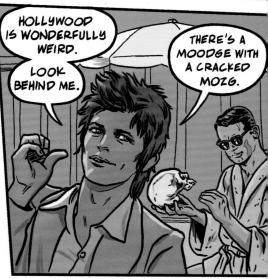

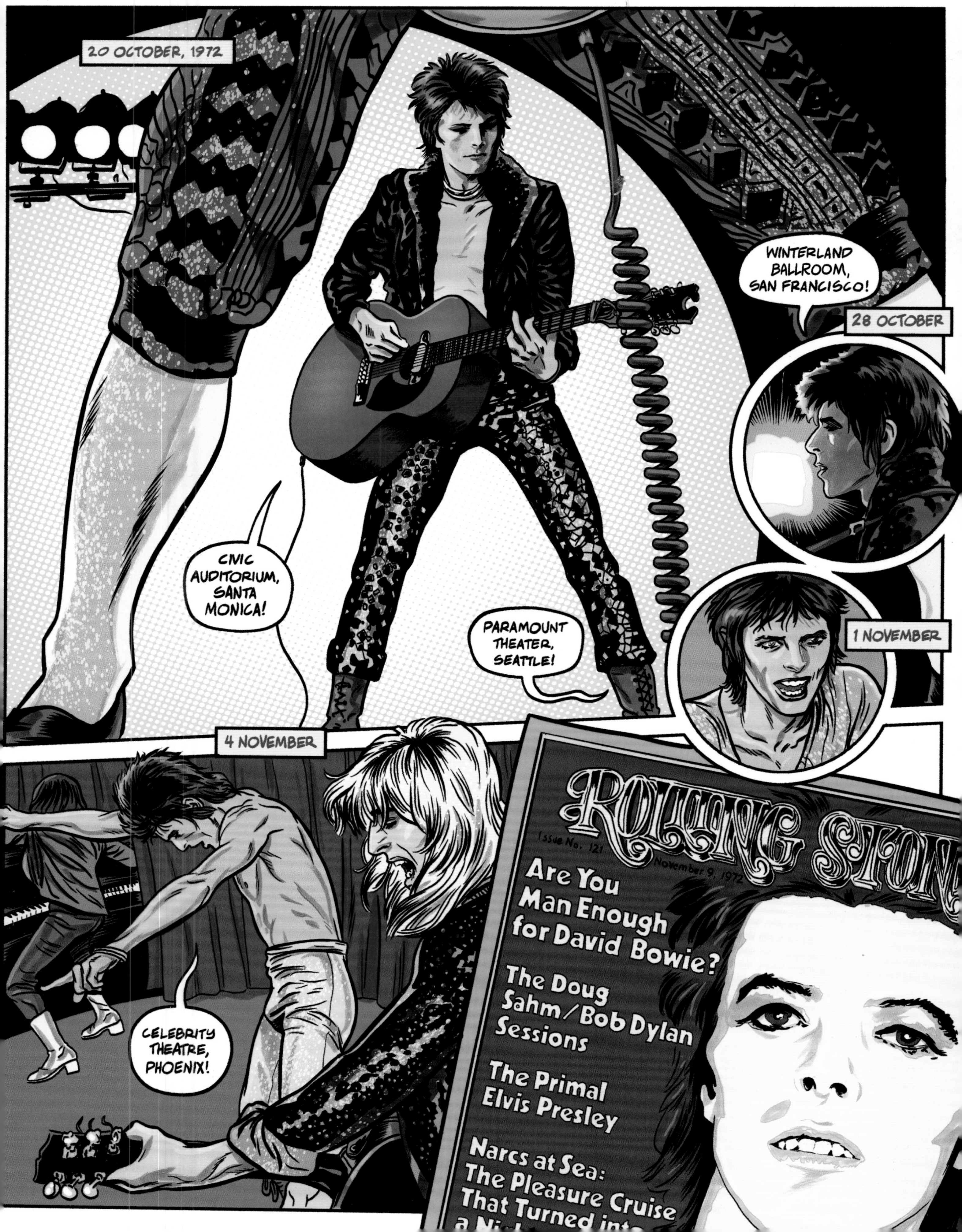

20 OCTOBER, 1972
CIVIC AUDITORIUM, SANTA MONICA!
PARAMOUNT THEATER, SEATTLE!
WINTERLAND BALLROOM, SAN FRANCISCO!
28 OCTOBER
1 NOVEMBER
4 NOVEMBER
CELEBRITY THEATRE, PHOENIX!
ROLLING STONE
Issue No. 121
November 9, 1972
Are You Man Enough for David Bowie?
The Doug Sahm/Bob Dylan Sessions
The Primal Elvis Presley
Narcs at Sea: The Pleasure Cruise That Turned into

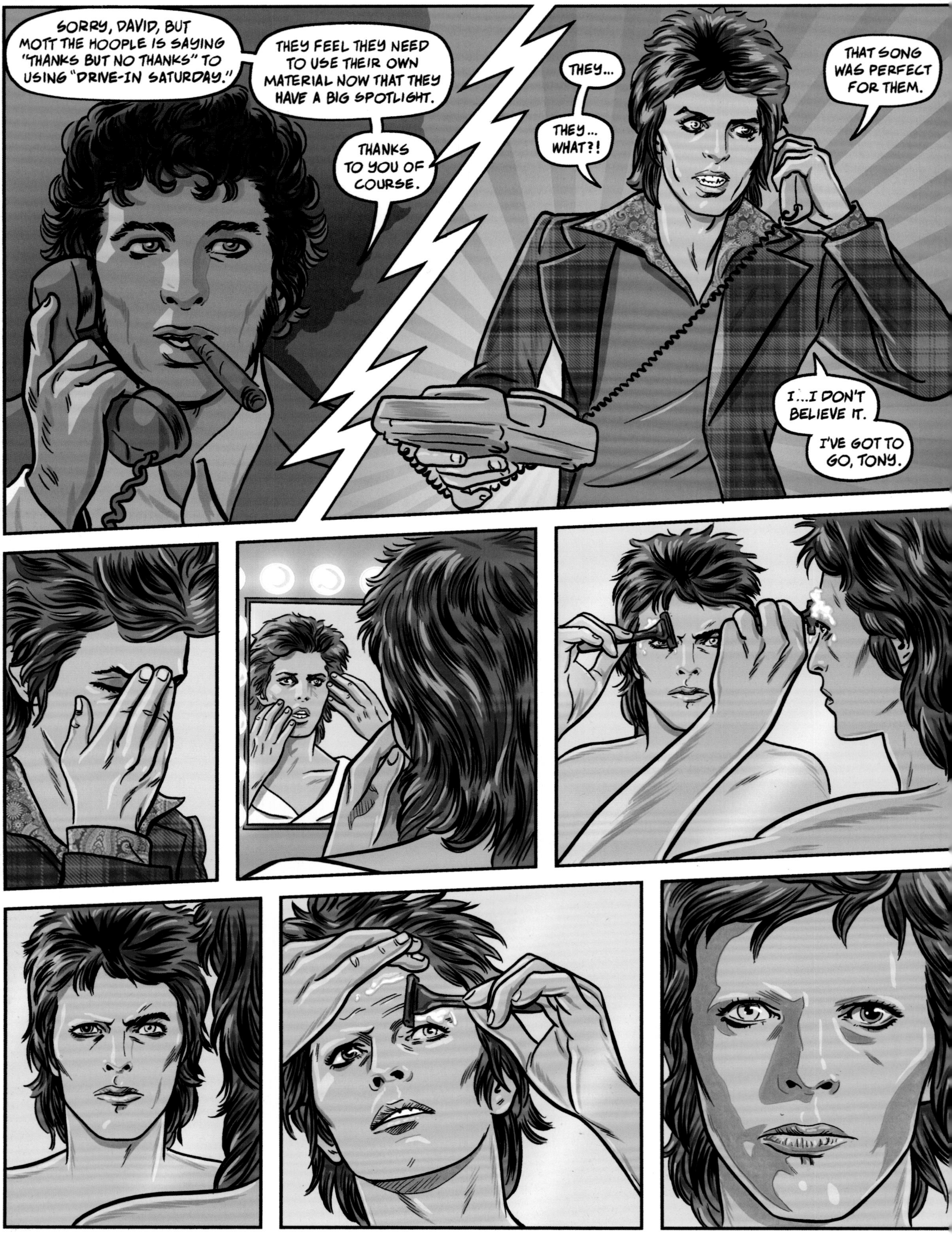
SORRY, DAVID, BUT MOTT THE HOOPLE IS SAYING "THANKS BUT NO THANKS" TO USING "DRIVE-IN SATURDAY."
THEY FEEL THEY NEED TO USE THEIR OWN MATERIAL NOW THAT THEY HAVE A BIG SPOTLIGHT.
THANKS TO YOU OF COURSE.
THEY...
THEY... WHAT?!
THAT SONG WAS PERFECT FOR THEM.
I...I DON'T BELIEVE IT.
I'VE GOT TO GO, TONY.

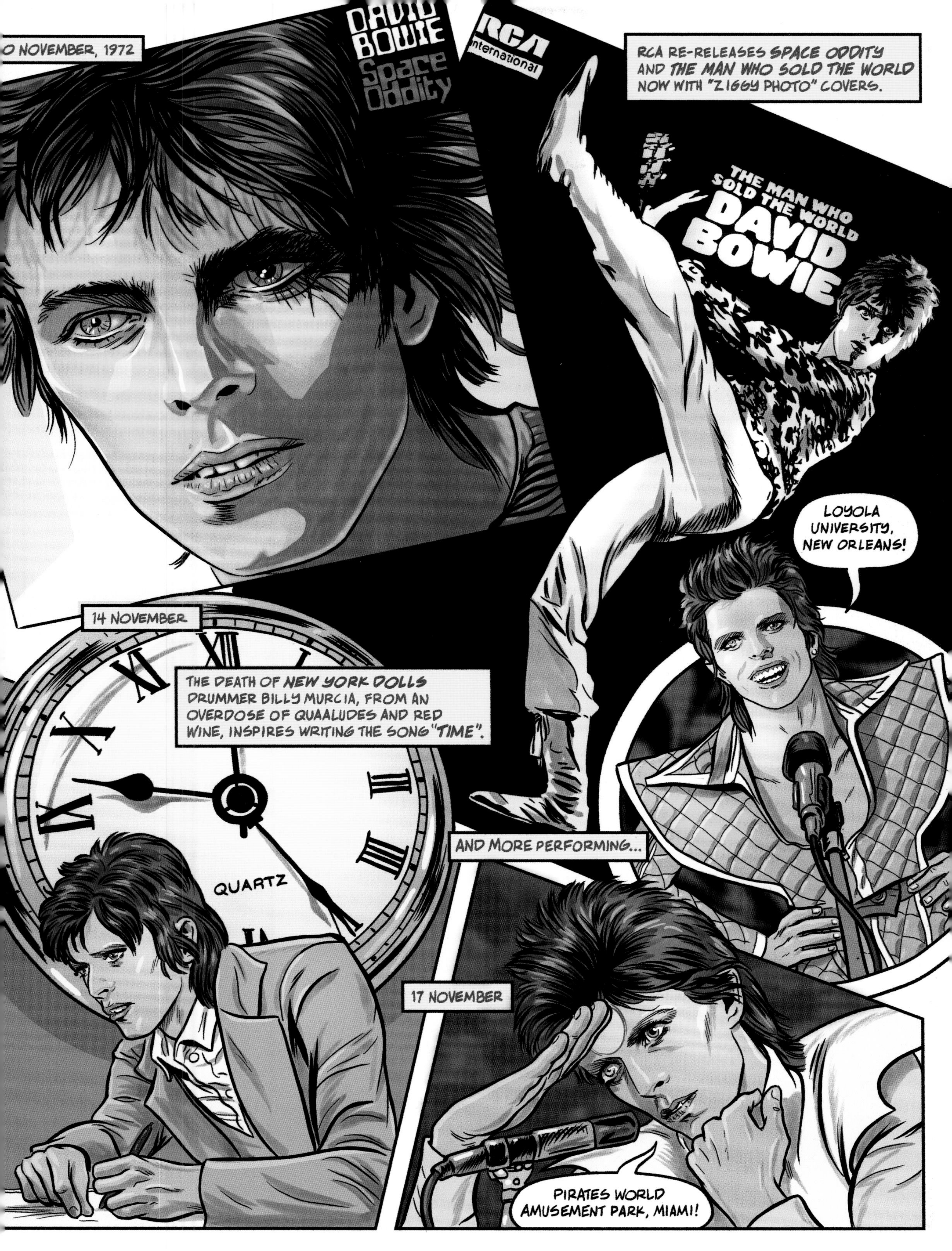

O NOVEMBER, 1972
DAVID BOWIE
Space Oddity
RCA
International
RCA RE-RELEASES SPACE ODDITY AND THE MAN WHO SOLD THE WORLD NOW WITH "ZIGGY PHOTO" COVERS.
THE MAN WHO SOLD THE WORLD
DAVID BOWIE
LOYOLA UNIVERSITY, NEW ORLEANS!
14 NOVEMBER
THE DEATH OF NEW YORK DOLLS DRUMMER BILLY MURCIA, FROM AN OVERDOSE OF QUAALUDES AND RED WINE, INSPIRES WRITING THE SONG "TIME".
QUARTZ
AND MORE PERFORMING...
17 NOVEMBER
PIRATES WORLD AMUSEMENT PARK, MIAMI!

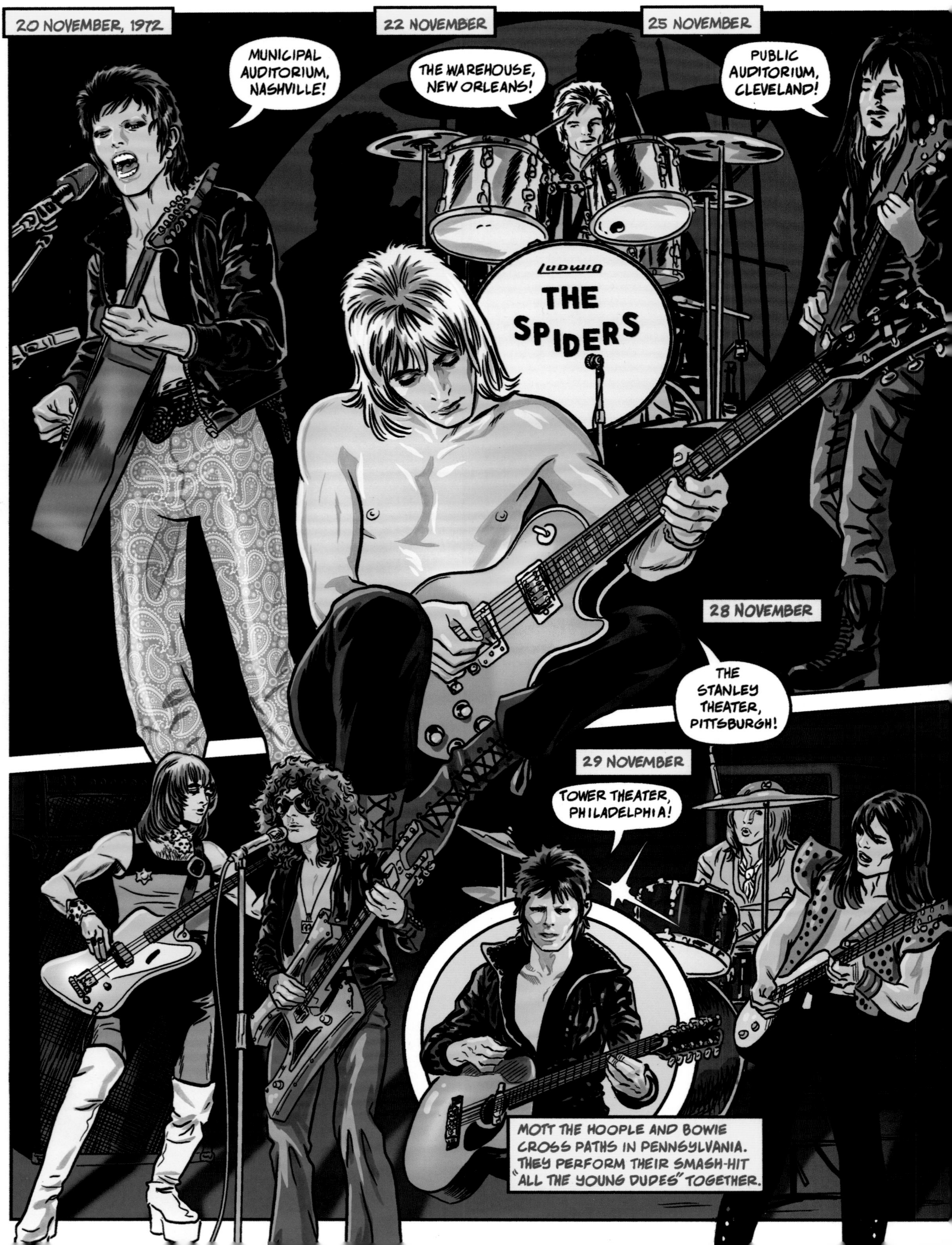
20 NOVEMBER, 1972
MUNICIPAL AUDITORIUM, NASHVILLE!
22 NOVEMBER
THE WAREHOUSE, NEW ORLEANS!
25 NOVEMBER
PUBLIC AUDITORIUM, CLEVELAND!
LUDWIG
THE SPIDERS
28 NOVEMBER
THE STANLEY THEATER, PITTSBURGH!
29 NOVEMBER
TOWER THEATER, PHILADELPHIA!
MOTT THE HOOPLE AND BOWIE CROSS PATHS IN PENNSYLVANIA. THEY PERFORM THEIR SMASH-HIT "ALL THE YOUNG DUDES" TOGETHER.

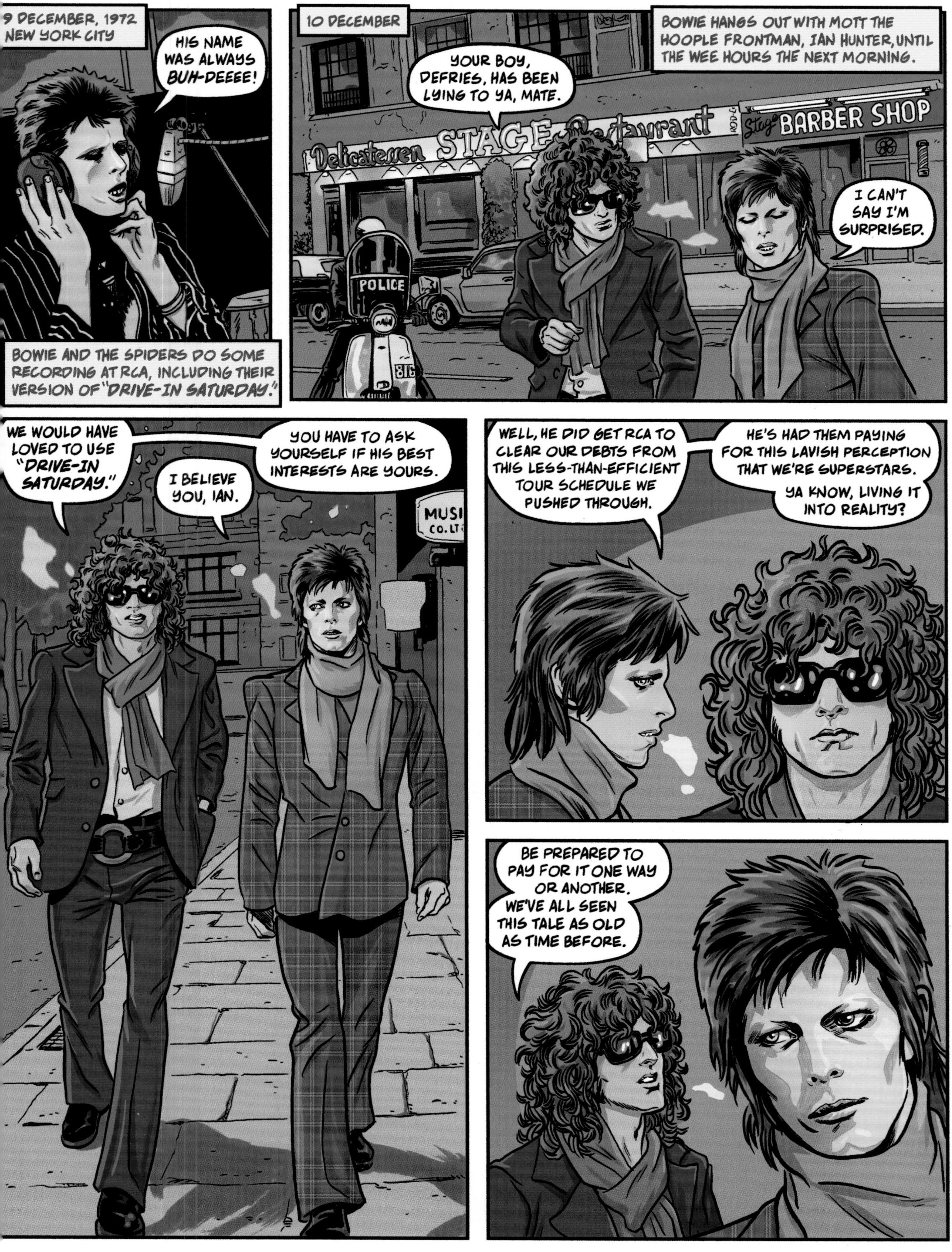
9 DECEMBER, 1972
NEW YORK CITY
HIS NAME WAS ALWAYS BUH-DEEEE!
BOWIE AND THE SPIDERS DO SOME RECORDING AT RCA, INCLUDING THEIR VERSION OF "DRIVE-IN SATURDAY."
10 DECEMBER
BOWIE HANGS OUT WITH MOTT THE HOOPLE FRONTMAN, IAN HUNTER, UNTIL THE WEE HOURS THE NEXT MORNING.
YOUR BOY, DEFRIES, HAS BEEN LYING TO YA, MATE.
Delicatessen STAGE Restaurant
Stage BARBER SHOP
POLICE
I CAN'T SAY I'M SURPRISED.
WE WOULD HAVE LOVED TO USE "DRIVE-IN SATURDAY."
I BELIEVE YOU, IAN.
YOU HAVE TO ASK YOURSELF IF HIS BEST INTERESTS ARE YOURS.
WELL, HE DID GET RCA TO CLEAR OUR DEBTS FROM THIS LESS-THAN-EFFICIENT TOUR SCHEDULE WE PUSHED THROUGH.
HE'S HAD THEM PAYING FOR THIS LAVISH PERCEPTION THAT WE'RE SUPERSTARS.
YA KNOW, LIVING IT INTO REALITY?
BE PREPARED TO PAY FOR IT ONE WAY OR ANOTHER.
WE'VE ALL SEEN THIS TALE AS OLD AS TIME BEFORE.

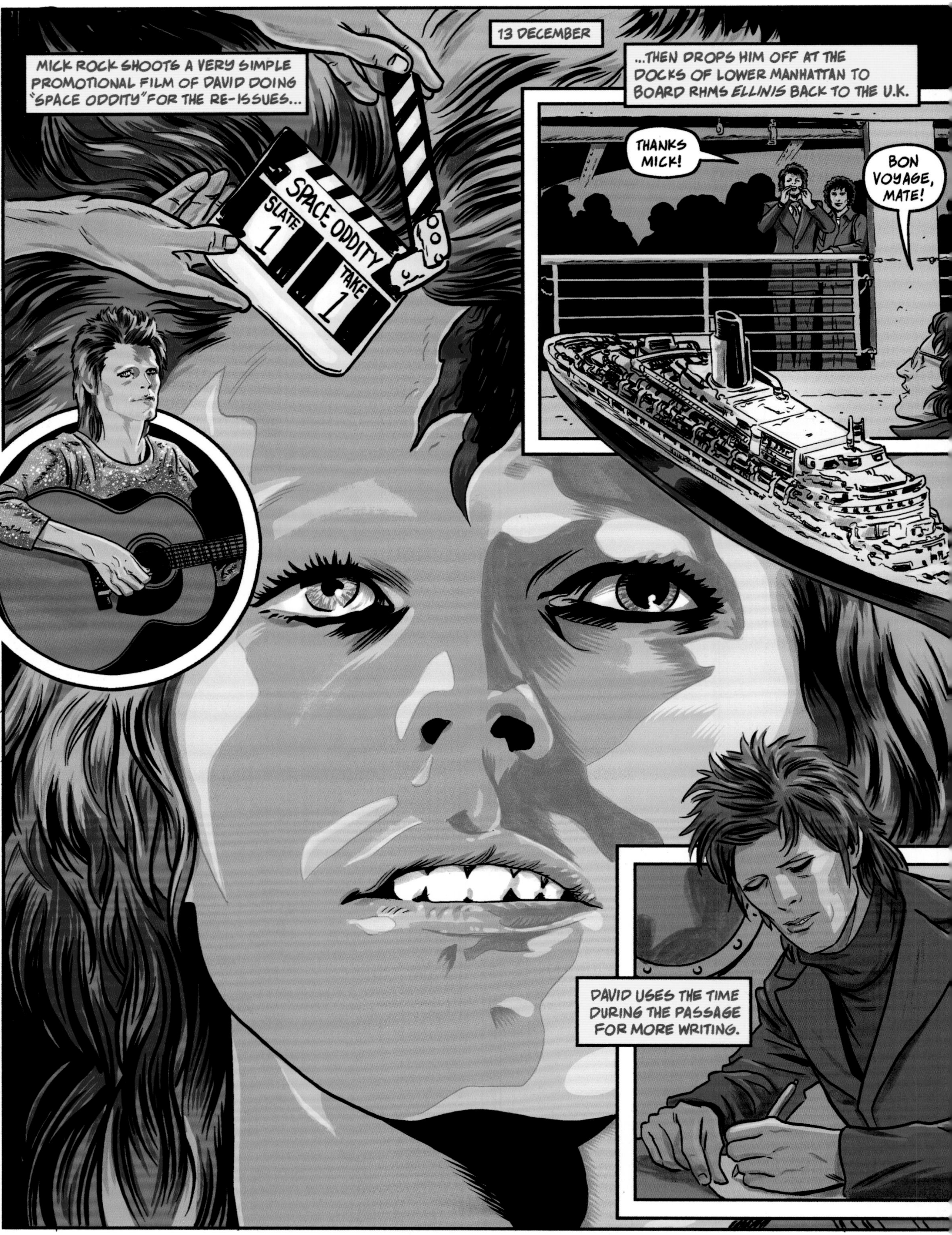
MICK ROCK SHOOTS A VERY SIMPLE PROMOTIONAL FILM OF DAVID DOING "SPACE ODDITY" FOR THE RE-ISSUES...
SPACE ODDITY
SLATE 1
TAKE 1
13 DECEMBER
...THEN DROPS HIM OFF AT THE DOCKS OF LOWER MANHATTAN TO BOARD RHMS *ELLINIS* BACK TO THE U.K.
THANKS MICK!
BON VOYAGE, MATE!
DAVID USES THE TIME DURING THE PASSAGE FOR MORE WRITING.

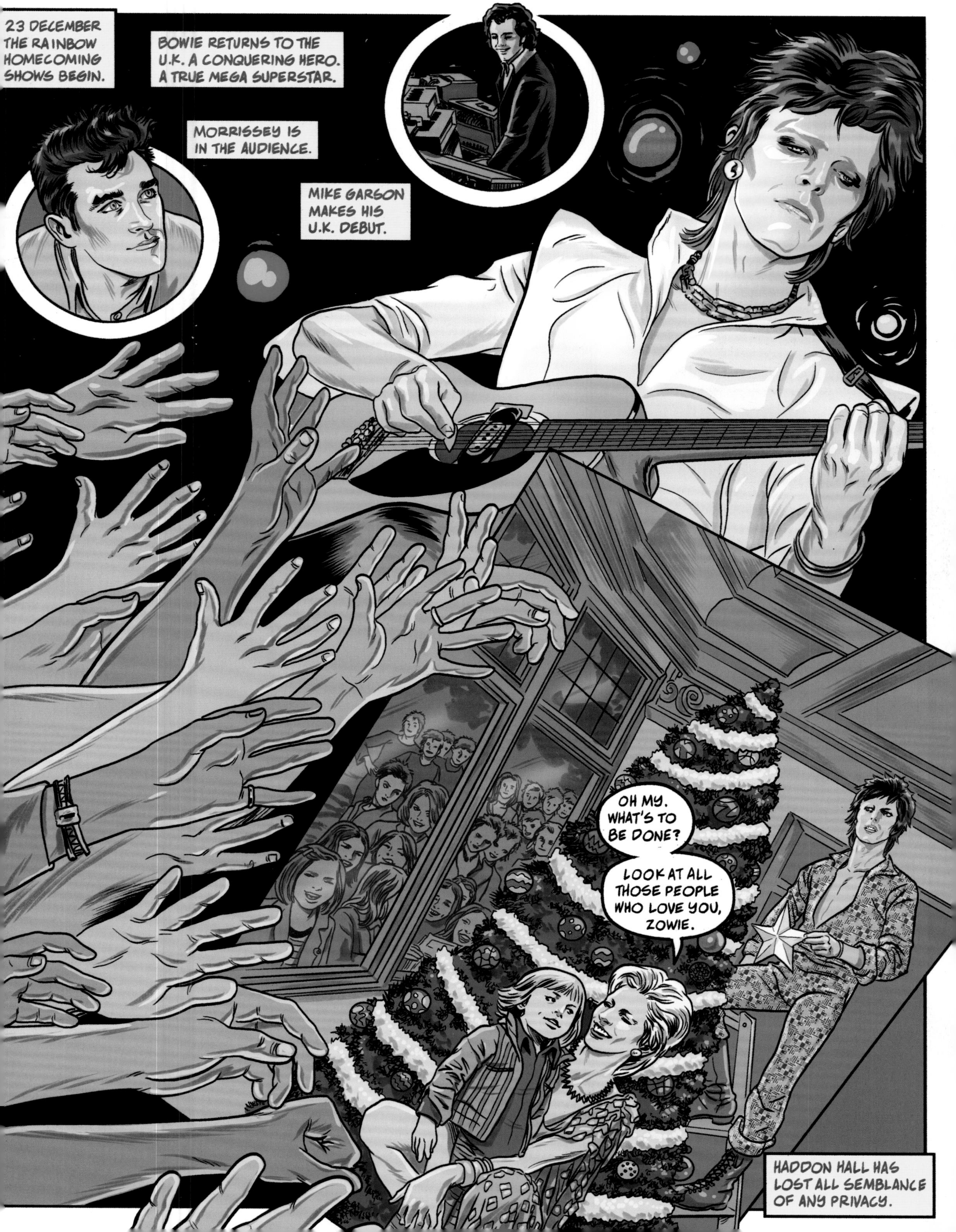

23 DECEMBER THE RAINBOW HOMECOMING SHOWS BEGIN.
BOWIE RETURNS TO THE U.K. A CONQUERING HERO. A TRUE MEGA SUPERSTAR.
MORRISSEY IS IN THE AUDIENCE.
MIKE GARSON MAKES HIS U.K. DEBUT.
OH MY. WHAT'S TO BE DONE?
LOOK AT ALL THOSE PEOPLE WHO LOVE YOU, ZOWIE.
HADDON HALL HAS LOST ALL SEMBLANCE OF ANY PRIVACY.

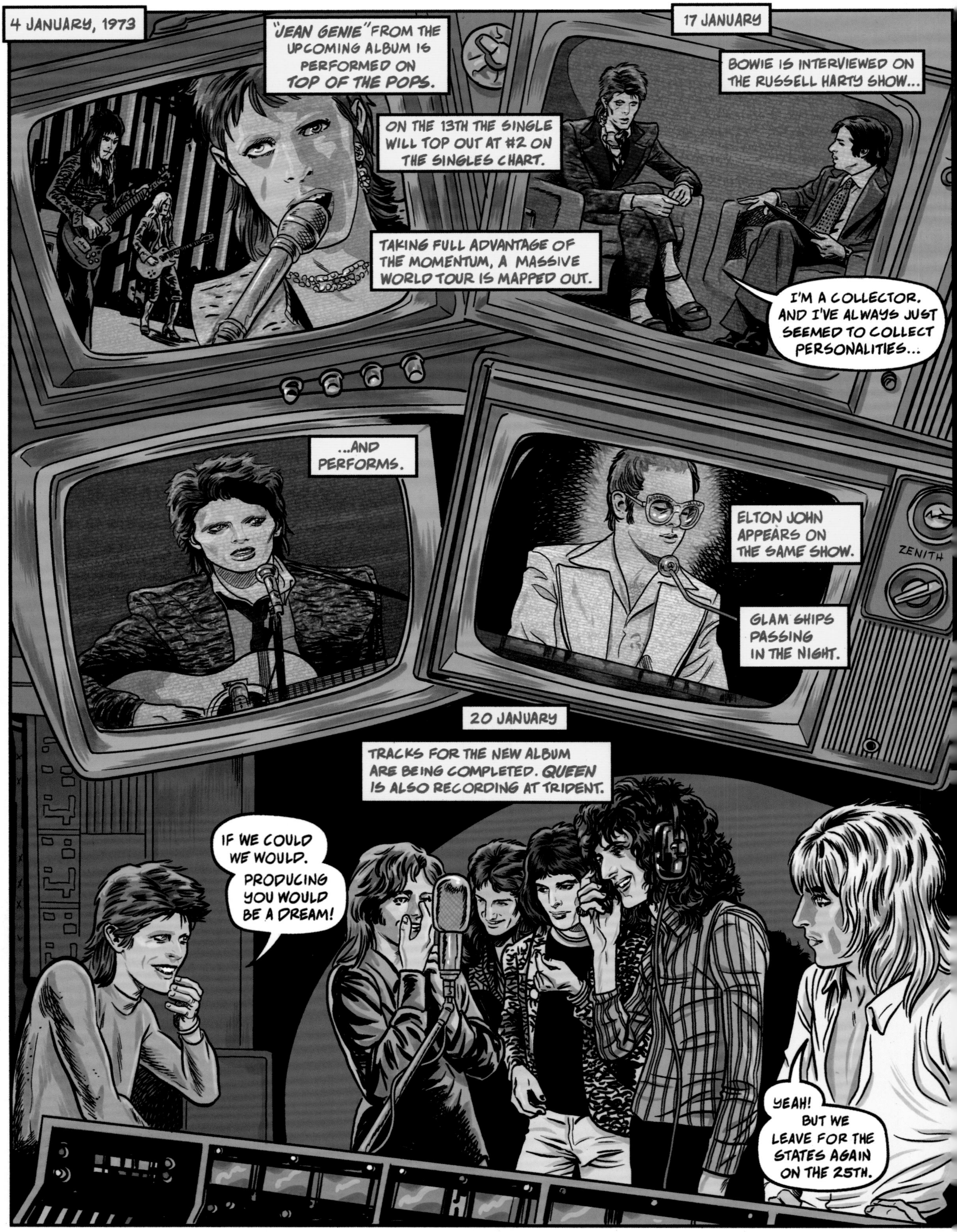
4 JANUARY, 1973
"JEAN GENIE" FROM THE UPCOMING ALBUM IS PERFORMED ON TOP OF THE POPS.
ON THE 13TH THE SINGLE WILL TOP OUT AT #2 ON THE SINGLES CHART.
TAKING FULL ADVANTAGE OF THE MOMENTUM, A MASSIVE WORLD TOUR IS MAPPED OUT.
17 JANUARY
BOWIE IS INTERVIEWED ON THE RUSSELL HARTY SHOW...
I'M A COLLECTOR. AND I'VE ALWAYS JUST SEEMED TO COLLECT PERSONALITIES...
...AND PERFORMS.
ELTON JOHN APPEARS ON THE SAME SHOW.
ZENITH
GLAM SHIPS PASSING IN THE NIGHT.
20 JANUARY
TRACKS FOR THE NEW ALBUM ARE BEING COMPLETED. QUEEN IS ALSO RECORDING AT TRIDENT.
IF WE COULD WE WOULD. PRODUCING YOU WOULD BE A DREAM!
YEAH! BUT WE LEAVE FOR THE STATES AGAIN ON THE 25TH.

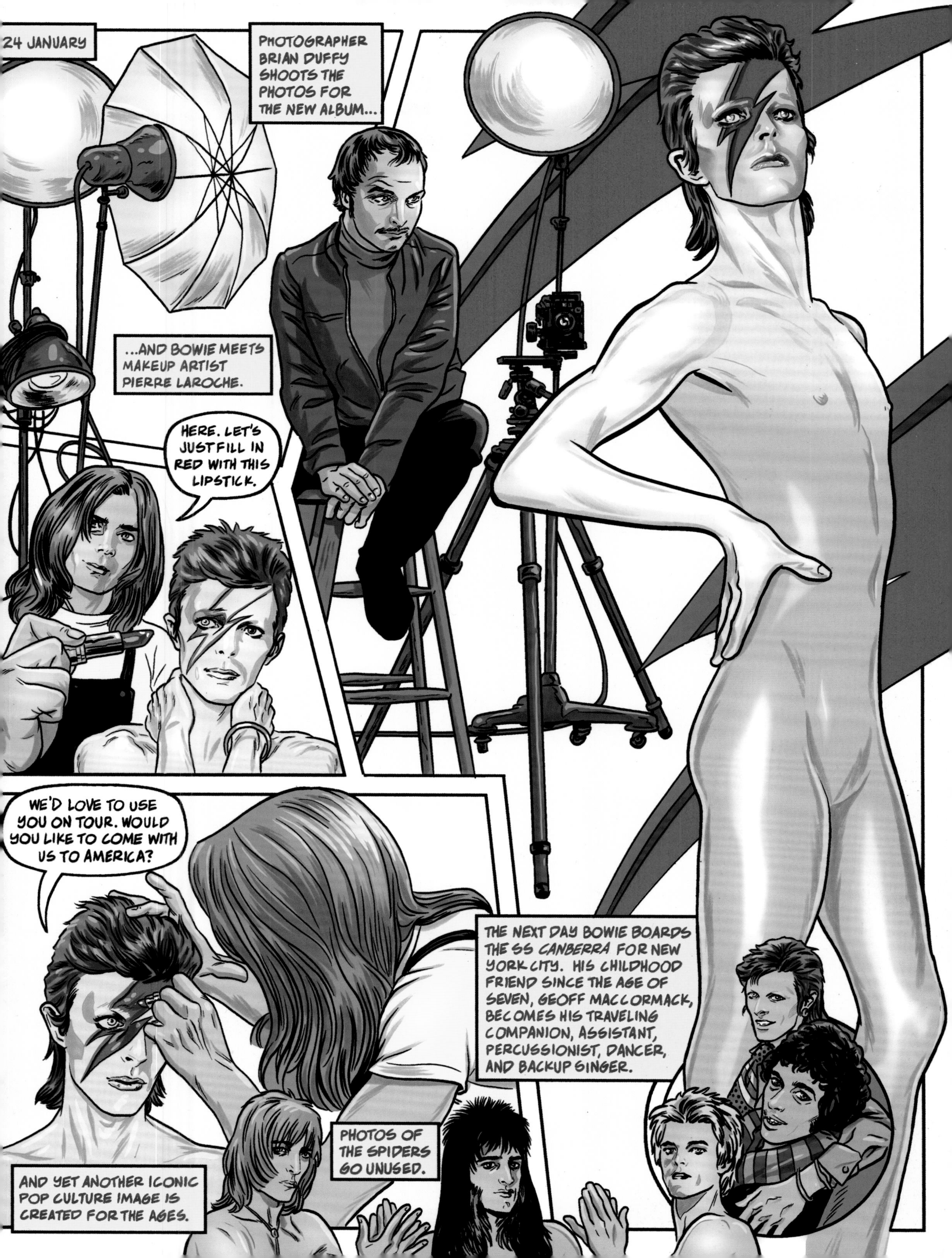

24 JANUARY
PHOTOGRAPHER BRIAN DUFFY SHOOTS THE PHOTOS FOR THE NEW ALBUM...
...AND BOWIE MEETS MAKEUP ARTIST PIERRE LAROCHE.
HERE. LET'S JUST FILL IN RED WITH THIS LIPSTICK.
WE'D LOVE TO USE YOU ON TOUR. WOULD YOU LIKE TO COME WITH US TO AMERICA?
THE NEXT DAY BOWIE BOARDS THE SS *CANBERRA* FOR NEW YORK CITY. HIS CHILDHOOD FRIEND SINCE THE AGE OF SEVEN, GEOFF MACCORMACK, BECOMES HIS TRAVELING COMPANION, ASSISTANT, PERCUSSIONIST, DANCER, AND BACKUP SINGER.
PHOTOS OF THE SPIDERS GO UNUSED.
AND YET ANOTHER ICONIC POP CULTURE IMAGE IS CREATED FOR THE AGES.

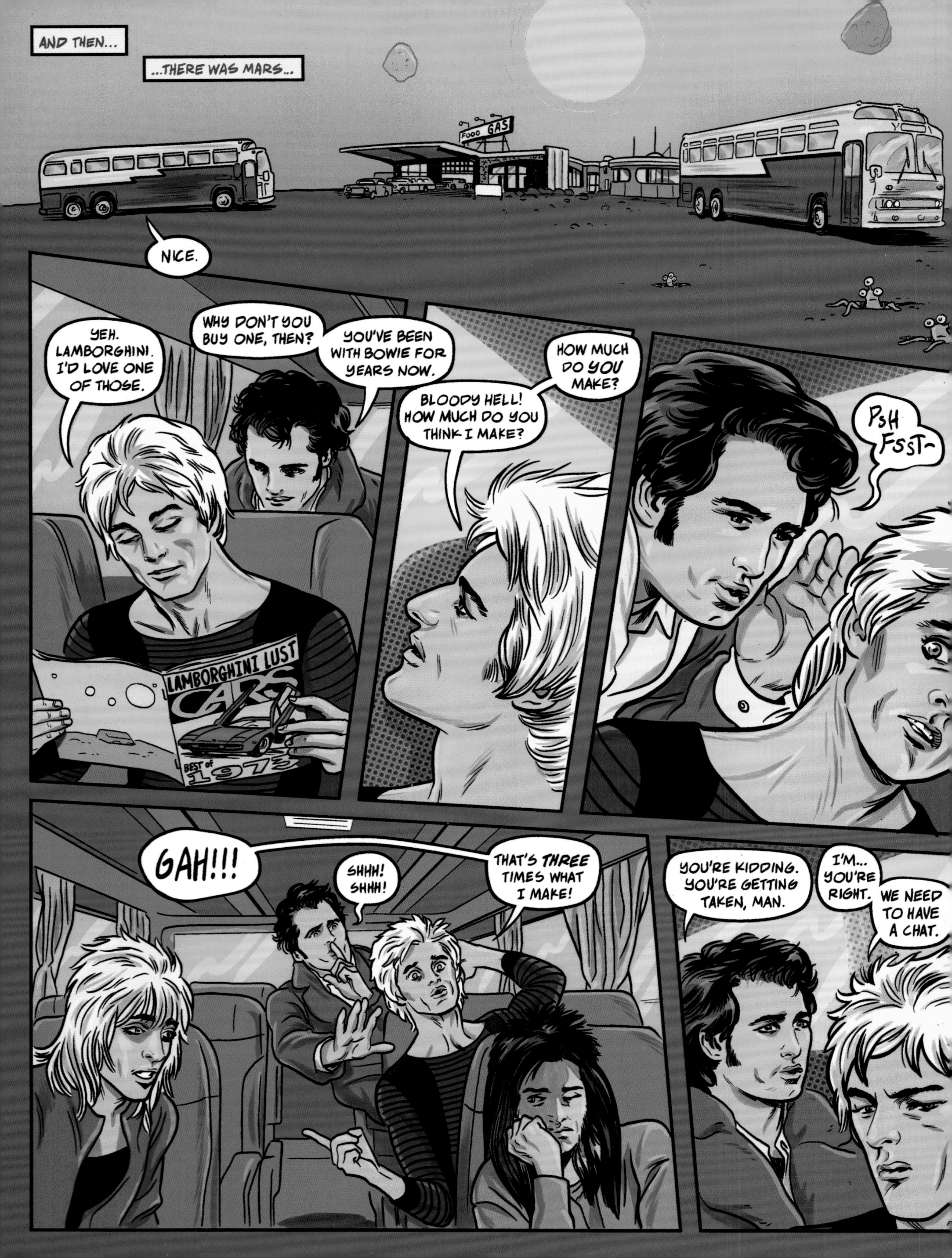
AND THEN...
...THERE WAS MARS...
FOOD GAS
NICE.
YEH. LAMBORGHINI. I'D LOVE ONE OF THOSE.
WHY DON'T YOU BUY ONE, THEN?
YOU'VE BEEN WITH BOWIE FOR YEARS NOW.
LAMBORGHINI LUST
CARS
BEST OF 1973
BLOODY HELL! HOW MUCH DO YOU THINK I MAKE?
HOW MUCH DO *YOU* MAKE?
PSH FSST-
GAH!!!
SHHH! SHHH!
THAT'S *THREE* TIMES WHAT I MAKE!
YOU'RE KIDDING. YOU'RE GETTING TAKEN, MAN.
I'M... YOU'RE RIGHT.
WE NEED TO HAVE A CHAT.

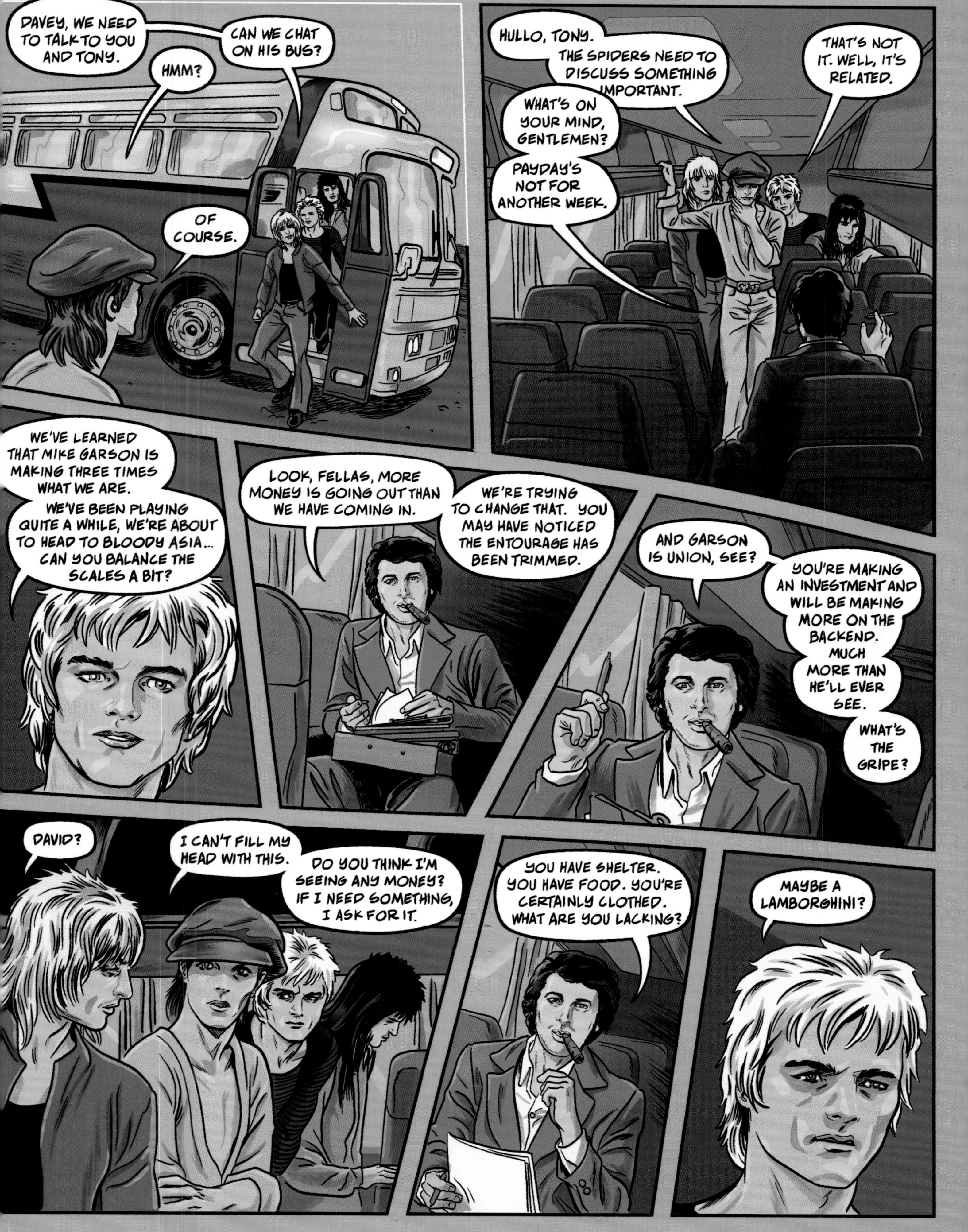
DAVEY, WE NEED TO TALK TO YOU AND TONY.
HMM?
CAN WE CHAT ON HIS BUS?
OF COURSE.
HULLO, TONY.
THE SPIDERS NEED TO DISCUSS SOMETHING IMPORTANT.
WHAT'S ON YOUR MIND, GENTLEMEN?
PAYDAY'S NOT FOR ANOTHER WEEK.
THAT'S NOT IT. WELL, IT'S RELATED.
WE'VE LEARNED THAT MIKE GARSON IS MAKING THREE TIMES WHAT WE ARE.
WE'VE BEEN PLAYING QUITE A WHILE, WE'RE ABOUT TO HEAD TO BLOODY ASIA... CAN YOU BALANCE THE SCALES A BIT?
LOOK, FELLAS, MORE MONEY IS GOING OUT THAN WE HAVE COMING IN.
WE'RE TRYING TO CHANGE THAT. YOU MAY HAVE NOTICED THE ENTOURAGE HAS BEEN TRIMMED.
AND GARSON IS UNION, SEE?
YOU'RE MAKING AN INVESTMENT AND WILL BE MAKING MORE ON THE BACKEND. MUCH MORE THAN HE'LL EVER SEE.
WHAT'S THE GRIPE?
DAVID?
I CAN'T FILL MY HEAD WITH THIS.
DO YOU THINK I'M SEEING ANY MONEY? IF I NEED SOMETHING, I ASK FOR IT.
YOU HAVE SHELTER. YOU HAVE FOOD. YOU'RE CERTAINLY CLOTHED. WHAT ARE YOU LACKING?
MAYBE A LAMBORGHINI?

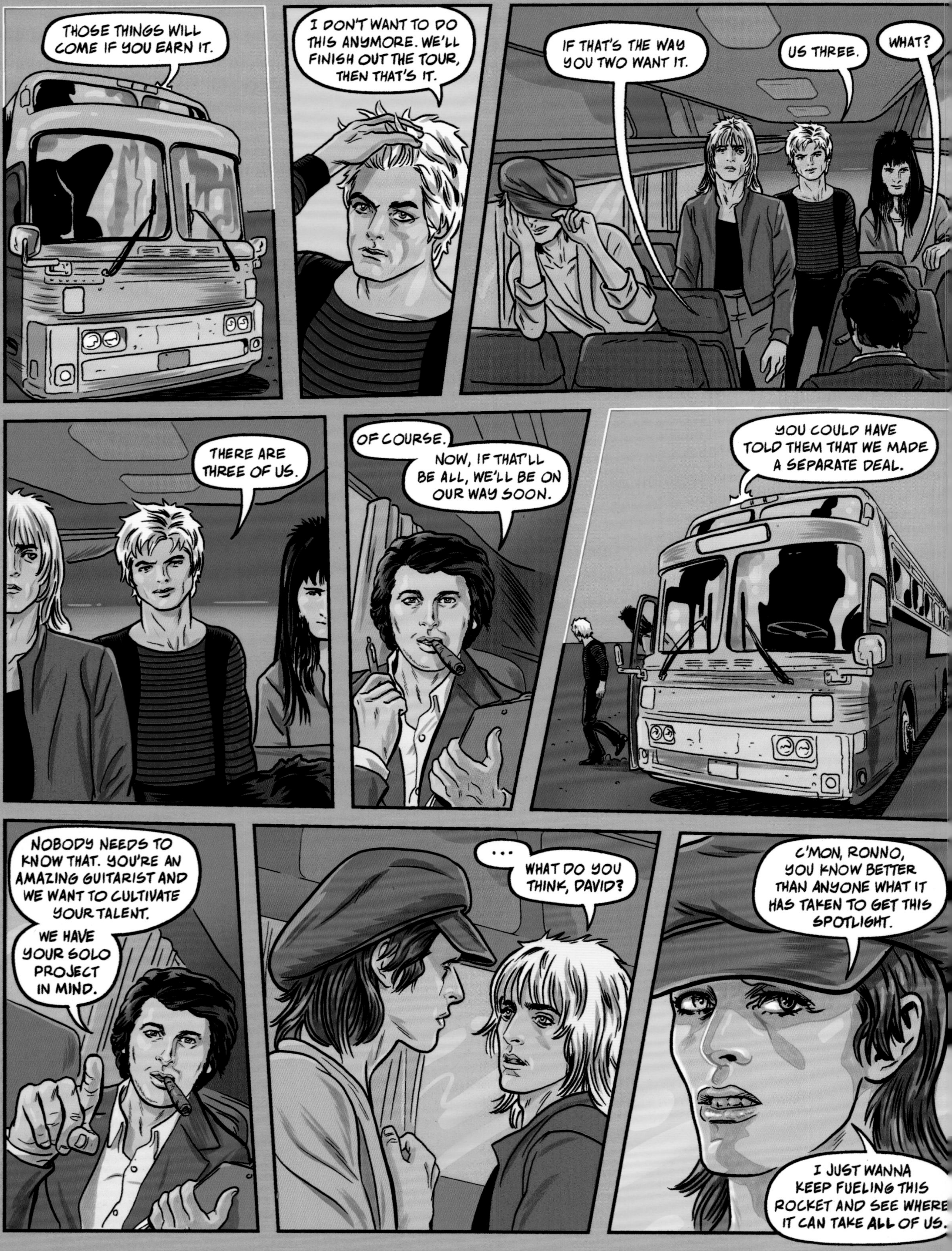
THOSE THINGS WILL COME IF YOU EARN IT.
I DON'T WANT TO DO THIS ANYMORE. WE'LL FINISH OUT THE TOUR, THEN THAT'S IT.
IF THAT'S THE WAY YOU TWO WANT IT.
US THREE.
WHAT?
THERE ARE THREE OF US.
OF COURSE.
NOW, IF THAT'LL BE ALL, WE'LL BE ON OUR WAY SOON.
YOU COULD HAVE TOLD THEM THAT WE MADE A SEPARATE DEAL.
NOBODY NEEDS TO KNOW THAT. YOU'RE AN AMAZING GUITARIST AND WE WANT TO CULTIVATE YOUR TALENT.
WE HAVE YOUR SOLO PROJECT IN MIND.
...
WHAT DO YOU THINK, DAVID?
C'MON, RONNO, YOU KNOW BETTER THAN ANYONE WHAT IT HAS TAKEN TO GET THIS SPOTLIGHT.
I JUST WANNA KEEP FUELING THIS ROCKET AND SEE WHERE IT CAN TAKE ALL OF US.

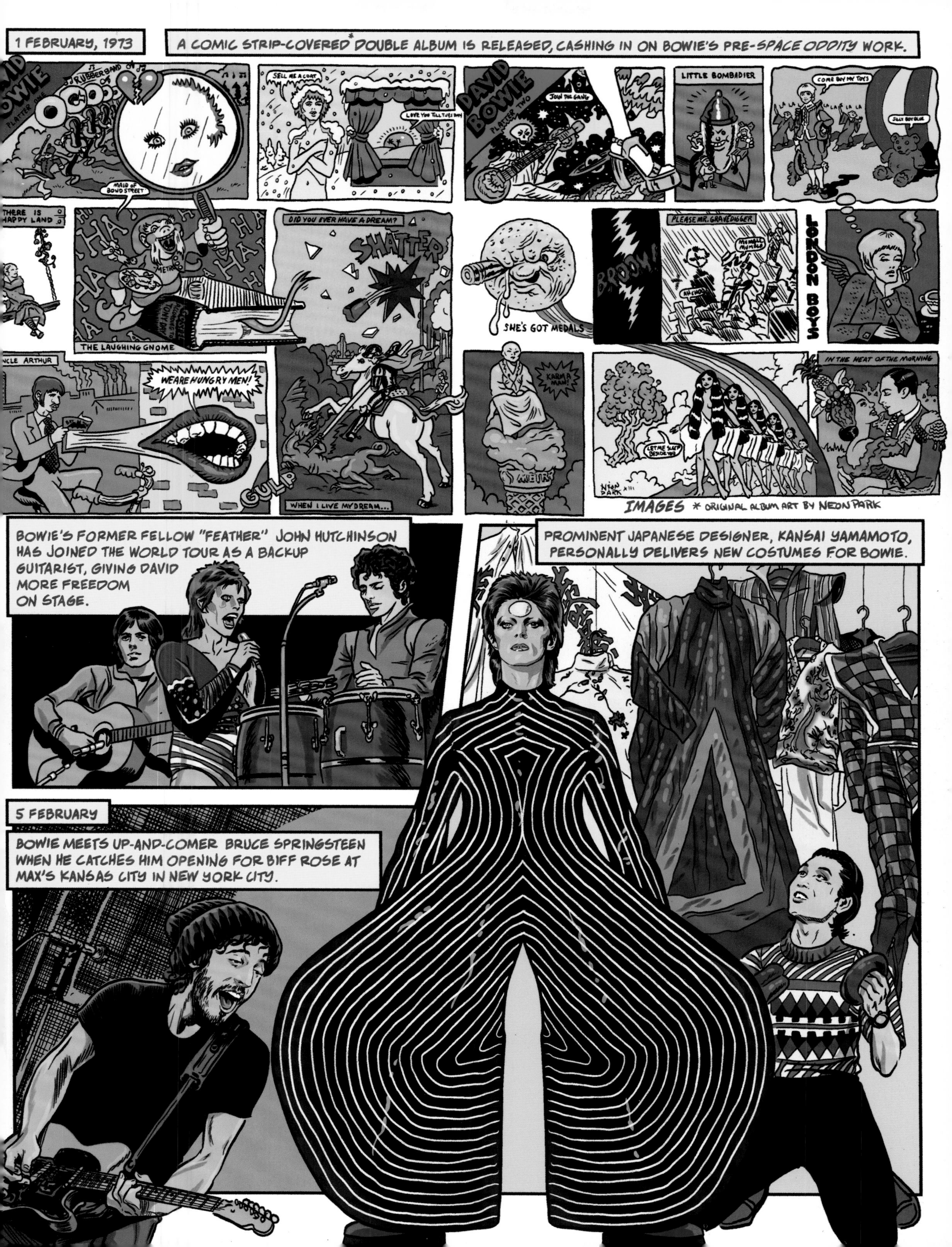

1 FEBRUARY, 1973
A COMIC STRIP-COVERED* DOUBLE ALBUM IS RELEASED, CASHING IN ON BOWIE'S PRE-SPACE ODDITY WORK.
DAVID BOWIE PLATTER ONE
RUBBERBAND
MAID OF BOND STREET
SELL ME A COAT
LOVE YOU TILL TUESDAY
DAVID BOWIE PLATTER TWO
JOIN THE GANG
LITTLE BOMBADIER
COME BUY MY TOYS
LA LA LA LA LA LA
SILLY BOY BLUE
THERE IS HAPPY LAND
THE LAUGHING GNOME
DID YOU EVER HAVE A DREAM?
SHATTER
SHE'S GOT MEDALS
BROOM!
PLEASE MR. GRAVEDIGGER
LONDON BOYS
UNCLE ARTHUR
WE ARE HUNGRY MEN!
GULP
WHEN I LIVE MY DREAM...
KARMA MAN!
LET ME SLEEP BESIDE YOU
IN THE HEAT OF THE MORNING
NEON PARK
IMAGES * ORIGINAL ALBUM ART BY NEON PARK
BOWIE'S FORMER FELLOW "FEATHER" JOHN HUTCHINSON HAS JOINED THE WORLD TOUR AS A BACKUP GUITARIST, GIVING DAVID MORE FREEDOM ON STAGE.
PROMINENT JAPANESE DESIGNER, KANSAI YAMAMOTO, PERSONALLY DELIVERS NEW COSTUMES FOR BOWIE.
5 FEBRUARY
BOWIE MEETS UP-AND-COMER BRUCE SPRINGSTEEN WHEN HE CATCHES HIM OPENING FOR BIFF ROSE AT MAX'S KANSAS CITY IN NEW YORK CITY.

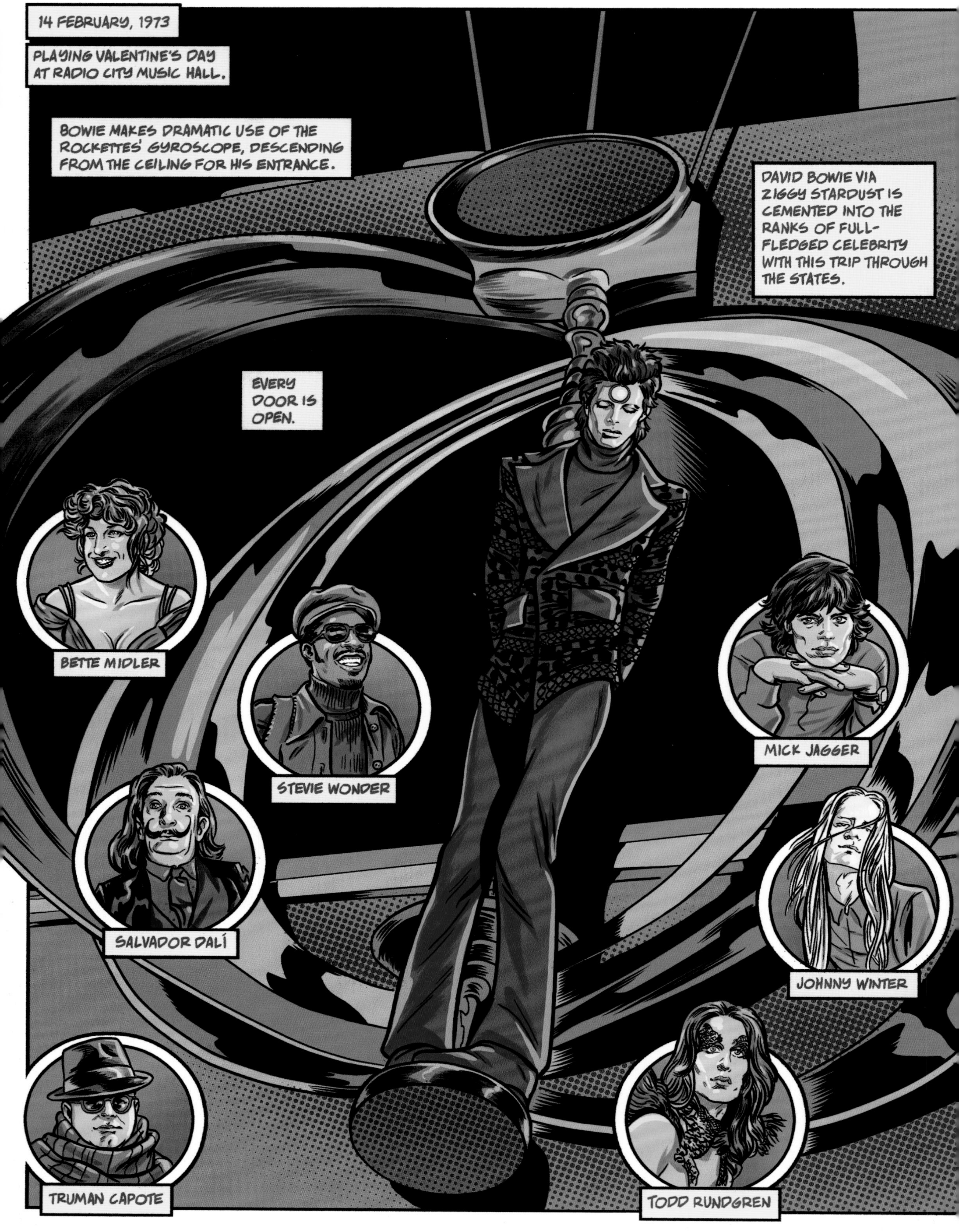
14 FEBRUARY, 1973
PLAYING VALENTINE'S DAY AT RADIO CITY MUSIC HALL.
BOWIE MAKES DRAMATIC USE OF THE ROCKETTES' GYROSCOPE, DESCENDING FROM THE CEILING FOR HIS ENTRANCE.
DAVID BOWIE VIA ZIGGY STARDUST IS CEMENTED INTO THE RANKS OF FULL-FLEDGED CELEBRITY WITH THIS TRIP THROUGH THE STATES.
EVERY DOOR IS OPEN.
BETTE MIDLER
STEVIE WONDER
MICK JAGGER
SALVADOR DALÍ
JOHNNY WINTER
TRUMAN CAPOTE
TODD RUNDGREN

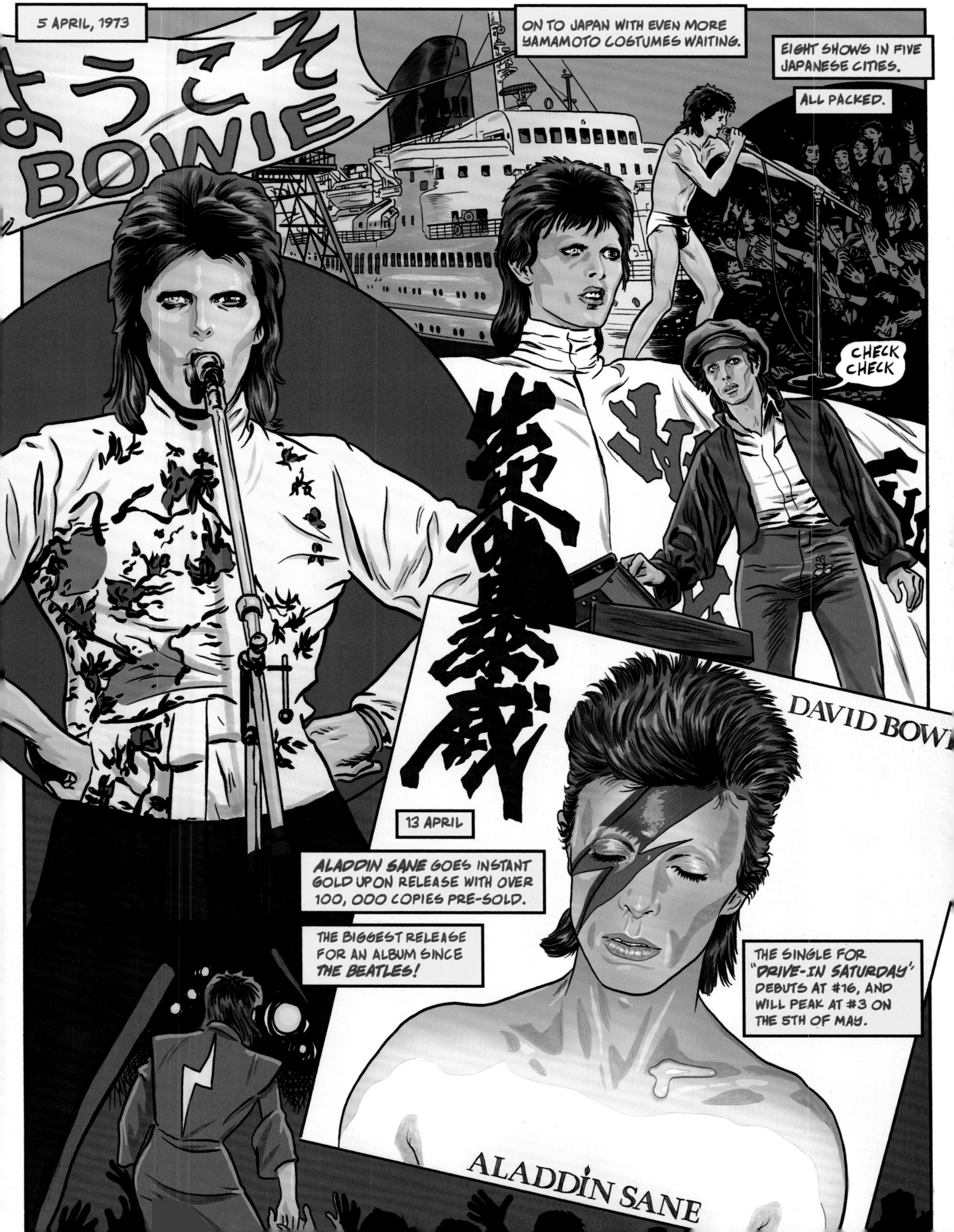

5 APRIL, 1973
ようこそ BOWIE
ON TO JAPAN WITH EVEN MORE YAMAMOTO COSTUMES WAITING.
EIGHT SHOWS IN FIVE JAPANESE CITIES.
ALL PACKED.
CHECK CHECK
DAVID BOWI
13 APRIL
ALADDIN SANE GOES INSTANT GOLD UPON RELEASE WITH OVER 100, 000 COPIES PRE-SOLD.
THE BIGGEST RELEASE FOR AN ALBUM SINCE *THE BEATLES!*
THE SINGLE FOR "*DRIVE-IN SATURDAY*" DEBUTS AT #16, AND WILL PEAK AT #3 ON THE 5TH OF MAY.
ALADDIN SANE

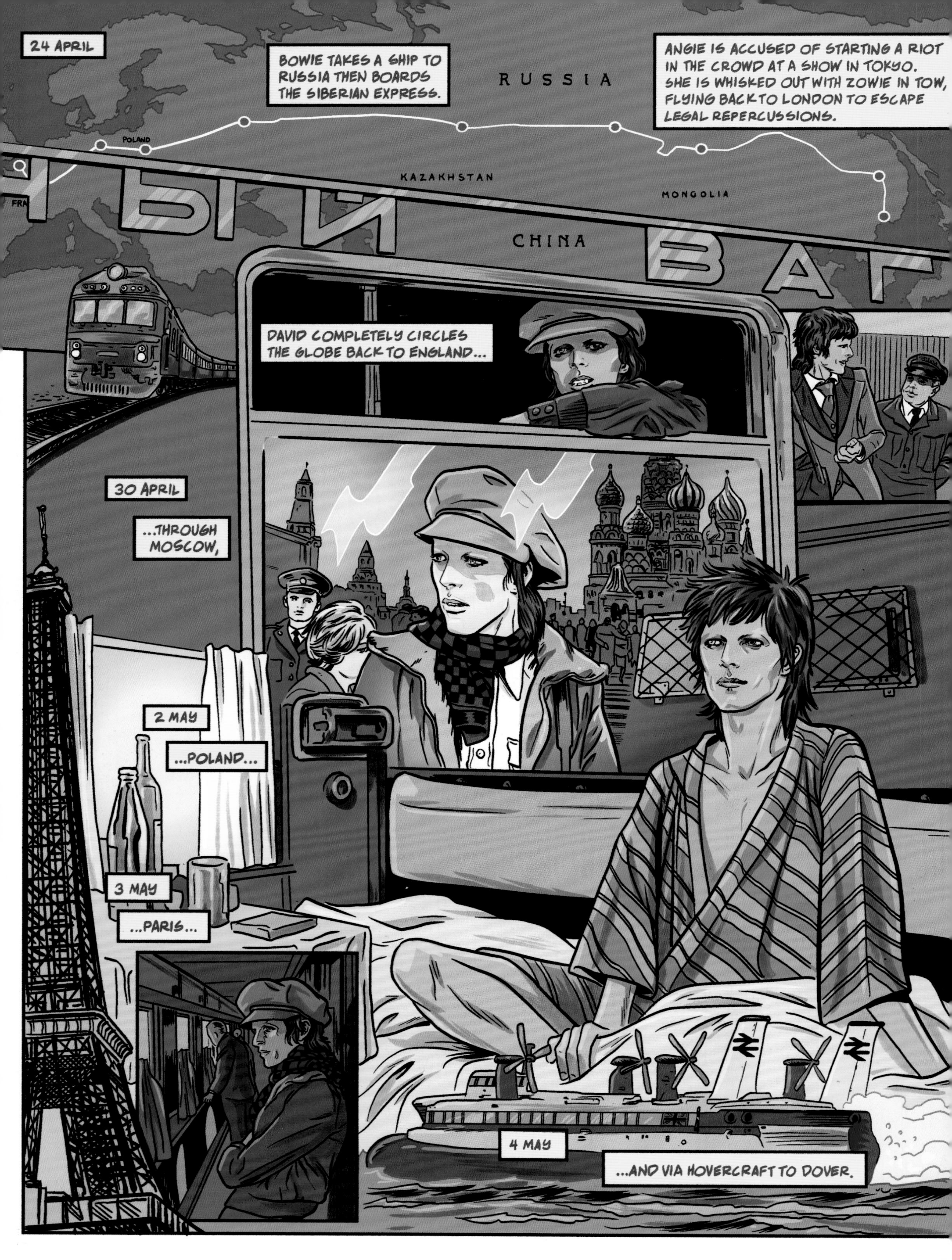
24 APRIL
BOWIE TAKES A SHIP TO RUSSIA THEN BOARDS THE SIBERIAN EXPRESS.
RUSSIA
ANGIE IS ACCUSED OF STARTING A RIOT IN THE CROWD AT A SHOW IN TOKYO. SHE IS WHISKED OUT WITH ZOWIE IN TOW, FLYING BACK TO LONDON TO ESCAPE LEGAL REPERCUSSIONS.
POLAND
KAZAKHSTAN
MONGOLIA
CHINA
DAVID COMPLETELY CIRCLES THE GLOBE BACK TO ENGLAND...
30 APRIL
...THROUGH MOSCOW,
2 MAY
...POLAND...
3 MAY
...PARIS...
4 MAY
...AND VIA HOVERCRAFT TO DOVER.

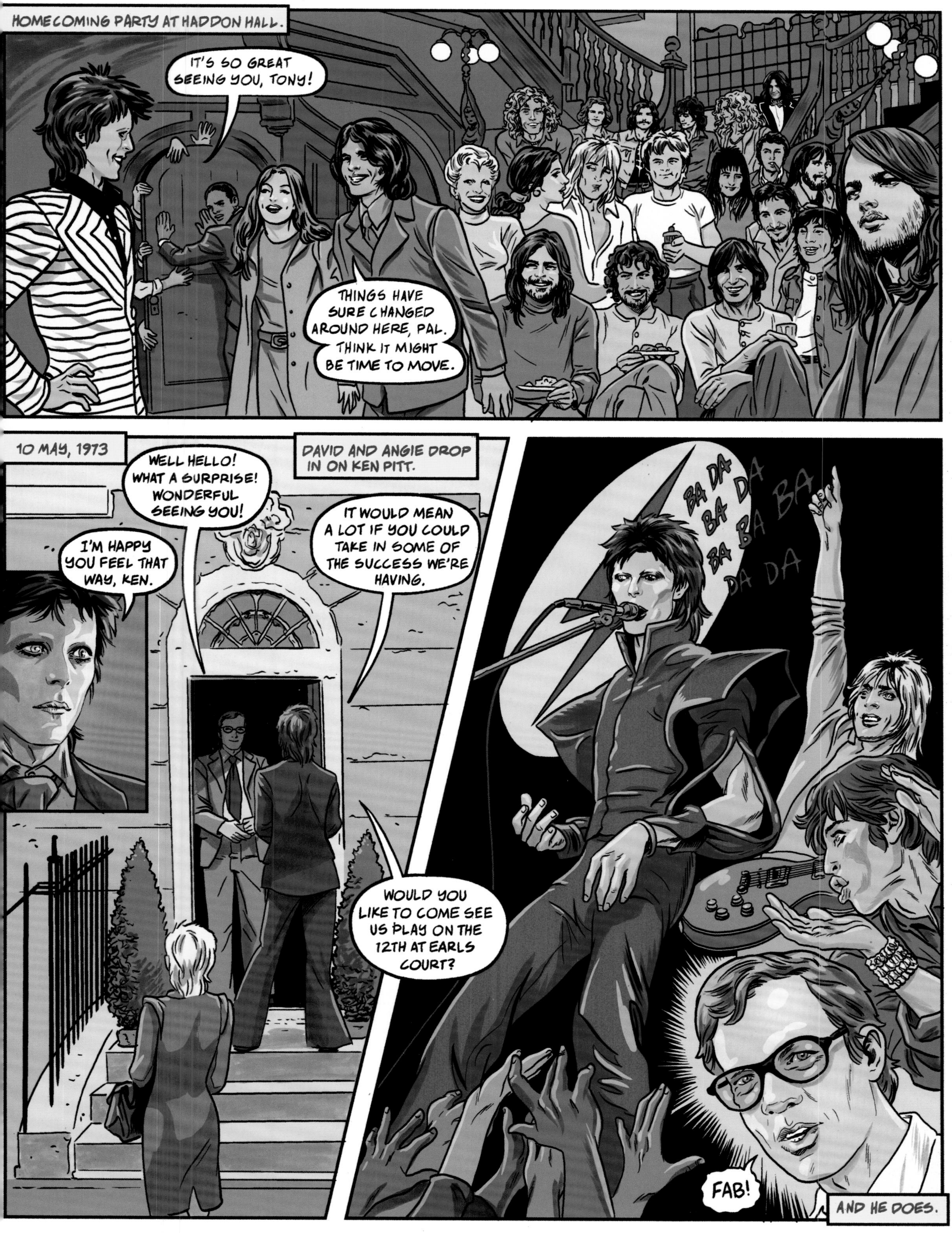
HOMECOMING PARTY AT HADDON HALL.
IT'S SO GREAT SEEING YOU, TONY!
THINGS HAVE SURE CHANGED AROUND HERE, PAL. THINK IT MIGHT BE TIME TO MOVE.
10 MAY, 1973
DAVID AND ANGIE DROP IN ON KEN PITT.
WELL HELLO! WHAT A SURPRISE! WONDERFUL SEEING YOU!
I'M HAPPY YOU FEEL THAT WAY, KEN.
IT WOULD MEAN A LOT IF YOU COULD TAKE IN SOME OF THE SUCCESS WE'RE HAVING.
WOULD YOU LIKE TO COME SEE US PLAY ON THE 12TH AT EARLS COURT?
BA DA BA DA BA BA BA BA BA DA DA
FAB!
AND HE DOES.

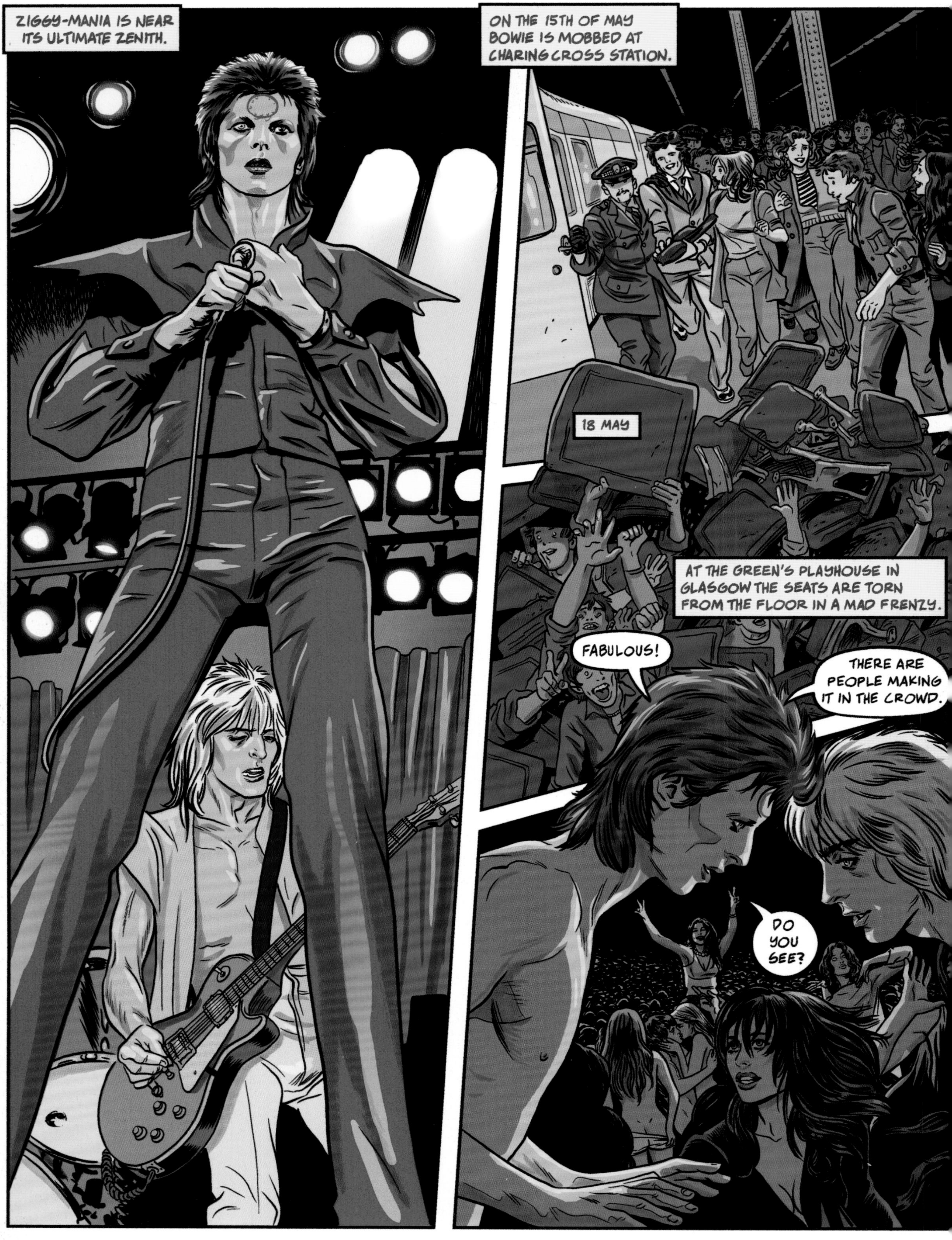
ZIGGY-MANIA IS NEAR ITS ULTIMATE ZENITH.
ON THE 15TH OF MAY BOWIE IS MOBBED AT CHARING CROSS STATION.
18 MAY
AT THE GREEN'S PLAYHOUSE IN GLASGOW THE SEATS ARE TORN FROM THE FLOOR IN A MAD FRENZY.
FABULOUS!
THERE ARE PEOPLE MAKING IT IN THE CROWD.
DO YOU SEE?

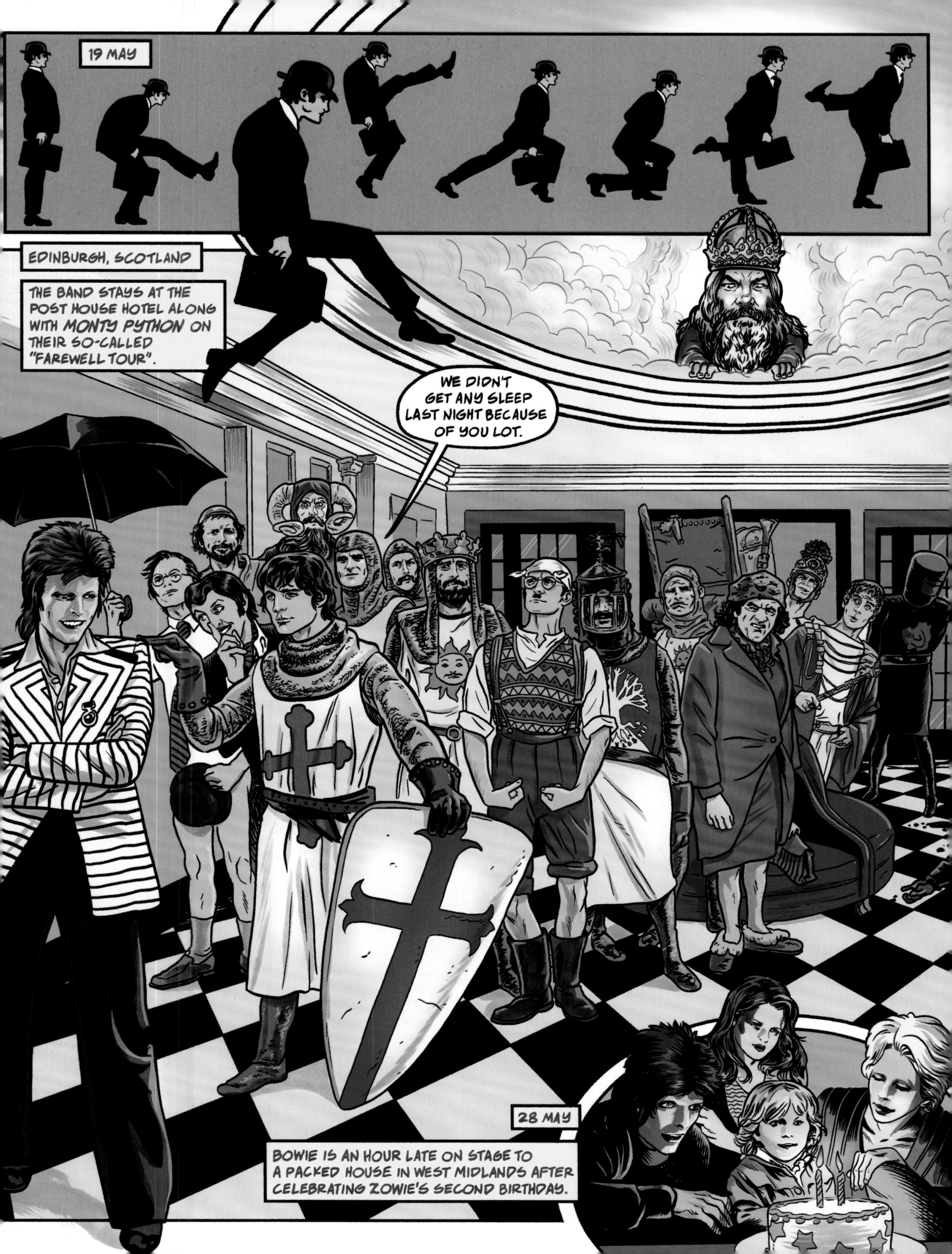

19 MAY
EDINBURGH, SCOTLAND
THE BAND STAYS AT THE POST HOUSE HOTEL ALONG WITH MONTY PYTHON ON THEIR SO-CALLED "FAREWELL TOUR".
WE DIDN'T GET ANY SLEEP LAST NIGHT BECAUSE OF YOU LOT.
28 MAY
BOWIE IS AN HOUR LATE ON STAGE TO A PACKED HOUSE IN WEST MIDLANDS AFTER CELEBRATING ZOWIE'S SECOND BIRTHDAY.

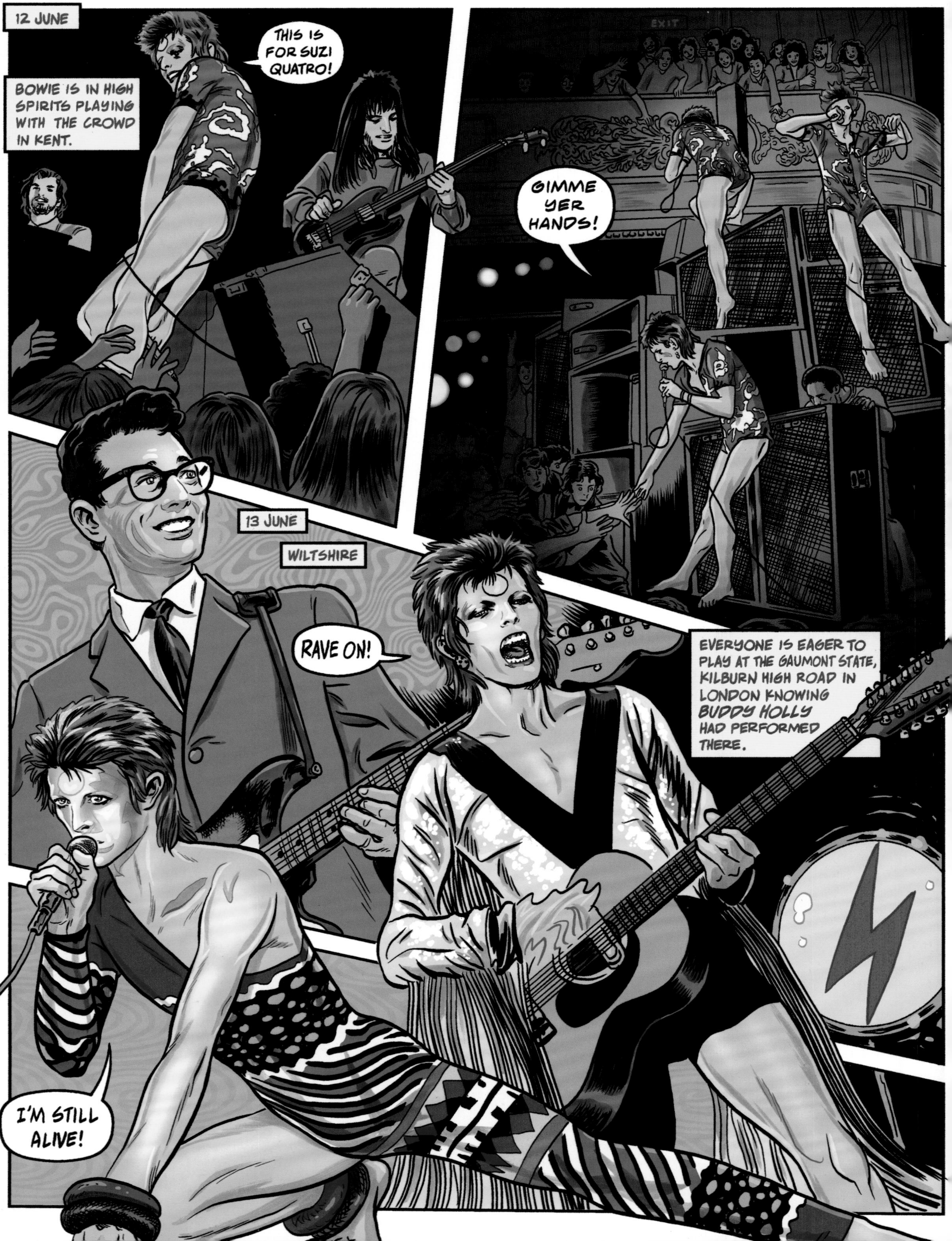
12 JUNE
BOWIE IS IN HIGH SPIRITS PLAYING WITH THE CROWD IN KENT.
THIS IS FOR SUZI QUATRO!
EXIT
GIMME YER HANDS!
13 JUNE
WILTSHIRE
RAVE ON!
EVERYONE IS EAGER TO PLAY AT THE GAUMONT STATE, KILBURN HIGH ROAD IN LONDON KNOWING BUDDY HOLLY HAD PERFORMED THERE.
I'M STILL ALIVE!

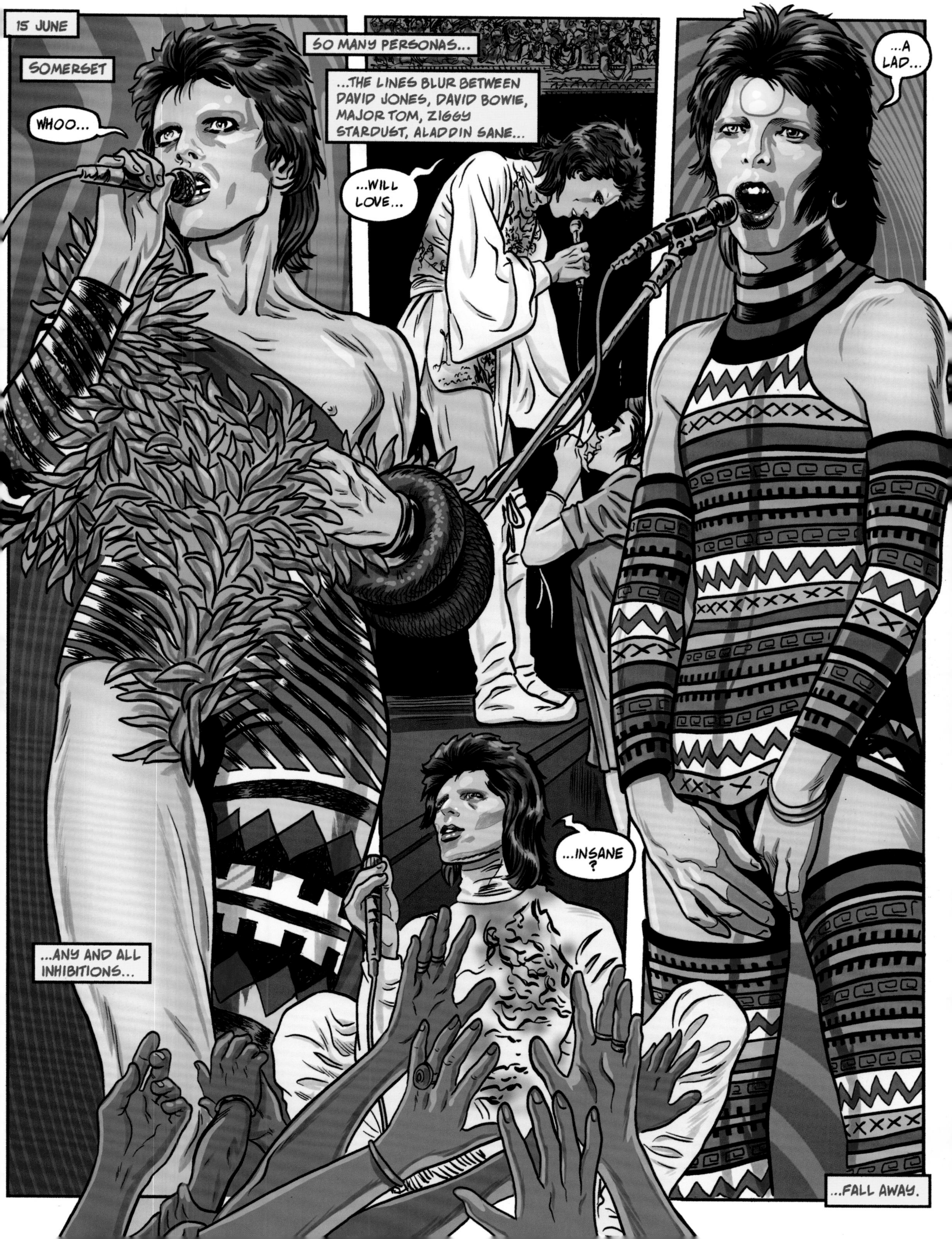
15 JUNE
SOMERSET
WHOO...
SO MANY PERSONAS...
...THE LINES BLUR BETWEEN DAVID JONES, DAVID BOWIE, MAJOR TOM, ZIGGY STARDUST, ALADDIN SANE...
...WILL LOVE...
...A LAD...
...INSANE?
...ANY AND ALL INHIBITIONS...
...FALL AWAY.

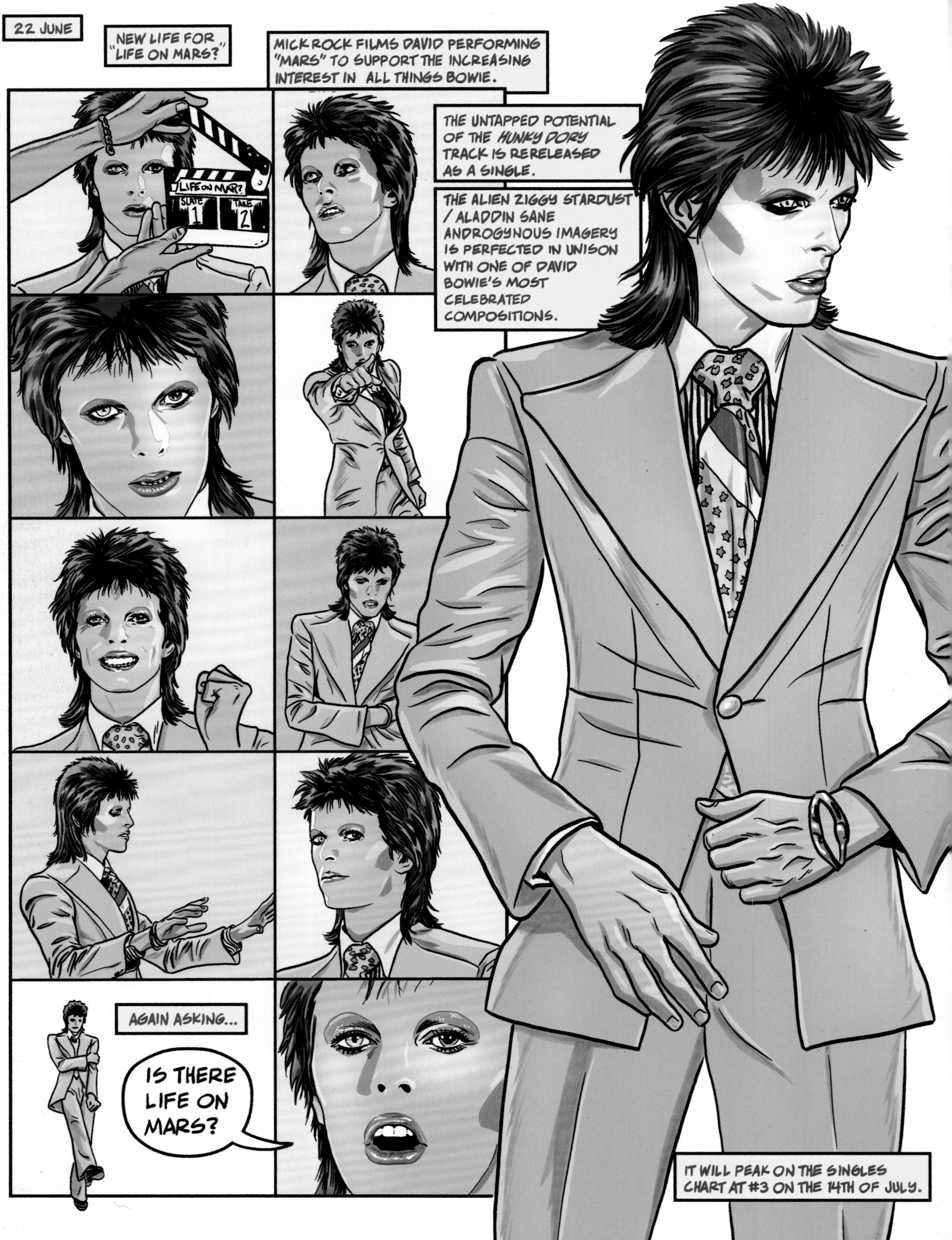
22 JUNE
"NEW LIFE FOR "LIFE ON MARS?"
MICK ROCK FILMS DAVID PERFORMING "MARS" TO SUPPORT THE INCREASING INTEREST IN ALL THINGS BOWIE.
LIFE ON MARS?
SLATE 1
TAKE 2
THE UNTAPPED POTENTIAL OF THE HUNKY DORY TRACK IS RERELEASED AS A SINGLE.
THE ALIEN ZIGGY STARDUST / ALADDIN SANE ANDROGYNOUS IMAGERY IS PERFECTED IN UNISON WITH ONE OF DAVID BOWIE'S MOST CELEBRATED COMPOSITIONS.
AGAIN ASKING...
IS THERE LIFE ON MARS?
IT WILL PEAK ON THE SINGLES CHART AT #3 ON THE 14TH OF JULY.

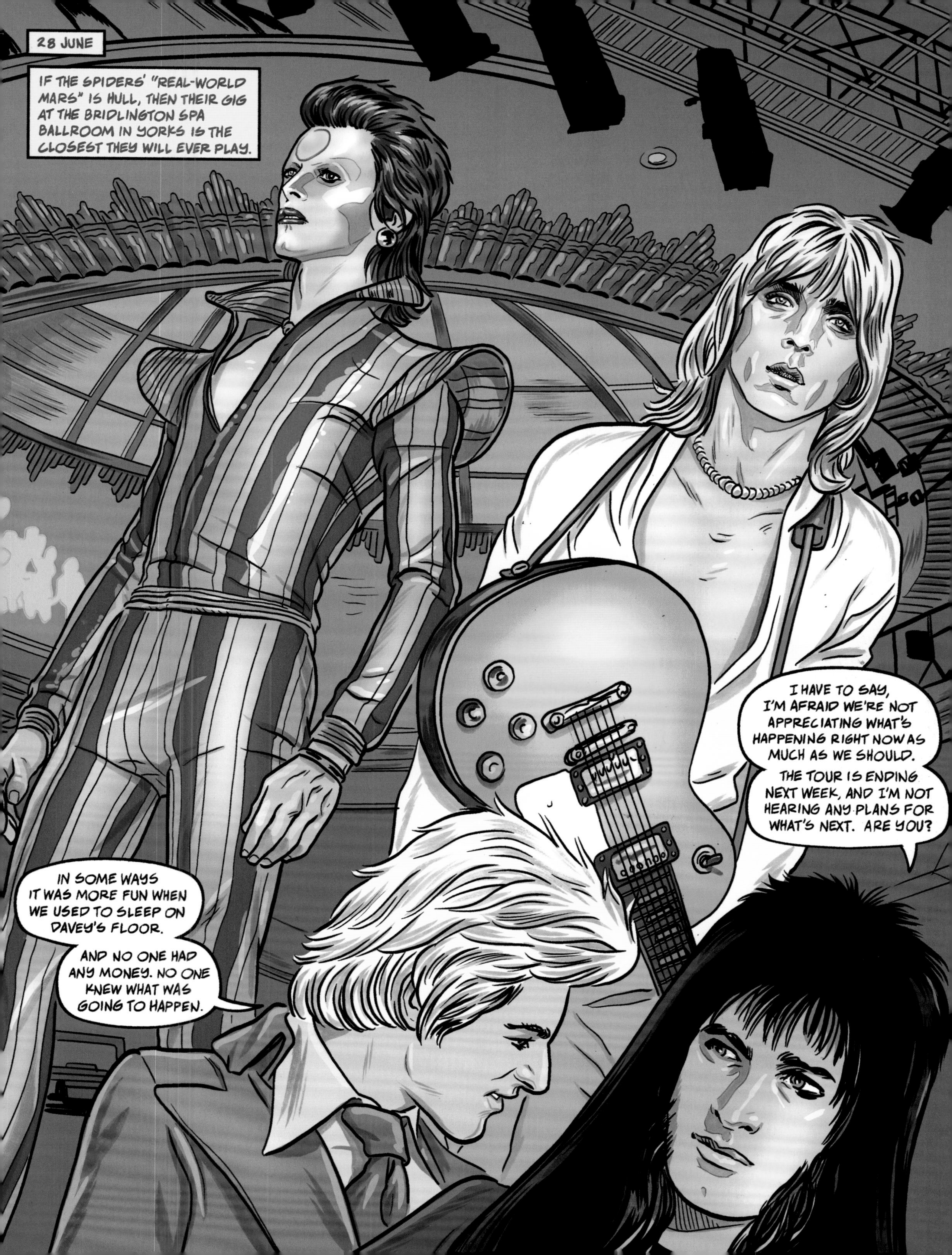
28 JUNE
IF THE SPIDERS' "REAL-WORLD MARS" IS HULL, THEN THEIR GIG AT THE BRIDLINGTON SPA BALLROOM IN YORKS IS THE CLOSEST THEY WILL EVER PLAY.
I HAVE TO SAY, I'M AFRAID WE'RE NOT APPRECIATING WHAT'S HAPPENING RIGHT NOW AS MUCH AS WE SHOULD.
THE TOUR IS ENDING NEXT WEEK, AND I'M NOT HEARING ANY PLANS FOR WHAT'S NEXT. ARE YOU?
IN SOME WAYS IT WAS MORE FUN WHEN WE USED TO SLEEP ON DAVEY'S FLOOR.
AND NO ONE HAD ANY MONEY. NO ONE KNEW WHAT WAS GOING TO HAPPEN.

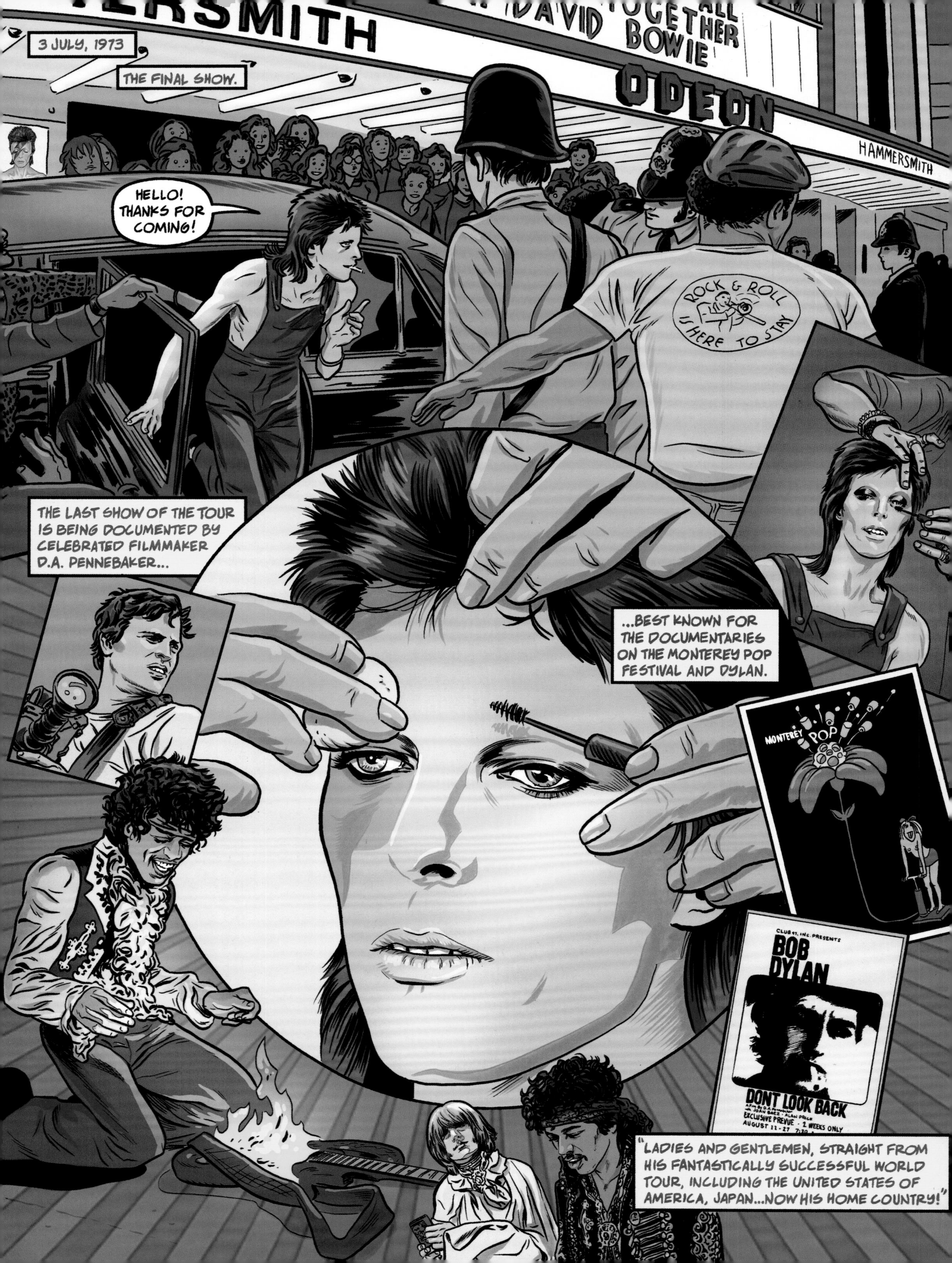

...RSMITH
DAVID BOWIE
TOGETHER
ODEON
HAMMERSMITH
3 JULY, 1973
THE FINAL SHOW.
HELLO! THANKS FOR COMING!
ROCK & ROLL IS HERE TO STAY
THE LAST SHOW OF THE TOUR IS BEING DOCUMENTED BY CELEBRATED FILMMAKER D.A. PENNEBAKER...
...BEST KNOWN FOR THE DOCUMENTARIES ON THE MONTEREY POP FESTIVAL AND DYLAN.
MONTEREY POP
BOB DYLAN
DONT LOOK BACK
EXCLUSIVE PREVUE · 2 WEEKS ONLY
"LADIES AND GENTLEMEN, STRAIGHT FROM HIS FANTASTICALLY SUCCESSFUL WORLD TOUR, INCLUDING THE UNITED STATES OF AMERICA, JAPAN...NOW HIS HOME COUNTRY!"

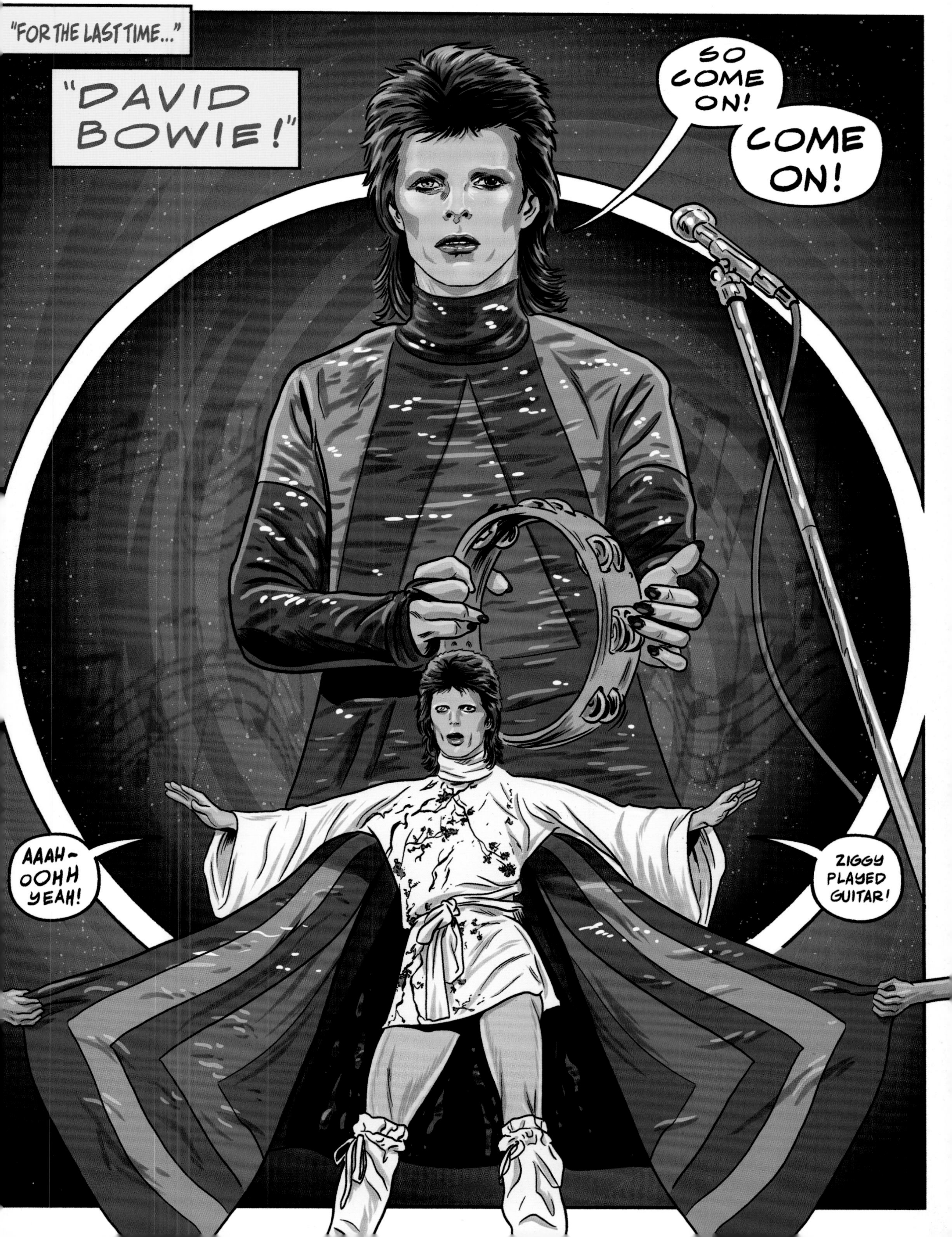
"FOR THE LAST TIME..."
"DAVID BOWIE!"
SO COME ON!
COME ON!
AAAH-OOHH YEAH!
ZIGGY PLAYED GUITAR!

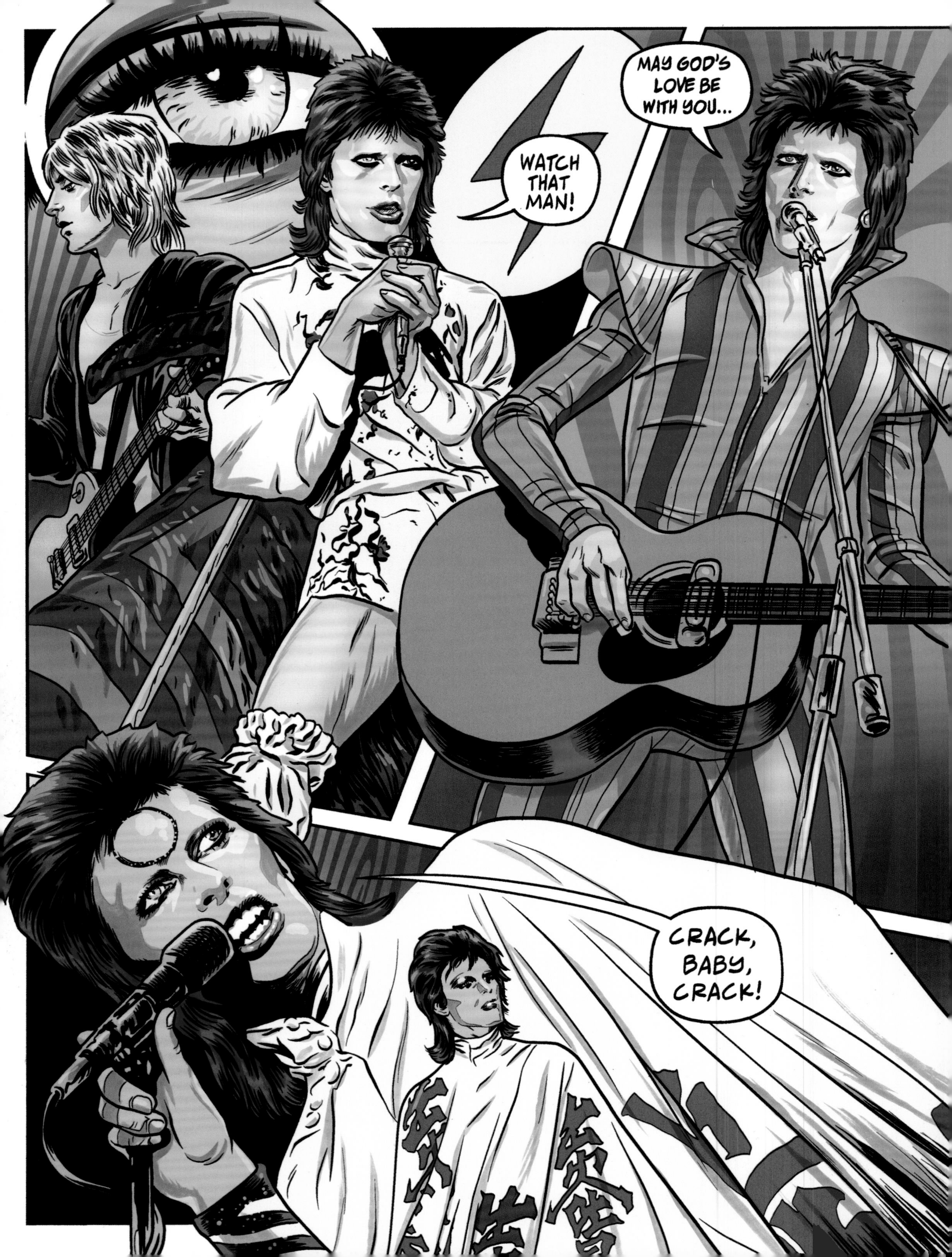
WATCH THAT MAN!
MAY GOD'S LOVE BE WITH YOU...
CRACK, BABY, CRACK!

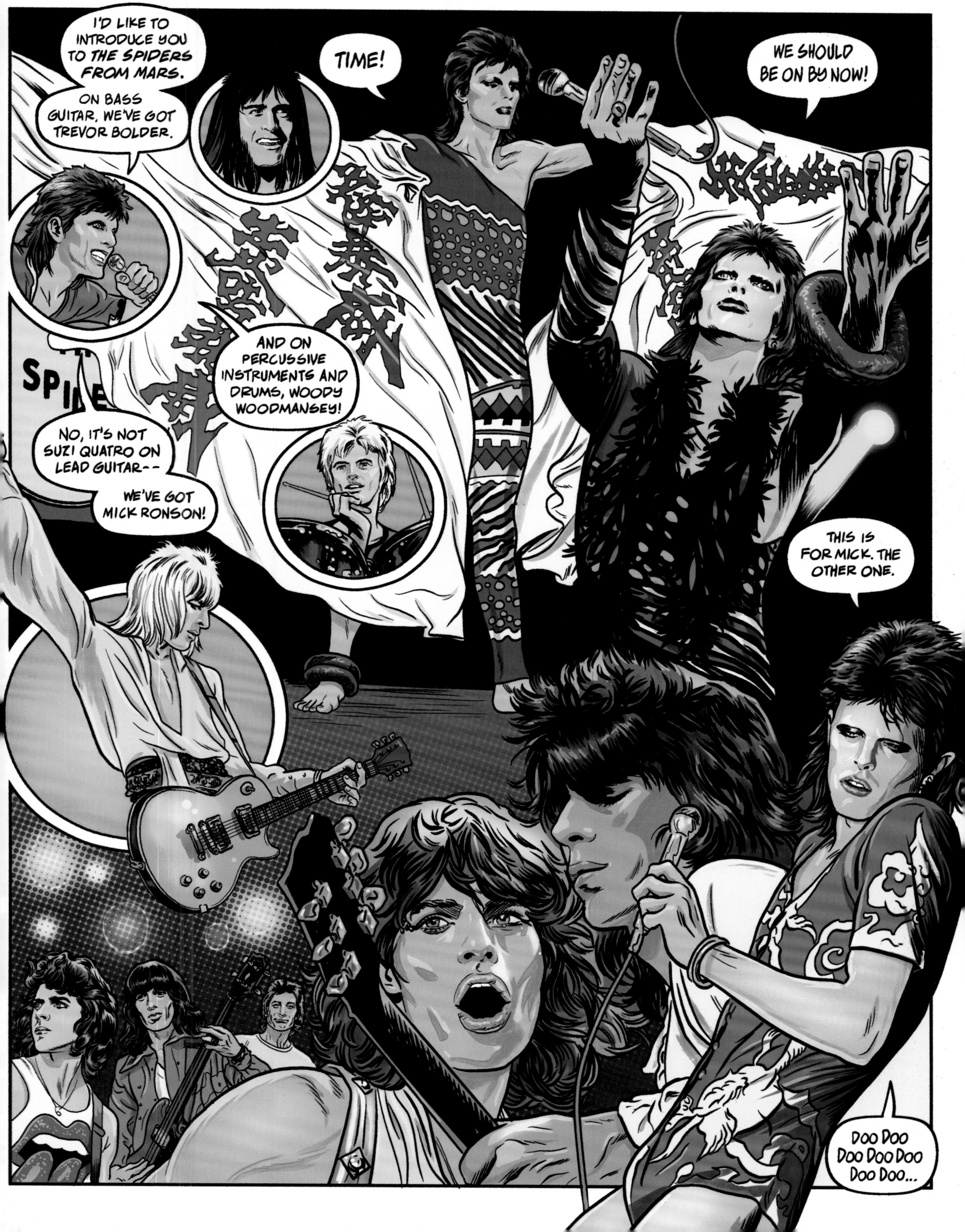

I'D LIKE TO INTRODUCE YOU TO THE SPIDERS FROM MARS.
ON BASS GUITAR, WE'VE GOT TREVOR BOLDER.
TIME!
WE SHOULD BE ON BY NOW!
AND ON PERCUSSIVE INSTRUMENTS AND DRUMS, WOODY WOODMANSEY!
NO, IT'S NOT SUZI QUATRO ON LEAD GUITAR--
WE'VE GOT MICK RONSON!
THIS IS FOR MICK. THE OTHER ONE.
DOO DOO DOO DOO DOO DOO DOO...

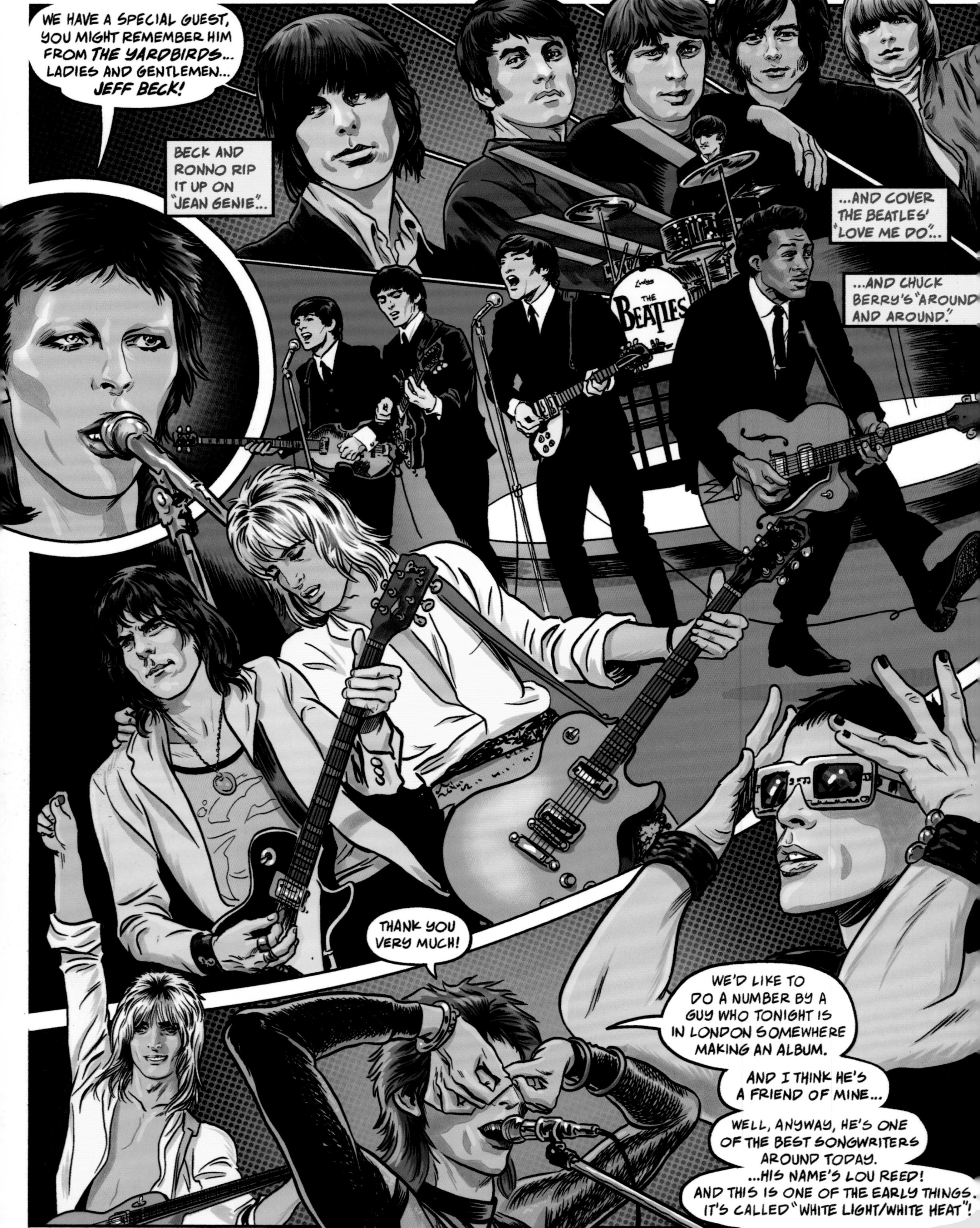

WE HAVE A SPECIAL GUEST, YOU MIGHT REMEMBER HIM FROM THE YARDBIRDS... LADIES AND GENTLEMEN... JEFF BECK!
BECK AND RONNO RIP IT UP ON "JEAN GENIE"...
...AND COVER THE BEATLES' "LOVE ME DO"...
...AND CHUCK BERRY'S "AROUND AND AROUND."
THE BEATLES
THANK YOU VERY MUCH!
WE'D LIKE TO DO A NUMBER BY A GUY WHO TONIGHT IS IN LONDON SOMEWHERE MAKING AN ALBUM.
AND I THINK HE'S A FRIEND OF MINE...
WELL, ANYWAY, HE'S ONE OF THE BEST SONGWRITERS AROUND TODAY. ...HIS NAME'S LOU REED! AND THIS IS ONE OF THE EARLY THINGS. IT'S CALLED "WHITE LIGHT/WHITE HEAT"!

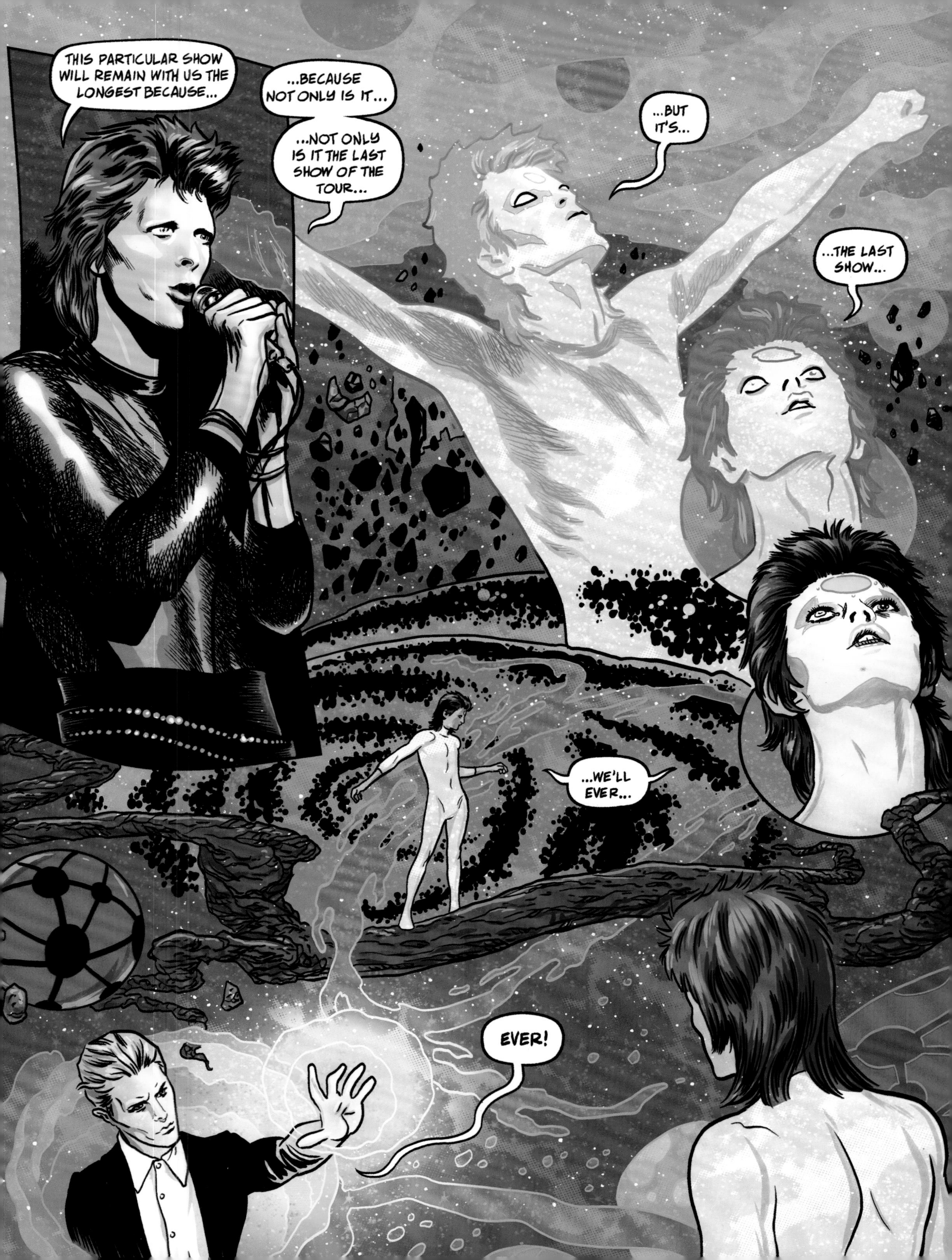
THIS PARTICULAR SHOW WILL REMAIN WITH US THE LONGEST BECAUSE...
...BECAUSE NOT ONLY IS IT...
...NOT ONLY IS IT THE LAST SHOW OF THE TOUR...
...BUT IT'S...
...THE LAST SHOW...
...WE'LL EVER...
EVER!

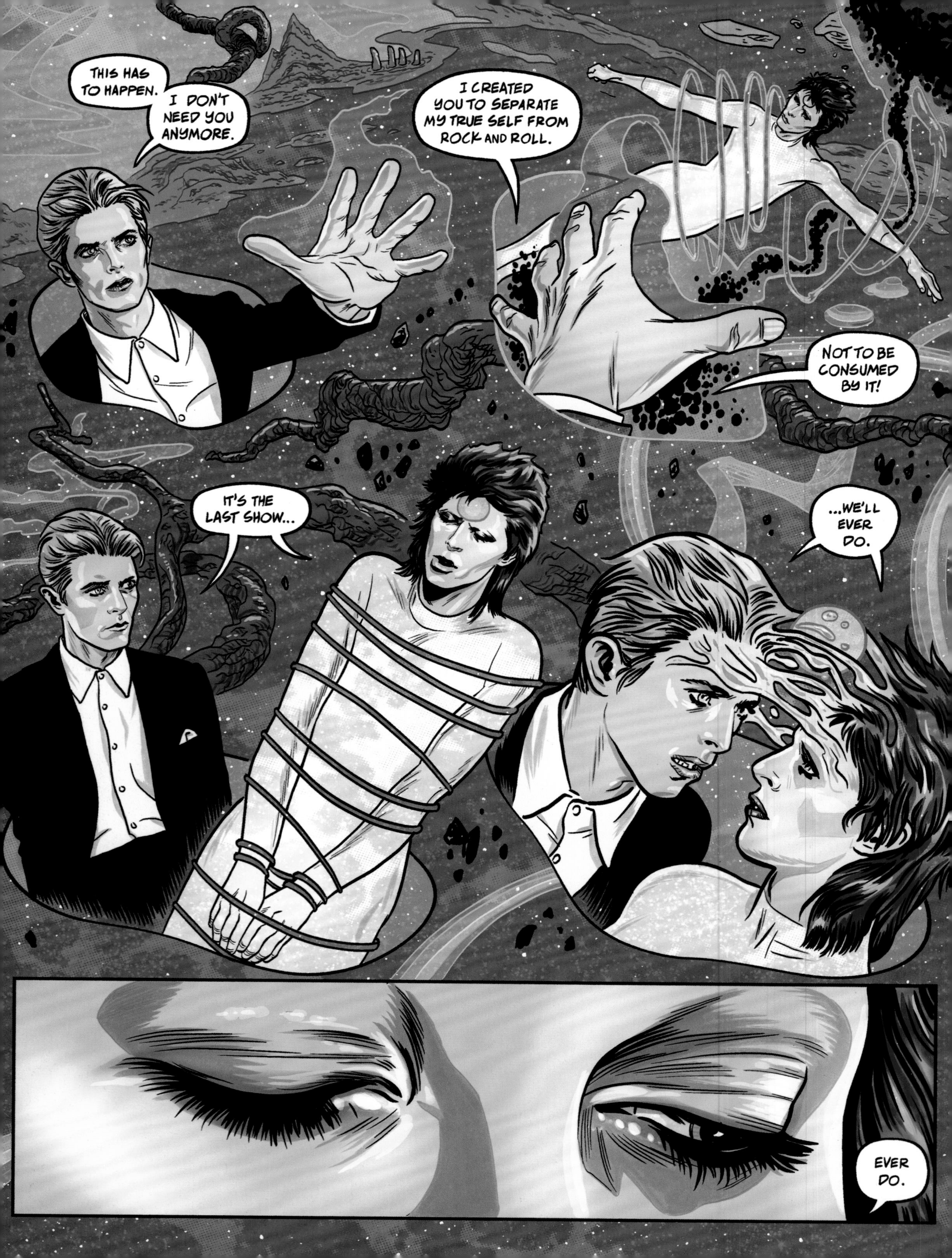
THIS HAS TO HAPPEN.
I DON'T NEED YOU ANYMORE.
I CREATED YOU TO SEPARATE MY TRUE SELF FROM ROCK AND ROLL.
NOT TO BE CONSUMED BY IT!
IT'S THE LAST SHOW...
...WE'LL EVER DO.
EVER DO.

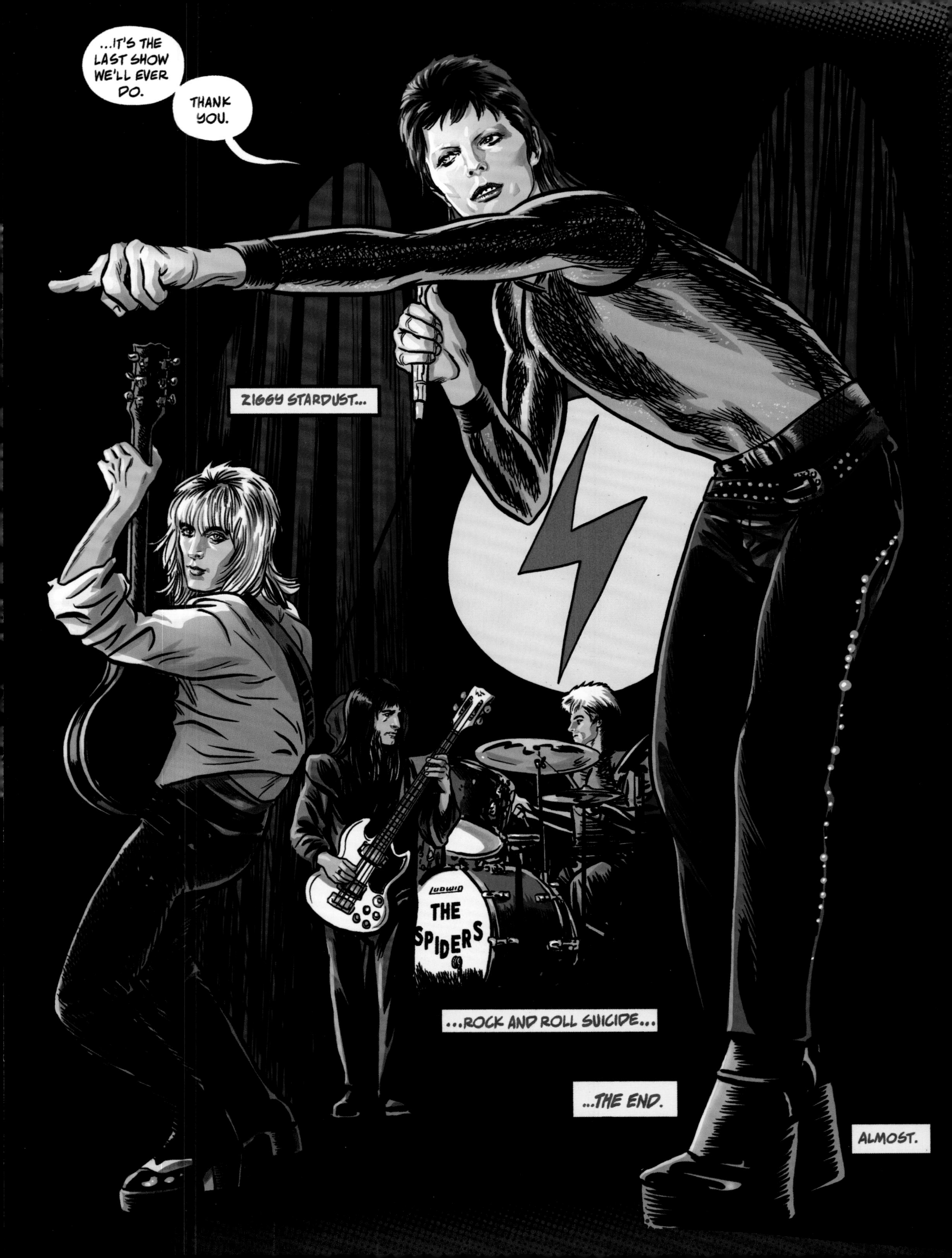
...IT'S THE LAST SHOW WE'LL EVER DO.
THANK YOU.
ZIGGY STARDUST...
THE SPIDERS
...ROCK AND ROLL SUICIDE...
...THE END.
ALMOST.

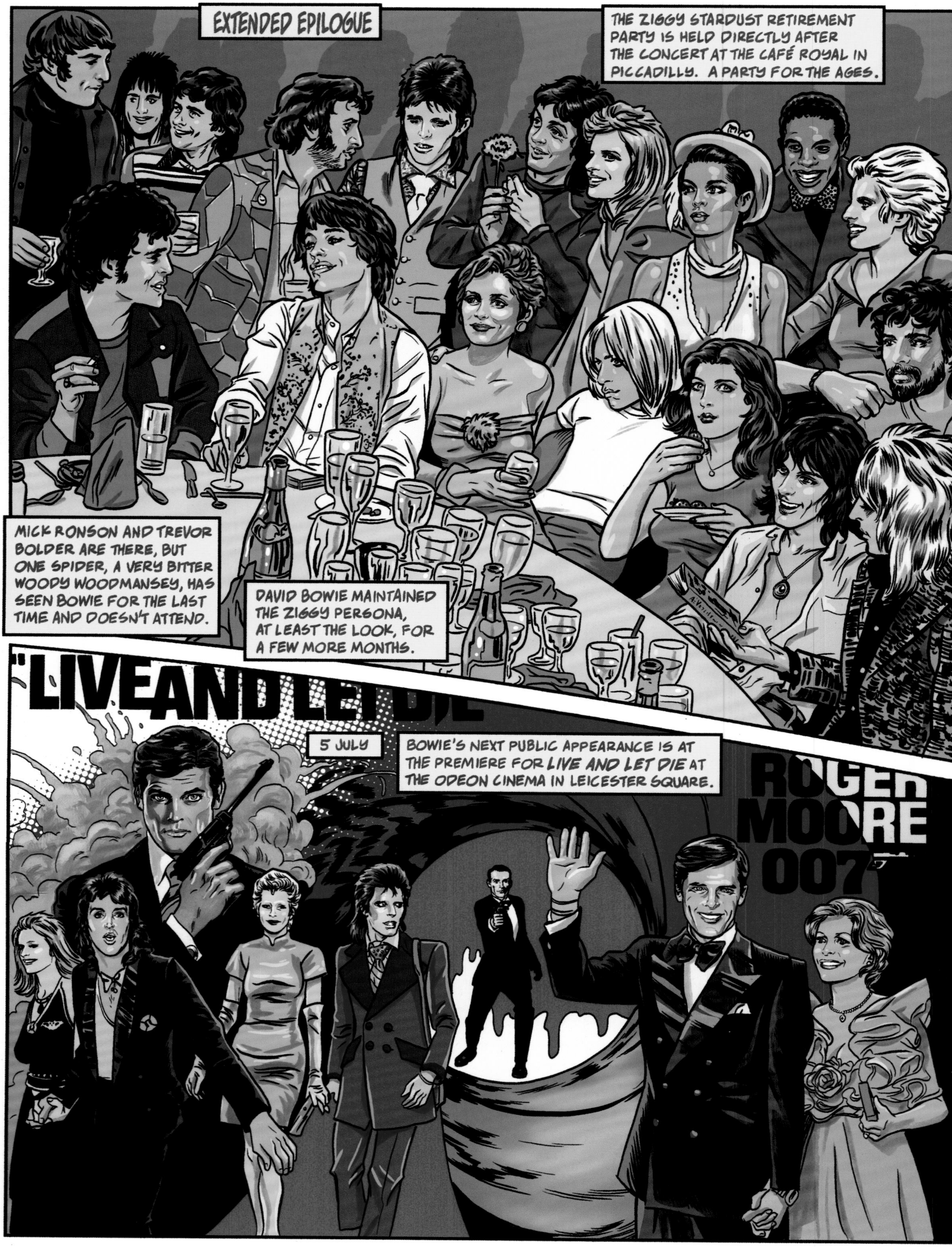
EXTENDED EPILOGUE
THE ZIGGY STARDUST RETIREMENT PARTY IS HELD DIRECTLY AFTER THE CONCERT AT THE CAFÉ ROYAL IN PICCADILLY. A PARTY FOR THE AGES.
MICK RONSON AND TREVOR BOLDER ARE THERE, BUT ONE SPIDER, A VERY BITTER WOODY WOODMANSEY, HAS SEEN BOWIE FOR THE LAST TIME AND DOESN'T ATTEND.
DAVID BOWIE MAINTAINED THE ZIGGY PERSONA, AT LEAST THE LOOK, FOR A FEW MORE MONTHS.
5 JULY
BOWIE'S NEXT PUBLIC APPEARANCE IS AT THE PREMIERE FOR LIVE AND LET DIE AT THE ODEON CINEMA IN LEICESTER SQUARE.
ROGER MOORE 007

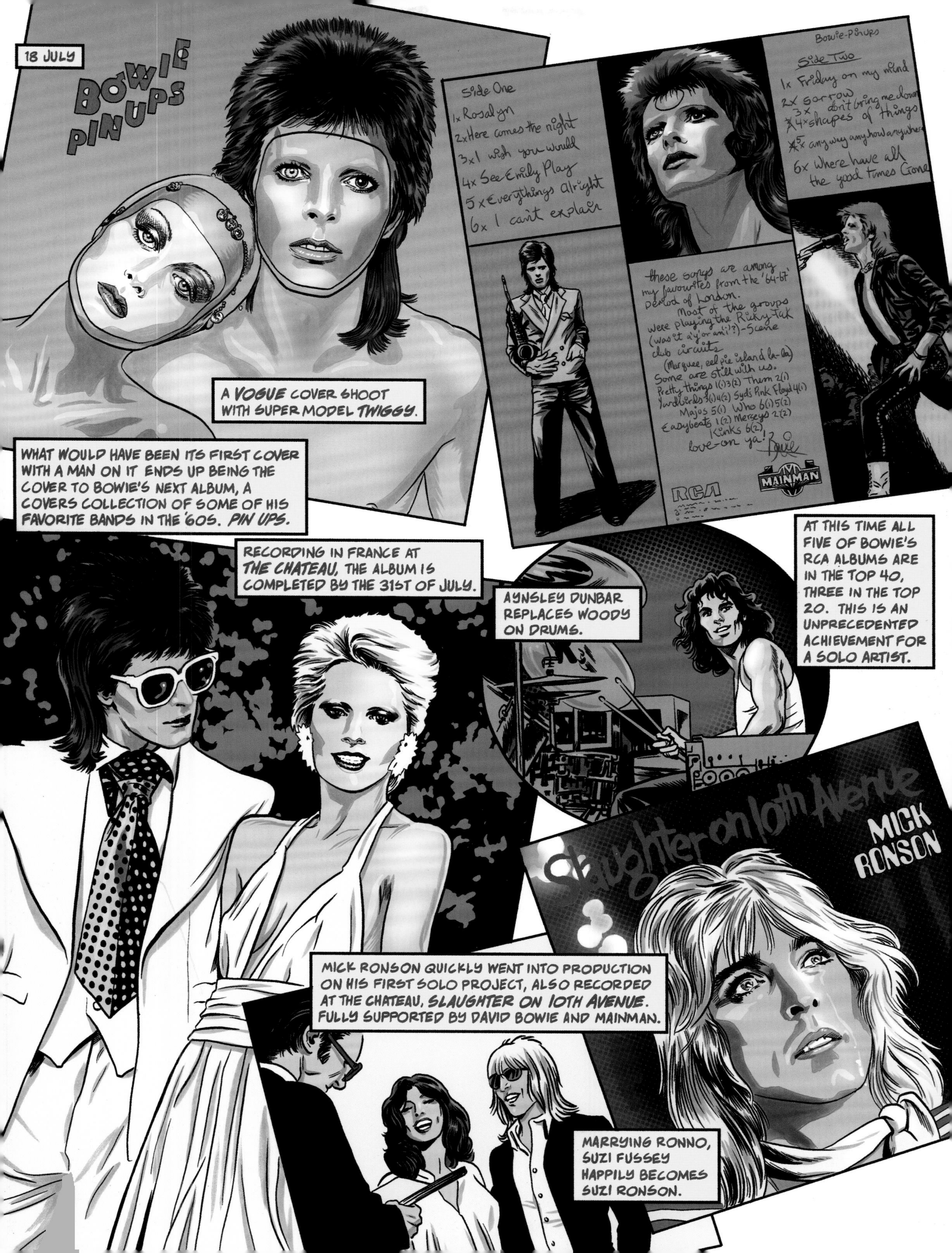

18 JULY
BOWIE PINUPS
A VOGUE COVER SHOOT WITH SUPER MODEL TWIGGY.
WHAT WOULD HAVE BEEN ITS FIRST COVER WITH A MAN ON IT ENDS UP BEING THE COVER TO BOWIE'S NEXT ALBUM, A COVERS COLLECTION OF SOME OF HIS FAVORITE BANDS IN THE '60S. PIN UPS.
Side One
1x Rosalyn
2x Here comes the night
3x I wish you would
4x See Emily Play
5x Everythings Alright
6x I can't explain
Bowie-Pinups
Side Two
1x Friday on my mind
2x Sorrow
3x don't bring me down
4x shapes of things
5x anyway anyhow anywhere
6x Where have all the good times Gone
these songs are among my favourites from the '64-67' period of London.
Most of the groups were playing the Ricky-Tick (was it a'yo'ani?)-Scene club circuits
(Marquee, eel pie island la-la)
Some are still with us.
Pretty things 1(1)3(2) Them 2(1)
Yardbirds 3(1)4(2) Syd's Pink Floyd 4(1)
Mojos 5(1) Who 6(1)5(2)
Easybeats 1(2) Merseys 2(2)
Kinks 6(2)
love-on ya!
Bowie
RCA
MAINMAN
RECORDING IN FRANCE AT THE CHATEAU, THE ALBUM IS COMPLETED BY THE 31ST OF JULY.
AYNSLEY DUNBAR REPLACES WOODY ON DRUMS.
AT THIS TIME ALL FIVE OF BOWIE'S RCA ALBUMS ARE IN THE TOP 40, THREE IN THE TOP 20. THIS IS AN UNPRECEDENTED ACHIEVEMENT FOR A SOLO ARTIST.
Slaughter on 10th Avenue
MICK RONSON
MICK RONSON QUICKLY WENT INTO PRODUCTION ON HIS FIRST SOLO PROJECT, ALSO RECORDED AT THE CHATEAU, SLAUGHTER ON 10TH AVENUE. FULLY SUPPORTED BY DAVID BOWIE AND MAINMAN.
MARRYING RONNO, SUZI FUSSEY HAPPILY BECOMES SUZI RONSON.

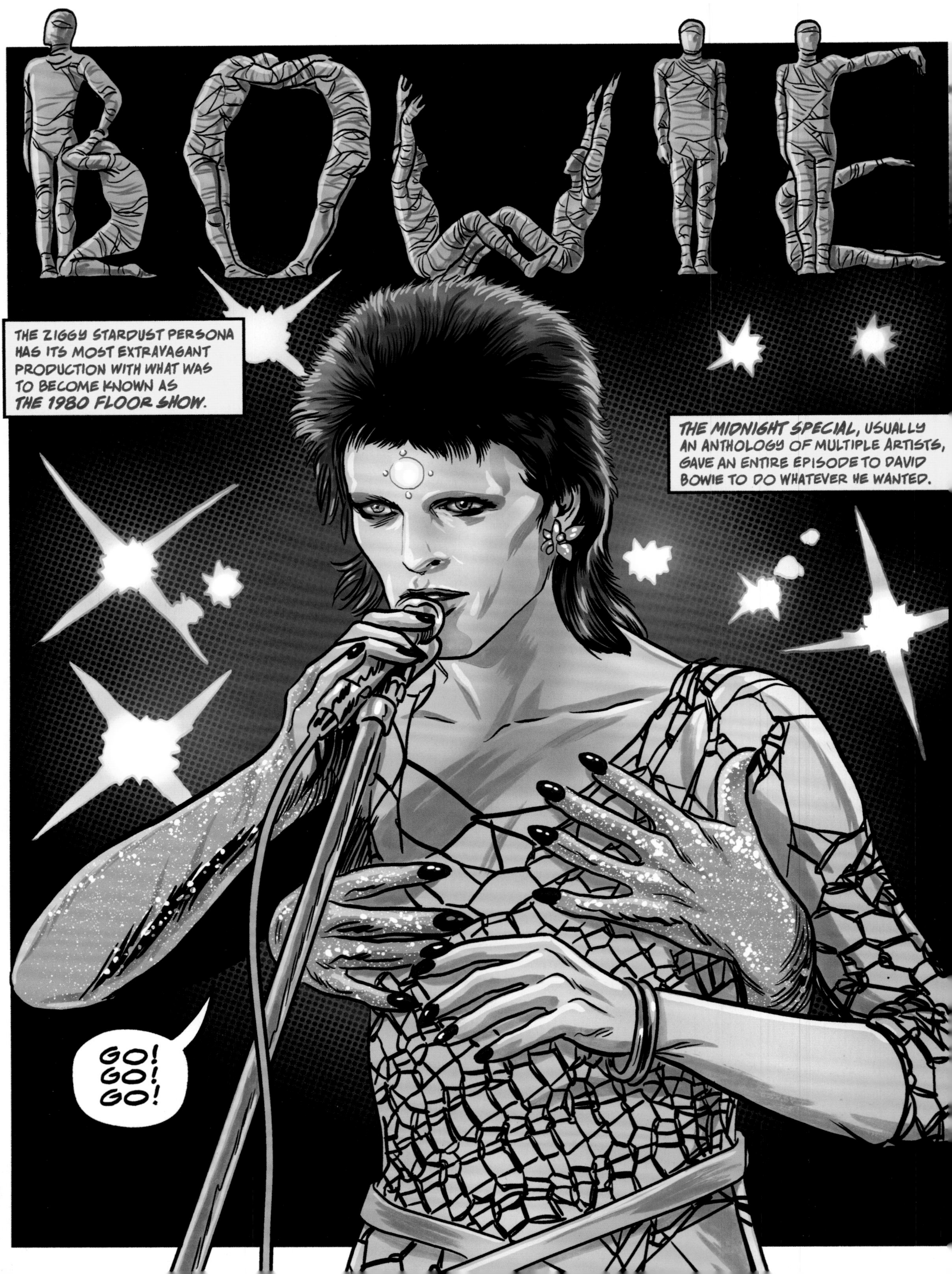
BOWIE
THE ZIGGY STARDUST PERSONA HAS ITS MOST EXTRAVAGANT PRODUCTION WITH WHAT WAS TO BECOME KNOWN AS *THE 1980 FLOOR SHOW*.
THE MIDNIGHT SPECIAL, USUALLY AN ANTHOLOGY OF MULTIPLE ARTISTS, GAVE AN ENTIRE EPISODE TO DAVID BOWIE TO DO WHATEVER HE WANTED.
GO! GO! GO!

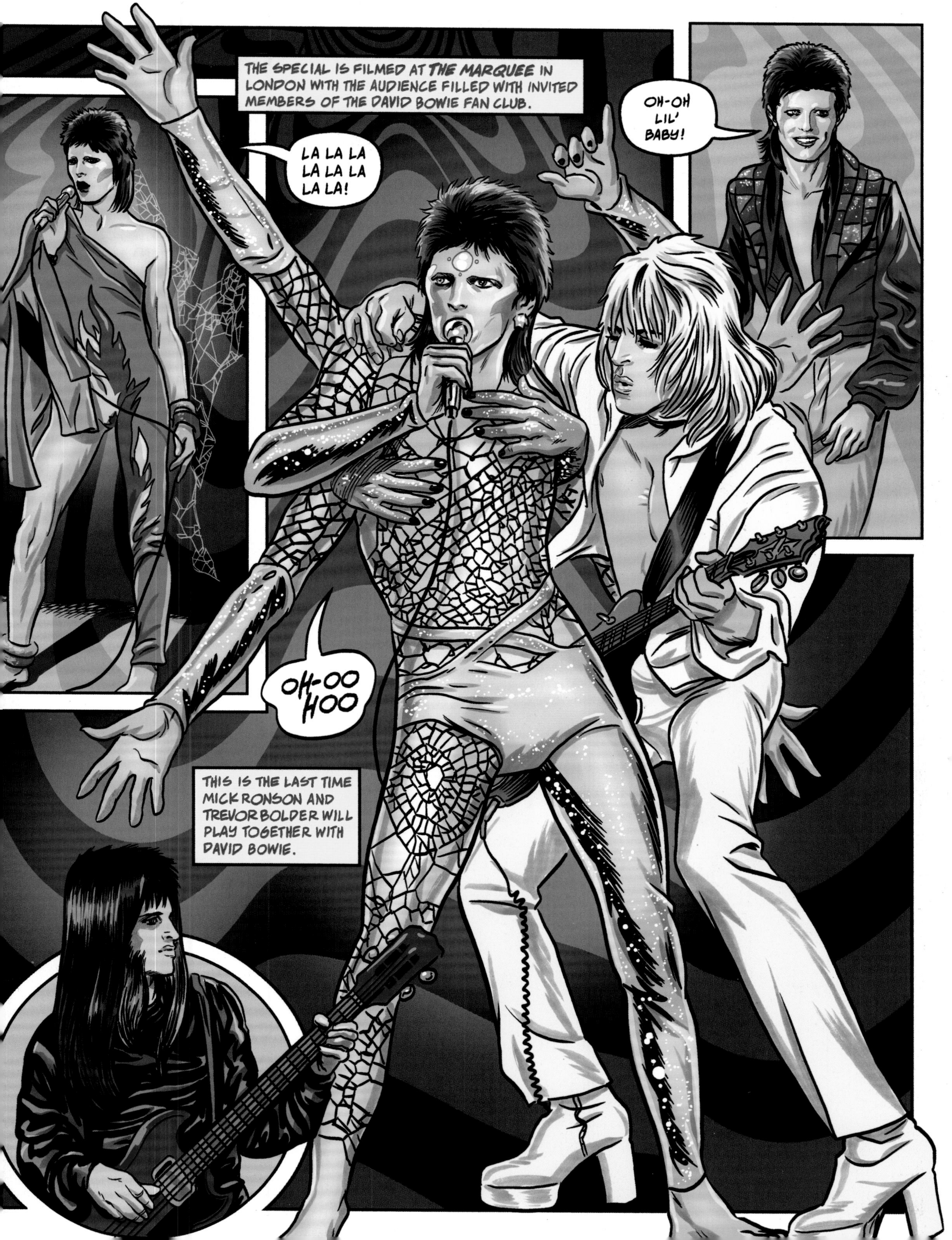
THE SPECIAL IS FILMED AT THE MARQUEE IN LONDON WITH THE AUDIENCE FILLED WITH INVITED MEMBERS OF THE DAVID BOWIE FAN CLUB.
LA LA LA LA LA LA LA LA!
OH-OH LIL' BABY!
OH-OO HOO
THIS IS THE LAST TIME MICK RONSON AND TREVOR BOLDER WILL PLAY TOGETHER WITH DAVID BOWIE.

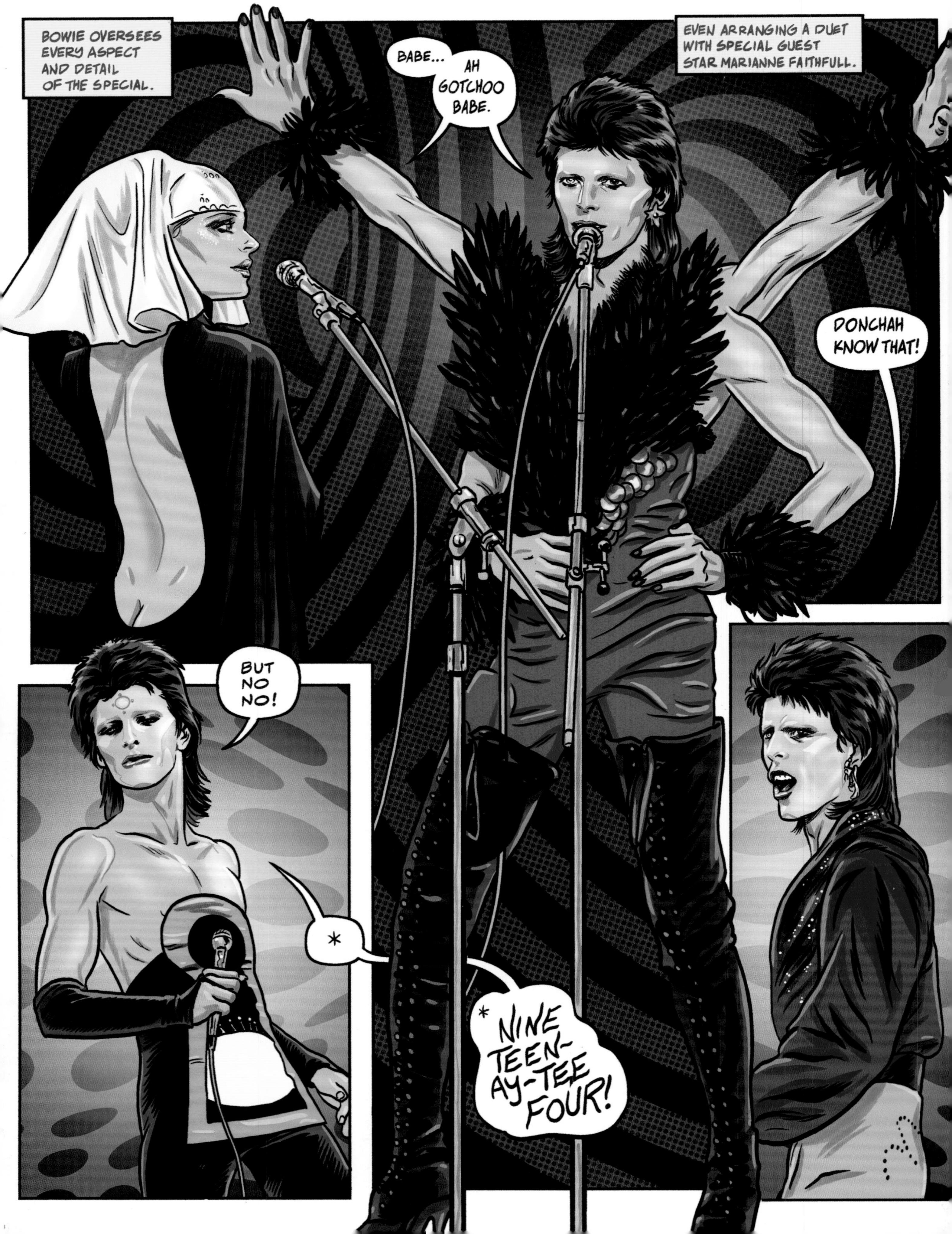
BOWIE OVERSEES EVERY ASPECT AND DETAIL OF THE SPECIAL.
BABE...
AH GOTCHOO BABE.
EVEN ARRANGING A DUET WITH SPECIAL GUEST STAR MARIANNE FAITHFULL.
DONCHAH KNOW THAT!
BUT NO NO!
*
* NINE TEEN-AY-TEE FOUR!

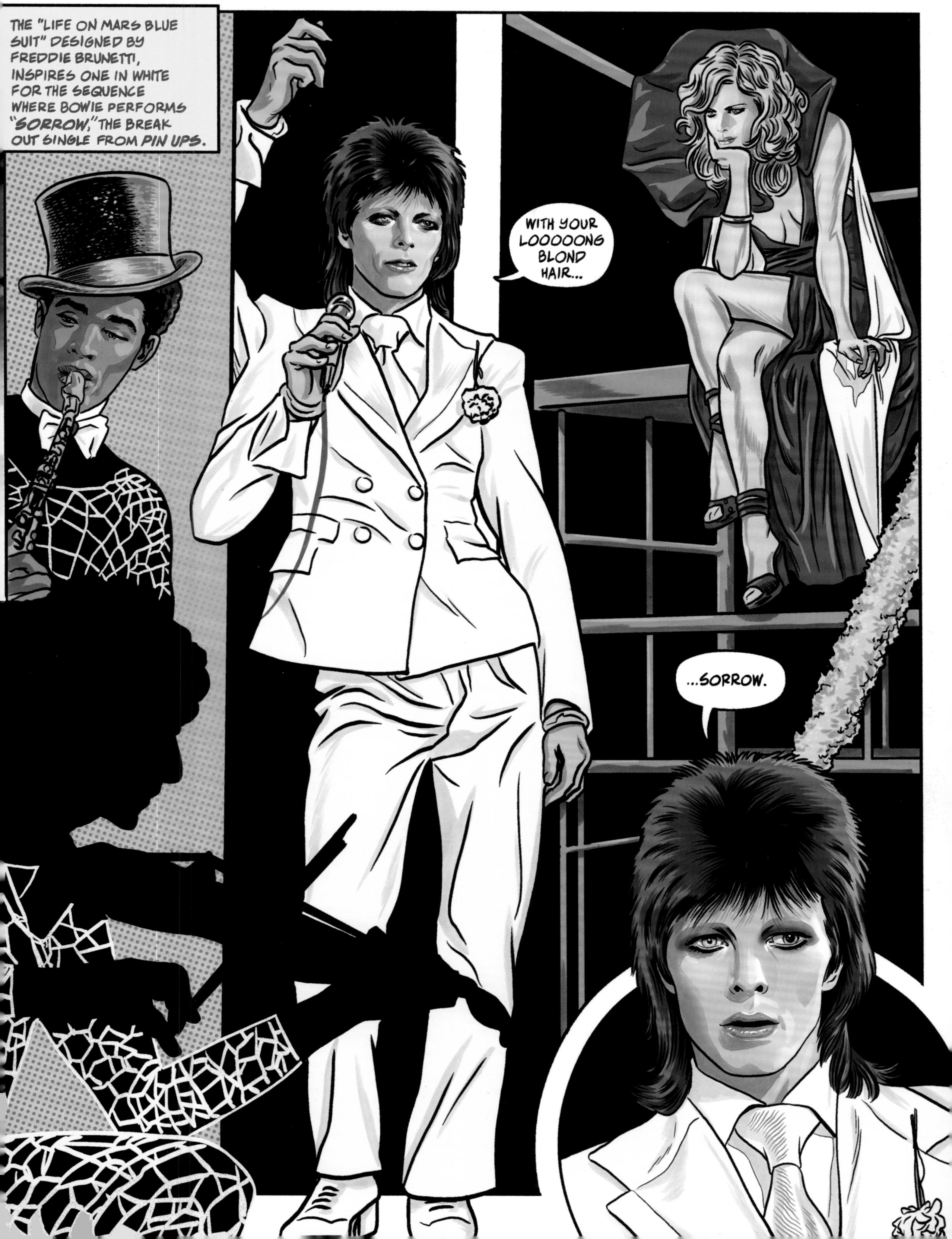
THE "LIFE ON MARS BLUE SUIT" DESIGNED BY FREDDIE BRUNETTI, INSPIRES ONE IN WHITE FOR THE SEQUENCE WHERE BOWIE PERFORMS "SORROW," THE BREAK OUT SINGLE FROM PIN UPS.
WITH YOUR LOOOOONG BLOND HAIR...
...SORROW.

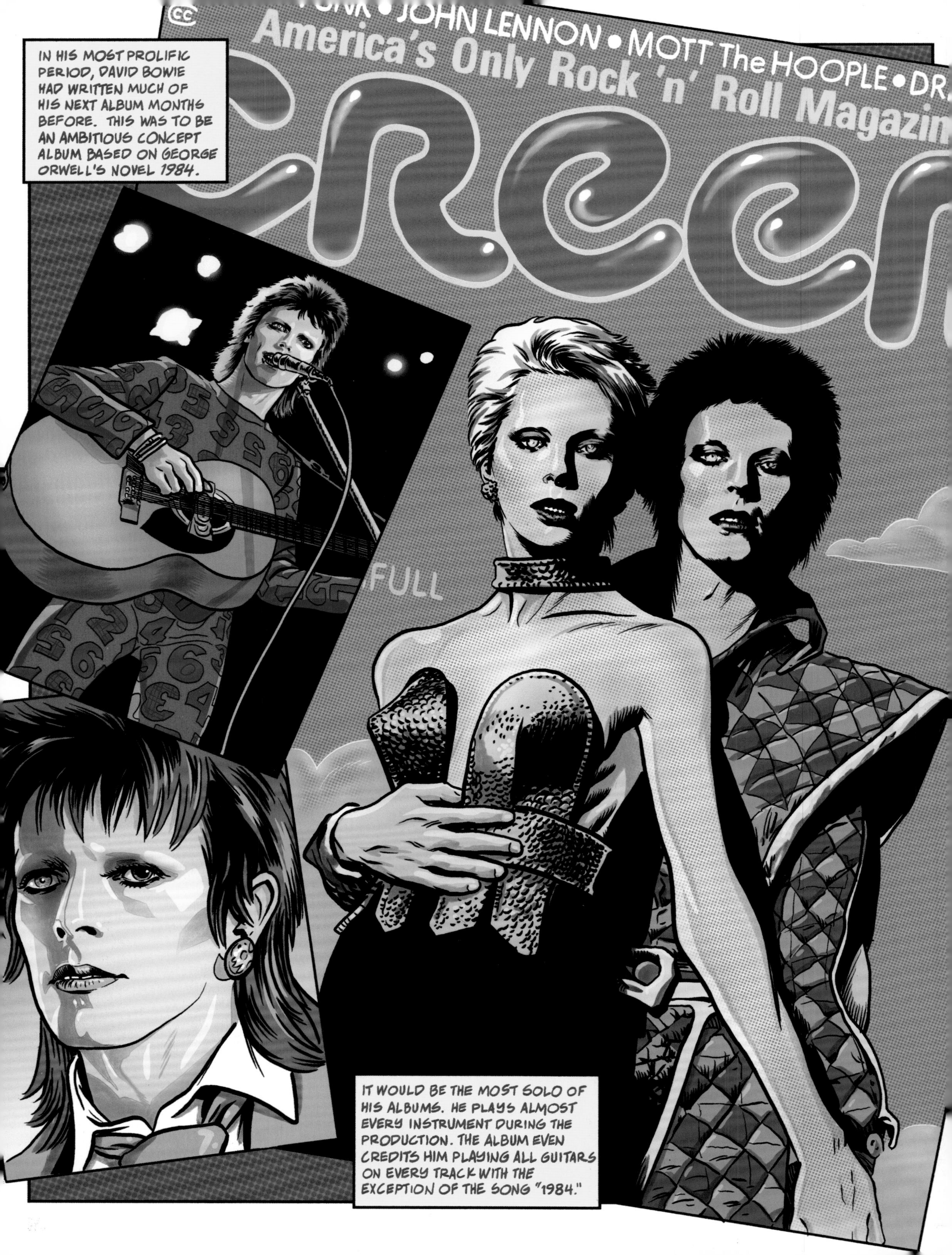

IN HIS MOST PROLIFIC PERIOD, DAVID BOWIE HAD WRITTEN MUCH OF HIS NEXT ALBUM MONTHS BEFORE. THIS WAS TO BE AN AMBITIOUS CONCEPT ALBUM BASED ON GEORGE ORWELL'S NOVEL 1984.
JOHN LENNON • MOTT The HOOPLE •
America's Only Rock 'n' Roll Magazin
FULL
IT WOULD BE THE MOST SOLO OF HIS ALBUMS. HE PLAYS ALMOST EVERY INSTRUMENT DURING THE PRODUCTION. THE ALBUM EVEN CREDITS HIM PLAYING ALL GUITARS ON EVERY TRACK WITH THE EXCEPTION OF THE SONG "1984."

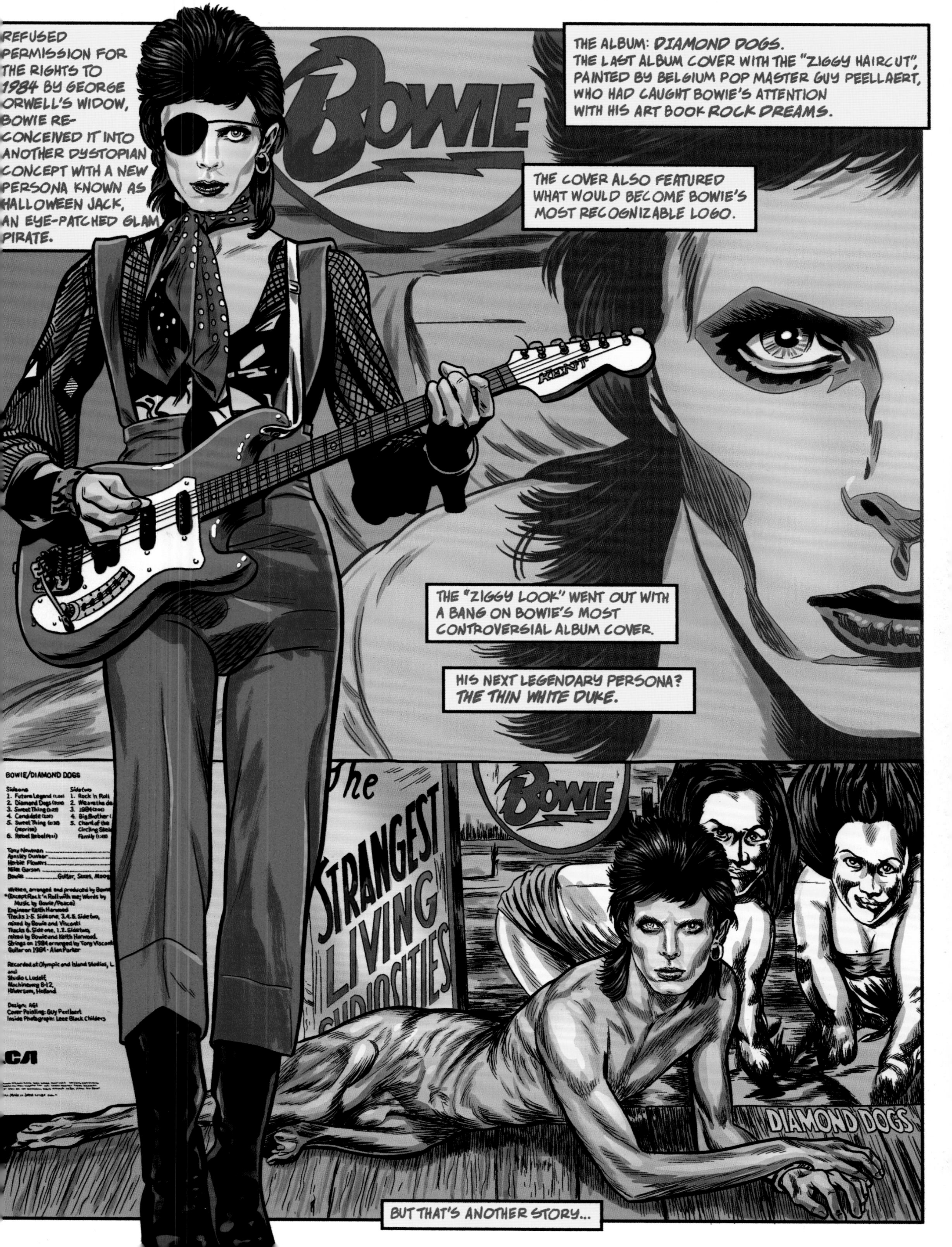

REFUSED PERMISSION FOR THE RIGHTS TO 1984 BY GEORGE ORWELL'S WIDOW, BOWIE RE-CONCEIVED IT INTO ANOTHER DYSTOPIAN CONCEPT WITH A NEW PERSONA KNOWN AS HALLOWEEN JACK, AN EYE-PATCHED GLAM PIRATE.
BOWIE
THE ALBUM: DIAMOND DOGS. THE LAST ALBUM COVER WITH THE "ZIGGY HAIRCUT", PAINTED BY BELGIUM POP MASTER GUY PEELLAERT, WHO HAD CAUGHT BOWIE'S ATTENTION WITH HIS ART BOOK ROCK DREAMS.
THE COVER ALSO FEATURED WHAT WOULD BECOME BOWIE'S MOST RECOGNIZABLE LOGO.
THE "ZIGGY LOOK" WENT OUT WITH A BANG ON BOWIE'S MOST CONTROVERSIAL ALBUM COVER.
HIS NEXT LEGENDARY PERSONA? THE THIN WHITE DUKE.
BOWIE/DIAMOND DOGS
Sideone
1. Future Legend
2. Diamond Dogs
3. Sweet Thing
4. Candidate
5. Sweet Thing (reprise)
6. Rebel Rebel
Sidetwo
1. Rock 'n Roll
3. 1984
Tony Newman
Aynsley Dunbar
Herbie Flowers
Mike Garson
Engineer Keith Harwood
Tracks 1-5. Side one, 3.4.5. Side two, mixed by Bowie and Visconti
Tracks 6. Side one, 1.2. Side two, mixed by Bowie and Keith Harwood.
Guitar on 1984 - Alan Parker
Studio L Ludolf, Machineweg 8-12, Hilversum, Holland
Design: AGI
Cover Painting: Guy Peellaert
Inside Photograph: Leee Black Childers
The
BOWIE
STRANGEST LIVING
DIAMOND DOGS
BUT THAT'S ANOTHER STORY...

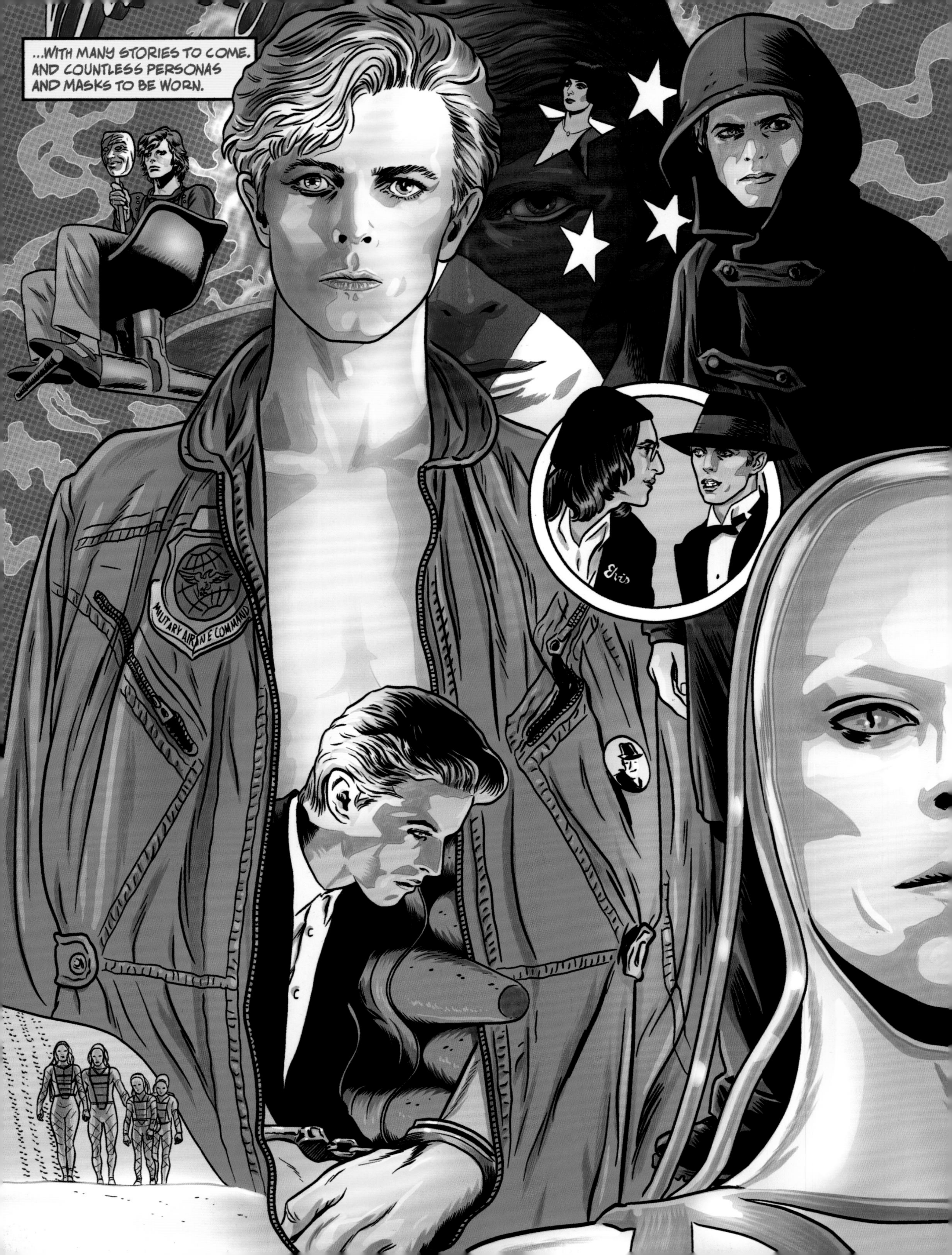
...WITH MANY STORIES TO COME. AND COUNTLESS PERSONAS AND MASKS TO BE WORN.
MILITARY AIRLINE COMMAND
Elvis

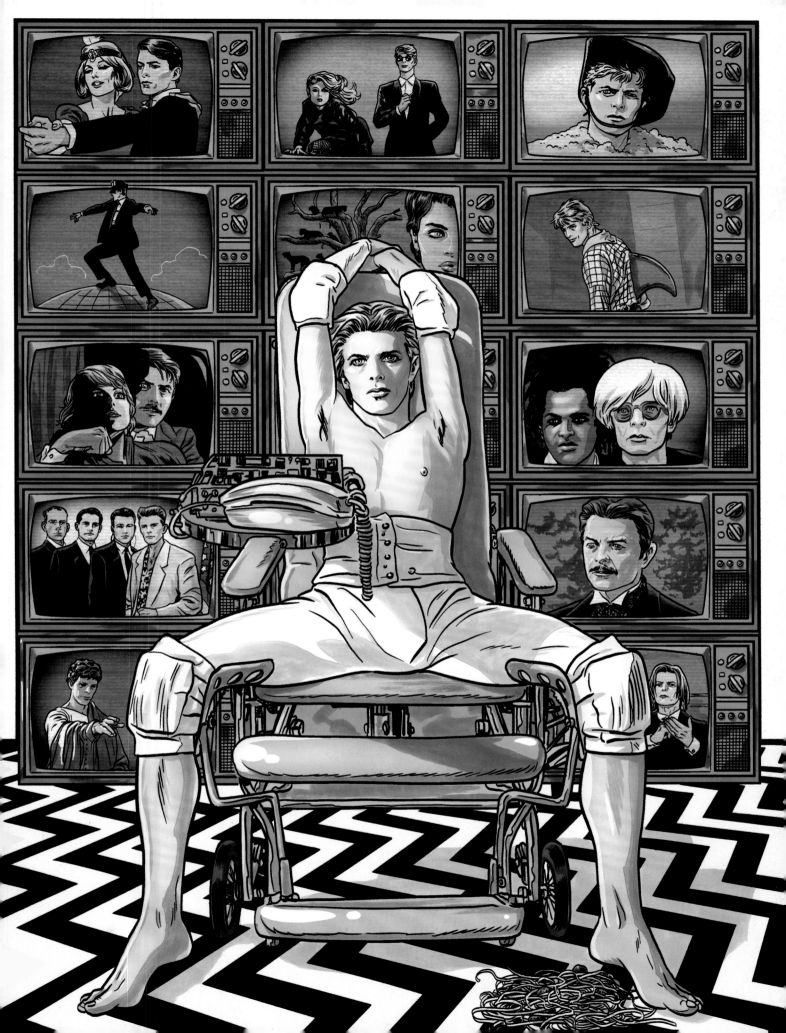

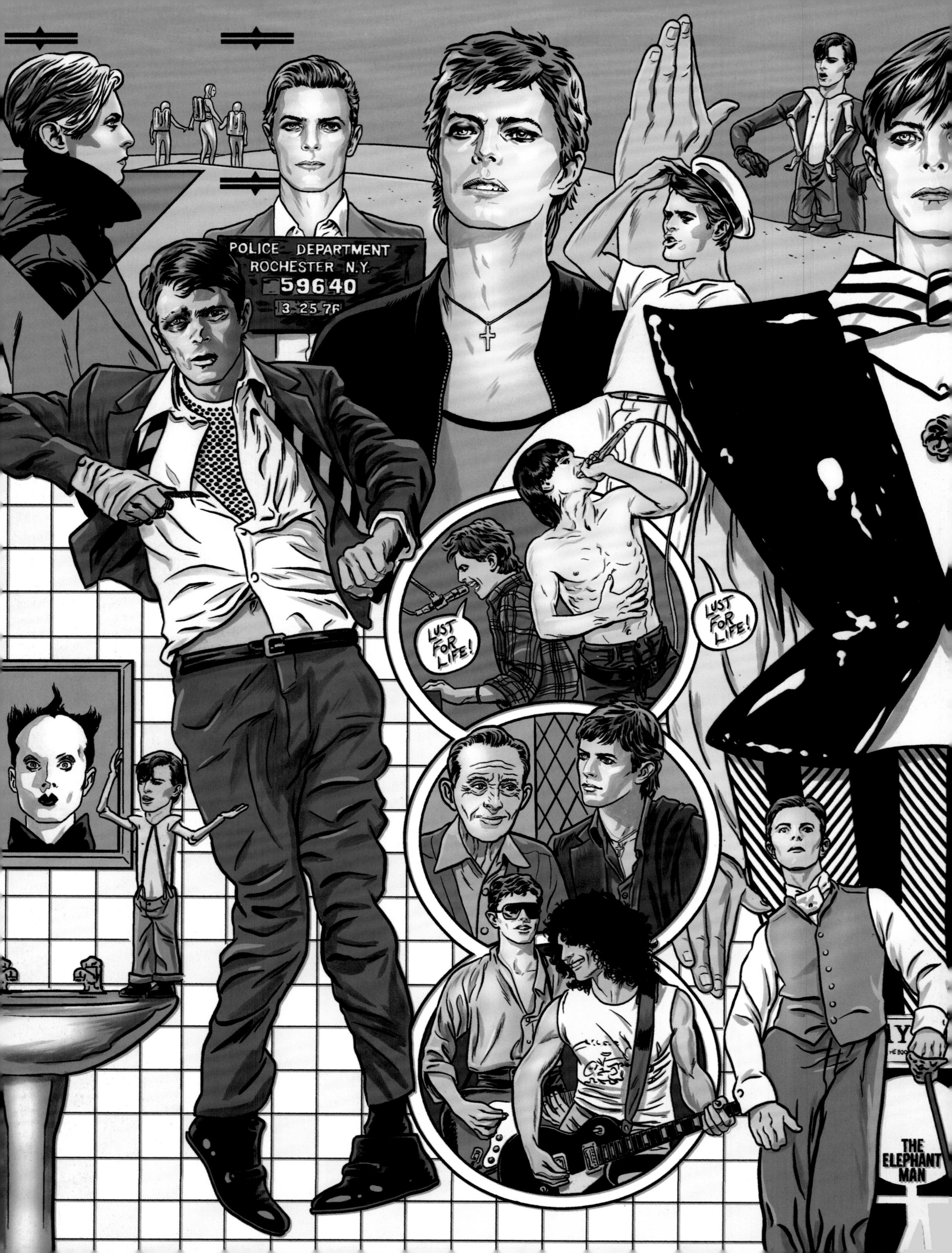
POLICE DEPARTMENT
ROCHESTER N.Y.
59640
3 25 76
LUST FOR LIFE!
LUST FOR LIFE!
THE ELEPHANT MAN

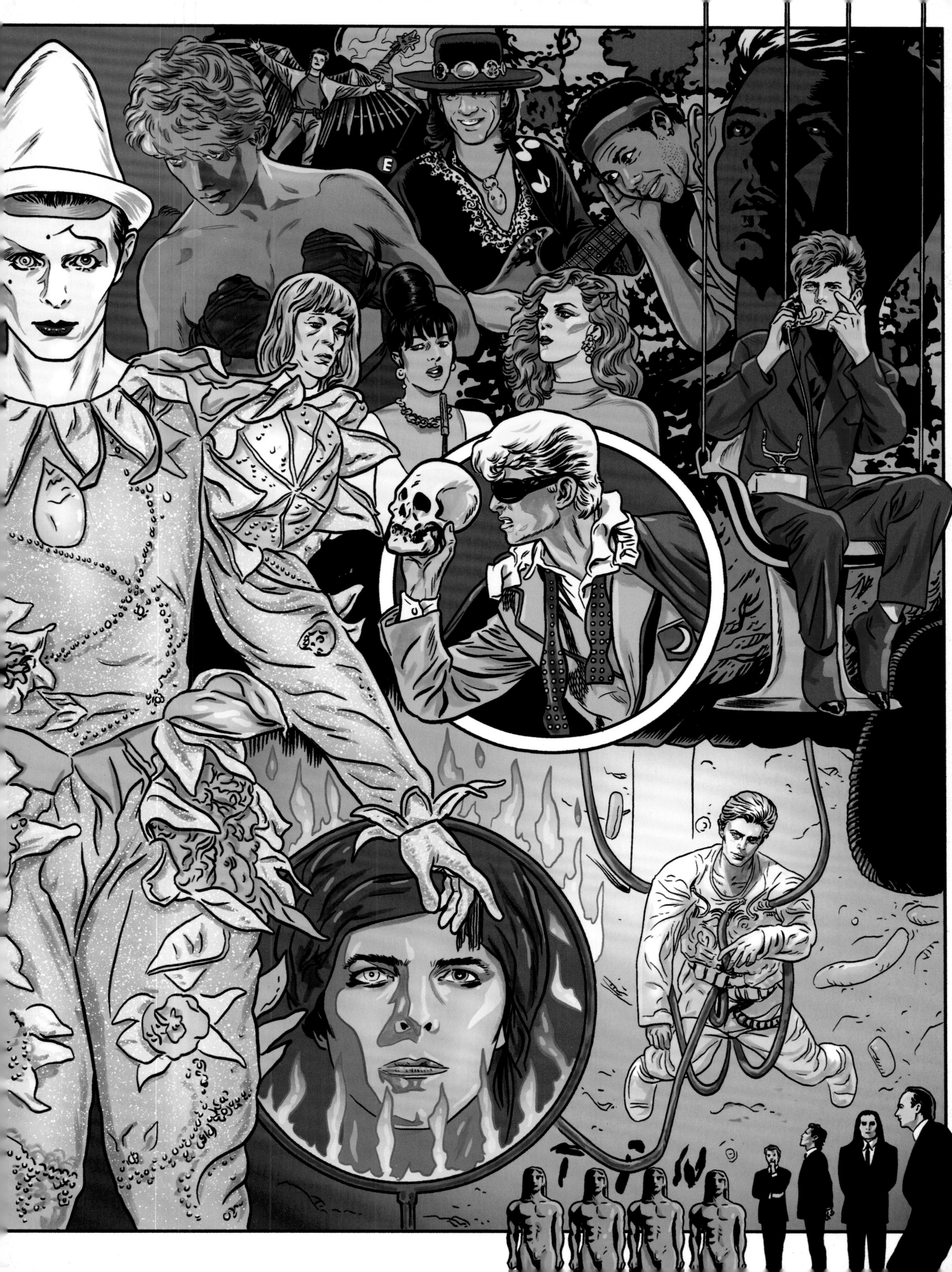

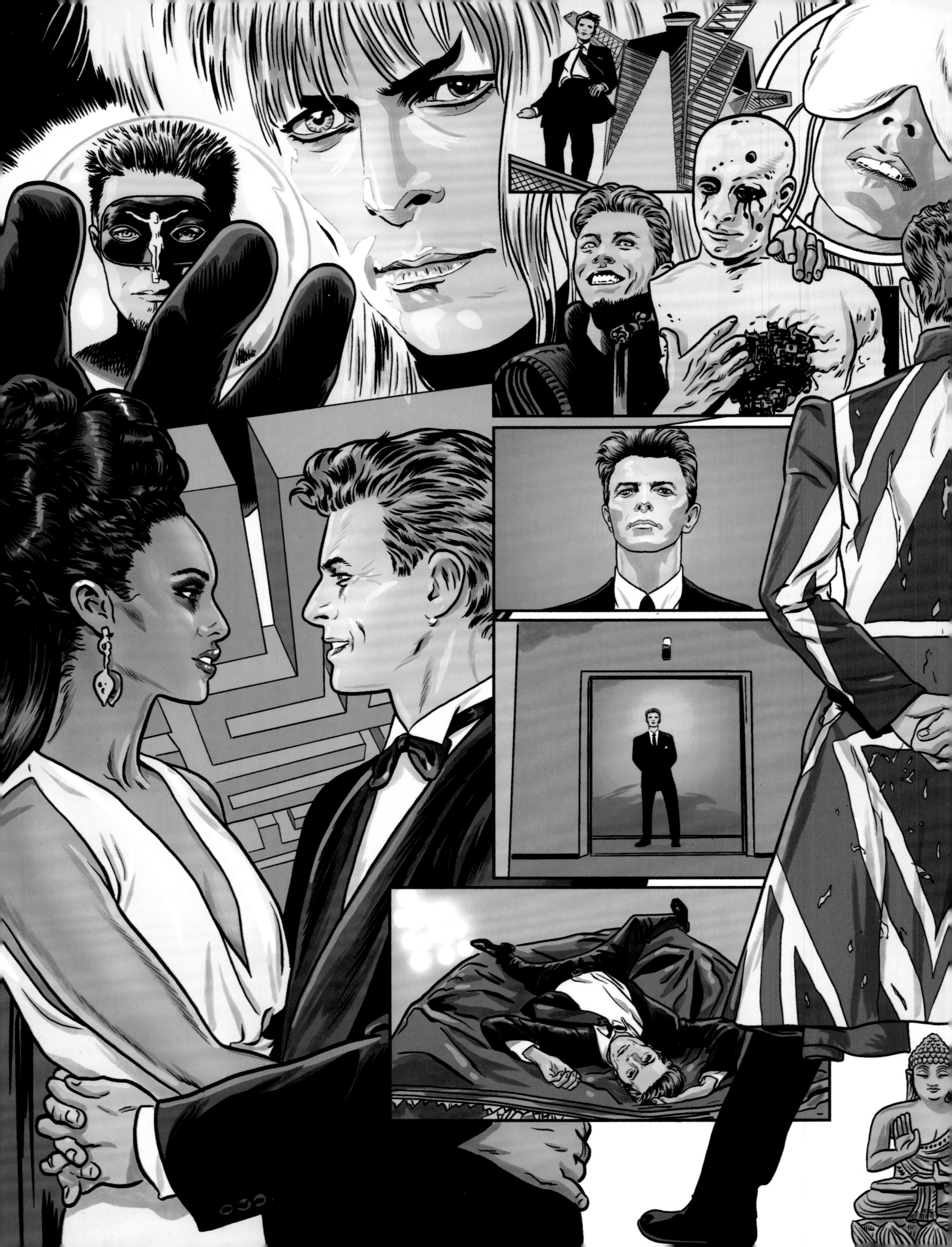

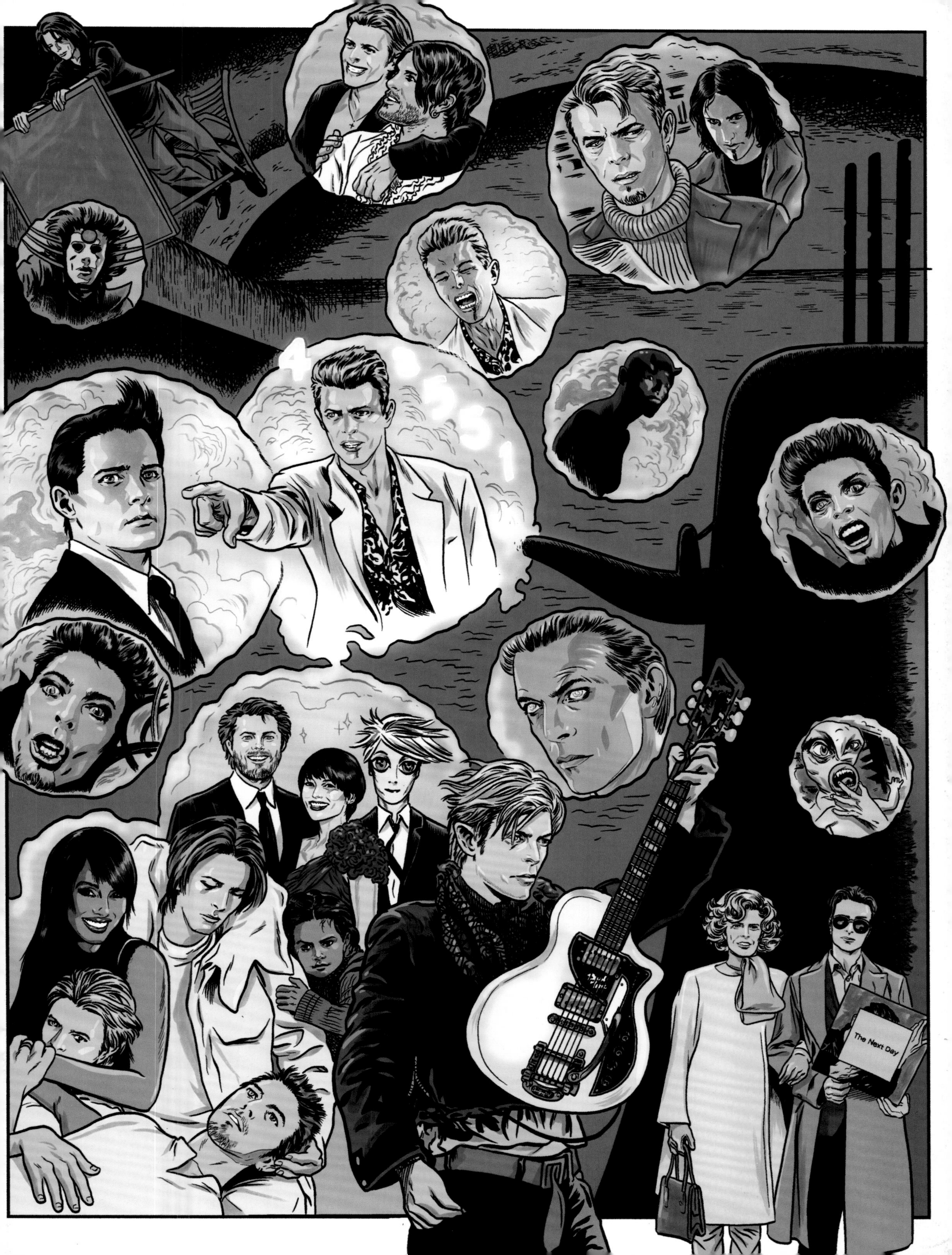
The Next Day

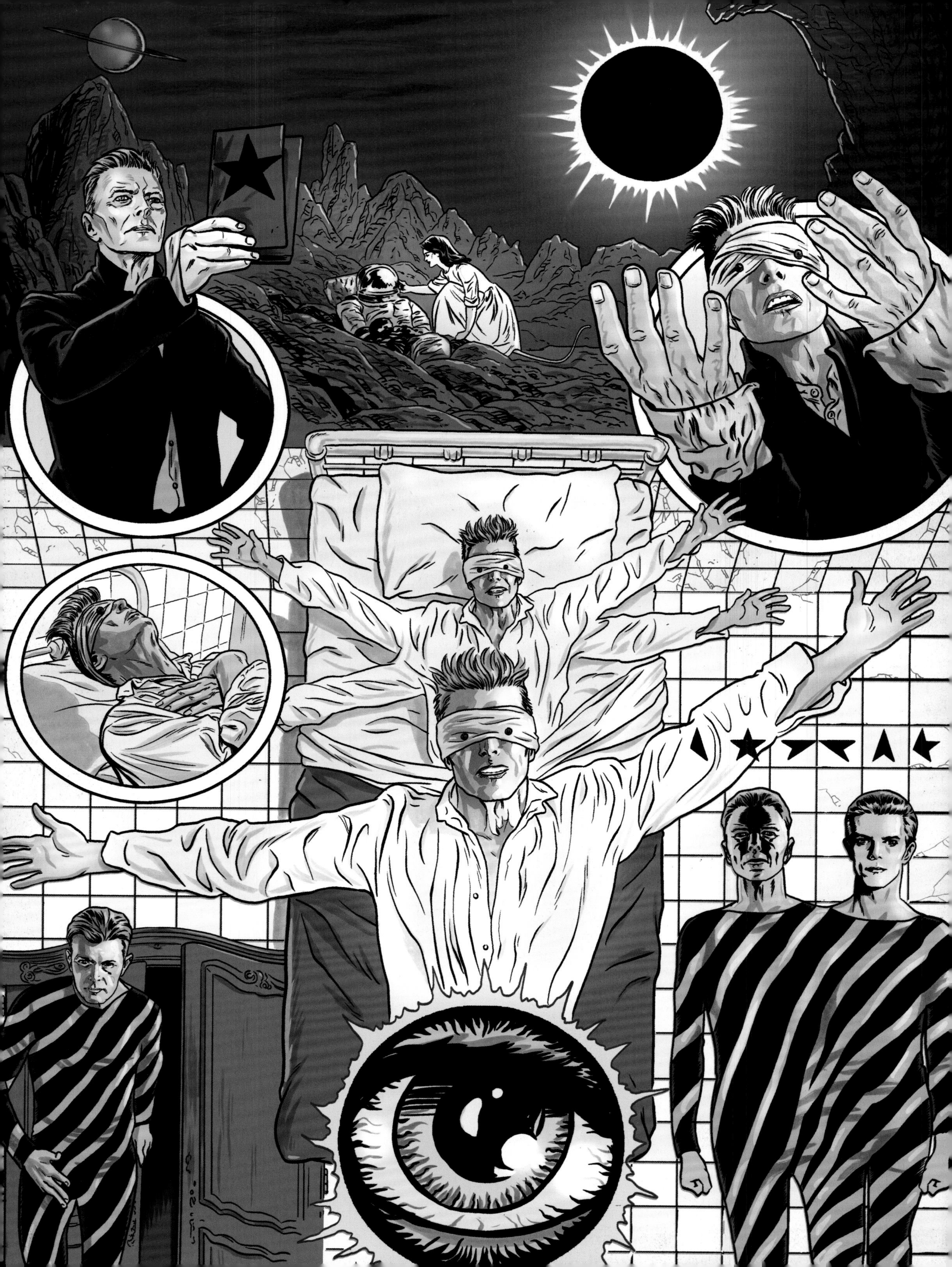

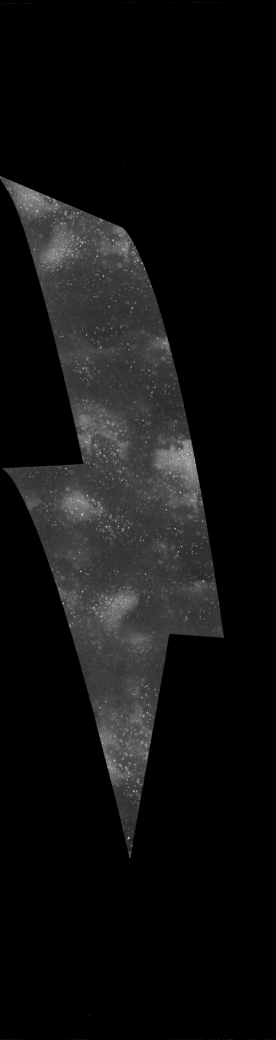

AFTER ALL

BY MICHAEL ALLRED

I've been drawing Bowie, and creating imaginary adventures for Ziggy Stardust, since 1974. At first, in school notebooks, and eventually, as a relatively successful professional writer and artist of comic books, I've been proposing a Ziggy Stardust comic book. But I was told by reps that David Bowie had plans of his own. So, like Bowie turning a proposed *1984* concept album into *Diamond Dogs*, I turned my Ziggy Stardust comic book into the graphic novel *Red Rocket 7*, in which I told the history of rock and roll through the eyes of a red-headed alien clone. Again, through reps, I was told that David saw it, liked it, and even referenced it in his song "New Killer Star" with the lyric "See my life in a comic . . ."

David Bowie's life: That's where all the real magic and mystery truly is!

After the deep dive into researching the history of rock and roll for *Red Rocket 7*, a work of fiction, the seed was planted for the ultimate expression of my obsessive David Bowie fandom. A sequel into "reality." But the time and research required would be insurmountable. So daunting was the task that I just shoved it into the back of my brain with all my other dream projects.

But writer/enabler Steve Horton was paying attention. Not only was he well aware of my crazed Bowie obsession (referenced throughout my entire career), but he also saw a path and cleared that path to make it happen. Approaching me in the most perfect, strapped-for-action kind of way, Steve sought and found the perfect home for the book with Insight Comics, ultimately uniting us with editor extraordinaire Mark Irwin.

I knew Steve and I were starting off on the same page when he suggested we mainly focus on David Bowie's stuttering explosion into stardom via Ziggy Stardust and the glam rock era—exactly the big bite that I was thinking. I suggested we open on the Ziggy Stardust farewell show for our framing device, and our game plan was set. But it was also infinitely important to me to make this book as definitive as possible, and I immediately planned an epilogue montage as a bonus overview of the rest David Bowie's life—a visual capper, if not a kind of preview of possible sequels to this volume.

Steve quickly finished a wonderful script. This was priceless, in that it revealed how wildly divergent the visual imagery of David Bowie's work can be interpreted by each fan, as well as which key events Steve felt held significance. I was thrilled to discover how he tapped into several elements that had been off my radar, amping up my enthusiasm. But at the same time, several of my favorite anecdotes—the creation of the Ziggy haircut and how its creator, Suzi Fussey, would end up marrying Mick "Ronno" Ronson; Bowie's mismatched eyes; the shaved eyebrows; and the various run-ins and interactions with other up-and-coming timeless icons—were missing and demanded inclusion.

Had I attacked this project completely on my own, it surely would exist as a singular personal love letter, but Steve's draft opened my eyes to valuable new perspectives I would have missed. It was clear that I needed to amplify my empathy for all of Bowie's fans. To look under every rock and make this as all-encompassing as possible. I tapped into my old-school journalism training (I was a TV reporter in Germany when the Wall came down during the late '80s): I started from scratch, double-checking Steve's research and discovering even more thrilling new insights along the way. I created "the shooting script," building off of what Steve had turned in. This effort increased my appreciation for Steve's contributions even further and provided the confidence that everything we could possibly squeeze into the allotted page count was in there. Even before we signed our final contract, I drew up my first *Bowie* cover idea and immediately started laying out the book. What a trip this has been!

In my research, I've almost doubled the number of Bowie books and magazines I've owned and read over the years—a crushing stack that could cause some serious damage if it tipped over. I turned the internet inside out and laid out all my reference for hairstyles, clothing, locations, etc., for the smoothest production possible. This was especially useful when Laura set out to faithfully re-create or reinterpret the colors for each era.

I found myself rediscovering all the same schoolboy passions that inspired countless hours of doodling on any available surface back in the day, crazily obsessed with the challenge of re-creating paraphernalia, album covers, instruments, and iconic images. I can't think of a project on which I've "worked/played" harder or had more fun with a single subject. This is a project that encapsulates, or at least taps into, the great majority of my life's creative passions and inspirations.

This is my ultimate gift to the kid who discovered David Bowie by chance in 1974 and started drawing pictures of the rock-and-roll alien, exploding with a love for creativity. It happened like this:

I grew up on comic books thanks to my older brother, Lee Allred, who had a miraculous knack for collecting all the best comics. One of my earliest memories is Lee shaking me off a card table when he wanted me to "dance faster!" I woke up in a hospital bed with a concussion. The bed was blanketed with comic books Lee had convinced Mom and Dad to buy for me in the hospital gift shop. Because of Lee, I was always surrounded by the best comics growing up.

But my introduction to David Bowie happened completely independently, with no outside influence from anyone, just as I was on the verge of bursting into puberty. In many ways, it is one of the most significant events in my life.

I was making the usual rounds walking downtown just off the hill from where I grew up in Roseburg, Oregon. I'd often hit the toy store and then check for new comics at the PayLess Drug Store. Among the magazines, next to the comic book spinner rack, an amazing image popped off the cover of something called *Creem* magazine that declared itself as "America's Only Rock 'n' Roll Magazine." On the cover was a photo of David Bowie and his wife, Angie, made up like bizarre aliens from outer space, airbrushed to accentuate and exaggerate Bowie's out-of-this-world appearance. (I've re-created this life-changing magazine cover on page 142.)

I immediately bought that magazine, and as I read it walking home, it inspired me to walk into Ricketts Music Store and see if they had anything on this rock star from outer space. They had his "Rebel Rebel" single on a 45 with "Lady Grinning Soul" on the flip side. When I got home, I played both sides over and over and over. From there, I dove deep into my very first obsessive pop-culture crash course. Before this, only the music and imagery of the Beatles and the Monkees had made a mark on me.

I started spending all my paper route money on records and more rock magazines. I bought the just-released *Diamond Dogs* album with that insane Guy Peellaert album cover. I was surprised that the album version of "Rebel Rebel" was completely different (longer and simpler) from the single version. This was my introduction to the concept album, with songs creating a cohesive theme and suggesting a story—a story that came together in my brain, igniting my imagination. From there, I went backward, discovering the treasure trove of more brain-exploding albums and visions, with everything that had come before: *Pin Ups*; *Aladdin Sane*; of course, the seminal *Ziggy Stardust* (and its wonderfully, epically long album title); *Hunky Dory*; *The Man Who Sold the World*; *Space Oddity*; and even the *Images* compilation that collected most of Bowie's pre–*Space Oddity* music. This was especially intriguing, with its gatefold comic-strip album cover. I went crazy for all this stuff, much of it containing posters, production notes, and lyric sheets to drink in while listening to the music. I've been a lad insane ever since!

And from all that, you now have this: *Bowie: Stardust, Rayguns & Moonage Daydreams*!

THIS BOOK TO BE PLAYED AT MAXIMUM VOLUME!

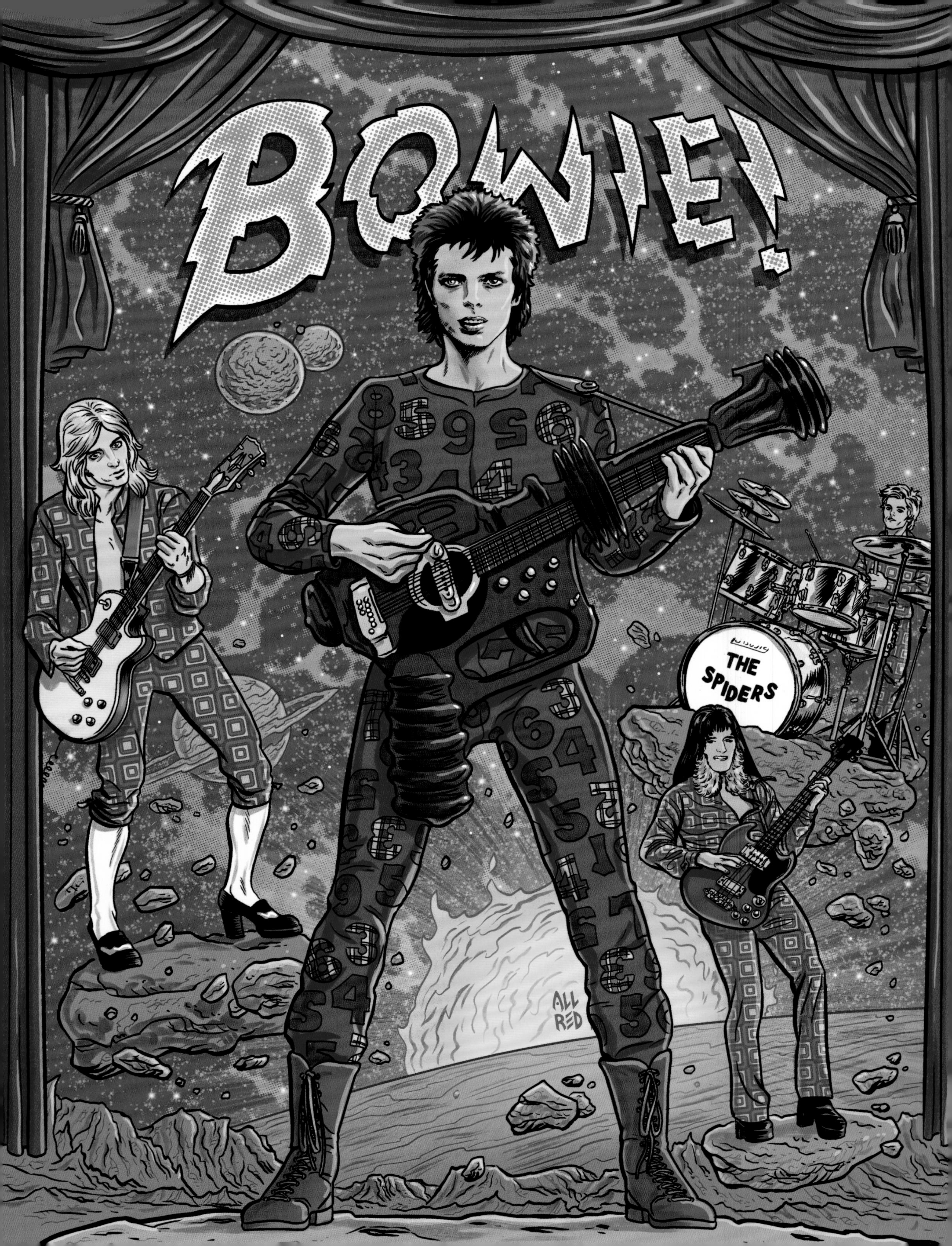
BOWIE!
THE SPIDERS
ALL RED

ACKNOWLEDGMENTS

Now for some infinite gratitude:

This being our love letter to the life, inspirations, influences, and creations of David Bowie, it's his existence that obviously gets all our endless appreciation.

We all especially want to give a huge "wham bam thank you man" to Neil Gaiman for introducing our effort. I first met Neil, as he describes, before my comic creator hobby turned into a career. When we next met, it was at the Harvey Awards, when I was nominated for Best New Talent, and Neil was nominated for Everything Else. Somehow, at the banquet, we both started enthusing over David Bowie and our affection for what we both felt was the underrated *Diamond Dogs* album. Spontaneously, we both recited the entire "Future Legend" intro in unison. This confirmed to everyone around us that we were certifiably insane. Listen or relisten to the cut to imagine what this must have sounded like as we excitedly got louder and louder, to its conclusion. Neil has been my "Bowie Brother" from that moment on.

Personally, I again want to thank Steve Horton for reaching out and grabbing me by the collar to "just do it already!", along with the energy-infusing Mark Irwin for opening the door, professionally and creatively, to this project. And, of course, Laura, the light of my life, for always making everything I do look way better than it has any right to. By the way, the first gift I ever gave her was David Bowie's *Hunky Dory* album. That may have sealed the deal on our future together.

Laura and I would very much like to thank our son, Han, for his creative heft, for keeping everything smooth and breezy, and for every other wonderful thing he does for us. And our other wonderful kids, and kids' kids: Bond, Kelby, Anakin, Frank Einstein, Ringo, Penny Rey, Bowie (yes, we have our own Bowie—Kelby's oldest daughter!), Ripley, Nicole, Adrian, Patti, and all the family and friends who make every day a party. Especially the "Framily Friday" crew, who help cap off each week with a burst of bliss: Brian, Elizabeth, Ben, Larisa, Bronwyn, Rowan, Matt, Julia, Brooks, Greg, Chloe, Cody, Tara, Abby, Tina, Tyler, Breanna, Jake, Kellyn, Brandon, Amber, Roya, Joëlle, Ryan, Michael, Taki, the Professor, and Mary Ann . . .

Special thanks to some of my gurus—Shelly Bond, Jamie S. Rich, Matt Wagner, Bob Schreck, Diana Schutz, Tom Brevoort, Charlie Custis, Steven T. Seagle, Mark Chiarello, Randy Bowen, Nate Piekos, Courtney Taylor-Taylor, Gerard Way, and Darwyn Cooke—for taking me to wonderful places I otherwise would not have gone. And a big thanks to everyone who has made a monumental impact in my life supporting all things creative. You should know who you are. And whether you do or not, I'll happily and gratefully write your name right here: _____.

Massive appreciation to my favorite Bowie artists: the brilliant Helen Green and the late, great Guy Peellaert, who inspired me to raise my game in every way possible for this project.

And finally, thank *you*! If this book inspires you to turn someone, anyone, on to the life and work of David Bowie, then it was all worth it.

—Michael Allred

Acknowledgment to the works of David Buckley, Nicholas Pegg, Woody Woodmansey, D. A. Pennebaker, and many many others.

For Brandon, Kaylee, Andrew, Loretta, and Sandy.

Thanks to Phil Hester.

And special thanks to the Starman himself.

—Steve Horton

OPPOSITE: Alternate cover art: *Space Curtains.*

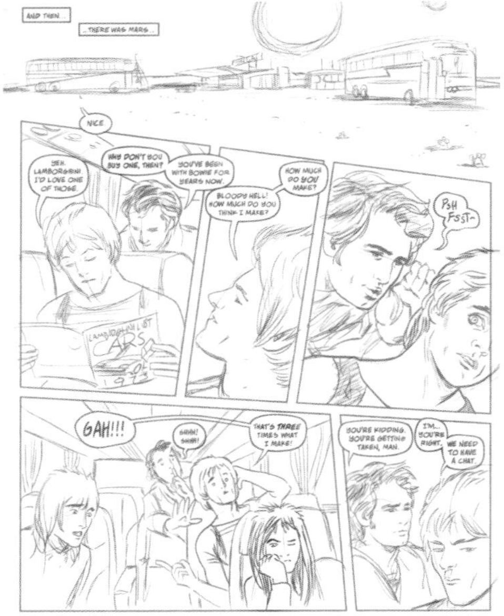
AND THEN...
...THERE WAS MARS...
NICE.
YEH. LAMBORGHINI. I'D LOVE ONE OF THOSE.
WHY DON'T YOU BUY ONE, THEN?
YOU'VE BEEN WITH BOWIE FOR YEARS NOW.
BLOODY HELL! HOW MUCH DO YOU THINK I MAKE?
HOW MUCH DO YOU MAKE?
PSH FSST-
GAH!!!
SHHH! SHHH!
THAT'S THREE TIMES WHAT I MAKE!
YOU'RE KIDDING. YOU'RE GETTING TAKEN, MAN.
I'M... YOU'RE RIGHT.
WE NEED TO HAVE A CHAT.

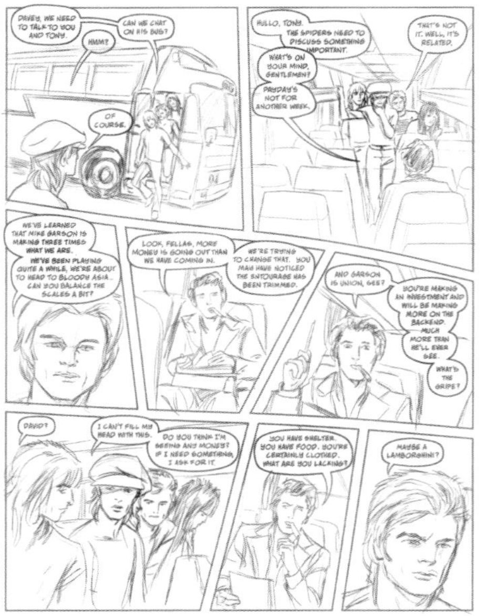
DAVEY, WE NEED TO TALK TO YOU AND TONY.
HMM?
CAN WE CHAT ON HIS BUS?
OF COURSE.
HULLO, TONY.
THE SPIDERS NEED TO DISCUSS SOMETHING IMPORTANT.
WHAT'S ON YOUR MIND, GENTLEMEN?
PAYDAY'S NOT FOR ANOTHER WEEK.
THAT'S NOT IT. WELL, IT'S RELATED.
WE'VE LEARNED THAT MIKE GARSON IS MAKING THREE TIMES WHAT WE ARE.
WE'VE BEEN PLAYING QUITE A WHILE, WE'RE ABOUT TO HEAD TO BLOODY ASIA... CAN YOU BALANCE THE SCALES A BIT?
LOOK, FELLAS, MORE MONEY IS GOING OUT THAN WE HAVE COMING IN.
WE'RE TRYING TO CHANGE THAT. YOU MAY HAVE NOTICED THE ENTOURAGE HAS BEEN TRIMMED.
AND GARSON IS UNION, SEE?
YOU'RE MAKING AN INVESTMENT AND WILL BE MAKING MORE ON THE BACKEND.
MUCH MORE THAN HE'LL EVER SEE.
WHAT'S THE GRIPE?
DAVID?
I CAN'T FILL MY HEAD WITH THIS.
DO YOU THINK I'M SEEING ANY MONEY? IF I NEED SOMETHING, I ASK FOR IT.
YOU HAVE SHELTER. YOU HAVE FOOD. YOU'RE CERTAINLY CLOTHED. WHAT ARE YOU LACKING?
MAYBE A LAMBORGHINI?

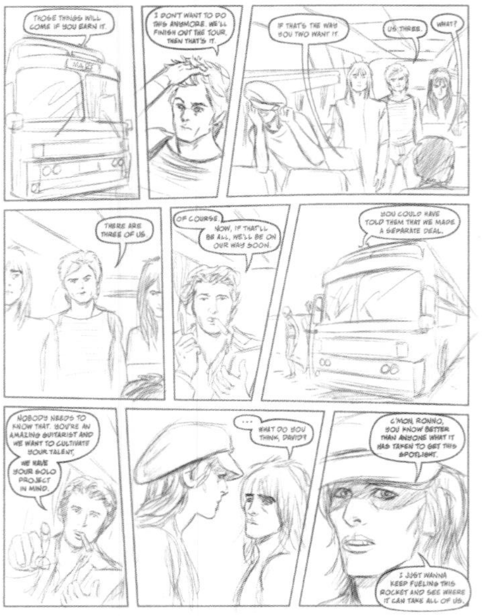
THOSE THINGS WILL COME IF YOU EARN IT.
I DON'T WANT TO DO THIS ANYMORE. WE'LL FINISH OUT THE TOUR, THEN THAT'S IT.
IF THAT'S THE WAY YOU TWO WANT IT.
US THREE.
WHAT?
THERE ARE THREE OF US.
OF COURSE.
NOW, IF THAT'LL BE ALL, WE'LL BE ON OUR WAY SOON.
YOU COULD HAVE TOLD THEM THAT WE MADE A SEPARATE DEAL.
NOBODY NEEDS TO KNOW THAT. YOU'RE AN AMAZING GUITARIST AND WE WANT TO CULTIVATE YOUR TALENT,
WE HAVE YOUR SOLO PROJECT IN MIND.
...
WHAT DO YOU THINK, DAVID?
C'MON, RONNO, YOU KNOW BETTER THAN ANYONE WHAT IT HAS TAKEN TO GET THIS SPOTLIGHT.
I JUST WANNA KEEP FUELING THIS ROCKET AND SEE WHERE IT CAN TAKE ALL OF US.

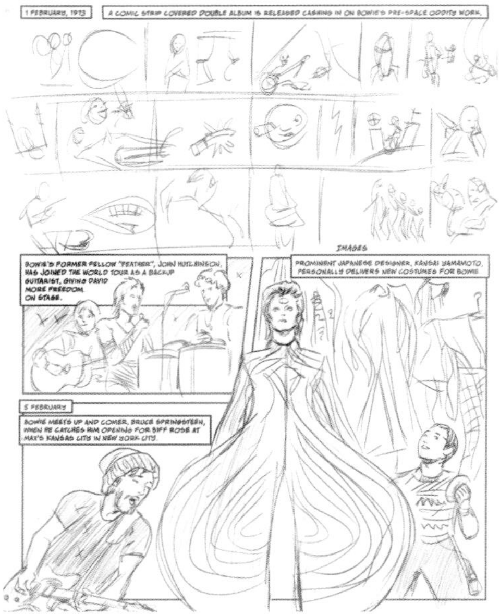
1 FEBRUARY, 1973
A COMIC STRIP COVERED DOUBLE ALBUM IS RELEASED CASHING IN ON BOWIE'S PRE-SPACE ODDITY WORK.
IMAGES
BOWIE'S FORMER FELLOW "FEATHER", JOHN HUTCHINSON, HAS JOINED THE WORLD TOUR AS A BACKUP GUITARIST, GIVING DAVID MORE FREEDOM ON STAGE.
PROMINENT JAPANESE DESIGNER, KANSAI YAMAMOTO, PERSONALLY DELIVERS NEW COSTUMES FOR BOWIE.
5 FEBRUARY
BOWIE MEETS UP AND COMER, BRUCE SPRINGSTEEN, WHEN HE CATCHES HIM OPENING FOR BIFF ROSE AT MAX'S KANSAS CITY IN NEW YORK CITY.

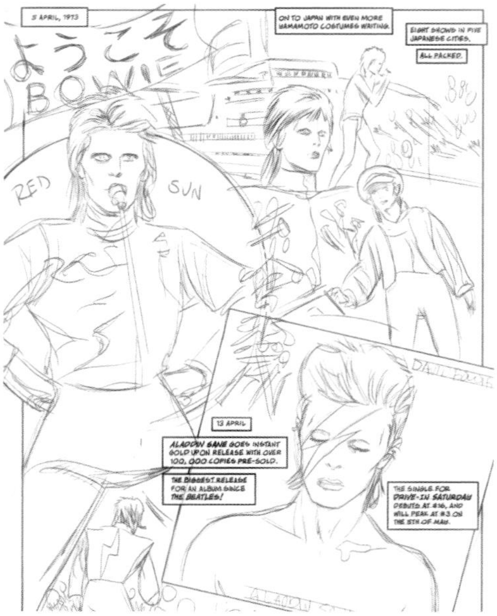
5 APRIL, 1973
ようこそ
BOWIE
RED
SUN
ON TO JAPAN WITH EVEN MORE YAMAMOTO COSTUMES WAITING.
EIGHT SHOWS IN FIVE JAPANESE CITIES.
ALL PACKED.
13 APRIL
ALADDIN SANE GOES INSTANT GOLD UPON RELEASE WITH OVER 100, 000 COPIES PRE-SOLD.
THE BIGGEST RELEASE FOR AN ALBUM SINCE THE BEATLES!
THE SINGLE FOR DRIVE-IN SATURDAY DEBUTS AT #16, AND WILL PEAK AT #3 ON THE 5TH OF MAY.

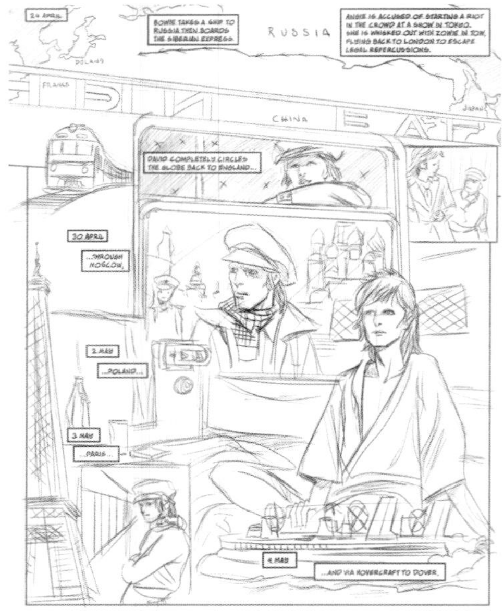
24 APRIL
POLAND
BOWIE TAKES A SHIP TO RUSSIA THEN BOARDS THE SIBERIAN EXPRESS.
RUSSIA
ANGIE IS ACCUSED OF STARTING A RIOT IN THE CROWD AT A SHOW IN TOKYO. SHE IS WHISKED OUT WITH ZOWIE IN TOW, FLYING BACK TO LONDON TO ESCAPE LEGAL REPERCUSSIONS.
FRANCE
CHINA
JAPAN
DAVID COMPLETELY CIRCLES THE GLOBE BACK TO ENGLAND...
30 APRIL
...THROUGH MOSCOW,
2 MAY
...POLAND...
3 MAY
...PARIS...
4 MAY
...AND VIA HOVERCRAFT TO DOVER.

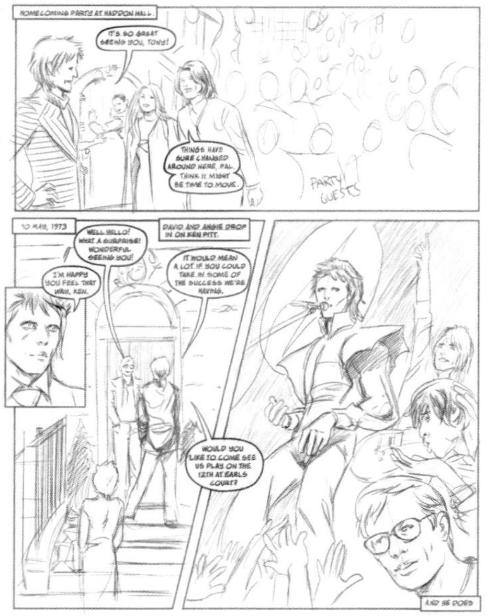
HOMECOMING PARTY AT HADDON HALL.
IT'S SO GREAT SEEING YOU, TONY!
THINGS HAVE SURE CHANGED AROUND HERE, PAL. THINK IT MIGHT BE TIME TO MOVE.
PARTY GUESTS
10 MAY, 1973
WELL HELLO! WHAT A SURPRISE! WONDERFUL SEEING YOU!
DAVID AND ANGIE DROP IN ON KEN PITT.
I'M HAPPY YOU FEEL THAT WAY, KEN.
IT WOULD MEAN A LOT IF YOU COULD TAKE IN SOME OF THE SUCCESS WE'RE HAVING.
WOULD YOU LIKE TO COME SEE US PLAY ON THE 12TH AT EARLS COURT?
AND HE DOES

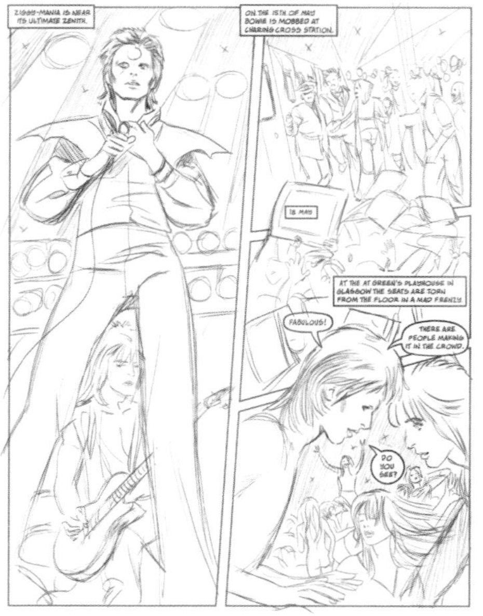
ZIGGY-MANIA IS NEAR ITS ULTIMATE ZENITH.
ON THE 15TH OF MAY BOWIE IS MOBBED AT CHARING CROSS STATION.
18 MAY
AT THE AT GREEN'S PLAYHOUSE IN GLASGOW THE SEATS ARE TORN FROM THE FLOOR IN A MAD FRENZY.
FABULOUS!
THERE ARE PEOPLE MAKING IT IN THE CROWD.
DO YOU SEE?

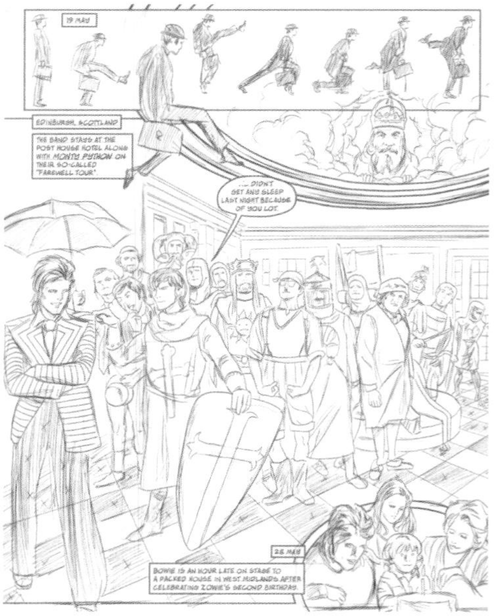
19 MAY
EDINBURGH, SCOTLAND
THE BAND STAYS AT THE POST HOUSE HOTEL ALONG WITH MONTY PYTHON ON THEIR SO-CALLED "FAREWELL TOUR".
... DIDN'T GET ANY SLEEP LAST NIGHT BECAUSE OF YOU LOT.
25 MAY
BOWIE IS AN HOUR LATE ON STAGE TO A PACKED HOUSE IN WEST MIDLANDS AFTER CELEBRATING ZOWIE'S SECOND BIRTHDAY.

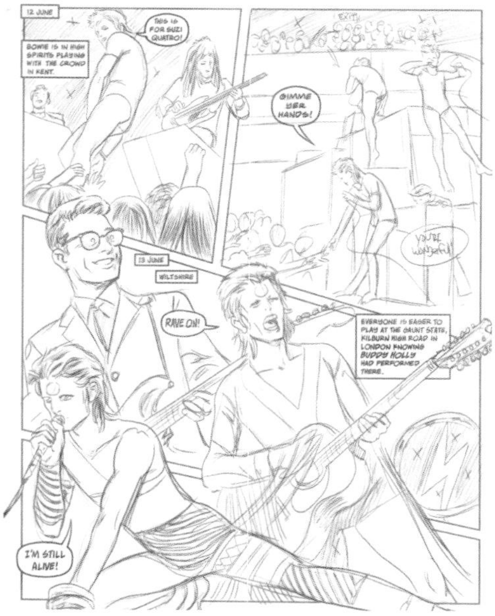
12 JUNE
BOWIE IS IN HIGH SPIRITS PLAYING WITH THE CROWD IN KENT.
THIS IS FOR SUZI QUATRO!
GIMME YER HANDS!
YOU'RE WONDERFUL!
13 JUNE
WILTSHIRE
RAVE ON!
EVERYONE IS EAGER TO PLAY AT THE GAUNT STATE, KILBURN HIGH ROAD IN LONDON KNOWING BUDDY HOLLY HAD PERFORMED THERE.
I'M STILL ALIVE!

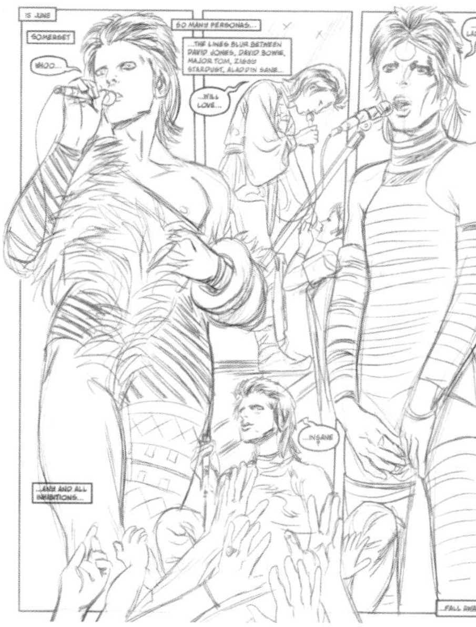
15 JUNE
SOMERSET
WHOO...
SO MANY PERSONAS...
...THE LINES BLUR BETWEEN DAVID JONES, DAVID BOWIE, MAJOR TOM, ZIGGY STARDUST, ALADDIN SANE...
...WILL LOVE...
...A LAD...
...INSANE
...FALL AWAY.

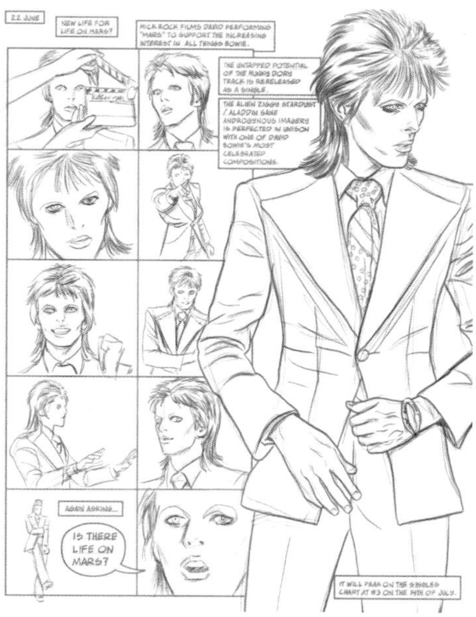
22 JUNE
NEW LIFE FOR LIFE ON MARS?
MICK ROCK FILMS DAVID PERFORMING "MARS" TO SUPPORT THE INCREASING INTEREST IN ALL THINGS BOWIE.
THE UNTAPPED POTENTIAL OF THE HUNKY DORY TRACK IS RERELEASED AS A SINGLE.
THE ALIEN ZIGGY STARDUST / ALADDIN SANE ANDROGYNOUS IMAGERY IS PERFECTED IN UNISON WITH ONE OF DAVID BOWIE'S MOST CELEBRATED COMPOSITIONS.
AGAIN ASKING...
IS THERE LIFE ON MARS?
IT WILL PEAK ON THE SINGLES CHART AT #3 ON THE 14TH OF JULY.

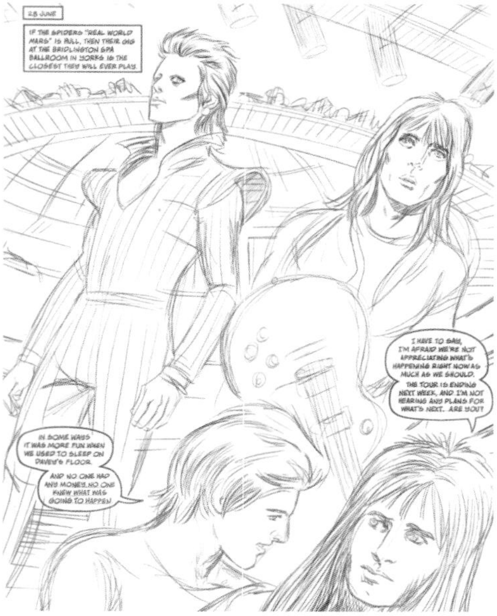
28 JUNE
IF THE SPIDERS "REAL WORLD MARS" IS HULL, THEN THEIR GIG AT THE BRIDLINGTON SPA BALLROOM IN YORKS IS THE CLOSEST THEY WILL EVER PLAY.
I HAVE TO SAY, I'M AFRAID WE'RE NOT APPRECIATING WHAT'S HAPPENING RIGHT NOW AS MUCH AS WE SHOULD.
THE TOUR IS ENDING NEXT WEEK, AND I'M NOT HEARING ANY PLANS FOR WHAT'S NEXT.. ARE YOU?
IN SOME WAYS IT WAS MORE FUN WHEN WE USED TO SLEEP ON DAVEY'S FLOOR.
AND NO ONE HAD ANY MONEY, NO ONE KNEW WHAT WAS GOING TO HAPPEN.

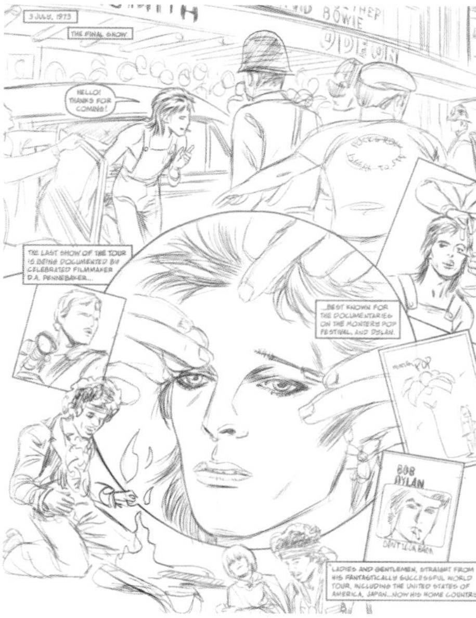
3 JULY, 1973
THE FINAL SHOW.
BOWIE
ODEON
HELLO! THANKS FOR COMING!
THE LAST SHOW OF THE TOUR IS BEING DOCUMENTED BY CELEBRATED FILMMAKER D.A. PENNEBAKER...
...BEST KNOWN FOR THE DOCUMENTARIES ON THE MONTEREY POP FESTIVAL, AND DYLAN.
BOB DYLAN
"LADIES AND GENTLEMEN, STRAIGHT FROM HIS FANTASTICALLY SUCCESSFUL WORLD TOUR, INCLUDING THE UNITED STATES OF AMERICA, JAPAN...NOW HIS HOME COUNTRY!"

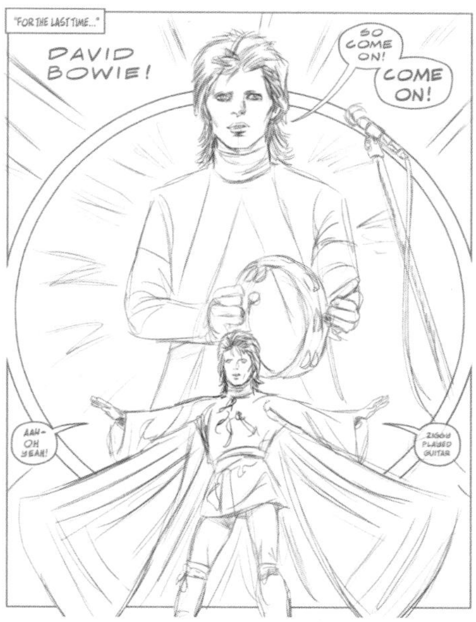
"FOR THE LAST TIME..."
DAVID BOWIE!
SO COME ON!
COME ON!
AAH-OH YEAH!
ZIGGY PLAYED GUITAR

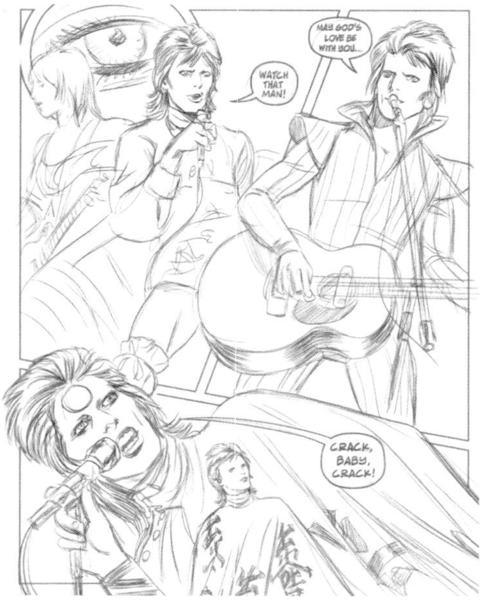
MAY GOD'S LOVE BE WITH YOU...
WATCH THAT MAN!
CRACK, BABY, CRACK!

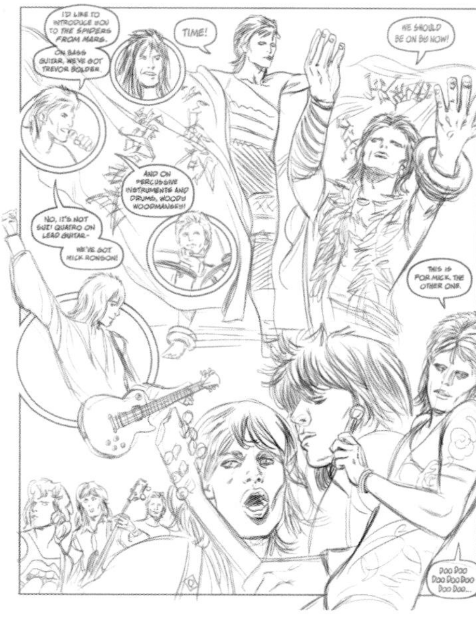
I'D LIKE TO INTRODUCE YOU TO THE SPIDERS FROM MARS.
ON BASS GUITAR, WE'VE GOT TREVOR BOLDER.
TIME!
WE SHOULD BE ON BY NOW!
AND ON PERCUSSIVE INSTRUMENTS AND DRUMS, WOODY WOODMANSEY!
NO, IT'S NOT SUZI QUATRO ON LEAD GUITAR-
WE'VE GOT MICK RONSON!
THIS IS FOR MICK, THE OTHER ONE.
DOO DOO DOO DOO DOO DOO DOO...

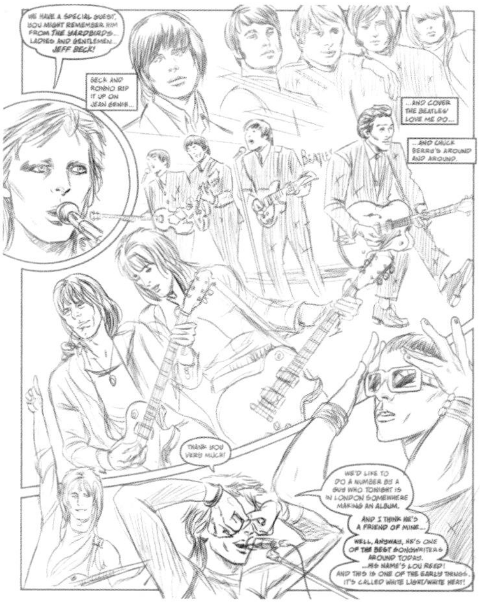
WE HAVE A SPECIAL GUEST, YOU MIGHT REMEMBER HIM FROM THE YARDBIRDS... LADIES AND GENTLEMEN... JEFF BECK!
BECK AND RONNO RIP IT UP ON JEAN GENIE...
...AND COVER THE BEATLES' LOVE ME DO...
...AND CHUCK BERRY'S AROUND AND AROUND.
THANK YOU VERY MUCH!
WE'D LIKE TO DO A NUMBER BY A GUY WHO TONIGHT IS IN LONDON SOMEWHERE MAKING AN ALBUM.
AND I THINK HE'S A FRIEND OF MINE...
WELL, ANYWAY, HE'S ONE OF THE BEST SONGWRITERS AROUND TODAY. ...HIS NAME'S LOU REED! AND THIS IS ONE OF THE EARLY THINGS. IT'S CALLED WHITE LIGHT/WHITE HEAT!

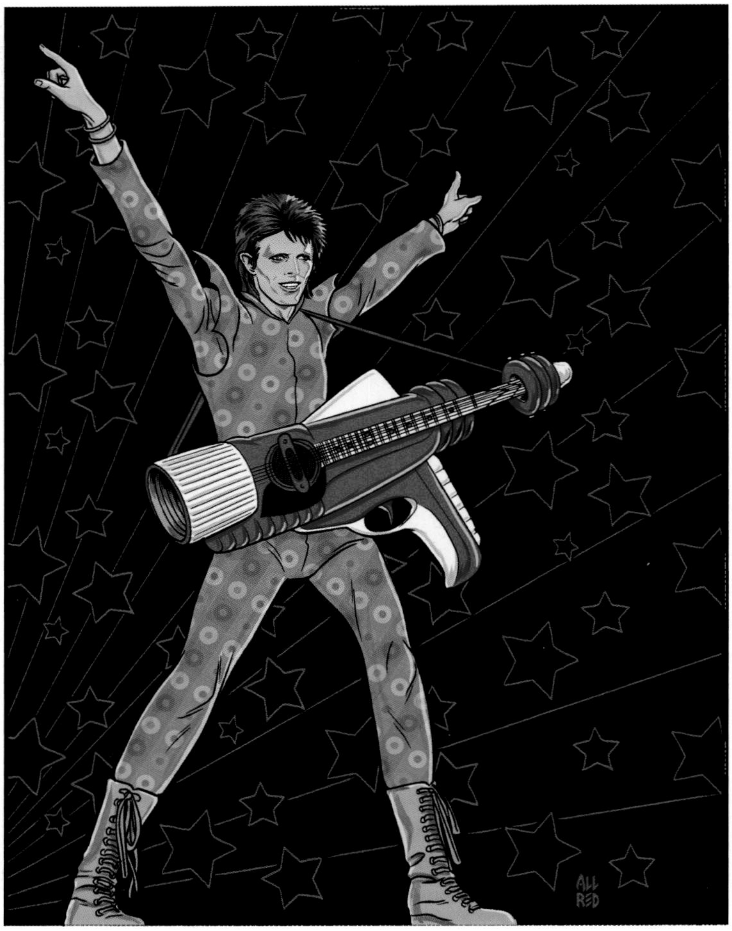
ALL
RED

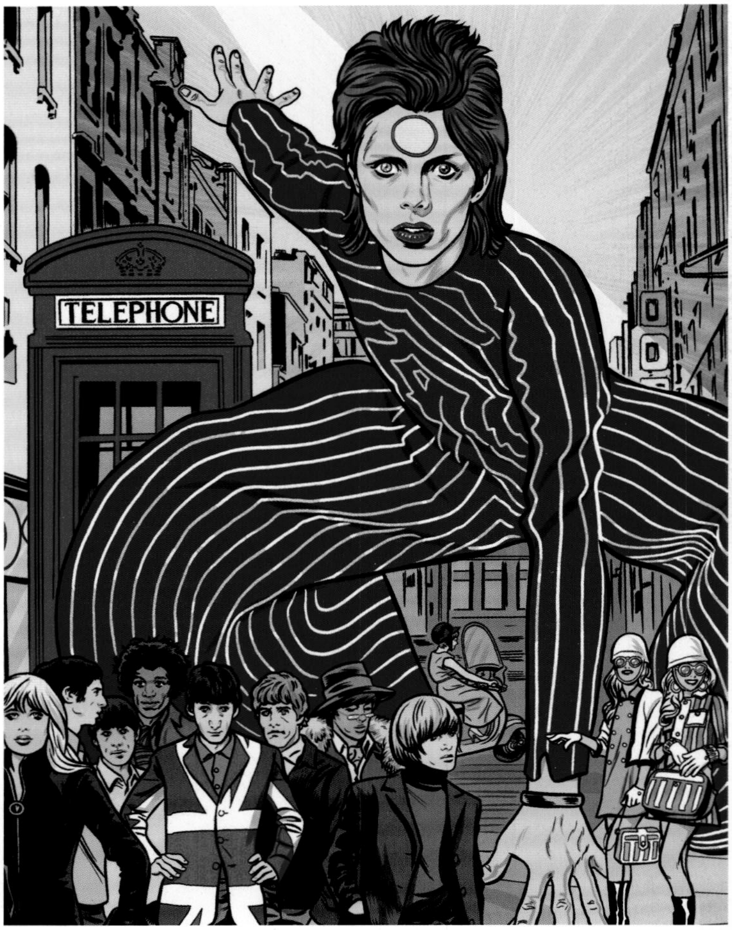
TELEPHONE

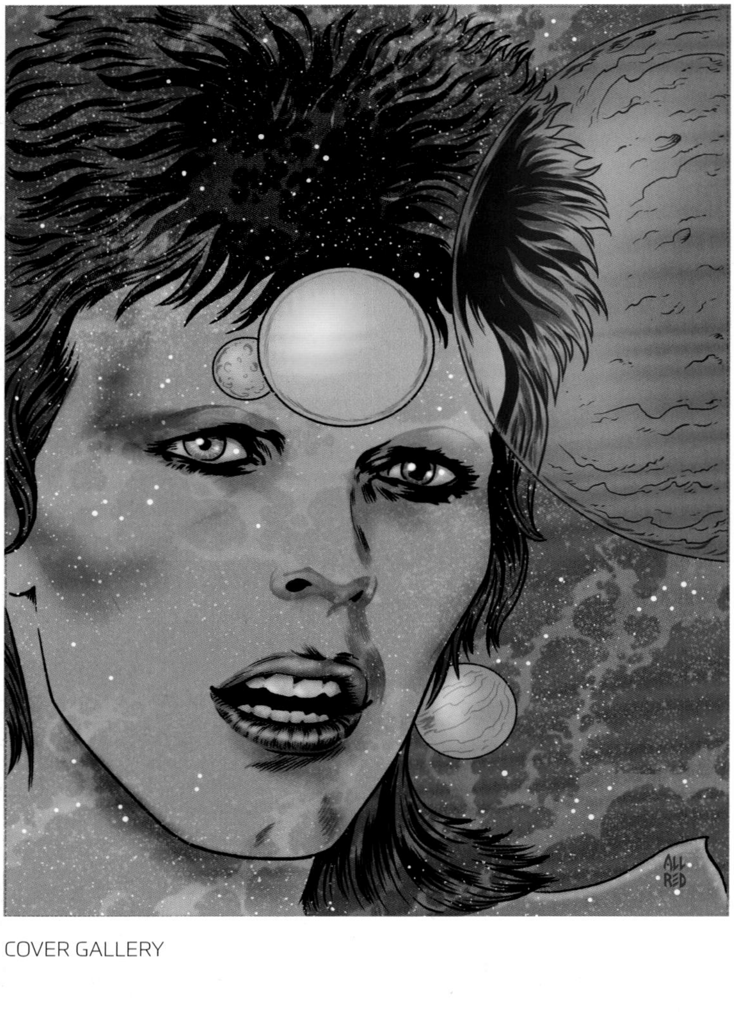
ALL
RED

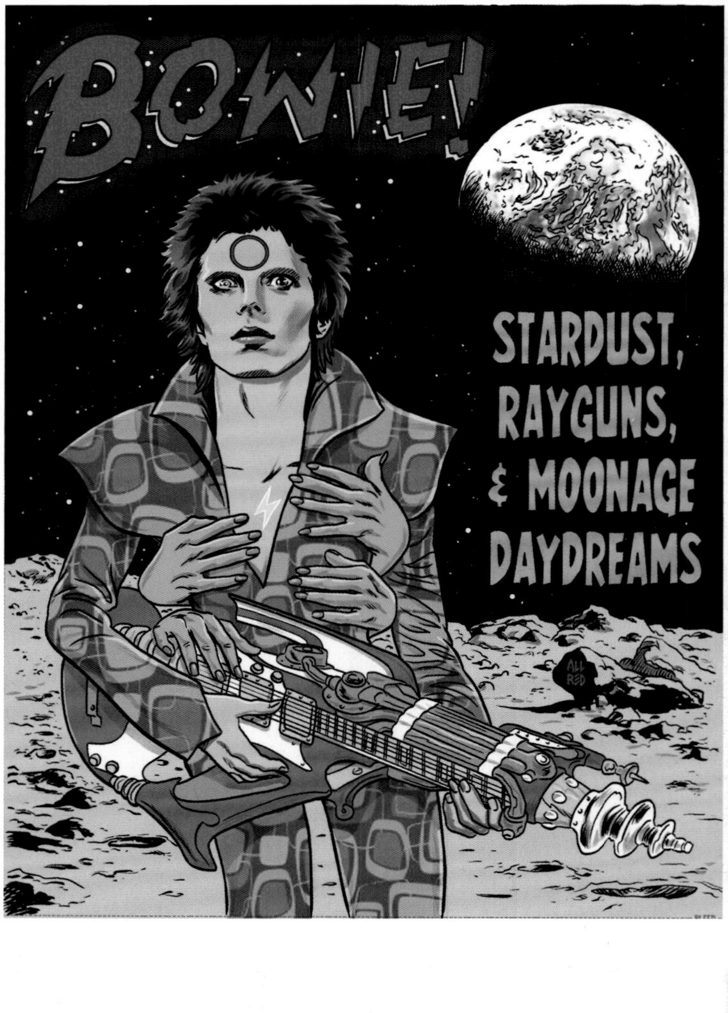
BOWIE!
STARDUST,
RAYGUNS,
& MOONAGE
DAYDREAMS
ALL
RED

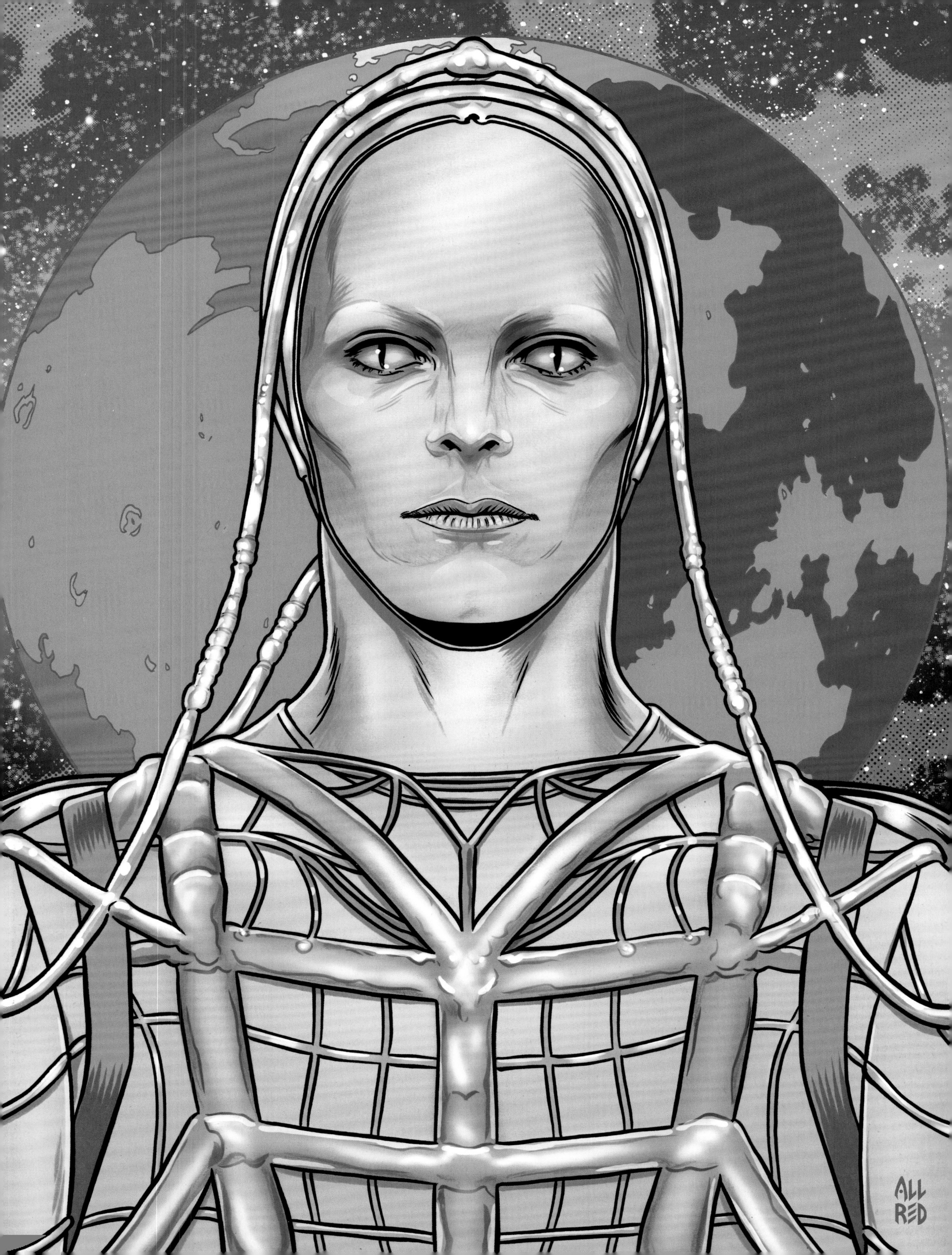
ALL
RED

An Imprint of Insight Editions
PO Box 3088
San Rafael, CA 94912
www.insightcomics.com

Find us on Facebook:
www.facebook.com/InsightEditionsComics

Follow us on Twitter:
@InsightComics

Follow us on Instagram:
Insight_Comics

Published by Insight Editions, San Rafael, California, in 2020.

Library of Congress Cataloging-in-Publication Data available.

ISBN: 978-1-68383-448-9

Publisher: Raoul Goff
President: Kate Jerome
Associate Publisher: Vanessa Lopez
Design Support: Brooke McCullum
Executive Editor: Mark Irwin
Associate Editor: Holly Fisher
Senior Production Editor: Elaine Ou
Production Director/Subsidiary Rights: Lina s Palma
Senior Production Manager: Greg Steffen
Production Coordinator: Eden Orlesky

ROOTS of PEACE   REPLANTED PAPER

Insight Editions, in association with Roots of Peace, will plant two trees for each tree used in the manufacturing of this book. Roots of Peace is an internationally renowned humanitarian organization dedicated to eradicating land mines worldwide and converting war-torn lands into productive farms and wildlife habitats. Roots of Peace will plant two million fruit and nut trees in Afghanistan and provide farmers there with the skills and support necessary for sustainable land use.

Manufactured in China by Insight Editions

10 9 8 7 6 5 4 3 2

SOURCES

Bowie, David, and Mick Rock. *Moonage Daydream: The Life & Times of Ziggy Stardust.* New York: Universe Publishing, 2005.

Broackes, Victoria, and Geoffrey Marsh, eds. *David Bowie Is.* London: V&A Publishing, 2013.

Cann, Kevin. *David Bowie: Any Day Now.* London: Adelita Ltd., 2010.

Cann, Kevin, and Chris Duffy. *Duffy Bowie: Five Sessions.* Woodbridge, UK: ACC Editions, 2014.

Carr, Roy, and Charles Shaar Murray. *David Bowie: An Illustrated Record.* Richmond: Eel Pie, 1981.

Currie, David, ed. *David Bowie: The Starzone Interviews.* London: Omnibus Press, 1995.

David Bowie: Glamour, January 2017.

David Bowie: Glamour, May 2017.

David Bowie: Glamour, January 2018.

David Bowie: Glamour, October 2018.

David Bowie: Glamour, April 2019.

Edwards, Henry, and Tony Zanetta. *Stardust: The David Bowie Story.* New York: McGraw-Hill, 1986.

Evans, Mike. *Bowie Treasures.* London: Carlton Books, 2016.

Gilbert, Pat. *Bowie: The Illustrated Story.* Minneapolis: Voyageur Press, 2017.

Griffin, Roger. *David Bowie: The Golden Years.* London: Omnibus Press, 2016.

Hewitt, Paolo. *Bowie: Album by Album.* San Rafael, CA: Insight Editions, 2016.

Hiatt, Brian, ed. *A Portrait of Bowie: A Tribute to Bowie by His Artistic Collaborators and Contemporaries.* London: Cassell, 2017.

Hudson, Jeff. *David Bowie.* New York: Sterling, 2010.

Jones, Dylan. *David Bowie: A Life.* New York: Crown Archetype, 2017.

Juby, Kerry, ed. *In Other Words . . . David Bowie.* New York: Music Sales Corporation, 1988.

Miles [Barry Miles], and Chris Charlesworth. *David Bowie Black Book.* London: Omnibus Press, 2016.

Néjib. *Haddon Hall: When David Invented Bowie.* Translated by Edward Gauvin. London: SelfMadeHero, 2017.

Spitz, Mark. *Bowie: A Biography.* New York: Three Rivers Press, 2010.

O'Leary, Chris. *Rebel Rebel: All the Songs of David Bowie from '64 to '76.* Alresford, UK: Zero Books, 2015.

O'Neill, Michael. *David Bowie on Reflection.* Knowle, UK: Danann Books, 2016.

O'Neill, Terry. *When Ziggy Played the Marquee: David Bowie's Last Performance as Ziggy Stardust.* Woodbridge, UK: ACC Editions, 2017.

Rock, Mick. *The Rise of David Bowie.* Cologne: Taschen, 2018.

———. *Ziggy Stardust: Bowie 1972–1973.* New York: St. Martin's Press, 1984.

Peellaert, Guy, and Nik Cohn. *Rock Dreams.* Cologne: Taschen, 2003.

Pegg, Nicholas. *The Complete David Bowie.* London: Titan, 2016.

Thomas, Gareth. *David Bowie: The Illustrated Biography.* London: Trans Atlantic Press, 2011.

Tremlett, George. *The David Bowie Story.* London: Futura Publications, 1974.

Visconti, Tony. *The Autobiography: Bowie, Bolan and the Brooklyn Boy.* London: HarperCollins UK, 2007.

Welch, Chris. *David Bowie Changes: His Life in Pictures 1947–2016.* London: Carlton Books, 2016.

Woodmansey, Woody. *Spider from Mars: My Life with Bowie.* New York: St. Martin's Press, 2017.